D1062842

DISCARDED

Collected Writings

DANTE GABRIEL
ROSSETTI

Collected Writings

Selected and Edited

by

JAN MARSH

NEW AMSTERDAM BOOKS
Ivan R. Dee, Publisher
Chicago

Public Library
Incorporated 1862
Barrie, Ontario

WITHDRAWN

COLLECTED WRITINGS OF DANTE GABRIEL ROSSETTI.
Introduction and other critical apparatus copyright © 2000 by Jan Marsh.

All rights reserved, including the right to reproduce
this book or portions thereof in any form.
For information, address: New Amsterdam Books,
c/o Ivan R. Dee, Publisher, 1332 North Halsted Street,
Chicago 60622.

First published in Great Britain by J. M. Dent

Library of Congress Cataloging-in-Publication Data

Rossettti, Dante Gabriel, 1828–1882.
  [Works. 2000]
  Collected writings of Dante Gabriel Rossetti / selected and edited by Jan Marsh.
    p. cm.
  Originally published: London : J.M. Dent, 1999.
  Includes bibliographical references (p.) and index.
  ISBN 1–56663–280–3 (alk. paper)
  I. Marsh, Jan 1942– II. Title.

PR 5241 .M37 2000
821'.8--dc21   99–047247

Typeset by Deltatype Ltd, Birkenhead, Merseyside
Printed and bound in Great Britain
by Butler & Tanner Ltd., Frome and London

CONTENTS

NOTE ON THE EDITOR

Dr Jan Marsh studied English Literature at the universities of Cambridge and Sussex. She is the author of a number of studies on women in the Pre-Raphaelite circle, as well as *Christina Rossetti: A Literary Biography*. For Everyman Paperbacks she edited *Christina Rossetti: Poems and Prose*, and with Pamela Gerrish Nunn she curated the 1997–8 exhibition 'Pre-Raphaelite Women Artists'. She recently published the biography *Dante Gabriel Rossetti: Painter and Poet*.

ABBREVIATIONS USED IN THE NOTES

ACS	Algernon Charles Swinburne
B&S	*Ballads & Sonnets*
CFM	Charles Fairfax Murray
Delaware	Rowland Elzea (ed.) *Correspondence between Samuel Bancroft Jnr and Charles Fairfax Murray 1892–1916*, Delaware Art Museum, Wilmington, 1980
DGR	Dante Gabriel Rossetti
DW	*The Letters of Dante Gabriel Rossetti*, edited by O. Doughty and J.R. Wahl, 1965–7, 4 vols (indicated by number, not page)
EBJ	Edward Burne-Jones
EIPs	*Early Italian Poets*, 1861
FLM	William Michael Rossetti, ed., *Dante Gabriel Rossetti: His Family-Letters with a Memoir*, 2 vols, London, 1895
HofL	*House of Life* sonnet sequence
JPRAS	*Journal of Pre-Raphaelite and Aesthetic Studies*
pub.	published
re-pub.	re-published
rev.	revised
RP	*Rossetti Papers 1862–1870*, ed. W.M. Rossetti, 1903
Sharp	William Sharp, *Dante Gabriel Rossetti*, 1882
TG 1894	*The Pre-Raphaelites*, Tate Gallery exhibition, 1984
THC	Thomas Hall Caine
TWD	Theodore Watts-Dunton
VP	*Victorian Poetry* vol. 20, 1982
VS	*Dante Gabriel Rossetti, Paintings and Drawings: A Catalogue Raisonné*, ed. Virginia Surtees, 2 vols, Oxford, 1971
WA	William Allingham
WHH	William Holman Hunt
WMR	William Michael Rossetti
WMR 1886	*The Collected Works of Dante Gabriel Rossetti*, vol. 1, ed. William M. Rossetti, 1886
WMR 1911	*The Works of Dante Gabriel Rossetti*, ed. William M. Rossetti, 1911
wr.	written

Anglo-Italian

Born Gabriel Charles Dante Rossetti in London on 5 May 1828, he had an Anglo-Italian inheritance. His father was the poet Gabriele Rossetti (1785–1854) from Naples, who composed popular odes to liberty during the 1820 revolt against absolutism, and arrived in Britain as a political refugee in 1824. His mother Frances (1800–1886) was the daughter of Gaetano Polidori, translator and linguist long settled in Britain. Their son, the second of four children, was thus three-quarters Italian, reared in a home that was a focal point for the politically active exile community. From 1830, his father was professor of Italian at newly founded King's College, London University; as well as language teaching, he pursued research into the works of Dante Alighieri, publishing lengthy commentaries in which erudition was sadly overwhelmed by idiosyncratic literary-political theories as to the encrypted meanings of medieval Italian literature.

Despite this early environment, most other influences were necessarily British, and while to the end of his life Dante Gabriel Rossetti remained, in his own words, 'an Italian who has never seen Italy',[2] in many respects he was more convincingly English, albeit always cosmopolitan in acquaintance. One of his first poems was on the defeated Napoleon at Waterloo, one of his last on the remaining survivors of Trafalgar. Though not wealthy, the family belonged to the cultured intelligentsia, where literature, scholarship and art were highly regarded and his mother confessed to a passionate desire that her husband and children be distinguished in some intellectual field. Her elder brother John Polidori had been Byron's travelling physician, and thereby also acquainted with the Shelleys.

The Rossettis lived in central London, in the first epoch of the economically prosperous Victorian age, when new technologies of rail transport, telegraph communication and mechanised production revolutionised Britain. As industry and commerce expanded, the urban population increased. Politically, power was transferred from lords and landowners to mercantile and bourgeois parliamentary rule, while the proletariat remained unenfranchised. Social rank determined by birth gave way to class distinctions based on wealth and education. Ireland remained an integral part of the United Kingdom. Social problems of poverty, ignorance, squalor and (in Ireland in the 1840s) famine were met by local and charitable provision, aided by energetic campaigners, and by large-scale emigration to North America and Australia.

Young Gabriel Rossetti showed a marked talent for drawing, but most of the home entertainment centred on books. Like his siblings,

INTRODUCTION

Throughout his life, Dante Gabriel Rossetti (1828–82) composed poetry in irregular bursts, which often coincided with the stimulus of projected publication. But at all periods his chief profession was painting, to which poetry effectively played second fiddle, albeit as it were within the same orchestra. From the start, he felt torn between the two arts, and in later life came to believe he had 'prostituted' his pictorial talents for professional reward, and that therefore his literary output was more purely expressive of personal thought and imagination. He saw himself as one who wrote under the stress or impulse of some idea or experience, but not as a confessional poet of immediate subjective feeling. In a projected note to his second collection, he wrote: 'To speak in the first person is often to speak most vividly: but these emotional poems are in no sense "occasional". The "Life" involved is life representative . . . Whether the recorded moment exist in the region of fact or of thought is a question indifferent to the Muse, so long only as her touch can quicken it.'[1]

Many of his pieces are carefully and complexly wrought. Others are simple in structure and substance. Most inhabit a 'poetic' realm, either that of a romantic, imaginary past, or that of archaic literary conventions where abstract entities like Love, Death and Song are personified as speaking subjects. Some are contemporary in style and content, a few political or satiric. In his youth, thanks to his position in the world of art, he was hailed as the leading 'Pre-Raphaelite' poet, developing Tennyson's modern-medieval mode of rendering romantic themes with vivid directness. Later, under the influence of Swinburne (1837–1909) and, particularly, the critical writings of Walter Pater (1839–94), he was identified as a key Aesthetic poet, in whose work form and style, language and metre were paramount. As such, and also owing to his colourful, doomed life, his work was influential on the writers of the 1890s and later, including those like T. S. Eliot (1888–1965) and Ezra Pound (1885–1972) who grew up in the late Victorian era. With the rise of Modernism in all the arts after 1920, his reputation declined, retaining a minor presence in the nineteenth century canon alongside, but distinct from, his sister Christina Rossetti. Latterly, with Victorian art and verse in general, his position has stabilised somewhat, though his painting now far outshines his poetry in general popularity.

he was encouraged to create his own compositions and, although the favoured elder son, was aware of a certain competition for the position of prodigy. In 1841 their father referred to his elder daughter Maria as 'my fourteen-year-old Sappho', while a short time later her younger sister Christina was hailed as the future 'poet of the family.'[3] Later in life, Rossetti dismissed his own literary juvenilia as showing no talent whatsoever – a judgement which posterity has largely endorsed. As Frances Rossetti kept a proud album of her children's productions, his youthful efforts can be chronicled, revealing the earliest influences on his imagination: the bloodier plays of Shakespeare, Sir Walter Scott, *The Arabian Nights* and tales of the supernatural. At the age of six he penned a brief drama entitled 'The Slave' whose characters include a Spanish Lord and an English Knight; 'no plot is apparent,' observed his brother William, 'only constant objurgation and fighting.'[4] In 1840, Gabriel was prime mover in a plan to write romance adventures set in the Middle Ages, of which his own was 'A Story of the Round Table' in three action-packed chapters within the confines of thirteen small manuscript pages.[5]

William and Marie. A Ballad is conjecturally dated to 1841, though one MS bears his mother's note 'written when he was fifteen.' Largely in Scots pastiche, its mode is borrowed from ballad anthologies like Scott's *Minstrelsy of the Scottish Border* (1802–3). Evidently deemed precociously competent, the verses were submitted for publication – an early example of the ambition for public recognition shared by the whole family. 'Sir,' wrote the young author to an unidentified editor, 'Should you consider the accompanying ballad not wholly unworthy of a place in your magazine, you would highly oblige me by inserting it ... P.S. I have also executed the enclosed sketch, which is intended, if considered sufficiently good, as a headpiece to the ballad.'[6] Neither was accepted, but in 1843 a companion piece named *Sir Hugh the Heron* was printed for private circulation by Gaetano Polidori, who encouraged his grandchildren's literary endeavours. Later, Gabriel tried to suppress all remaining copies of *Sir Hugh*, calling it 'absurd trash' that displayed 'absolutely no promise at all – less than should even exist at twelve'.[7] Both juvenile efforts are however noteworthy for the fact that the historical ballad remained one of Rossetti's favourite poetic forms, as in *The White Ship* and *The King's Tragedy*, written at the very end of his life.

By 1843 Rossetti had left King's College School to start a professional career in art and from 1846 to 1849 he attended the Royal Academy Schools. He continued to read widely, discovering Byron, Shelley, Keats, Goethe's *Faust* and other Romantic literature, but his compositional talents were mainly deployed in translation. Thanks to lessons in German from Prof. Adolf Heimann of University College, he translated Bürger's *Lenore* into verse, followed by a lost rendering of the Niebelungenlied and in 1845–6 by *Henry the Leper*, translated into Chaucerian couplets from the twelfth century German of Hartmann von Auë's *Der Arme Heinrich*. A fluent if sometimes cavalier linguist, Rossetti believed translation should render the spirit and style of the original as much as the meaning. He also at this date began his verse versions from Dante and other early Italian poets of *il dolce stil nuovo* that would eventually be issued in 1861. 'Glowing from the flame-breath of Dante Alighieri, Rossetti made continual incursions into the Old Reading-room of the British Museum hunting up volumes of the most ancient Italian lyrists,' wrote his brother later. 'No doubt this pursuit involved some partial neglect of his artistic studies. When he found an Italian poem that pleased him he set-to translating it . . .'[8]

These exercises effectively formed his poetic apprenticeship, together with practice at the literary parlour game of writing *bouts rimés* sonnets against the clock, at which he excelled. Meanwhile, their grandfather had printed a translation and a moral allegory by his elder sister Maria Rossetti (1827–76) and a collection of poems by the younger Christina Rossetti (1830–94). Gabriel's next serious literary endeavours came when boredom with his art studies led to ample daytime leisure and acquaintance with men on the fringes of Grub Street. As well as Italian literature, he sought out old English poetry, imitating its archaic diction and quaint forms. Reading omnivorously, he also devoured modern writers like Coleridge, Keats, Tennyson, Victor Hugo, Longfellow and Edgar Allan Poe.

Some of his own efforts perished, including one called 'Rose Mary' ('You may remember my using the name long ago for some rubbish destroyed,' he reminded William in the 1870s.)[9] Some survived in draft form to be later re-cast, like *Jenny* and *The Bride's Prelude*. The earliest of the complete poems was *The Blessed Damozel*, which he later stated was written before he was nineteen – that is, before 12 May 1847[10] – and inspired by the Gothickry of Poe's *Lenore* and *The Raven*. 'I saw that Poe had done the utmost it was possible to do with the grief of the lover on earth,' he said in 1882, 'and I determined to reverse the conditions, and give utterance to the yearning of the loved one in heaven.'[11] In due course *The Blessed Damozel* became Rossetti's most anthologised 'signature poem'. As befits a young man's verses, it is suffused with discreet sexual desire, giving fleshly warmth to the heavenly damozel's bosom. Other influences include the sensuous style of Keats, and the mock-antique ballads of Elizabeth Barrett's 1844 *Poems*.

Most importantly, however, the *Damozel* is inspired by the *stil novisti* poets and especially by Rossetti's namesake Dante, whose *Vita Nuova* he adopted as a text of personal import, supplying repeated inspiration for drawings and paintings. Signalling a new professional identity, Rossetti altered the order of his baptismal names so that 'Dante' came first. Informally, owing to his use of initials and monogram he became known as 'DGR', a useful contraction given the number of literary Rossettis. In contrast to his father, who held to an allegorical understanding of Dante's unfulfilled love for Beatrice as personifying a disguised ideal, DGR saw Beatrice as a real woman, representative of all beauty and goodness, and Dante's passion as the expression of idealised desire.

In 1848, baulked of an exhibition debut at the Royal Academy summer show, he sent a selection of his translations and original pieces (which by inference included *The Blessed Damozel*) to Leigh Hunt, doyen of the Romantic movement in Britain. Friend of Keats and Shelley and influential critic, Hunt was author of *The Story of Rimini* (1844) and *Captain Sword and Captain Pen* (1835). He replied on 31 March 1948 with praise to enrapture a beginner:

> I felt perplexed, it is true, at first, by the translations, which, though containing evidences of a strong feeling of the truth and simplicity of the originals, appeared to me harsh, and want correctness in the versification. I guess indeed that you are altogether not so musical as pictorial. But, when I came to the originals of your own, I recognized an unquestionable poet, thoughtful, imaginative, and with rare powers of expression. I hailed you as such at once, without any misgiving; and, besides your Dantesque heavens (without any hell to spoil them) admired the complete and genial round of your sympathies with humanity . . . If you paint as well as you write, you may be a rich man; or, at all events, if you do not care to be rich, may get leisure enough to cultivate your writing. But I hardly need tell you that poetry, even the very best – nay, the best, in this respect, is apt to be the worst – is not a thing for a man to live upon while he is in the flesh, however immortal it may render him in spirit.[12]

Family finances being severely straitened owing to Professor Rossetti's ill-health, Gabriel returned to his artistic studies. But by the same token, he kept a lifelong vision of poetry as his true vocation. Painting was a career, a livelihood; poetry was untrammelled, uncompromised creativity. It is a theme still worth debating, as is the issue whether the literary-pictorial interplay in both arts is a strength or weakness in his oeuvre.

Art-Catholic and Pre-Raphaelite

At an early date Rossetti discovered Robert Browning (1812–89), becoming one of the first admirers of this poet's dense dramatic style, with *Sordello* as an especial favourite. He also responded to writers of the so-called Spasmodic School – P. J. Bailey, Sydney Dobell, Westland Marston – as much as anything for their deliberate obscurity and over-wrought manner. In 1847, while haunting the British Museum, he had acquired from Samuel Palmer's brother an original notebook belonging to William Blake, poet and painter, whose works were then regarded as too eccentric for serious attention, but whom Rossetti hailed as an imaginative genius and creative exemplar; in 1861–3 he would help prepare Alexander Gilchrist's *Life of Blake*, which took the first step to establish Blake's rightful place in the history of British art and literature. Generally speaking, in this period Rossetti responded to 'all things counter, original, spare, strange' (to quote Hopkins) in the literary line.

In painting, he worked first with Ford Madox Brown (1821–1890) and then with William Holman Hunt (1827–1910). With other young artists, he formed a short-lived 'literary club' whose members read out original pieces. Published anonymously in September 1848, his own *My Sister's Sleep* was a death-bed piece of a familiar sentimental type, sharpened by a mood of intense piety and simplicity derived from the contemporary 'Oxford Movement' whose recovery of Catholic religious imagery is also strongly visible in *Ave*. Though he formally adhered to no church, Rossetti was powerfully affected by the Anglo-Catholic fervour that profoundly influenced both his sisters. In 1848 he gave his poems the group title 'Songs of an Art-Catholic', while his first major picture, *The Girlhood of Mary Virgin*, was exhibited with explanatory sonnets de-coding iconography unfamiliar to British viewers.

In 1848, nations across Europe strove to overthrow outmoded forms of government in a sequence of revolutions, in France, Italy, and Germany, bringing a real possibility that Professor Rossetti might at last return to his homeland. Caught up in the excitement, DGR composed a sonnet hailing the new dawn in Italy and drafted *A Last Confession*, a dramatic monologue in the voice of a young, outlawed Italian patriot. When revolutionary hopes collapsed later in the year, he turned consciously away from political engagement, perhaps owing to too-acute disillusion, instead steeping himself in art and poetry.

At the end of the year he led his brother and five student friends including Holman Hunt and John Everett Millais (1829–96) into the foundation of the Pre-Raphaelite Brotherhood or PRB, according to the boyishly cryptic insignia used by its members. The idea was loosely inspired by the German Lukasbrüder or Nazarene painters and by the writings of John Ruskin, who urged artists to 'return to nature, in all simplicity of heart'. Despite the choice of name the young artists were poorly acquainted with art before the time of Raphael, as all their training looked to high Renaissance exemplars, but in the revolutionary year an iconoclastic return to 'primitive' inspiration was an energizing principle. At around the time of the PRB, Rossetti composed the sonnet trio later published as *Old and New Art*, the last of which was originally addressed 'To the Young Painters of England, in memory of those before Raphael,' and may stand as a PRB manifesto.

Though the mystic initials went unnoticed during the 1849 exhibition season, *The Girlhood of Mary Virgin* was well received, as a manifestation of new religious sincerity in art. In the autumn a trip with Holman Hunt to Paris and Belgium brought fresh enthusiasm, and screeds of new writing, including a travel diary in verse. Back in Britain, a monthly magazine called *The Germ* was launched, carrying in its four issues ten poems by DGR, including *The Blessed Damozel* and six sonnets on paintings. In addition, he wrote *Hand and Soul*, a prose tale whose hero Chiaro dell'Erma is a real, if fictional, pre-Raphaelite painter, and also a figure of the author as an artist who aspires to draw inspiration from within his soul, rather than work for worldly fame or religious faith.

Like his pictures in this period, Rossetti's early writings are marked by an immediacy that is sometimes abrupt but very modern and goes to the heart of the Brotherhood's spirit in art, reaching through conventional forms to direct expression of experience in poems like *The Woodspurge*. In maturity, DGR seems to have felt this was too naive; compare for example the revision of his *Germ* poem *From the Cliffs: Noon*, with its 1870 incarnation as *The Sea-Limits*, where the poet's initial, awed response to the eternal motion of waves is overlaid by later philosophising. Other poems were deliberately 'quaint', in a pastiche manner inspired by medieval romances that reflects his half-wishful belief that art, and particularly poetry, belonged to a timeless realm that spoke across the ages, linking – for example – thirteenth century Florence, fifteenth century France and nineteenth century Britain. Provocatively, he would ask what did it

matter whether the earth went round the sun, and hail Keats's toast to
the confusion of Newton for having reduced the poetry of the
rainbow to a prism. But he also pondered the differences between
eras, as in *The Burden of Nineveh*, inspired by seeing the great
Winged Bull sculptures from Assyria arrive at the British Museum.
And always his verse is replete with allusive, implicit commentary on
other poems.

A clutch of poems was prompted by a solitary walking tour in
summer 1853 through Warwickshire, chiefly in order to visit
Shakespeare's Stratford-upon-Avon. At this date his closest literary
acquaintance was the Irish poet William Allingham (1824–89), author
of *Day & Night Songs* (1854) and *The Music Master* (1856), with
whom he shared a liking for traditional balladry, although works like
The Bride's Prelude and *Sister Helen* owe obvious debts to Barrett
Browning's *Romaunt of the Page* and *Rime of the Duchess May*. In
this period, Rossetti got to know the Brownings well, and was
present on one memorable occasion when Tennyson read *Maud* and
Browning *Fra Lippo Lippi*. From 1855 he was a friend and
professional associate of John Ruskin, during the composition of
Modern Painters 3 & 4.

From the end of 1852 Rossetti lived and worked at Chatham Place,
just north of Blackfriars Bridge. Within sight of St Paul's Cathedral,
this was also in easy reach of the home of Elizabeth Siddal, the young
woman who acted as model for several PRB paintings, notably
Millais's *Ophelia* (1852, Tate Gallery) and who this year became
Rossetti's 'love and pupil'. The unconventional, informal arrangement
allowed them to spend much time together, although Gabriel's love
for his 'dear dove divine' was at this date mainly expressed through
delicate and beautiful drawings rather than verses. In 1854 they were
on holiday together at Hastings. Lizzie – as she was commonly
known – spent the winter of 1855–6 on the Riviera, for the sake of
her health, during which time Rossetti's adoration appears to have
cooled; quarrels over marriage followed, and after several months
together in Derbyshire in 1857–8 there was a parting, which seems
reflected in certain brief poems of this date. In May 1860 however
they were finally married.

Later, Rossetti would cite 1853 as the date he gave up poetry, aged
twenty-five, 'on finding that it impeded attention to what constituted
another aim and a livelihood into the bargain – i.e. painting'. From
that date to 1869, he claimed to have written 'extremely little – I
might almost say nothing except the renovated *Jenny* in 1858 or
/59'.[13] This is not wholly true, however, for 1854 is the date of the
finely accomplished ode *Love's Nocturn*, while 1856 saw his meeting

with Edward Burne-Jones (1833–98) and William Morris (1834–96), in whose *Germ*-inspired magazine DGR re-printed *The Blessed Damozel*, and first published *The Burden of Nineveh* and *The Staff and Scrip*. These three poems then furnished his literary debut in the United States, when re-published in *The Crayon* (New York) in 1857. These accompanied a distinctly chivalric phase in his art, largely inspired by Malory's *Morte d'Arthur*.

Much influenced by Browning's *Men and Women* (1856) he subsequently re-worked *Jenny* into an outstanding dramatic mono-logue on the topical subject of male responsibility for prostitution, which he projected submitting to the *Cornhill Magazine*, and also composed a number of new poems, including several with explicitly sexual themes such as the *Song of the Bower* and the notorious sonnet later known as *Nuptial Sleep*. In addition he set about the task of revising and editing his translations with a view to publication. Through *Early Italian Poets*, issued in 1861, almost entirely unknown works to complement early Italian painting were introduced to English-speaking audiences. Being the first to attempt such a project, he was proud to claim innovation, while acknowledging that his versions were not scholarly. As he explained in his preface, the aim was not literality. 'I there meant to refer entirely to fidelity of main meaning,' he further explained in response to queries from Richard Burton. 'Though adhering to the character of each metre I did not follow the individualities of separate Sonnets, since some freedom of action was necessary to my aim at harmonious English.'[14] Thus, the poems must largely stand on their own merits, and as the works that introduced a generation of readers to the lyric poetry of medieval Europe. Ezra Pound's account of his first reading of *Early Italian Poets* is contained in his essay on Cavalcanti, first published in *Make it New* (1934) and subsequently in his *Literary Essays*, edited and introduced by T. S. Eliot (1954).

While seeing his translations through the press, Rossetti also prepared a collection of original verse, advertised at the end of 1861 as 'Dante at Verona and Other Poems'. The contents of this can be roughly reconstructed from the pieces known to have been composed by this date; as well as the title poem they included *Jenny*, *A Last Confession*, *Nineveh*, and *Sister Helen*. All were copied into a calf-bound exercise book and shown to Ruskin and Allingham, among others. Then, following the death of their stillborn daughter the previous year, in February 1862 Rossetti's wife Lizzie died of an overdose of the opiate drug laudanum. In a grief-struck gesture, Rossetti consigned his manuscript book to her coffin, buried in the family grave at Highgate cemetery.

This act has sometimes been interpreted as a Romantic sacrifice of love poems to the tomb of the beloved, but in truth few of DGR's verses at this date can be so classified; even *Love's Nocturn* is more of a Miltonic or Keatsian ode than a romantic declaration, and while several of the shorter pieces may have a personal element, the general inference is mistaken. It is true however that from this date, he abandoned plans to publish, and gave up writing poetry. He left Blackfriars for Cheyne Walk, Chelsea, where he concentrated on painting.

Painter and Poet

To begin with, the Cheyne Walk house was shared with William, with Algernon Swinburne (1837–1909) then at the outset of his poetic career, and briefly with George Meredith (1828–1909), novelist and author of *Modern Love* (1862). Another inmate was Rossetti's buxom model and mistress, former prostitute Fanny Cornforth, who sat for many of the alluring depictions of sensuous female beauty that now formed the staple of his art. Having been an abstemious and idealistic young man, he now grew more worldly – though still preferring water to alcohol or coffee – and cultivated a wide acquaintance among London clubs and dinner tables. The 1860s saw a loosening of social morals and an increase in entertainment and self-indulgence that may accurately be called permissive. In 1864, a trip to Paris amid the *grand luxe* of the Second Empire introduced Rossetti to the work of Millet, which he admired, and Manet, which he loathed. Simultaneously, ideas of *l'art pour l'art*, in which aesthetic aims ousted narrative or moral content from painting and poetry began to reach Britain from the writings of Théophile Gautier and Charles Baudelaire. The only thing worth attention 'is simply excellence of verse or colour', wrote Swinburne. 'Artists should not take part in saving souls or helping humanity.'[15]

In this period, Rossetti was an active member of the design partnership later known as Morris & Co, with Brown, Burne-Jones and Philip Webb as well as William Morris. Launched in 1861, the Firm (as it was dubbed) provided the nucleus of a social circle in which Rossetti was a natural leader, as he had been in the PRB, and frequently a genial host. In respect of the business, however, he left management matters to others; and within a few years his design work, mainly for stained glass, was crowded out by painting commissions. As regards poetry, he wrote little or nothing, but he advised his sister Christina with her second collection (1866) and watched admiringly as Morris's literary reputation developed through the volumes of the *Earthly Paradise* sequence (1868–70.)

In 1868, personal and professional crises led Rossetti back to literature. The latter was caused by problems of vision that impeded his painting and plunged him into insomniac depression, to combat which he began to take whisky and, later, the narcotic drug chloral hydrate. The personal crisis arose from his growing love for Janey Morris, wife of his friend and partner, who from this date became the main model for his visual art, in a long sequence of portrait drawings and subject pictures. Under this combined influence, DGR began producing sonnets, including *Willowwood* and *The Kiss*, which at some unrecorded date he started to conceive as elements in a sequence of 100 – as in the lost 'century of sonnets' said to have been written by Raphael whose art was held up to the young PRBs as highest of all in the Western canon. (Note, in this connection, Browning's poem to his wife, *One Word More*, on Raphael's poetry and Dante's drawing.)

Friends who lamented Rossetti's lost volume urged him to publish, and poetic re-birth was signalled in March 1869 in the pages of the *Fortnightly Review*, edited by John Morley. Thereafter, sonnets and longer pieces began to flow, including *Troy Town* and *Eden Bower*, based on curious legends from Greek and Hebrew mythology, in response to the contemporary interest in such sources, together with emerging theories of archetype and symbol. In the autumn of this year, he obtained permission to exhume his wife's coffin and retrieve his manuscript, thereby regaining possession of otherwise lost texts.

After a number of further delays – always, Rossetti hoped for the masterpiece-to-come which would lift the collection to another plane – the volume entitled simply *Poems* was published in April 1870. Intermingling old and new pieces, it included a sequence of sonnets and songs under the heading 'Towards a work to be called "The House of Life" ' of which half were declared to 'treat of love'. Apprehensive over a literary debut in his forties, he secured friendly reviews from Swinburne and Morris, and found the volume generally well received. Sales were good, and when younger writers started to regard him as a beacon, Rossetti began to re-fashion his identity as a poet rather than painter. 'I have often said that to be an artist is just the same thing as to be a whore, as far as dependence on the whims and fancies of individuals is concerned,' he told Brown, in respect of the painter's relationship with patrons.[16] However, simultaneously with publication, his sight improved, allowing him to resume painting. Optimistically refreshed, he planned to exhibit his keynote work, *Dante's Dream of the Death of Beatrice*, and also to prepare a new collection of poems. He and Jane Morris spent summer 1871 in romantic seclusion at the stone-built manorhouse at Kelmscott, in Oxfordshire, hard by the upper Thames, where several of his most passionately lyrical love sonnets were written, together with *The Cloud Confines*, an Arnoldian meditation on the limits of knowledge and faith, and the fantastical narrative *Rose Mary*, an elaborate throwback to the days of supernatural balladry which is most nearly indebted to Coleridge's *Geraldine*.

In early summer 1872, there followed a catastrophic mental and emotional breakdown, when DGR became temporarily deranged by delusions and aural hallucinations, convinced he was the victim of a conspiracy to hound him out of society. The immediate cause was an adverse critique of *Poems* in the *Contemporary Review*, entitled 'The Fleshly School of Poetry', which mockingly attacked the sensuality of *The House of Life* and accused Rossetti of being the chief of a self-serving, jealous coterie whose art was 'infected' with indecent, foreign, and pretentiously affected ideas. The author, at first under a pseudonym, was rival author Robert Buchanan, who had previously clashed swords with both Swinburne and William Rossetti. DGR drafted a reply, published in December 1871, which provoked his critic to enlarge his article into a pamphlet, expanding especially on the sexual sonnets. Soon after this appeared, Rossetti's mind gave way. He spent six months in seclusion in Scotland, and then went to live at Kelmscott, where he resumed painting. Once again, however, he gave up writing, and the projected second collection was put aside.

Steadily, over the next decade, his physical as well as mental health declined, although in this period he produced several major canvases, including *Proserpine*, *Astarte Syriaca*, and *La Bella Mano* (for all of which he composed accompanying sonnets) as well as that illustrating his own *Blessed Damozel*. Chronically depressed, he grew more and more reclusive, pathetically dependent on a few close and tolerant friends. Among the latter were a lawyer named Theodore Watts, who in 1879 rescued Swinburne from suicidal alcoholism, and a young man named Hall Caine, who went on to be a popular novelist. With their encouragement, Rossetti returned again to verse, and by the beginning of 1881 had sufficient new material to prepare a new collection, *Ballads and Sonnets*, which included an expanded *House of Life* (omitting the contentious *Nuptial Sleep*) and the historical narratives *The White Ship* and *The King's Tragedy*. At the same time, he re-issued *Poems*, adding the still unfinished *Bride's Prelude* to fill up the space vacated by *The House of Life*. By the time both volumes appeared in October, however, he was too sick in mind and body to take much interest; and after a long lingering decline he died of organ failure in April 1882, aged fifty-four.

Poetic methods and aims

In 1870 DGR wrote to an acquaintance and potential reviewer:

> My own belief is that I am a poet (within the limit of my powers) primarily, and that it is my poetic tendencies that chiefly give value to my pictures: only painting being – what poetry is not – a livelihood – I have put my poetry chiefly in that form. On the other hand, the bread-and-cheese question has led to a good deal of my painting being pot-boiling and no more – whereas my verse, being unprofitable, has remained (as much as I have found time for) unprostituted.
>
>   ... I am glad you like *Eden Bower*. I think that poem, *Jenny, A Last Confession*, and *The House of Life*, are the things I would wish to be known by ... As with recreated forms in painting, so I should wish to deal in poetry chiefly with personified emotions; and in carrying out my scheme of the '*House of Life*' (if ever I do so) I shall try to put in action a complete *dramatis personae* of the soul.
>
>   ... I hope one thing most sincerely – and that is, that you will not in the least hesitate to dwell on the weak side of my work, as well as on such strength as it may possess. Also if you could in some way refer to the book of Translations, it might remind people of what I hope ere long to republish and perhaps get better remembered for the future.'[17]

His favoured poetic forms were the narrative ballad and the sonnet, as the title of his 1881 collection indicates. He also employed the dramatic monologue in blank verse, the ode and the shorter lyric or 'song'. For the ballad, he used a variety of formal structures, including the traditional stanza of eight- and six-syllable lines rhyming *abcb*, octosyllabic sestinas rhyming *abbacc*, terza rima with a varying burden, and nine-syllable couplets. The triplets of *Eden Bower* use feminine rhymes throughout, and careful diversification of form appears to have been one of Rossetti's goals. For sonnets, however, he always preferred the Italian or Petrarchan form, with a *volta* break between octave and sestina; frequently each part is a single sentence, to be delivered in a single breath. Such formalities are not rigidly adhered to, but on the whole DGR was a correct sonneteer. The same cannot be said of his rhymes, which are notoriously loose, and moreover often wrenched against the correct inflexion, with the metrical accent falling on unstressed syllables, in a Romantic affectation frequent in Victorian verse but trying to the modern ear. *The Stream's Secret*, however, deploys mellifluous and plangent versification, subtly imitative of water flowing over rocks.

His own view was that conception – the intellectual idea behind a poem, or what he referred to as 'fundamental brainwork' – was more important than correctness. 'Work your metal as much as you like, but first take care that it is gold and worth working. A Shakespearean sonnet is better than the most perfect in form because Shakespeare wrote it,' he told a correspondent in 1880.[18] His notion of the *House of Life* as 'a complete *dramatis personae* of the soul' suggests that he conceived of the sequence as expressive of an interior 'life-drama' of interacting experiences and emotions, perhaps with the additional image of each occupying a separate room (*stanza* in Italian) in the house of the poet's soul.

Poetic writing was often laborious, as he was the first to acknowledge, telling a correspondent in 1871 that in 'the ardour of composition' he sometimes found he had overlooked 'imperfections of phraseology' that had subsequently to be corrected. This was, he felt, in contrast to the methods used by his sister, who was altogether a more natural and instinctive poet. Though himself critical of the Della Cruscan manner, his work is not entirely free of such tendencies. According to his brother, writing in 1869, DGR's 'practice with poetry is first to write the thing in the rough, and then turn over dictionaries of rhymes and synonyms so as to bring the poem into the most perfect form'. He himself wrote later of 'the first and highest' quality in poetic composition being 'where the work has been all mentally "cartooned" as it were, beforehand, by a process intensely conscious, but patient and silent – an occult evolution of life.'[19] Whether 'occult' or not, this process is comparable to that of pictorial composition: beginning with a subject sketched out, then elaborated or simplified into a full 'cartoon' to be worked up with appropriate materials before being finished and polished, and perhaps laid aside for a while, to be finally completed and presented to the public. In relation to longer poems, this was DGR's method, as prose summaries for a number of never-executed poems attest. With sonnets and lyrics, the process was slightly different. 'I hardly ever do produce a sonnet except on some basis of special momentary emotion, but I think there is another class admissible also – and that is the only other one I practise, viz. the class depending on a line or two clearly given you, you know not whence, and calling up a sequence of ideas. This also is a just *raison d'être* for a sonnet,' he wrote in 1871.[20] In practice, he appears usually to have responded to the 'momentary emotion' by raising a correlative poetic figure or motif as a conceit on which to structure the poem. This method is fully in keeping with Renaissance poetic practice, as also practised by Shakespeare and Donne – and in more than a few cases, the contrived nature of the motif is equally challenging to the reader. In addition, DGR followed his Italian models in deploying Love, Hope, Death, etc. as active rather than abstract figures in a sometimes awkward and old-fashioned way. As Death is virtually the only such personification to remain familiar today, present-day readers struggle to accommodate 'love' as a corporeal, speaking Eros; as Browning wrote privately, in response to *Poems* 1870: 'Then, how I hate "love" as a lubberly, naked young man putting his arms there & his wings there, about a pair of lovers – a fellow they would kick away in the reality.'[21] Understanding of the Dantescan origins of this device removes some of the difficulty, but the result can be undeniably comic, as when in *Sleepless Dreams* Joy and Ruth shoo away Sleep, who tiptoes round the poet's bed.

Compared to the highly wrought diction and imagery of the sonnets, that of the narrative poems, from *A Last Confession* through *Sister Helen* and *Rose Mary* to *The King's Tragedy*, is remarkably simple and direct, with little use of simile or metaphorical language. In 1880 he told a correspondent with a taste for the purple style that 'seriously, simple English in prose writing and in all narrative poetry (however monumental language may become in abstract verse) seems to me a treasure not to be forgone.'

Heavily revised proofs demonstrate how he endeavoured to hit upon the exact choice and order of words. Reading Rossetti's correspondence, one is conscious of perennial striving which he himself described as 'vain longings for perfectibility' through 'repeated condensation and revision'[22] so that the work might match up to the projected or platonic ideal. Perfect they may not be (should such a thing exist) but the density of some of his work, with its packed, compound words and phrases, is often reminiscent of Gerard Manley Hopkins (1844–89), and it is an ironic sadness that in 1880 their mutual friend R. W. Dixon forwarded some of Hopkins' plainer sonnets for inclusion in an anthology being edited by Hall Caine, which were summarily rejected by Rossetti.

In literary histories, as indicated above, Rossetti is positioned as a 'late Romantic' or 'Aesthetic' poet, and as a proto-Symbolist or Decadent. His collections published in 1870 and 1881 were influential on the next generation, including Oscar Wilde (1854–1900) and most notably W. B. Yeats (1869–1939). In the United States, Pound and Eliot were also profoundly marked by the 'Rossettian' style, until they rebelled against their literary elders and cast him out of the poetic pantheon (Pound however retaining his admiration for Rossetti's translations, as aforementioned). Following the Modernist lead, in 1952 F. R. Leavis damned the Rossettian 'religion of Beauty'

as 'a shameless cheap evocation of a romantic and bogus Platonism
... in which "significance" is vagueness, and profundity an uninhi-
bited proffer of large drafts on a merely nominal account ... nullity
of thought made aggressively vulgar by a wordy pretentiousness.'[23]

Over the past generation, as Victorian poetry has returned to
critical favour, D. G. Rossetti has been more studied in selected texts
– especially *The Blessed Damozel, Jenny* and some of the *House of
Life* sonnets – than through his oeuvre as a whole. Recent critics
however are steadily discovering more points of interest, and are less
inclined to dismiss textual difficulties as poetic failure. Increasingly,
his work is seen in the context of its time. 'Far from being
preternaturally independent of his age, Rossetti was profoundly in
touch with some of its deepest currents of feeling, and his art was
deeply satisfying to some of its most urgent needs', writes David
Riede.[24] Whereas once it was thought necessary to hail him uncriti-
cally as a great, if flawed, genius in order to respond to his aesthetic
sensibility, today his imaginative practices yield many other intellec-
tual rewards. According to Jerome McGann, author of some of the
most stimulating recent criticism on both the poems and pictures,[25]
'should we desire to reimagine the cultural horizon framed by
institutional Modernism, Rossetti becomes an interesting point of
departure.' Antony H. Harrison has rewardingly explored the
metaliterary implications of Rossetti's dense intertextuality, a dialecti-
cal activity that becomes in his verse 'the pre-eminent mode of self-
definition, intellectual inquiry, social understanding and spiritual self-
generation'.[26]

One obstacle to reading and studying Rossetti's literary output in
order to appreciate its diversity and depth as well as its aspirations
and achievements has been the absence of easily accessible modern
editions, which the present publication is intended to supply. For
dedicated and casual students, there is, or will shortly be, available by
internet the multi-media *Complete Writings and Pictures of Dante
Gabriel Rossetti: A Hypermedia Research Archive*, created by Jerome
McGann at the University of Virginia, together with the late W. E.
Fredman's forthcoming edition of the *Complete Letters*, also available
in electronic form. An invigorating phase of Rossettian criticism is
poised to open.

1 See *Victorian Poetry*, 1982, plate 1.
2 Joaquin Miller, 'Recollections of the Rossetti Dinner', *Overland Monthly*,
   February 1920, 141.
3 See R. D. Waller, *The Rossetti Family, 1824–1854*, Manchester University Press,
   1932, 173; and William Sharp, *Papers Critical and Reminiscent*, 1912, 73.

4 *FLM*, I, 66.
5 Two or three years later, this was revised and retitled 'The Free Companions. A Tale of the Days of King Stephen'.
6 DW 11.
7 *FLM*, I, 105.
8 *FLM*, I, 105.
9 DW 1165.
10 *FLM*, I, 107. If so, it is surprising that it was not offered for publication at that date – especially as in autumn 1847 both Christina and William Rossetti had poems published in the *Athenaeum*, the leading literary weekly.
11 T. H. Caine, *Recollections of Rossetti*, 1882, quoted *FLM*, I, 107.
12 *FLM*, I, 123.
13 April 1880, quoted in T. H. Caine, *Recollections of Rossetti*, 1928 (1990 edn, 11)
14 DGR to Richard Burton, n.d. University of Texas.
15 Algernon Charles Swinburne, *William Blake*, 1868.
16 DW 1345.
17 To T. G. Hake, 21 April 1870, DW 992.
18 Quoted THC, *Recollections*, 1928 (1990 edn, 71).
19 *RP*, 393; and see Sharp, 410.
20 DW 1153.
21 Robert Browning, *Letters to Isa Blagden*, ed. E. C. McAleer, Austin, 1951, 336–7.
22 Bryson no. 12.
23 F. R. Leavis, *The Common Pursuit*, 1952, 48.
24 David G. Riede, *Dante Gabriel Rossetti Revisited*, 1992, 167.
25 See the forthcoming study, *Rossetti and the Game that Must be Lost*.
26 Antony H. Harrison, *Victorian Poets and Romantic Poems*, University Press of Virginia 1990, 91.

NOTE ON THE TEXTS

DGR left a few unpublished poems, mainly from his youth, together with a number of couplets, drafts, fragments, and subjects schemed out as potential narratives. The present edition contains everything published in DGR's lifetime, in texts authorised by himself, together with the more significant items published after DGR's death by his brother and editor WMR. It includes the prose story *Hand and Soul* (1850) and the critical defence of his verse 'The Stealthy School of Criticism' (1871). A selection of translations, primarily of texts by Dante and his peers, are also reprinted, together with a handful of fragments that for one reason or other have entered the canon of DGR's work during the past hundred years.

Because DGR was a constant reviser of texts prior to re-publication, it is sometimes difficult to select the most 'canonical' version of any piece – especially as the earlier (1870) versions of several continued to be available, for example in the 1912 Everyman Library edition from J. M. Dent, and that of 1913 from OUP (both of which also included the *Early Italian Poets* from the edition of 1861). In the present edition, where 'early' and 'late' published versions of the same poem differ markedly, both are included; otherwise, the first published version has generally been selected, in order to convey a better sense of DGR's poetic development and the position of each piece within it. There are however a few exceptions, as with *Sister Helen*, where a whole new element was inserted at the end of DGR's life, altering the narrative but not justifying the inclusion of both versions in full. MS versions and variations are largely ignored, as are minor amendments made by WMR in his various editions between 1886 and 1911. The vexed question of the versions contained in the so-called 'Trial Books' of 1869 (in actuality proof sheets ordered from the printer ahead of publication, for the purpose of revision) has been resolved by treating these as drafts, in accordance with R. C. Lewis's advice in *T. J. Wise and the Trial Book Fallacy*, 1995, 117 that 'We should . . . regard the heavily revised proof copies not as books but as manuscripts. Unlike most poets, Rossetti had some of his most creative moments labouring over proofsheets.'

The texts are arranged in chronological order of publication, for simpler comparison with the publication dates of works by other authors.

Poems
first published
1848–62

My Sister's Sleep

[TEXT A, 1850]

She fell asleep on Christmas Eve.
  Upon her eyes' most patient calms
  The lids were shut; her uplaid arms
Covered her bosom, I believe.

Our mother, who had leaned all day   5
  Over the bed from chime to chime,
  Then raised herself for the first time,
And as she sat her down, did pray.

Her little work-table was spread
  With work to finish. For the glare   10
  Made by her candle, she had care
To work some distance from the bed.

Without, there was a good moon up,
  Which left its shadow far within;
  The depth of light that it was in   15
Seemed hollow like an altar-cup.

Through the small room, with subtle sound
  Of flame, by vents the fireshine drove
  And reddened. In its dim alcove
The mirror shed a clearness round.   20

I had been sitting up some nights,
  And my tir'd mind felt weak and blank;
  Like a sharp strengthening wine, it drank
The stillness and the broken lights.

Silence was speaking at my side   25
  With an exceedingly clear voice:
  I knew the calm as of a choice
Made in God for me, to abide.

I said, "Full knowledge does not grieve:
  This which upon my spirit dwells   30
  Perhaps would have been sorrow else:
But I am glad 'tis Christmas Eve."

Twelve struck. That sound, which all the years
  Hear in each hour, crept off; and then
  The ruffled silence spread again,   35
Like water that a pebble stirs.

Our mother rose from where she sat.
  Her needles, as she laid them down,
  Met lightly, and her silken gown
Settled: no other noise than that.   40

"Glory unto the Newly Born!"
  So, as said angels, she did say;
  Because we were in Christmas-day,
Though it would still be long till dawn.

She stood a moment with her hands   45
  Kept in each other, praying much;
  A moment that the soul may touch
But the heart only understands.

Almost unwittingly, my mind
  Repeated her words after her;   50
  Perhaps tho' my lips did not stir;
It was scarce thought, or cause assign'd.

Just then in the room over us
  There was a pushing back of chairs,
  As some who had sat unawares   55
So late, now heard the hour, and rose.

Anxious, with softly stepping haste,
  Our mother went where Margaret lay,
  Fearing the sounds o'erhead – should they
Have broken her long-watched for rest!   60

She stooped an instant, calm, and turned;
  But suddenly turned back again;
  And all her features seemed in pain
With woe, and her eyes gazed and yearned.

For my part, I but hid my face,   65
  And held my breath, and spake no word:
  There was none spoken; but *I heard*
The silence for a little space.

Our mother bowed herself and wept.
  And both my arms fell, and I said: 70
  "God knows I knew that she was dead."
And there, all white, my sister slept.

Then kneeling, upon Christmas morn
   A little after twelve o'clock
   We said, ere the first quarter struck,   75
"Christ's blessing on the newly born!"

My Sister's Sleep¹
[TEXT B, 1870]

She fell asleep on Christmas Eve:
   At length the long-ungranted shade
   Of weary eyelids overweigh'd
The pain nought else might yet relieve.

Our mother, who had leaned all day   5
   Over the bed from chime to chime,
   Then raised herself for the first time,
And as she sat her down, did pray.

Her little work-table was spread
   With work to finish. For the glare   10
   Made by her candle, she had care
To work some distance from the bed.

Without, there was a cold moon up,
   Of winter radiance sheer and thin;
   The hollow halo it was in   15
Was like an icy crystal cup.

Through the small room, with subtle sound
   Of flame, by vents the fireshine drove
   And reddened. In its dim alcove
The mirror shed a clearness round.   20

I had been sitting up some nights,
   And my tired mind felt weak and blank;
   Like a sharp strengthening wine it drank
The stillness and the broken lights.

Twelve struck. That sound, by dwindling years   25
   Heard in each hour, crept off; and then
   The ruffled silence spread again,
Like water that a pebble stirs.

Our mother rose from where she sat:
    Her needles, as she laid them down,   30
    Met lightly, and her silken gown
Settled: no other noise than that.

'Glory unto the Newly Born!'
    So, as said angels, she did say;
    Because we were in Christmas Day,   35
Though it would still be long till morn.

Just then in the room over us
    There was a pushing back of chairs,
    As some who had sat unawares
So late, now heard the hour, and rose.   40

With anxious softly-stepping haste
    Our mother went where Margaret lay,
    Fearing the sounds o'erhead – should they
Have broken her long watched-for rest!

She stooped an instant, calm, and turned;   45
    But suddenly turned back again;
    And all her features seemed in pain
With woe, and her eyes gazed and yearned.

For my part, I but hid my face,
    And held my breath, and spoke no word: 50
    There was none spoken; but I heard
The silence for a little space.

Our mother bowed herself and wept:
    And both my arms fell, and I said,
    'God knows I knew that she was dead.'   55
And there, all white, my sister slept.

Then kneeling, upon Christmas morn
    A little after twelve o'clock
    We said, ere the first quarter struck,
'Christ's blessing on the newly born!'   60

1 This little poem, written in 1847, was printed in a periodical at the outset of 1850.
The metre, which is used by several old English writers, became celebrated a month
or two later on the publication of *In Memoriam.*

Mary's Girlhood

[FOR A PICTURE]

I

This is that blessed Mary, pre-elect
 God's Virgin. Gone is a great while, and she
 Dwelt young in Nazareth of Galilee.
Unto God's will she brought devout respect,
Profound simplicity of intellect,   5
 And supreme patience. From her mother's knee
 Faithful and hopeful; wise in charity;
Strong in grave peace; in pity circumspect.

So held she through her girlhood; as it were
 An angel-watered lily, that near God   10
  Grows and is quiet. Till, one dawn at home
She woke in her white bed, and had no fear
 At all, – yet wept till sunshine, and felt awed:
  Because the fulness of the time was come.

II

These are the symbols. On that cloth of red 15
 I' the centre is the Tripoint: perfect each,
 Except the second of its points, to teach
That Christ is not yet born. The books – whose head
Is golden Charity, as Paul hath said –
 Those virtues are wherein the soul is rich: 20
 Therefore on them the lily standeth, which
Is Innocence, bring interpreted.

The seven-thorn'd briar and the palm seven-leaved
 Are her great sorrow and her great reward.
  Until the end be full, the Holy One 25
Abides without. She soon shall have achieved
 Her perfect purity: yea, God the Lord
  Shall soon vouchsafe His Son to be her Son.

The Blessed Damozel
[TEXT A, 1850]

The blessed Damozel leaned out
  From the gold bar of Heaven:
Her blue grave eyes were deeper much
  Than a deep water, even.
She had three lilies in her hand,   5
  And the stars in her hair were seven.

Her robe, ungirt from clasp to hem,
  No wrought flowers did adorn,
But a white rose of Mary's gift
  On the neck meetly worn;   10
And her hair, lying down her back,
  Was yellow like ripe corn.

Herseemed she scarce had been a day
  One of God's choristers;
The wonder was not yet quite gone   15
  From that still look of hers;
Albeit to them she left, her day
  Had counted as ten years.

(To *one* it is ten years of years:
  .... Yet now, here in this place   20
Surely she leaned o'er me, – her hair
  Fell all about my face........
Nothing: the Autumn-fall of leaves.
  The whole year sets apace.)

It was the terrace of God's house   25
  That she was standing on, –
By God built over the sheer depth
  In which Space is begun;
So high, that looking downward thence,
  She could scarce see the sun.   30

It lies from Heaven across the flood
  Of ether, as a bridge.
Beneath, the tides of day and night
  With flame and blackness ridge
The void, as low as where this earth   35
  Spins like a fretful midge.

But in those tracts, with her, it was
    The peace of utter light
And silence. For no breeze may stir
    Along the steady flight   40
Of seraphim; no echo there,
    Beyond all depth or height.

Heard hardly, some of her new friends,
    Playing at holy games,
Spake, gentle-mouthed, among themselves,   45
    Their virginal chaste names;
And the souls, mounting up to God,
    Went by her like thin flames.

And still she bowed herself, and stooped
    Into the vast waste calm;   50
Till her bosom's pressure must have made
    The bar she leaned on warm,
And the lilies lay as if asleep
    Along her bended arm.

From the fixt lull of heaven, she saw   55
    Time, like a pulse, shake fierce
Through all the worlds. Her gaze still strove,
    In that steep gulph, to pierce
The swarm: and then she spake, as when
    The stars sang in their spheres.   60

"I wish that he were come to me,
    For he will come," she said.
"Have I not prayed in solemn heaven?
    On earth, has he not prayed?
Are not two prayers a perfect strength?   65
    And shall I feel afraid?

"When round his head the aureole clings,
    And he is clothed in white,
I'll take his hand, and go with him
    To the deep wells of light,   70
And we will step down as to a stream
    And bathe there in God's sight.

"We two will stand beside that shrine,
    Occult, withheld, untrod,
Whose lamps tremble continually   75
    With prayer sent up to God;

And where each need, revealed, expects
  Its patient period.

"We two will lie i' the shadow of
  That living mystic tree   80
Within whose secret growth the Dove
  Sometimes is felt to be,
While every leaf that His plumes touch
  Saith His name audibly.

"And I myself will teach to him –   85
  I myself, lying so, –
The songs I sing here; which his mouth
  Shall pause in, hushed and slow,
Finding some knowledge at each pause
  And some new thing to know."   90

(Alas! to *her* wise simple mind
  These things were all but known
Before: they trembled on her sense, –
  Her voice had caught their tone.
Alas for lonely Heaven! Alas   95
  For life wrung out alone!

Alas, and though the end were reached?........
  Was *thy* part understood
Or borne in trust? And for her sake
  Shall this too be found good? –   100
May the close lips that knew not prayer
  Praise ever, though they would?)

"We two," she said, "will seek the groves
  Where the lady Mary is,
With her five handmaidens, whose names   105
  Are five sweet symphonies: –
Cecily, Gertrude, Magdalen,
  Margaret, and Rosalys.

"Circle-wise sit they, with bound locks
  And bosoms covered;   110
Into the fine cloth, white like flame,
  Weaving the golden thread,
To fashion the birth-robes for them
  Who are just born, being dead.

"He shall fear haply, and be dumb. 115
  Then I will lay my cheek
To his, and tell about our love,
  Not once abashed or weak:
And the dear Mother will approve
  My pride, and let me speak. 120

"Herself shall bring us, hand in hand,
  To Him round whom all souls
Kneel – the unnumber'd solemn heads
  Bowed with their aureoles:
And Angels, meeting us, shall sing 125
  To their citherns and citoles.

"There will I ask of Christ the Lord
  Thus much for him and me: –
To have more blessing than on earth
  In nowise; but to be 130
As then we were, – being as then
  At peace. Yea, verily.

"Yea, verily; when he is come
  We will do thus and thus:
Till this my vigil seem quite strange 135
  And almost fabulous;
We two will live at once, one life;
  And peace shall be with us."

She gazed, and listened, and then said,
  Less sad of speech than mild: 140
"All this is when he comes." She ceased;
  The light thrilled past her, filled
With Angels, in strong level lapse.
  Her eyes prayed, and she smiled.

(I saw her smile.) But soon their flight 145
  Was vague 'mid the poised spheres.
And then she cast her arms along
  The golden barriers,
And laid her face between her hands,
  And wept. (I heard her tears.) 150

The Blessed Damozel

[TEXT B, 1870]

The blessed damozel leaned out
   From the gold bar of Heaven;
Her eyes were deeper than the depth
   Of waters stilled at even;
She had three lilies in her hand,   5
   And the stars in her hair were seven.

Her robe, ungirt from clasp to hem,
   No wrought flowers did adorn,
But a white rose of Mary's gift
   For service meetly worn;   10
Her hair that lay along her back
   Was yellow like ripe corn.

Herseemed she scarce had been a day
   One of God's choristers;
The wonder was not yet quite gone   15
   From that still look of hers;
Albeit, to them she left, her day
   Had counted as ten years.

(To one, it is ten years of years:
   ... Yet now, and in this place   20
Surely she leaned o'er me – her hair
   Fell all about my face....
Nothing: the autumn fall of leaves.
   The whole year sets apace.)

It was the rampart of God's house   25
   That she was standing on;
By God built over the sheer depth
   The which is Space begun;
So high, that looking downward thence
   She scarce could see the sun.   30

It lies in Heaven, across the flood
   Of ether, as a bridge.
Beneath, the tides of day and night
   With flame and darkness ridge
The void, as low as where this earth   35
   Spins like a fretful midge.

Heard hardly, some of her new friends
  Amid their loving games
Spake evermore among themselves
Their virginal chaste names;   40
And the souls mounting up to God
  Went by her like thin flames.

And still she bowed herself and stooped
  Out of the circling charm;
Until her bosom must have made   45
  The bar she leaned on warm,
And the lilies lay as if asleep
  Along her bended arm.

From the fixed place of Heaven she saw
  Time like a pulse shake fierce   50
Through all the worlds. Her gaze still strove
  Within the gulf to pierce
Its path: and now she spoke as when
  The stars sang in their spheres.

The sun was gone now; the curled moon   55
  Was like a little feather
Fluttering far down the gulf; and now
  She spoke through the still weather.
Her voice was like the voice the stars
  Had when they sang together.   60

(Ah sweet! Even now, in that bird's song,
  Strove not her accents there,
Fain to be hearkened? When those bells
  Possessed the mid-day air,
Strove not her steps to reach my side   65
  Down all the echoing stair?)

'I wish that he were come to me,
  For he will come,' she said.
'Have I not prayed in Heaven? – on earth,
  Lord, Lord, has he not pray'd?   70
Are not two prayers a perfect strength?
  And shall I feel afraid?

'When round his head the aureole clings,
  And he is clothed in white,
I'll take his hand and go with him   75

To the deep wells of light;
We will step down as to a stream,
    And bathe there in God's sight.

'We two will stand beside that shrine,
    Occult, withheld, untrod,   80
Whose lamps are stirred continually
    With prayer sent up to God;
And see our old prayers, granted, melt
    Each like a little cloud.

'We two will lie i' the shadow of   85
    That living mystic tree
Within whose secret growth the Dove
    Is sometimes felt to be,
While every leaf that His plumes touch
    Saith His Name audibly.   90

'And I myself will teach to him,
    I myself, lying so,
The songs I sing here; which his voice
    Shall pause in, hushed and slow,
And find some knowledge at each pause,   95
    Or some new thing to know.'

(Alas! We two, we two, thou say'st!
    Yea, one wast thou with me
That once of old. But shall God lift
    To endless unity   100
The soul whose likeness with thy soul
    Was but its love for thee?)

'We two,' she said, 'will seek the groves
    Where the lady Mary is,
With her five handmaidens, whose names   105
    Are five sweet symphonies,
Cecily, Gertrude, Magdalen,
    Margaret and Rosalys.

'Circlewise sit they, with bound locks
    And foreheads garlanded;   110
Into the fine cloth white like flame
    Weaving the golden thread,

To fashion the birth-robes for them
   Who are just born, being dead.

'He shall fear, haply and be dumb: 115
   Then will I lay my cheek
To his, and tell about our love,
   Not once abashed or weak:
And the dear Mother will approve
   My pride, and let me speak.   120

'Herself shall bring us, hand in hand,
   To Him round whom all souls
Kneel, the clear-ranged unnumbered heads
   Bowed with their aureoles:
And angels meeting us shall sing   125
   To their citherns and citoles.

'There will I ask of Christ the Lord
   Thus much for him and me:—
Only to live as once on earth
   With Love, – only to be,   130
As then awhile, for ever now
   Together, I and he.'

She gazed and listened and then said,
   Less sad of speech than mild, –
'All this is when he comes.' She ceased.   135
   The light thrilled towards her, fill'd
With angels in strong level flight.
   Her eyes prayed, and she smil'd.

(I saw her smile.) But soon their path
   Was vague in distant spheres: 140
And then she cast her arms along
   The golden barriers,
And laid her face between her hands,
   And wept. (I heard her tears.)

The Carillon

ANTWERP AND BRUGES

(In these and others of the Flemish towns, the *Carillon*, or
chimes which have a most fantastic and delicate music, are
played almost continuously. The custom is very ancient.)

At Antwerp, there is a low wall
   Binding the city, and a moat
   Beneath, that the wind keeps afloat.
You pass the gates in a slow drawl
Of wheels. If it is warm at all   5
   The Carillon will give you thought.

I climbed the stair in Antwerp church,
   What time the urgent weight of sound
   At sunset seems to heave it round.
Far up, the Carillon did search   10
The wind; and the birds came to perch
   Far under, where the gables wound.

In Antwerp harbour on the Scheldt
   I stood along, a certain space
   Of night. The mist was near my face: 15
Deep on, the flow was heard and felt.
The Carillon kept pause, and dwelt
   In music through the silent place.

At Bruges, when you leave the train,
   – A singing numbness in your ears, –   20
   The Carillon's first sound appears
Only the inner moil. Again
A little minute though – your brain
   Takes quiet, and the whole sense hears.

John Memmeling and John Van Eyck   25
   Hold state at Bruges. In sore shame
   I scanned the works that keep their name.
The Carillon, which then did strike
Mine ears, was heard of theirs alike:
   It set me closer unto them.   30

I climbed at Bruges all the flight
   The Belfry has of ancient stone.
   For leagues I saw the east wind blown:

The earth was grey, the sky was white.
I stood so near upon the height   35
    That my flesh felt the Carillon.

October, 1849

From the Cliffs: Noon
[TEXT A, 1850]

The sea is in its listless chime:
    Time's lapse it is, made audible, –
    The murmur of the earth's large shell.
In a sad blueness beyond rhyme
    It ends: sense, without thought, can pass   5
    No stadium further. Since time was,
This sound hath told the lapse of time.

No stagnance that death wins, – it hath
    The mournfulness of ancient life,
    Always enduring at dull strife.   10
As the world's heart of rest and wrath,
    Its painful pulse is in the sands.
    Last utterly, the whole sky stands,
Grey and not known, along its path.

The Sea-Limits
[TEXT B, 1870]

Consider the sea's listless chime:
    Time's self it is, made audible, –
    The murmur of the earth's own shell.
Secret continuance sublime
    Is the sea's end: our sight may pass   5
    No furlong further. Since time was,
This sound hath told the lapse of time.

No quiet, which is death's, – it hath
    The mournfulness of ancient life,
    Enduring always at dull strife.   10
As the world's heart of rest and wrath,
    Its painful pulse is in the sands.

Last utterly, the whole sky stands,
Grey and not known, along its path.

Listen alone beside the sea,   15
  Listen alone among the woods;
  Those voices of twin solitudes
Shall have one sound alike to thee:
  Hark where the murmurs of thronged men
  Surge and sink back and surge again, –   20
Still the one voice of wave and tree.

Gather a shell from the strown beach
  And listen at its lips: they sigh
  The same desire and mystery,
The echo of the whole sea's speech.   25
  And all mankind is thus at heart
  Not anything but what thou art:
And Earth, Sea, Man, are all in each.

Pax Vobis

[TEXT A, 1850]

'Tis of the Father Hilary.
  He strove, but could not pray; so took
  The darkened stair, where his feet shook
A sad blind echo. He kept up
  Slowly. 'Twas a chill sway of air   5
  That autumn noon within the stair,
Sick, dizzy, like a turning cup.
  His brain perplexed him, void and thin:
  He shut his eyes and felt it spin;
  The obscure deafness hemmed him in.   10
He said: 'The air is calm outside.'

He leaned unto the gallery
  Where the chime keeps the night and day:
  It hurt his brain, – he could not pray.
He had his face upon the stone: 15
  Deep 'twixt the narrow shafts, his eye
  Passed all the roofs unto the sky
Whose greyness the wind swept alone.
  Close by his feet he saw it shake

With wind in pools that the rains make: 20
The ripple set his eyes to ache.
He said: 'Calm hath its peace outside.'

He stood within the mystery
  Girding God's blessed Eucharist:
  The organ and the chaunt had ceased: 25
A few words paused against his ear,
  Said from the altar: drawn round him,
  The silence was at rest and dim.
He could not pray. The bell shook clear
  And ceased. All was great awe, – the breath   30
  Of God in man, that warranteth
Wholly the inner things of Faith.
He said: 'There is the world outside.'

Ghent: Church of St Bavon

World's Worth

[TEXT B, 1870]

'Tis of the Father Hilary.
  He strove, but could not pray; so took
  The steep-coiled stair, where his feet shook
A sad blind echo. Ever up
  He toiled. 'Twas a sick sway of air   5
  That autumn noon within the stair,
As dizzy as a turning cup.
  His brain benumbed him, void and thin;
  He shut his eyes and felt it spin;
  The obscure deafness hemmed him in.   10
He said: 'O world, what world for me?'

He leaned unto the balcony
  Where the chime keeps the night and day;
  It hurt his brain, he could not pray.
He had his face upon the stone: 15
  Deep 'twixt the narrow shafts, his eye
  Passed all the roofs to the stark sky,
Swept with no wing, with wind alone.
  Close to his feet the sky did shake
  With wind in pools that the rains make: 20

The ripple set his eyes to ache.
He said: 'O world, what world for me?'

He stood within the mystery
   Girding God's blessed Eucharist:
   The organ and the chaunt had ceas'd: 25
The last words paused against his ear
   Said from the altar: drawn round him,
   The gathering rest was dumb and dim.
And now the sacring-bell rang clear
   And ceased; and all was awe, – the breath   30
   Of God in man that warranteth
The inmost utmost things of faith.
He said: 'O God, my world in Thee!'

An Allegorical Dance of Women, by Andrea Mantegna
in the Louvre

Scarcely, I think; yet it indeed *may* be
   The meaning reached him, when this music rang
   Clear through his frame, a sweet possessive pang,
And he beheld these rocks and that ridged sea.
But I believe that, leaning tow'rds them, he   5
   Just felt their hair carried across his face
   As each girl passed him; nor gave ear to trace
How many feet; nor bent assuredly
His eyes from the blind fixedness of thought
   To know the dancers. It is bitter glad   10
   Even unto tears. Its meaning filleth it,
   A secret of the wells of Life: to wit:—
The heart's each pulse shall keep the sense it had
With all, though the mind's labour run to nought.

A Virgin and Child, by Hans Memmeling
in the Academy of Bruges

Mystery: God, Man's Life, born into man
  Of woman. There abideth on her brow
  The ended pang of knowledge, the which now
Is calm assured. Since first her task began,
She hath known all. What more of anguish than   5
  Endurance oft hath lived through, the whole space
  Through night till night, passed weak upon her face
While like a heavy flood the darkness ran?
All hath been told her touching her dear Son,
  And all shall be accomplished. Where he sits   10
    Even now, a babe, he holds the symbol fruit
Perfect and chosen. Until God permits,
    His soul's elect still have the absolute
Harsh nether darkness, and make painful moan.

A Marriage of St Katharine, by the same
in the Hospital of St John at Bruges

Mystery: Katharine, the bride of Christ.
  She kneels, and on her hand the holy Child
  Setteth the ring. Her life is sad and mild,
Laid in God's knowledge – ever unenticed
From Him, and in the end thus fitly priced.   5
  Awe, and the music that is near her, wrought
  Of Angels, hath possessed her eyes in thought:
Her utter joy is her's, and hath sufficed.
There is a pause while Mary Virgin turns
  The leaf, and reads. With eyes on the spread book,   10
    That damsel at her knees reads after her.
    John whom He loved and John His harbinger
Listen and watch. Whereon soe'er thou look,
The light is starred in gems, and the gold burns.

A Venetian Pastoral, by Giorgione
in the Louvre
[TEXT A, 1850]

(In this picture, two cavaliers and an undraped woman are
seated in the grass, with musical instruments, while another
woman dips a vase into a well hard by, for water.)

Water, for anguish of the solstice, – yea,
  Over the vessel's mouth still widening
  Listlessly dipt to let the water in
With slow vague gurgle. Blue, and deep away,
The heat lies silent at the brink of day.   5
  Now the hand trails upon the viol-string
  That sobs; and the brown faces cease to sing,
Mournful with complete pleasure. Her eyes stray
In distance; through her lips the pipe doth creep
  And leaves them pouting; the green shadowed grass   10
  Is cool against her naked flesh. Let be:
Do not now speak unto her lest she weep, –
  Nor name this ever. Be it as it was –
  Silence of heat, and solemn poetry.

A Venetian Pastoral, by Giorgione
in the Louvre
[TEXT B, 1870]

Water, for anguish of the solstice: – nay,
  But dip the vessel slowly, – nay, but lean
  And hark how at its verge the wave sighs in
Reluctant. Hush! Beyond all depth away
The heat lies silent at the brink of day: 5
  Now the hand trails upon the viol-string
  That sobs, and the brown faces cease to sing,
Sad with the whole of pleasure. Whither stray
Her eyes now, from whose mouth the slim pipes creep
  And leave it pouting, while the shadowed grass   10
  Is cool against her naked side? Let be:–
Say nothing now unto her lest she weep,
  Nor name this ever. Be it as it was, –
  Life touching lips with Immortality.

Ruggiero and Angelica, by Ingres

I

A remote sky, prolonged to the sea's brim:
  One rock-point standing buffeted alone,
  Vexed at its base with a foul beast unknown,
Hell-birth of geomaunt and teraphim:
A knight, and a winged creature bearing him,   5
  Reared at the rock: a woman fettered there,
  Leaning into the hollow with loose hair
And throat let back and heartsick trail of limb.

The sky is harsh, and the sea shrewd and salt:
  Under his lord the griffin-horse ramps blind   10
    With rigid wings and tail. The spear's lithe stem
  Thrills in the roaring of those jaws: behind,
That evil length of body chafes at fault.
    She doth not hear nor see – she knows of them.

II

Clench thine eyes now, – 'tis the last instant, girl: 15
  Draw in thy senses, set thy knees, and take
  One breath for all: thy life is keen awake, –
Thou mayst not swoon. Was that the scattered whirl
Of its foam drenched thee? – or the waves that curl
  And split, bleak spray wherein thy temples ache?   20
  Or was it his the champion's blood to flake
Thy flesh? – or thine own blood's anointing, girl?

Now, silence: for the sea's is such a sound
  As irks not silence; and except the sea,
    All now is still. Now the dead thing doth cease   25
  To writhe, and drifts. He turns to her: and she,
Cast from the jaws of Death, remains there, bound,
  Again a woman in her nakedness.

The Card-Dealer

Could you not drink her gaze like wine?
  Yet though its splendour swoon
Into the silence languidly
  As a tune into a tune,
Those eyes unravel the coiled night   5
  And know the stars at noon.

The gold that's heaped beside her hand,
  In truth rich prize it were;
And rich the dreams that wreathe her brows
  With magic stillness there;   10
And he were rich who should unwind
  That woven golden hair.

Around her, where she sits, the dance
  Now breathes its eager heat;
And not more lightly or more true   15
  Fall there the dancers' feet
Than fall her cards on the bright board
  As 'twere an heart that beat.

Her fingers let them softly through,
  Smooth polished silent things;   20
And each one as it falls reflects
  In swift light-shadowings,
Blood-red and purple, green and blue
  The great eyes of her rings.

Whom plays she with? With thee, who lov'st   25
  Those gems upon her hand;
With me, who search her secret brows;
  With all men, bless'd or bann'd.
We play together, she and we,
  Within a vain strange land: 30

A land without any order, –
  Day even as night, (one saith,) –
Where who lieth down ariseth not
  Nor the sleeper awakeneth;
A land of darkness as darkness itself   35
  And of the shadow of death.

What be her cards, you ask? Even these:–
    The heart, that doth but crave
More, having fed; the diamond,
    Skilled to make base seem brave;   40
The club, for smiting in the dark;
    The spade, to dig a grave.

And do you ask what game she plays?
    With me 'tis lost or won;
With thee it is playing still; with him   45
    It is not well begun;
But 'tis a game she plays with all
    Beneath the sway o' the sun.

Thou seest the card that falls, – she knows
    The card that followeth: 50
Her game in thy tongue is called Life,
    As ebbs thy daily breath:
When she shall speak, thou'lt learn her tongue
    And know she calls it Death.

Sister Helen

"Why did you melt your waxen man,
                        Sister Helen?
To-day is the third since you began."
"The time was long, yet the time ran,
                        Little brother."   5
            (*O Mother, Mary Mother,*
Three days to-day, between Hell and Heaven!)

"But if you have done your work aright,
                        Sister Helen,
You'll let me play, for you said I might."   10
"Be very still in your play to-night,
                        Little brother."
            (*O Mother, Mary Mother,*
Third night, tonight, between Hell and Heaven!)

"You said it must melt ere vesper-bell,   15
                        Sister Helen;
If now it be molten, all is well."

"Even so, – nay, peace! you cannot tell,
           Little brother."
          (O Mother, Mary Mother,   20
O what is this, between Hell and Heaven?)

"Oh the waxen knave was plump to-day,
           Sister Helen;
How like dead folk he has dropped away!"
"Nay now, of the dead what can you say,   25
           Little brother?"
          (O Mother, Mary Mother,
What of the dead, between Hell and Heaven?)

"See, see, the sunken pile of wood,
           Sister Helen,   30
Shines through the thinned wax red as blood!"
"Nay now, when looked you yet on blood,
           Little brother?"
          (O Mother, Mary Mother,
How pale she is, between Hell and Heaven!)   35

"Now close your eyes, for they're sick and sore,
           Sister Helen,
And I'll play without the gallery door."
"Aye, let me rest, – I'll lie on the floor,
           Little brother."   40
          (O Mother, Mary Mother,
What rest to-night between Hell and Heaven?)

"Here high up in the balcony,
           Sister Helen;
The moon flies face to face with me."   45
"Aye, look and say whatever you see,
           Little brother."
          (O Mother, Mary Mother,
What sight to-night, between Hell and Heaven?)

"Outside it's merry in the wind's wake,   50
           Sister Helen,
In the shaken trees the chill stars shake."
"Hush, heard you a horse-tread as you spake,
           Little brother?"
          (O Mother, Mary Mother,   55
What sound to-night, between Hell and Heaven?)

"I hear a horse-tread, and I see,
                    Sister Helen,
Three horsemen that ride terribly."
"Little brother, whence come the three,   60
                    Little brother?"
            (*O Mother, Mary Mother,*
Whence should they come, between Hell and Heaven?)

"They come by the hill-verge from Boyne Bar,
                    Sister Helen,   65
And one draws nigh, but two are afar."
"Look, look, do you know them who they are,
                    Little brother?"
            (*O Mother, Mary Mother,*
Who should they be, between Hell and Heaven?)   70

"Oh, it's Keith of Eastholm rides so fast,
                    Sister Helen,
For I know the white mane on the blast."
"The hour has come, has come at last,
                    Little brother!"   75
            (*O Mother, Mary Mother,*
Her hour at last, between Hell and Heaven!)

"He has made a sign and called Halloo!
                    Sister Helen,
And he says that he would speak with you."   80
"Oh tell him I fear the frozen dew,
                    Little brother."
            (*O Mother, Mary Mother,*
Why laughs she thus, between Hell and Heaven?)

"The wind is loud, but I hear him cry,   85
                    Sister Helen,
That Keith of Ewern's like to die."
"And he and thou, and thou and I,
                    Little brother."
            (*O Mother, Mary Mother,*   90
And they and we, between Hell and Heaven!)

"Three days ago, on his marriage-morn,
                    Sister Helen,
He sickened, and lies since then forlorn."
"For bridegroom's side is the bride a thorn,   95
                    Little brother?"

(O Mother, Mary Mother,
Cold bridal cheer, between Hell and Heaven!)

"Three days and nights he has lain abed,
        Sister Helen,   100
And he prays in torment to be dead."
"The thing may chance, if he have prayed,
        Little brother!"
        (O Mother, Mary Mother,
If he have prayed, between Hell and Heaven!)   105

"But he has not ceased to cry to-day,
        Sister Helen,
That you should take your curse away."
"*My* prayer was heard, – he need but pray,
        Little brother!"   110
        (O Mother, Mary Mother,
Shall God not hear, between Hell and Heaven?)

"But he says, till you take back your ban,
        Sister Helen,
His soul would pass, yet never can."   115
"Nay then, shall I slay a living man,
        Little brother?"
        (O Mother, Mary Mother,
A living soul, between Hell and Heaven!)

"But he calls for ever on your name,   120
        Sister Helen,
And says that he melts before a flame."
"My heart for his pleasure fared the same,
        Little brother."
        (O Mother, Mary Mother,   125
Fire at the heart, between Hell and Heaven!)

"Here's Keith of Westholm riding fast,
        Sister Helen,
For I know the white plume on the blast."
"The hour, the sweet hour I forecast,   130
        Little brother!"
        (O Mother, Mary Mother,
Is the hour sweet, between Hell and Heaven?)

"He stops to speak, and he stills his horse,
        Sister Helen;   135

But his words are drowned in the wind's course."
"Nay hear, nay hear, you must hear perforce,
            Little brother!"
        (*O Mother, Mary Mother,*
What word now heard, between Hell and Heaven?)   140

"Oh he says that Keith of Ewern's cry,
            Sister Helen,
Is ever to see you ere he die.'
"In all that his soul sees, there am I,
            Little brother!"   145
        (*O Mother, Mary Mother,*
The soul's one sight, between Hell and Heaven!)

"He sends a ring and a broken coin,
            Sister Helen,
And bids you mind the banks of Boyne."   150
"What else he broke will he ever join,
            Little brother?"
        (*O Mother, Mary Mother,*
No, never joined, between Hell and Heaven!)

"He yields you these and craves full fain,   155
            Sister Helen,
You pardon him in his mortal pain."
"What else he took will he give again,
            Little brother?"
        (*O Mother, Mary Mother,*   160
Not twice to give, between Hell and Heaven!)

"He calls your name in an agony,
            Sister Helen,
That even dead Love must weep to see."
"Hate, born of Love, is blind as he,   165
            Little brother!"
        (*O Mother, Mary Mother,*
Love turned to hate, between Hell and Heaven!)

"Oh it's Keith of Keith now that rides fast,
            Sister Helen,   170
For I know the white hair on the blast."
"The short short hour will soon be past,
            Little brother!"
        (*O Mother, Mary Mother,*
Will soon be past, between Hell and Heaven!)   175

"He looks at me and he tries to speak,
                    Sister Helen,
But oh! his voice is sad and weak!"
"What here should the mighty Baron seek,
                    Little brother?"   180
          (*O Mother, Mary Mother,*
Is this the end, between Hell and Heaven?)

"Oh his son still cries, if you forgive,
                    Sister Helen,
The body dies but the soul shall live."   185
"Fire shall forgive me as I forgive,
                    Little brother!"
          (*O Mother, Mary Mother,*
As she forgives, between Hell and Heaven!)

"Oh he prays you, as his heart would rive,   190
                    Sister Helen,
To save his dear son's soul alive."
"Fire cannot slay it, it shall thrive,
                    Little brother!"
          (*O Mother, Mary Mother,*   195
Alas, alas, between Hell and Heaven!)

"He cries to you, kneeling in the road,
                    Sister Helen,
To go with him for the love of God!"
"The way is long to his son's abode,   200
                    Little brother."
          (*O Mother, Mary Mother,*
The way is long, between Hell and Heaven!)

"A lady's here, by a dark steed brought,
                    Sister Helen,   205
So darkly clad, I saw her not."
"See her now or never see aught,
                    Little brother!"
          (*O Mother, Mary Mother,*
What more to see, between Hell and Heaven?)   210

"Her hood falls back, and the moon shines fair,
                    Sister Helen,
On the Lady of Ewern's golden hair."
"Blest hour of my power and her despair,
                    Little brother!"   215

(O Mother, Mary Mother,
Hour blest and bann'd, between Hell and Heaven!)

"Pale, pale her cheeks, that in pride did glow,
      Sister Helen,
'Neath the bridal-wreath three days ago."   220
"One morn for pride and three days for woe,
      Little brother!"
      (O Mother, Mary Mother,
Three days, three nights, between Hell and Heaven!)

"Her clasped hands stretch from her bending head,   225
      Sister Helen;
With the loud wind's wail her sobs are wed."
"What wedding-strains hath her bridal-bed,
      Little brother?"
      (O Mother, Mary Mother,   230
What strain but death's, between Hell and Heaven!)

"She may not speak, she sinks in a swoon,
      Sister Helen, –
She lifts her lips and gasps on the moon."
"Oh! might I but hear her soul's blithe tune,   235
      Little brother!"
      (O Mother, Mary Mother,
Her woe's dumb cry, between Hell and Heaven!)

"They've caught her to Westholm's saddle-bow,
      Sister Helen,   240
And her moonlit hair gleams white in its flow."
"Let it turn whiter than winter snow,
      Little brother!"
      (O Mother, Mary Mother,
Woe-withered gold, between Hell and Heaven!)   245

"O Sister Helen, you heard the bell.
      Sister Helen!
More loud than the vesper-chime it fell."
"No vesper-chime, but a dying knell,
      Little brother!"   250
      (O Mother, Mary Mother,
His dying knell, between Hell and Heaven!)

"Alas! but I fear the heavy sound,
      Sister Helen;

Is it in the sky or in the ground?"   255
"Say, have they turned their horses round,
                    Little brother?"
            (O Mother, Mary Mother,
What would she more, between Hell and Heaven?)

"They have raised the old man from his knee,   260
                    Sister Helen,
And they ride in silence hastily."
"More fast the naked soul doth flee,
                    Little brother!"
            (O Mother, Mary Mother,   265
The naked soul, between Hell and Heaven!)

"Flank to flank are the three steeds gone,
                    Sister Helen,
But the lady's dark steed goes alone."
"And lonely her bridegroom's soul hath flown,   270
                    Little brother."
            (O Mother, Mary Mother,
The lonely ghost, between Hell and Heaven!)

"Oh the wind is sad in the iron chill,
                    Sister Helen,   275
And weary sad they look by the hill."
"But he and I are sadder still,
                    Little brother!"
            (O Mother, Mary Mother,
Most sad of all, between Hell and Heaven!)   280

"See, see, the wax has dropped from its place,
                    Sister Helen,
And the flames are winning up apace!"
"Yet here they burn but for a space,
                    Little brother!"   285
            (O Mother, Mary Mother,
Here for a space, between Hell and Heaven!)

"Ah! what white thing at the door has cross'd,
                    Sister Helen?
Ah! what is this that sighs in the frost?"   290
"A soul that's lost as mine is lost,
                    Little brother!"
            (O Mother, Mary Mother,
Lost, lost, all lost, between Hell and Heaven!)

The Burden of Nineveh

In our Museum galleries
To-day I lingered o'er the prize
Dead Greece vouchsafes to living eyes, –
Her Art for ever in fresh wise
   From hour to hour rejoicing me.   5
Sighing I turned at last to win
Once more the London dirt and din;
And as I made the swing-door spin
And issued, they were hoisting in
   A wingèd beast from Nineveh.   10

A human face the creature wore,
And hoofs behind and hoofs before,
And flanks with dark runes fretted o'er.
'Twas bull, 'twas mitred Minotaur,
   A dead disbowelled mystery;   15
The mummy of a buried faith
Stark from the charnel without scathe,
Its wings stood for the light to bathe, –
Such fossil cerements as might swathe
   The very corpse of Nineveh.   20

The print of its first rush-wrapping,
Wound ere it dried, still ribbed the thing.
What song did the brown maidens sing,
From purple mouths alternating,
   When that was woven languidly?   25
What vows, what rites, what prayers preferr'd,
What songs has the strange image heard?
In what blind vigil stood interr'd
For ages, till an English word
   Broke silence first at Nineveh?   30

Oh when upon each sculptured court,
Where even the wind might not resort, –
O'er which Time passed, of like import
With the wild Arab boys at sport, –
   A living face looked in to see: –   35
Oh seemed it not – the spell once broke –
As though the carven warriors woke,
As though the shaft the string forsook,

The cymbals clashed, the chariots shook,
   And there was life in Nineveh?   40

On London stones our sun anew
The beast's recovered shadow threw.
(No shade that plague of darkness knew,
No light, no shade, while older grew
   By ages the old earth and sea.)   45
Lo thou! could all thy priests have shown
Such proof to make thy godhead known?
From their dead Past thou liv'st alone;
And still thy shadow is thine own
   Even as of yore in Nineveh.   50

That day whereof we keep record,
When near thy city-gates the Lord
Sheltered his Jonah with a gourd,
This sun, (I said) here present, pour'd
   Even thus this shadow that I see.   55
This shadow has been shed the same
From sun and moon, – from lamps which came
For prayer, – from fifteen days of flame,
The last, while smouldered to a name
   Sardanapalus' Nineveh.   60

Within thy shadow, haply, once
Sennacherib has knelt, whose sons
Smote him between the altar-stones:
Or pale Semiramis her zones
   Of gold, her incense brought to thee,   65
In love for grace, in war for aid: . . .
Ay, and who else? . . . till 'neath thy shade
Within his trenches newly made
Last year the Christian knelt and pray'd –
   Not to thy strength – in Nineveh.[1]   70

Now, thou poor god, within this hall
Where the blank windows blind the wall
From pedestal to pedestal,
The kind of light shall on thee fall
   Which London takes the day to be: 75
While school-foundations in the act
Of holiday, three files compact,

---

1 During the excavations, the Tiyari workmen held their services in the shadow of
the great bulls. (Layard's *Nineveh*, ch. ix.)

Shall learn to view thee as a fact
Connected with that zealous tract:
   'Rome, – Babylon and Nineveh.'   80

Deemed they of this, those worshippers,
When, in some mythic chain of verse
Which man shall not again rehearse,
The faces of thy ministers
   Yearned pale with bitter ecstasy?   85
Greece, Egypt, Rome, – did any god
Before whose feet men knelt unshod
Deem that in this unblest abode
Another scarce more unknown god
   Should house with him, from Nineveh?   90

Ah! in what quarries lay the stone
From which this pillared pile has grown,
Unto man's need how long unknown,
Since those thy temples, court and cone,
   Rose far in desert history?   95
Ah! what is here that does not lie
All strange to thine awakened eye?
Ah! what is here can testify
(Save that dumb presence of the sky)
   Unto thy day and Nineveh?   100

Why, of those mummies in the room
Above, there might indeed have come
One out of Egypt to thy home,
An alien. Nay, but were not some
   Of these thine own antiquity?   105
And now, – they and their gods and thou
All relics here together – now
Whose profit? whether bull or cow,
Isis or Ibis, who or how,
   Whether of Thebes or Nineveh?   110

The consecrated metals found,
And ivory tablets, underground,
Winged teraphim and creatures crown'd,
When air and daylight filled the mound,
   Fell into dust immediately.   115
And even as these, the images
Of awe and worship, – even as these, –

So, smitten with the sun's increase,
Her glory mouldered and did cease
  From immemorial Nineveh.   120

The day her builders made their halt,
Those cities of the lake of salt
Stood firmly 'stablished without fault
Made proud with pillars of basalt,
  With sardonyx and porphyry.   125
The day that Jonah bore abroad
To Nineveh the voice of God,
A brackish lake lay in his road,
Where erst Pride fixed her sure abode
  As then in royal Nineveh.   130

The day when he, Pride's lord and Man's,
Showed all the kingdoms at a glance
To Him before whose countenance
The years recede, the years advance,
  And said, Fall down and worship me: –   135
'Mid all the pomp beneath that look,
Then stirred there, haply, some rebuke,
Where to the wind the Salt Pools shook,
And in those tracts, of life forsook,
  That knew thee not, O Nineveh!   140

Delicate harlot! On thy throne
Thou with a world beneath thee prone
In state for ages sat'st alone;
And needs were years and lustres flown
  Ere strength of man could vanquish thee: 145
Whom even thy victor foes must bring,
Still royal, among maids that sing
As with doves' voices, taboring
Upon their breasts, unto the King, –
  A kingly conquest, Nineveh!   150

... Here woke my thought. The wind's slow sway
Had waxed; and like the human play
Of scorn that smiling spreads away,
The sunshine shivered off the day:
  The callous wind, it seemed to me,   155
Swept up the shadow from the ground:
And pale as whom the Fates astound,

The god forlorn stood winged and crown'd:
Within I knew the cry lay bound
   Of the dumb soul of Nineveh.   160

And as I turned, my sense half shut
Still saw the crowds of kerbs and rut
Go past as marshalled to the strut
Of ranks in gypsum quaintly cut.
   It seemed in one same pageantry   165
They followed forms which had been erst;
To pass, till on my sight should burst
That future of the best or worst
When some may question which was first,
   Of London or of Nineveh.   170

For as that Bull-god once did stand
And watched the burial-clouds of sand,
Till these at last without a hand
Rose o'er his eyes, another land,
   And blinded him with destiny: –   175
So may he stand again; till now,
In ships of unknown sail and prow,
Some tribe of the Australian plough
Bear him afar, – a relic now
   Of London, not of Nineveh!   180

Or it may chance indeed that when
Man's age is hoary among men, –
His centuries threescore and ten, –
His furthest childhood shall seem then
   More clear than later times may be: 185
Who, finding in this desert place
This form, shall hold us for some race
That walked not in Christ's lowly ways,
But bowed its pride and vowed its praise
   Unto the God of Nineveh.   190

The smile rose first, – anon drew nigh
The thought: ... Those heavy wings spread high
So sure of flight, which do not fly;
That set gaze never on the sky;
   Those scriptured flanks it cannot see;   195
Its crown, a brow-contracting load;
Its planted feet which trust the sod: ...

(So grew the image as I trod:)
O Nineveh, was this thy God, –
Thine also, mighty Nineveh?   200

The Staff and Scrip

'Who owns these lands?' the Pilgrim said.
  'Stranger, Queen Blanchelys.'
'And who has thus harried them?' he said.
  'It was Duke Luke did this:
      God's ban be his!'   5

The Pilgrim said: 'Where is your house?
  I'll rest there, with your will.'
'You've but to climb these blackened boughs
  And you'll see it over the hill,
      For it burns still.'   10

'Which road, to seek your Queen?' said he.
  'Nay, nay, but with some wound
You'll fly back hither, it may be,
  And by your blood i' the ground
      My place be found.'   15

'Friend, stay in peace. God keep your head,
  And mine, where I will go;
For He is here and there,' he said.
  He passed the hill-side, slow,
      And stood below.   20

The Queen sat idle by her loom:
  She heard the arras stir,
And looked up sadly: through the room
  The sweetness sickened her
      Of musk and myrrh.   25

Her women, standing two and two,
  In silence combed the fleece.
The pilgrim said, 'Peace be with you,
  Lady;' and bent his knees.
      She answered, 'Peace.'   30

Her eyes were like the wave within;
   Like water-reeds the poise
Of her soft body, dainty thin;
   And like the water's noise
      Her plaintive voice. 35

For him, the stream had never well'd
   In desert tracts malign
So sweet; nor had he ever felt
   So faint in the sunshine
      Of Palestine. 40

Right so, he knew that he saw weep
   Each night through every dream
The Queen's own face, confused in sleep
   With visages supreme
      Not known to him. 45

'Lady,' he said, 'your lands lie burnt
   And waste: to meet your foe
All fear: this I have seen and learnt.
   Say that it shall be so,
      And I will go.' 50

She gazed at him. 'Your cause is just,
   For I have heard the same:'
He said: 'God's strength shall be my trust.
   Fall it to good or grame,
      'Tis in His name.' 55

'Sir, you are thanked. My cause is dead.
   Why should you toil to break
A grave, and fall therein?' she said.
   He did not pause but spake:
      'For my vow's sake.' 60

'Can such vows be, Sir – to God's ear,
   Not to God's will?' 'My vow
Remains: God heard me there as here,'
   He said with reverent brow,
      'Both then and now.' 65

They gazed together, he and she,
   The minute while he spoke;
And when he ceased, she suddenly

Looked round upon her folk
  As though she woke.   70

'Fight, Sir,' she said: 'my prayers in pain
  Shall be your fellowship.'
He whispered one among her train, –
  'To-morrow bid her keep
    This staff and scrip.'   75

She sent him a sharp sword, whose belt
  About his body there
As sweet as her own arms he felt.
  He kissed its blade, all bare,
    Instead of her.   80

She sent him a green banner wrought
  With one white lily stem,
To bind his lance with when he fought.
  He writ upon the same
    And kissed her name.   85

She sent him a white shield, whereon
  She bade that he should trace
His will. He blent fair hues that shone,
  And in a golden space
    He kissed her face.   90

Right so, the sunset skies unseal'd,
  Like lands he never knew,
Beyond to-morrow's battle-field
  Lay open out of view
    To ride into.   95

Next day till dark the women pray'd:
  Nor any might know there
How the fight went: the Queen has bade
  That there do come to her
    No messenger.   100

Weak now to them the voice o' the priest
  As any trance affords;
And when each anthem failed and ceas'd,
  It seemed that the last chords
    Still sang the words.   105

Lo, Father, is thine ear inclin'd,
  And hath thine angel pass'd?

For these thy watchers now are blind
  With vigil, and at last
    Dizzy with fast.   110

'Oh what is the light that shines so red?
  'Tis long since the sun set;'
Quoth the youngest to the eldest maid:
  ''Twas dim but now, and yet
    The light is great.'   115

Quoth the other: ''Tis our sight is dazed
  That we see flame i' the air.'
But the Queen held her brows and gazed,
  And said, 'It is the glare
    Of torches there.'   120

'Oh what are the sounds that rise and spread?
  All day it was so still;'
Quoth the youngest to the eldest maid;
  'Unto the furthest hill
    The air they fill.'   125

Quoth the other; ''Tis our sense is blurr'd
  With all the chants gone by.'
But the Queen held her breath and heard,
  And said, 'It is the cry
    Of Victory.'   130

The first of all the rout was sound,
  The next were dust and flame,
And then the horses shook the ground:
  And in the thick of them
    A still band came.   135

'Oh what do ye bring out of the fight,
  Thus hid beneath these boughs?'
'Even him, thy conquering guest to-night,
  Who yet shall not carouse,
    Queen, in thy house.'   140

'Uncover ye his face,' she said.
  'O changed in little space!'
She cried, 'O pale that was so red!
  O God, O God of grace!
    Cover his face.'   145

His sword was broken in his hand
  Where he had kissed the blade.
'O soft steel that could not withstand!
  O my hard heart unstayed,
    That prayed and prayed!'   150

His bloodied banner crossed his mouth
  Where he had kissed her name.
'O east, and west, and north, and south,
  Fair flew my web, for shame,
    To guide Death's aim!'   155

The tints were shredded from his shield
  Where he had kissed her face.
'Oh, of all gifts that I could yield,
  Death only keeps its place,
    My gift and grace!'   160

Then stepped a damsel to her side,
  And spoke, and needs must weep:
'For his sake, lady, if he died,
  He prayed of thee to keep
    This staff and scrip.'   165

That night they hung above her bed,
  Till morning wet with tears.
Year after year above her head
  Her bed his token wears,
    Five years, ten years.   170

That night the passion of her grief
  Shook them as there they hung.
Each year the wind that shed the leaf
  Shook them and in its tongue
    A message flung.   175

And once she woke with a clear mind
  That letters writ to calm
Her soul lay in the scrip; to find
  Only a torpid balm
    And dust of palm.   180

They shook far off with palace sport
  When joust and dance were rife;
And the hunt shook them from the court;

For hers, in peace or strife,
  Was a Queen's life.   185

A Queen's death now: as now they shake
  To gusts in chapel dim, –
Hung where she sleeps, not seen to wake,
  (Carved lovely white and slim,)
    With them by him.   190

Stand up to-day, still armed, with her,
  Good knight, before His brow
Who then as now was here and there,
  Who had in mind thy vow
    Then even as now.   195

The lists are set in Heaven to-day,
  The bright pavilions shine;
Fair hangs thy shield, and none gainsay;
  The trumpets sound in sign
    That she is thine.   200

Not tithed with days' and years' decrease
  He pays thy wage He owed,
But with imperishable peace
  Here in His own abode,
    Thy jealous God.   205

Sudden Light

I have been here before,
  But when or how I cannot tell:
I know the grass beyond the door,
  The sweet keen smell,
The sighing sound, the lights around the shore.   5

You have been mine before, –
  How long ago I may not know:
But just when at that swallow's soar
  Your neck turned so,
Some veil did fall, – I knew it all of yore.   10

Then, now, – perchance again! . . .
  O round mine eyes your tresses shake!

Shall we not lie as we have lain
Thus for Love's sake,
And sleep, and wake, yet never break the chain?   15

Fiction,
published 1850

Hand and Soul

Rivolsimi in quel lato
Là 'nde venia la voce,
E parvemi una luce
Che lucca quanto stella:
La mia mente era quella.
                    Bonaggiunta Urbiciani (1250)

Before any knowledge of painting was brought to Florence, there were already painters in Lucca, and Pisa, and Arezzo, who feared God and loved the art. The keen, grave workmen from Greece, whose trade it was to sell their own works in Italy and teach Italians to imitate them, had already found rivals of the soil with skill that could forestall their lessons and cheapen their crucifixes and *addolorate*, more years than is supposed before the art came at all into Florence. The pre-eminence to which Cimabue was raised at once by his contemporaries, and which he still retains to a wide extent even in the modern mind, is to be accounted for, partly by the circumstances under which he arose, and partly by that extraordinary *purpose of fortune* born with the lives of some few, and through which it is not a little thing for any who went before, if they are even remembered as the shadows of the coming of such an one, and the voices which prepared his way in the wilderness. It is thus, almost exclusively, that the painters of whom I speak are now known. They have left little, and but little heed is taken of that which men hold to have been surpassed; it is gone like time gone, – a track of dust and dead leaves that merely led to the fountain.

Nevertheless, of very late years and in very rare instances, some signs of a better understanding have become manifest. A case in point is that of the triptic and two cruciform pictures at Dresden, by Chiaro di Messer Bello dell' Erma, to which the eloquent pamphlet of Dr Aemmster has at length succeeded in attracting the students. There is another still more solemn and beautiful work, now proved to be by the same hand, in the gallery at Florence. It is the one to which my narrative will relate.

This Chiaro dell' Erma was a young man of very honourable family in Arezzo; where, conceiving art almost, as it were, for himself, and loving it deeply, he endeavoured from early boyhood towards the imitation of any objects offered in nature. The extreme longing after a visible embodiment of his thoughts strengthened as his years increased, more even than his sinews or the blood of his life; until he would feel faint in sunsets and at the sight of stately persons. When he had lived nineteen years, he heard of the famous Giunta Pisano; and, feeling much of admiration, with, perhaps, a little of that envy which youth always feels until it has learned to measure success by time and opportunity, he determined that he would seek out Giunta, and, if possible, become his pupil.

Having arrived in Pisa, he clothed himself in humble apparel, being unwilling that any other thing than the desire he had for knowledge should be his plea with the great painter; and then, leaving his baggage at a house of entertainment, he took his way along the street, asking whom he met for the lodging of Giunta. It soon chanced that one of that city, conceiving him to be a stranger and poor, took him into his house, and refreshed him; afterwards directing him on his way.

When he was brought to speech of Giunta, he said merely that he was a student, and that nothing in the world was so much at his heart as to become that which he had heard told of him with whom he was speaking. He was received with courtesy and consideration, and shown into the study of the famous artist. But the forms he saw there were lifeless and incomplete; and a sudden exultation possessed him as he said within himself, 'I am the master of this man.' The blood came at first into his face, but the next moment he was quite pale and fell to trembling. He was able, however, to conceal his emotion; speaking very little to Giunta, but, when he took his leave, thanking him respectfully.

After this, Chiaro's first resolve was, that he would work out thoroughly some of his thoughts, and let the world know him. But the lesson which he had now learned, of how small a greatness might win fame, and how little there was to strive against, served to make him torpid, and rendered his exertions less continual. Also Pisa was a larger and more luxurious city than Arezzo; and when, in his walks, he saw the great gardens laid out for pleasure, and the beautiful women who passed to and fro, and heard the music that was in the groves of the city at evening, he was taken with wonder that he had never claimed his share of the inheritance of those years in which his youth was cast. And women loved Chiaro; for, in despite of the burthen of study, he was well-favoured and very manly in his walking; and, seeing his face in front, there was a glory upon it, as upon the face of one who feels a light round his hair.

So he put thought from him, and partook of his life. But, one night,

being in a certain company of ladies, a gentleman that was there with
him began to speak of the paintings of a youth named Bonaventura,
which he had seen in Lucca; adding that Giunta Pisano might now
look for a rival. When Chiaro heard this, the lamps shook before him
and the music beat in his ears and made him giddy. He rose up,
alleging a sudden sickness, and went out of that house with his teeth
set.

He now took to work diligently; not returning to Arezzo, but
remaining in Pisa, that no day more might be lost; only living entirely
to himself. Sometimes, after nightfall, he would walk abroad in the
most solitary places he could find; hardly feeling the ground under
him, because of the thoughts of the day which held him in fever.

The lodging he had chosen was in a house that looked upon
gardens fast by the Church of San Rocco. During the offices, as he sat
at work, he could hear the music of the organ and the long murmur
that the chanting left; and if his window were open, sometimes, at
those parts of the mass where there is silence throughout the church,
his ear caught faintly the single voice of the priest. Beside the matters
of his art and a very few books, almost the only object to be noticed
in Chiaro's room was a small consecrated image of St Mary Virgin
wrought out of silver, before which stood always, in summer-time, a
glass containing a lily and a rose.

It was here, and at this time, that Chiaro painted the Dresden
pictures; as also, in all likelihood, the one – inferior in merit, but
certainly his – which is now at Munich. For the most part, he was
calm and regular in his manner of study; though often he would
remain at work through the whole of a day, not resting once so long
as the light lasted; flushed, and with the hair from his face. Or, at
times, when he could not paint, he would sit for hours in thought of
all the greatness the world had known from of old; until he was weak
with yearning, like one who gazes upon a path of stars.

He continued in this patient endeavour for about three years, at the
end of which his name was spoken throughout all Tuscany. As his
fame waxed, he began to be employed, besides easel-pictures, upon
paintings in fresco; but I believe that no traces remain to us of any of
these latter. He is said to have painted in the Duomo; and
D'Agincourt mentions having seen some portions of a fresco by him
which originally had its place above the high altar in the Church of
the Certosa; but which, at the time he saw it, being very dilapidated,
had been hewn out of the wall, and was preserved in the stores of the
convent. Before the period of Dr Aemmster's researches, however, it
had been entirely destroyed.

Chiaro was now famous. It was for the race of fame that he had girded up his loins; and he had not paused until fame was reached: yet now, in taking breath, he found that the weight was still at his heart. The years of his labour had fallen from him, and his life was still in its first painful desire.

With all that Chiaro had done during these three years, and even before, with the studies of his early youth, there had always been a feeling of worship and service. It was the peace-offering that he made to God and to his own soul for the eager selfishness of his aim. There was earth, indeed, upon the hem of his raiment; but *this* was of the heaven, heavenly. He had seasons when he could endure to think of no other feature of his hope than this: and sometimes, in the ecstasy of prayer, it had even seemed to him to behold that day when his mistress – his mystical lady (now hardly in her ninth year, but whose solemn smile at meeting had already lighted on his soul like the dove of the Trinity) – even she, his own gracious and holy Italian Art – with her virginal bosom, and her unfathomable eyes, and the thread of sunlight round her brows – should pass, through the sun that never sets, into the circle of the shadow of the tree of life, and be seen of God, and found good: and then it had seemed to him that he, with many who, since his coming, had joined the band of whom he was one (for, in his dream, the body he had worn on earth had been dead an hundred years), were permitted to gather round the blessed maiden, and to worship with her through all ages and ages of ages, saying, Holy, holy, holy. This thing he had seen with the eyes of his spirit; and in this thing had trusted, believing that it would surely come to pass.

But now (being at length led to inquire closely into himself), even as, in the pursuit of fame, the unrest abiding after attainment had proved to him that he had misinterpreted the craving of his own spirit – so also, now that he would willingly have fallen back on devotion, he became aware that much of that reverence which he had mistaken for faith had been no more than the worship of beauty. Therefore, after certain days passed in perplexity, Chiaro said within himself, 'My life and my will are yet before me: I will take another aim to my life.'

From that moment Chiaro set a watch on his soul, and put his hand to no other works but only to such as had for their end the presentment of some moral greatness that should impress the beholder: and, in doing this, he did not choose for his medium the action and passion of human life, but cold symbolism and abstract impersonation. So the people ceased to throng about his pictures as heretofore; and, when they were carried through town and town to their destination, they were no longer delayed by the crowds eager to gaze and admire: and no prayers or offerings were brought to them on their path, as to his Madonnas, and his Saints, and his Holy Children. Only the critical audience remained to him; and these, in default of more worthy matter, would have turned their scrutiny on a puppet or a mantle. Meanwhile, he had no more of fever upon him; but was calm and pale each day in all that he did and in his goings in and out. The works he produced at this time have perished – in all likelihood, not unjustly. It is said (and we may easily believe it), that, though more laboured than his former pictures, they were cold and unemphatic; bearing marked out upon them, as they must certainly have done, the measure of that boundary to which they were made to conform.

And the weight was still close at Chiaro's heart: but he held in his breath, never resting (for he was afraid), and would not know it.

Now it happened, within these days, that there fell a great feast in Pisa, for holy matters: and each man left his occupation; and all the guilds and companies of the city were got together for games and rejoicings. And there were scarcely any that stayed in the houses, except ladies who lay or sat along their balconies between open windows which let the breeze beat through the rooms and over the spread tables from end to end. And the golden cloths that their arms lay upon drew all eyes upward to see their beauty; and the day was long; and every hour of the day was bright with the sun.

So Chiaro's model, when he awoke that morning on the hot pavement of the Piazza Nunziata, and saw the hurry of people that passed him, got up and went along with them; and Chiaro waited for him in vain.

For the whole of that morning, the music was in Chiaro's room from the Church close at hand; and he could hear the sounds that the crowd made in the streets; hushed only at long intervals while the processions for the feast-day chanted in going under his windows. Also, more than once, there was a high clamour from the meeting of factious persons: for the ladies of both leagues were looking down; and he who encountered his enemy could not choose but draw upon him. Chiaro waited a long time idle; and then knew that his model was gone elsewhere. When at his work, he was blind and deaf to all else; but he feared sloth: for then his stealthy thoughts would begin, as it were, to beat round and round him, seeking a point for attack. He now rose, therefore, and went to the window. It was within a short space of noon; and underneath him a throng of people was coming out through the porch of San Rocco.

The two greatest houses of the feud in Pisa had filled the church for that mass. The first to leave had been the Gherghiotti; who, stopping on the threshold, had fallen back in ranks along each side of the archway: so that now, in passing outward, the Marotoli had to walk between two files of men whom they hated, and whose fathers had hated theirs. All the chiefs were there and their whole adherence; and each knew the name of each. Every man of the Marotoli, as he came forth and saw his foes, laid back his hood and gazed about him, to show the badge upon the close cap that held his hair. And of the Gherghiotti there were some who tightened their girdles; and some shrilled and threw up their wrists scornfully, as who flies a falcon; for that was the crest of their house.

On the walls within the entry were a number of tall narrow frescoes, presenting a moral allegory of Peace, which Chiaro had painted that year for the Church. The Gherghiotti stood with their backs to these frescoes; and among them Golzo Ninuccio, the youngest noble of the faction, called by the people Golaghiotta, for his debased life. This youth had remained for some while talking listlessly to his fellows, though with his sleepy sunken eyes fixed on them who passed: but now, seeing that no man jostled another, he drew the long silver shoe off his foot, and struck the dust out of it on the cloak of him who was going by, asking him how far the tides rose at Viderza. And he said so because it was three months since, at that place, the Gherghiotti had beaten the Marotoli to the sands, and held them there while the sea came in; whereby many had been drowned. And, when he had spoken, at once the whole archway was dazzling with the light of confused swords; and they who had left turned back; and they who were still behind made haste to come forth: and there was so much blood cast up the walls on a sudden, that it ran in long streams down Chiaro's paintings.

Chiaro turned himself from the window; for the light felt dry between his lids, and he could not look. He sat down, and heard the noise of contention driven out of the church-porch and a great way through the streets; and soon there was a deep murmur that heaved and waxed from the other side of the city, where those of both parties were gathering to join in the tumult.

Chiaro sat with his face in his open hands. Once again he had wished to set his foot on a place that looked green and fertile; and once again it seemed to him that the thin rank mask was about to spread away, and that this time the chill of the water must leave leprosy in his flesh. The light still swam in his head, and bewildered him at first; but when he knew his thoughts, they were these: –

'Fame failed me: faith failed me: and now this also, – the hope that I nourished in this my generation of men, – shall pass from me, and leave my feet and my hands groping. Yet, because of this, are my feet become slow and my hands thin. I am as one who, through the whole night, holding his way diligently, hath smitten the steel unto the flint, to lead some whom he knew darkling; who hath kept his eyes always on the sparks that himself made, lest they should fail; and who, towards dawn, turning to bid them that he had guided God speed, sees the wet grass untrodden except of his own feet. I am as the last hour of the day, whose chimes are a perfect number; whom the next followeth not, nor light ensueth from him; but in the same darkness is the old order begun afresh. Men, say, "This is not God nor man; he is not as we are, neither above us: let him sit beneath us, for we are many." Where I write Peace, in that spot is the drawing of swords, and there men's footprints are red. When I would sow, another harvest is ripe. Nay, it is much worse with me than thus much. Am I not as a cloth drawn before the light, that the looker may not be blinded? but which showeth thereby the grain of its own coarseness; so that the light seems defiled, and men say, "We will not walk by it." Wherefore through me they shall be doubly accursed, seeing that through me they reject the light. May one be a devil and not know it?'

As Chiaro was in these thoughts, the fever encroached slowly on his veins, till he could sit no longer and would have risen; but suddenly he found awe within him, and held his head bowed, without stirring. The warmth of the air was not shaken; but there seemed a pulse in the light, and a living freshness, like rain. The silence was a painful music, that made the blood ache in his temples; and he lifted his face and his deep eyes.

A woman was present in his room, clad to the hands and feet with a green and grey raiment, fashioned to that time. It seemed that the first thoughts he had ever known were given him as at first from her eyes, and he knew her hair to be the golden veil through which he beheld his dreams. Though her hands were joined, her face was not lifted, but set forward; and though the gaze was austere, yet her mouth was supreme in gentleness. And as he looked, Chiaro's spirit appeared abashed of its own intimate presence, and his lips shook with the thrill of tears; it seemed such a bitter while till the spirit might be indeed alone.

She did not move closer towards him, but he felt her to be as much with him as his breath. He was like one who, scaling a great steepness, hears his own voice echoed in some place much higher than he can see, and the name of which is not known to him. As the woman stood, her speech was with Chiaro: not, as it were, from her mouth or in his ears; but distinctly between them.

'I am an image, Chiaro, of thine own soul within thee. See me, and know me as I am. Thou sayest that fame has failed thee, and faith failed thee; but because at least thou hast not laid thy life unto riches, therefore, though thus late, I am suffered to come into thy knowledge. Fame sufficed not, for that thou didst seek fame: seek thine own conscience (not thy mind's conscience, but thine heart's), and all shall approve and suffice. For Fame, in noble soils, is a fruit of the Spring: but not therefore should it be said: "Lo! my garden that I planted is barren: the crocus is here, but the lily is dead in the dry ground, and shall not lift the earth that covers it: therefore I will fling my garden together, and give it unto the builders." Take heed rather that thou trouble not the wise secret earth; for in the mould that thou throwest up shall the first tender growth lie to waste; which else had been strong in its season. Yea, and even if the year fall past in all its months, and the soil be indeed, to thee, peevish and incapable, and though thou indeed gather all thy harvest, and it suffice for others, and thou remain vext with emptiness; and others drink of thy streams, and the drouth rasp thy throat; – let it be enough that these have found the feast good, and thanked the giver: remembering that, when the winter is striven through, there is another year, whose wind is meek, and whose sun fulfilleth all.'

While he heard, Chiaro went slowly on his knees. It was not to her that spoke, for the speech seemed within him and his own. The air brooded in sunshine, and though the turmoil was great outside, the air within was at peace. But when he looked in her eyes, he wept. And she came to him, and cast her hair over him, and took her hands about his forehead, and spoke again: –

'Thou hast said,' she continued gently, 'that faith failed thee. This cannot be so. Either thou hadst it not, or thou hast it. But who bade thee strike the point betwixt love and faith? Wouldst thou sift the warm breeze from the sun that quickens it? Who bade thee turn upon God and say: "Behold, my offering is of earth, and not worthy: thy fire comes not upon it; therefore, though I slay not my brother whom thou acceptest, I will depart before thou smite me." Why shouldst thou rise up and tell God He is not content? Had He, of His warrant, certified so to thee? Be not nice to seek out division; but possess thy love in sufficiency: assuredly this is faith, for the heart must believe first. What He hath set in thine heart to do, that do thou; and even though thou do it without thought of Him, it shall be well done; it is this sacrifice that He asketh of thee, and His flame is upon it for a sign. Think not of Him; but of His love and thy love. For God is no morbid exactor: He hath no hand to bow beneath, nor a foot, that thou shouldst kiss it.'

And Chiaro held silence, and wept into her hair which covered his face; and the salt tears that he shed ran through her hair upon his lips;

and he tasted the bitterness of shame.

Then the fair woman, that was his soul, spoke again to him, saying:

'And for this thy last purpose, and for those unprofitable truths of thy teaching, – thine heart hath already put them away, and it needs not that I lay my bidding upon thee. How is it that thou, a man, wouldst say coldly to the mind what God hath said to the heart warmly? Thy will was honest and wholesome; but look well lest this also be folly, – to say, "I, in doing this, do strengthen God among men." When at any time hath he cried unto thee, saying, "My son, lend me thy shoulder, for I fall?" Deemest thou that the men who enter God's temple in malice, to the provoking of blood, and neither for his love nor for his wrath will abate their purpose, – shall afterwards stand with thee in the porch, midway between Him and themselves, to give ear unto thy thin voice, which merely the fall of their visors can drown, and to see thy hands, stretched feebly, tremble among their swords? Give thou to God no more than he asketh of thee; but to man also, that which is man's. In all that thou doest, work from thine own heart, simply; for his heart is as thine, when thine is wise and humble; and he shall have understanding of thee. One drop of rain is as another, and the sun's prism in all: and shalt not thou be as he, whose lives are the breath of One? Only by making thyself his equal can he learn to hold communion with thee, and at last own thee above him. Not till thou lean over the water shalt thou see thine image therein: stand erect, and it shall slope from thy feet and be lost. Know that there is but this means whereby thou may'st serve God with man: – Set thine hand and thy soul to serve man with God.'

And when she that spoke had said these words within Chiaro's spirit, she left his side quietly, and stood up as he had first seen her: with her fingers laid together, and her eyes steadfast, and with the breadth of her long dress covering her feet on the floor. And, speaking again, she said:

'Chiaro, servant of God, take now thine Art unto thee, and paint me thus, as I am, to know me: weak, as I am, and in the weeds of this time; only with eyes which seek out labour, and with a faith, not learned, yet jealous of prayer. Do this; so shall thy soul stand before thee always, and perplex thee no more.'

And Chiaro did as she bade him. While he worked, his face grew solemn with knowledge: and before the shadows had turned, his work was done. Having finished, he lay back where he sat, and was asleep immediately; for the growth of that strong sunset was heavy about him, and he felt weak and haggard; like one just come out of a dusk, hollow country, bewildered with echoes, where he had lost himself, and who has not slept for many days and nights. And when she saw him lie back, the beautiful woman came to him, and sat at his head, gazing, and quieted his sleep with her voice.

The tumult of the factions had endured all that day through all Pisa, though Chiaro had not heard it: and the last service of that Feast was a mass sung at midnight from the windows of all the churches for the many dead who lay about the city, and who had to be buried before morning, because of the extreme heats.

In the Spring of 1847 I was in Florence. Such as were there at the same time with myself – those, at least, to whom Art is something – will certainly recollect how many rooms of the Pitti Gallery were closed through that season, in order that some of the pictures they contained might be examined and repaired without the necessity of removal. The hall, the staircases, and the vast central suite of apartments, were the only accessible portions; and in these such paintings as they could admit from the sealed *penetralia* were profanely huddled together, without respect of dates, schools, or persons.

I fear that, through this interdict, I may have missed seeing many of the best pictures. I do not mean *only* the most talked of: for these, as they were restored, generally found their way somehow into the open rooms, owing to the clamours raised by the students; and I remember how old Ercoli's, the curator's, spectacles used to be mirrored in the reclaimed surface, as he leaned mysteriously over these works with some of the visitors, to scrutinize and elucidate.

One picture that I saw that Spring, I shall not easily forget. It was among those, I believe, brought from the other rooms, and had been hung, obviously out of all chronology, immediately beneath that head by Raphael so long known as the 'Berrettino', and now said to be the portrait of Cecco Ciulli.

The picture I speak of is a small one, and represents merely the figure of a woman, clad to the hands and feet with a green and grey raiment, chaste and early in its fashion, but exceedingly simple. She is standing: her hands are held together lightly, and her eyes set earnestly open.

The face and hands in this picture, though wrought with great delicacy, have the appearance of being painted at once, in a single sitting: the drapery is unfinished. As soon as I saw the figure, it drew an awe upon me, like water in shadow. I shall not attempt to describe it more than I have already done; for the most absorbing wonder of it was its literality. You knew that figure, when painted, had been seen; yet it was not a thing to be seen of men. This language will appear ridiculous to such as have never looked on the work; and it may be even to some among those who have. On examining it closely, I perceived in one corner of the canvas the words *Manus Animam pinxit*, and the date 1239.

I turned to my Catalogue, but that was useless, for the pictures were all displaced. I then stepped up to the Cavaliere Ercoli, who was in the room at the moment, and asked him regarding the subject and authorship of the painting. He treated the matter, I thought, somewhat slightingly, and said that he could show me the reference in the Catalogue, which he had compiled. This, when found, was not of much value, as it merely said, 'Schizzo d'autore incerto,' adding the inscription.[1] I could willingly have prolonged my inquiry, in the hope that it might somehow lead to some result; but I had disturbed the curator from certain yards of Guido, and he was not communicative. I went back therefore, and stood before the picture till it grew dusk.

The next day I was there again; but this time a circle of students was round the spot, all copying the 'Berrettino'. I contrived, however, to find a place whence I could see *my* picture, and where I seemed to be in nobody's way. For some minutes I remained undisturbed; and then I heard, in an English voice: 'Might I beg of you, sir, to stand a little more to this side, as you interrupt my view?'

I felt vext, for, standing where he asked me, a glare struck on the picture from the windows, and I could not see it. However, the request was reasonably made, and from a countryman; so I complied, and turning away, stood by his easel. I knew it was not worth while; yet I referred in some way to the work underneath the one he was copying. He did not laugh, but he smiled as we do in England. '*Very odd, is it not?*' said he.

The other students near us were all continental; and seeing an Englishman select an Englishman to speak with, conceived, I suppose, that he could understand no language but his own. They had evidently been noticing the interest which the little picture appeared to excite in me.

One of them, an Italian, said something to another who stood next to him. He spoke with a Genoese accent, and I lost the sense in the villainous dialect. 'Che so?' replied the other, lifting his eyebrows

---

1 I should here say, that in the catalogue for the year just over, (owing, as in cases before mentioned, to the zeal and enthusiasm of Dr Aemmster) this, and several other pictures, have been more competently entered. The work in question is now placed in the Sala Sessagona, a room I did not see – under the number 161. It is described as 'Figura mistica di Chiaro dell' Erma', and there is a brief notice of the author appended.

towards the figure: 'roba mistica: 'st' Inglesi son matti sul misticismo: somiglia alle nebbie di là. Li fa pensare alla patria,

> "E intenerisce il core
> Lo dì ch' han detto ai dolci amici adio." '

'La notte, vuoi dire,' said a third.

There was a general laugh. My compatriot was evidently a novice in the language, and did not take in what was said. I remained silent, being amused.

'Et toi donc?' said he who had quoted Dante, turning to a student, whose birthplace was unmistakable, even had he been addressed in any other language: 'que dis-tu de ce genre-là?'

'Moi?' returned the Frenchman, standing back from his easel, and looking at me and at the figure, quite politely, though with an evident reservation: 'Je dis, mon cher, que c'est une spécialité dont je me fiche pas mal. Je tiens que quand on ne comprend pas une chose, c'est qu'elle ne signifie rien.'

My reader thinks possibly that the French student was right.

From
Early Italian Poets,
published 1861

PREFACE

I need not dilate here on the characteristics of the first epoch of Italian Poetry; since the extent of my translated selections is sufficient to afford a complete view of it. Its great beauties may often remain unapproached in the versions here attempted; but, at the same time, its imperfections are not all to be charged to the translator. Among these I may refer to its limited range of subject and continual obscurity, as well as to its monotony in the use of rhymes or frequent substitution of assonances. But to compensate for much that is incomplete and inexperienced, these poems possess, in their degree, beauties of a kind which can never again exist in art; and offer, besides, a treasure of grace and variety in the formation of their metres. Nothing but a strong impression, first of their poetic value, and next of the biographical interest of some of them (chiefly of those in my second division), would have inclined me to bestow the time and trouble which have resulted in this collection.

Much has been said, and in many respects justly, against the value of metrical translation. But I think it would be admitted that the tributary art might find a not illegitimate use in the case of poems which come down to us in such a form as do these early Italian ones. Struggling originally with corrupt dialect and imperfect expression, and hardly kept alive through centuries of neglect, they have reached that last and worst state in which the *coup-de-grace* has almost been dealt them by clumsy transcription and pedantic superstructure. At this stage the task of talking much more about them in any language is hardly to be entered upon; and a translation (involving, as it does, the necessity of settling many points without discussion,) remains perhaps the most direct form of commentary.

The life-blood of rhymed translation is this, – that a good poem shall not be turned into a bad one. The only true motive for putting poetry into a fresh language must be to endow a fresh nation, as far as possible, with one more possession of beauty. Poetry not being an exact science, literality of rendering is altogether secondary to this chief aim. I say *literality*, – not fidelity, which is by no means the same thing. When literality can be combined with what is thus the primary condition of success, the translator is fortunate, and must strive his utmost to unite them; when such object can only be attained by paraphrase, that is his only path.

Any merit possessed by these translations is derived from an effort to follow this principle; and, in some degree, from the fact that such painstaking in arrangement and descriptive heading as is often indispensable to old and especially to 'occasional' poetry, has here been bestowed on these poets for the first time.

That there are many defects in these translations, or that the above merit is their defect, or that they have no merits but only defects, are discoveries so sure to be made if necessary (or perhaps here and there in any case), that I may safely leave them in other hands. The collection has probably a wider scope than some readers might look for, and includes now and then (though I believe in rare instances) matter which may not meet with universal approval; and whose introduction, needed as it is by the literary aim of my work, is I know inconsistent with the principles of pretty bookmaking. My wish has been to give a full and truthful view of early Italian poetry; not to make it appear to consist only of certain elements to the exclusion of others equally belonging to it.

Of the difficulties I have had to encounter, – the causes of imperfections for which I have no other excuse, – it is the reader's best privilege to remain ignorant; but I may perhaps be pardoned for briefly referring to such among these as concern the exigencies of translation. The task of the translator (and with all humility be it spoken) is one of some self-denial. Often would he avail himself of any special grace of his own idiom and epoch, if only his will belonged to him: often would some cadence serve him but for his author's structure – some structure but for his author's cadence: often the beautiful turn of a stanza must be weakened to adopt some rhyme which will tally, and he sees the poet revelling in abundance of language where himself is scantily supplied. Now he would slight the matter for the music, and now the music for the matter; but no, he must deal to each alike. Sometimes too a flaw in the work galls him, and he would fain remove it, doing for the poet that which his age denied him; but no, – it is not in the bond. His path is like that of Aladdin through the enchanted vaults: many are the precious fruits and flowers which he must pass by unheeded in search for the lamp alone; happy if at last, when brought to light, it does not prove that his old lamp has been exchanged for a new one, – glittering indeed to the eye, but scarcely of the same virtue nor with the same genius at its summons.

In relinquishing this work (which, small as it is, is the only contribution I expect to make to our English knowledge of old Italy), I feel, as it were, divided from my youth. The first associations I have are connected with my father's devoted studies, which, from his own point of view, have done so much towards the general investigation of Dante's writings. Thus, in those early days, all around me partook of the influence of the great Florentine; till, from viewing it as a natural element, I also, growing older, was drawn within the circle. I trust that from this the reader may place more confidence in a work not carelessly undertaken, though produced in the spare-time of other pursuits more closely followed. He should perhaps be told that it has occupied the leisure moments of not a few years; thus affording, often at long intervals, every opportunity for consideration and revision; and that on the score of care, at least, he has no need to mistrust it.

Nevertheless, I know there is no great stir to be made by launching afresh, on high-seas busy with new traffic, the ships which have been long outstripped and the ensigns which are grown strange. The feeling of self-doubt inseparable from such an attempt has been admirably expressed by a great living poet, in words which may be applied exactly to my humbler position, though relating in his case to a work all his own.

> 'Still, what if I approach the august sphere
> Named now with only one name, – disentwine
> That under current soft and argentine
> From its fierce mate in the majestic mass
> Leaven'd as the sea whose fire was mix'd with glass
> In John's transcendent vision, – launch once more
> That lustre? Dante, pacer of the shore
> Where glutted Hell disgorges filthiest gloom,
> Unbitten by its whirring sulphur-spume –
> Or whence the grieved and obscure waters slope
> Into a darkness quieted by hope –
> Plucker of amaranths grown beneath God's eye
> In gracious twilights where His chosen lie, –
> I would do this! If I should falter now! . . .'

(*Sordello*, by Robert Browning, B[ook] 1)

FROM PART I:
POETS CHIEFLY BEFORE DANTE

GUIDO GUINICELLI

Of the Gentle Heart
CANZONE

Within the gentle heart Love shelters him
   As birds within the green shade of the grove.
Before the gentle heart, in Nature's scheme,
   Love was not, nor the gentle Heart ere Love.
     For with the sun, at once,   5
So sprang the light immediately; nor was
     Its birth before the sun's.
   And Love hath his effect in gentleness
     Of very self; even as
   Within the middle fire the heart's excess.   10

The fire of Love comes to the gentle heart
   Like as its virtue to a precious stone;
To which no star its influence can impart
   Till it is made a pure thing by the sun:
     For when the sun hath smit   15
From out its essence that which there was vile,
     The star endoweth it.
   And so the heart created by God's breath
     Pure, true, and clean from guile,
A woman, like a star, enamoureth.   20

In gentle heart Love for like reason is
   For which the lamp's high flame is fann'd and bow'd:
Clear, piercing bright, it shines for its own bliss;
   Nor would it burn there else, it is so proud.
     For evil natures meet   25
With Love as it were water met with fire,
     As cold abhorring heat.

Through gentle heart Love doth a track divine,
   Like knowing like; the same
As diamond runs through iron in the mine.   30

The sun strikes full upon the mud all day;
  It remains vile, nor the sun's worth is less.
'By race I am gentle,' the proud man doth say:
  He is the mud, the sun is gentleness.
     Let no man predicate   35
That aught the name of gentleness should have,
   Even in a king's estate,
Except the heart there be a gentle man's.
   The star-beam lights the wave,
Heaven holds the star and the star's radiance.   40

God, in the understanding of high heaven,
  Burns more than in our sight the living sun:
There to behold His Face unveil'd is given;
  And Heaven, whose will is homage paid to One,
   Fulfils the things which live   45
In God, from the beginning excellent.
   So should my lady give
That truth which in her eyes is glorified,
   On which her heart is bent,
To me whose service waiteth at her side.   50

My lady, God shall ask, 'What dared'st thou?'
  (When my soul stands with all her acts review'd;)
'Thou passed'st heaven, into My sight, as now,
  To make Me of vain love similitude.
   To me doth praise belong,   55
And to the Queen of all the realm of grace
   Who endeth fraud and wrong.'
Then may I plead: 'As though from Thee he came,
   Love wore an Angel's face;
Lord, if I loved her, count it not my shame.'   60

JACOPO DA LENTINO

To his Lady in Heaven
SONNET

I have it in my heart to serve God so
  That into Paradise I shall repair,
  The holy place through the which everywhere
I have heard say that joy and solace flow.
Without my lady I were loth to go,   5
  She who has the bright face and the bright hair;
  Because if she were absent, I being there,
My pleasure would be less than nought, I know.
Look you, I say not this to such intent
  As that I there would deal in any sin: 10
  I only would behold her gracious mien,
    And beautiful soft eyes, and lovely face,
That so it should be my complete content
  To see my lady joyful in her place.

Of his Lady's Face
SONNET

Her face has made my life most proud and glad;
  Her face has made my life quite wearisome;
  It comforts me when other troubles come,
And amid other joys it strikes me sad.
Truly I think her face can drive me mad;   5
  For now I am too loud, and anon dumb.
  There is no second face in Christendom
Has a like power, nor shall have, nor has had.
What man in living face has seen such eyes,
  Or such a lovely bending of the head,   10
    Or mouth that opens to so sweet a smile?
In speech, my heart before her faints and dies,
  And into heaven seems to be spirited;
    So that I count me blest a certain while.

NICCOLÒ DEGLI ALBIZZI

When the Troops were Returning from Milan
PROLONGED SONNET

If you could see, fair brother, how dead beat
  The fellows look who come through Rome today,
  Black yellow smoke-dried visages, you'd say
They thought their haste at going all too fleet.
Their empty victual-waggons up the street   5
  Over the bridge dreadfully sound and sway;
  Their eyes, as hang'd men's, turning the wrong way;
And nothing on their backs, or heads, or feet.
One sees the ribs and all the skeletons
  Of their gaunt horses; and a sorry sight   10
Are the torn saddles, cramm'd with straw and stones.
  They are ashamed, and march throughout the night;
Stumbling, for hunger, on their marrowbones;
  Like barrels rolling, jolting, in this plight.
Their arms all gone, not even their swords are saved;   15
And each as silent as a man being shaved.

GIACOMINO PUGLIESI

Of his Dead Lady
CANZONE

Death, why hast thou made life so hard to bear,
  Taking my lady hence? Hast thou no whit
Of shame? The youngest flower and the most fair
  Thou hast pluck'd away, and the world wanteth it.
O leaden Death, hast thou no pitying?   5
Our warm love's very spring
  Thou stopp'st, and endest what was holy and meet;
And of my gladdening
Mak'st a most woeful thing,
And in my heart dost bid the bird not sing   10
  That sang so sweet.

Once the great joy and solace that I had
  Was more than is with other gentlemen:
Now is my love gone hence, who made me glad.
  With her that hope I lived in she hath ta'en,   15
And left me nothing but these sighs and tears,
Nothing of the old years
  That come not back again,
Wherein I was so happy, being her's.
Now to mine eyes her face no more appears,   20
Nor doth her voice make music in mine ears,
  As it did then.

O God, why hast thou made my grief so deep?
  Why set me in the dark to grope and pine?
Why parted me from her companionship,   25
  And crush'd the hope that was a gift of thine?
To think, dear, that I never any more
Can see thee as before!
  Who is it shuts thee in?
Who hides that smile for which my heart is sore,   30
And drowns those words that I am longing for,
  Lady of mine?

Where is my lady, and the lovely face
  She had, and the sweet motion when she walk'd?
Her chaste, mild favour – her so delicate grace –   35
  Her eyes, her mouth, and the dear way she talk'd? –
  Her courteous bending – her most noble air –
The soft fall of her hair? . . .
My lady – she who to my soul so rare
  A gladness brought!   40
Now I do never see her anywhere,
And I may not, looking in her eyes, gain there
  The blessing which I sought.

So if I had the realm of Hungary,
  With Greece and all the Almayn even to France,   45
Or Saint Sophia's treasure-hoard, you see
  All could not give me back her countenance.
For since the day when my dear lady died
From us (with God being born and glorified)
  No more pleasaunce   50

Her image bringeth, seated at my side,
But only tears. Ay me! the strength and pride
   Which it brought once.
   Had I my will, beloved, I would say
To God, unto whose bidding all things bow,   55
That we were still together night and day:
   Yet be it done as His behests allow.
I do remember that while she remain'd
With me, she often called me her sweet friend;
   But does not now,   60
Because God drew her towards Him, in the end.
Lady, that peace which none but He can send
   Be thine. Even so.

FRA GUITTONE D'AREZZO

To the Blessed Virgin Mary
SONNET

Lady of Heaven, the mother glorified
   Of glory, which is Jesus, – He whose death
   Us from the gates of Hell delivereth
And our first parents' error sets aside: –
Behold this earthly Love, how his darts glide –   5
   How sharpen'd – to what fate – throughout this earth!
   Pitiful Mother, partner of our birth,
Win these from following where his flight doth guide.
And O, inspire in me that holy love
   Which leads the soul back to its origin,   10
      Till of all other love the link do fail.
This water only can this fire reprove, –
   Only such cure suffice for such like sin;
      As nail from out a plank is struck by nail.

FAZIO DEGLI UBERTI

His Portrait of his Lady, Angiola of Verona
CANZONE

I look at the crisp golden-threaded hair
   Whereof, to thrall my heart, Love twists a net;
   Using at times a string of pearls for bait,
   And sometimes with a single rose therein.
I look into her eyes which unaware   5
   Through mine own eyes to my heart penetrate;
   Their splendour, that is excellently great,
     To the sun's radiance seeming near akin,
     Yet from herself a sweeter light to win.
So that I, gazing on that lovely one,   10
   Discourse in this wise with my secret thought: —
   'Woe's me! why am I not,
Even as my wish, alone with her alone? —
   That hair of hers, so heavily uplaid,
   To shed down braid by braid,   15
And make myself two mirrors of her eyes
Within whose light all other glory dies.'

I look at the amorous beautiful mouth,
   The spacious forehead which her locks enclose,
   The small white teeth, the straight and shapely nose,   20
   And the clear brows of a sweet pencilling.
And then the thought within me gains full growth,
   Saying, 'Be careful that thy glance now goes
   Between her lips, red as an open rose,
     Quite full of every dear and precious thing;   25
   And listen to her gracious answering,
Born of the gentle mind that in her dwells,
   Which from all things can glean the nobler half.
   Look thou when she doth laugh
How much her laugh is sweeter than aught else.   30
   Thus evermore my spirit makes avow
   Touching her mouth; till now
I would give anything that I possess,
Only to hear her mouth say frankly, 'Yes.'

I look at her white easy neck, so well   35
   From shoulders and from bosom lifted out;
     And at her round cleft chin, which beyond doubt
       No fancy in the world could have design'd.
And then, with longing grown more voluble,
   'Were it not pleasant now,' pursues my thought,   40
   'To have that kiss within thy two arms caught
     And kiss it till the mark were left behind?'
     Then, urgently: 'The eyelids of thy mind
Open thou: if such loveliness be given
   To sight here, – what of that which she doth hide?   45
   Only the wondrous ride
Of suns and planets through the visible heaven
   Tells us that there beyond is Paradise.
   Thus, if thou fix thine eyes,
Of a truth certainly thou must infer   50
That every earthly joy abides in her.'

I look at the large arms, so lithe and round, –
   At the hands, which are white and rosy too, –
   At the long fingers, clasp'd and woven through,
     Bright with the ring which one of them doth wear.   55
Then my thought whispers: 'Were thy body wound
   Within those arms, as loving women's do
   In all thy veins were born a life made new
     Which thou couldst find no language to declare.
     Behold if any picture can compare   60
With her just limbs, each fit in shape and size,
   Or match her angel's colour like a pearl.
   She is a gentle girl
To see; yet when it needs her, scorn can rise.
   Meek, bashful, and in all things temperate,   65
   Her virtue holds its state;
In whose least act there is that gift express'd
Which of all reverence makes her worthiest.'

Soft as a peacock steps she, or as a stork
   Straight on herself, taller and statelier: 70
   'Tis a good sight how every limb doth stir
     For ever in a womanly sweet way.
'Open thy soul to see God's perfect work,'
   (My thought begins afresh,) 'and look at her
   When with some lady-friend exceeding fair   75
     She bends and mingles arms and locks in play.

Even as all lesser lights vanish away,
When the sun moves, before his dazzling face,
  So is this lady brighter than all these.
  How should she fail to please, –   80
Love's self being no more than her loveliness?
  In all her ways some beauty springs to view;
  All that she loves to do
Tends alway to her honour's single scope;
And only from good deeds she draws her hope.'   85

Song, thou canst surely say, without pretence,
  That since the first fair woman ever made,
  Not one can have display'd
    More power upon all hearts than this one doth;
    Because in her are both   90
Loveliness and the soul's true excellence: –
And yet (woe's me!) is pity absent thence?

FRANCO SACCHETTI

His Talk with certain Peasant Girls
BALLATA

'Ye graceful peasant-girls and mountain-maids,
Whence come ye homeward through these evening shades?'

'We come from where the forest skirts the hill;
  A very little cottage is our home,
Where with our father and our mother still   5
  We live, and love our life, nor wish to roam.
  Back every evening from the field we come
And bring with us our sheep from pasturing there.'

'Where, tell me, is the hamlet of your birth,
  Whose fruitage is the sweetest by so much?   10
Ye seem to me as creatures worship-worth,
  The shining of your countenance is such.
  No gold about your clothes, coarse to the touch,
Nor silver; yet with such an angel's air!

'I think your beauties might make great complaint   15
  Of being thus shown over mount and dell;
Because no city is so excellent

But that your stay therein were honourable.
  In very truth, now, does it like ye well
To live so poorly on the hill-side here?'   20

'Better it liketh one of us, pardiè,
  Behind her flock to seek the pasture-stance,
Far better than it liketh one of ye
  To ride unto your curtain'd rooms and dance.
  We seek no riches, neither golden chance   25
Save wealth of flowers to weave into our hair.'

Ballad, if I were now as once I was,
  I'd make myself a shepherd on some hill,
And, without telling anyone, would pass
  Where these girls went, and follow at their will;   30
  And 'Mary' and 'Martin' we would murmur still,
And I would be for ever where they were.

On a Fine Day

CATCH

'Be stirring, girls! we ought to have a run:
  Look, did you ever see so fine a day?
Fling spindles right away
    And rocks and reels and wools:
    Now don't be fools, –   5
To-day your spinning's done.
Up with you, up with you!' So, one by one,
  They caught hands, catch who can,
  Then singing, singing, to the river they ran,
  They ran, they ran   10
To the river, the river:
    And the merry-go-round
    Carries them at a bound
To the mill o'er the river.
'Miller, miller, miller,   15
    Weigh me this lady
    And this other. Now steady!'
'You weigh a hundred, you,
And this one weighs two.'
    'Why, dear you do get stout!'   20
    'You think so, dear, no doubt:
    Are you in a decline?'

'Keep your temper and I'll keep mine.'
'Come, girls,' ('O thank you, miller!')
'We'll go home when you will.'   25
So, as we cross'd the hill,
A clown came in great grief,
Crying, 'Stop thief! stop thief!
O what a wretch I am!'
'Well, fellow, here's a clatter!   30
Well, what's the matter?'
'O Lord, O Lord, the wolf has got my lamb!'
Now at that word of woe,
The beauties came and clung about me so
That if wolf had but shown himself, may be   35
I too had caught a lamb that fled to me.

On a Wet Day

CATCH

As I walk'd thinking through a little grove,
Some girls that gather'd flowers kept passing me,
Saying, 'Look here! look there!' delightedly.
'Oh here it is!' 'What's that?' 'A lily, love.'
'And there are violets!'   5
'Further for roses! Oh the lovely pets –
The darling beauties! Oh the nasty thorn!
Look here, my hand's all torn!'
'What's that that jumps?' 'Oh don't! it's a grasshopper!'
'Come run, come run,   10
Here's bluebells!' 'Oh what fun!'
'Not that way! Stop her!'
'Yes, this way!' 'Pluck them, then!'
'Oh, I've found mushrooms! Oh look here!' 'Oh I'm
Quite sure that further on we'll get wild thyme.'   15

'Oh, we shall stay too long, it's going to rain!
There's lightning, oh there's thunder!'
'Oh, shan't we hear the vesper-bell, I wonder?'
'Why it's not nones, you silly little thing;
And don't you hear the nightingales that sing   20
Fly away O die away?'
'I feel so funny! Hush!'
'Why, where? what is it then?' 'Ah! in that bush!'

So every girl here knocks it, shakes and shocks it,
Till with the stir they make 25
Out skurries a great snake.
'O Lord! O me! Alack! Ah me! alack!'
They scream, and then all run and scream again,
And then in heavy drops comes down the rain.

Each running at the other in a fright, 30
Each trying to get before the others, and crying
And flying, stumbling, tumbling, wrong or right;
One sets her knee
There where her foot should be;
One has her hands and dress 35
All smother'd up with mud in a fine mess;
And one gets trampled on by two or three.
What's gather'd is let fall
About the wood and not pick'd up at all.
The wreaths of flowers are scatter'd on the ground; 40
And still as screaming, hustling without rest
They run this way and that and round and round,
She thinks herself in luck who runs the best.

I stood quite still to have a perfect view,
And never noticed till I got wet through. 45

ANONYMOUS

Of True and False Singing
BALLATA

A little wild bird sometimes at my ear
Sings his own little verses very clear.
Others sing louder that I do not hear.

For singing loudly is not singing well;
But ever by the song that's soft and low 5
The master-singer's voice is plain to tell.
Few have it, and yet all are masters now,
And each of them can trill out what he calls
His ballads, canzonets and madrigals.

The world with masters is so cover'd o'er 10
There is no room for pupils any more.

FROM PART II:
DANTE AND HIS CIRCLE

Introduction to Part II
[Introduction to the *Vita Nuova*]

In the second division of this volume are included all the poems I could find which seemed to have value as being personal to the circle of Dante's friends, and as illustrating their intercourse with each other. Those who know the Italian collections from which I have drawn these pieces (many of them most obscure) will perceive how much which is in fact elucidation is here attempted to be embodied in themselves, as to their rendering, arrangement, and heading: since the Italian editors have never yet paid any of them, except of course those by Dante, any such attention; but have printed and reprinted them in a jumbled and disheartening form, by which they can serve little purpose except as *testi di lingua* – dead stock by whose help the makers of dictionaries may smother the language with decayed words. Appearing now I believe for the first time in print, though in a new idiom, from their once living writers to such living readers as they may find, they require some preliminary notice.

The *Vita Nuova* (the Autobiography or Autopsychology of Dante's youth till about his twenty-seventh year) is already well known to many in the original, or by means of essays and of English versions partial or entire. It is, therefore, and on all accounts, unnecessary to say much more of the work here than it says for itself. Wedded to its exquisite and intimate beauties are personal peculiarities which excite wonder and conjecture, best replied to in the words which Beatrice herself is made to utter in the *Commedia*: 'Questi *fu tal* nella sua vita nuova.'[1] Thus then young Dante *was*. All that seemed possible to be done here for the work was to translate it in as free and clear a form as was consistent with fidelity to its meaning; to ease it, as far as possible, from notes and encumbrances; and to accompany it for the first time with those poems from Dante's own lyrical series which have reference to its events, as well as with such native commentary (so to speak) as might be afforded by the writings

---

1 *Purgatorio,* C[anto] xxx.

of those with whom its author was at that time in familiar intercourse. Not chiefly to Dante, then, of whom so much is known to all or may readily be found written, but to the various other members of his circle, these few pages should be devoted.

It may be noted here, however, how necessary a knowledge of the *Vita Nuova* is to the full comprehension of the part borne by Beatrice in the *Commedia*. Moreover, it is only from the perusal of its earliest and then undivulged self-communings that we can divine the whole bitterness of wrong to such a soul as Dante's, its poignant sense of abandonment, or its deep and jealous refuge in memory. Above all, it is here that we find the first manifestations of that wisdom of obedience, that natural breath of duty, which afterwards, in the *Commedia*, lifted up a mighty voice for warning and testimony. Throughout the *Vita Nuova* there is a strain like the first falling murmur which reaches the ear in some remote meadow, and prepares us to look upon the sea.

Boccaccio, in his 'Life of Dante', tells us that the great poet, in later life, was ashamed of this work of his youth. Such a statement hardly seems reconcilable with the allusions to it made or implied in the *Commedia*; but it is true that the *Vita Nuova* is a book which only youth could have produced, and which must chiefly remain sacred to the young; to each of whom the figure of Beatrice, less lifelike than lovelike, will seem the friend of his own heart. Nor is this, perhaps, its least praise. To tax its author with effeminacy on account of the extreme sensitiveness evinced by this narrative of his love, would be manifestly unjust, when we find that, though love alone is the theme of the *Vita Nuova*, war already ranked among its author's experiences at the period to which it relates. In the year 1289, the one preceding the death of Beatrice, Dante served with the foremost cavalry in the great battle of Campaldino, on the eleventh of June, when the Florentines defeated the people of Arezzo. In the autumn of the next year, 1290, when for him, by the death of Beatrice, the city as he says 'sat solitary', such refuge as he might find from his grief was sought in action and danger: for we learn from the *Commedia* (*Hell*, C. xxi) that he served in the war then waged by Florence upon Pisa, and was present at the surrender of Caprona. He says, using the reminiscence to give life to a description, in his great way: —

I've seen the troops out of Caprona go
  On terms, affrighted thus, when on the spot
They found themselves with foemen compass'd so.

(Cayley's Translation)

A word should be said here of the title of Dante's autobiography. The adjective *Nuovo, nuova*, or *Novello, novella*, literally *New*, is often used by Dante and other early writers in the sense of *young*. This has induced some editors of the *Vita Nuova* to explain the title as meaning *Early Life*. I should be glad on some accounts to adopt this supposition, as everything is a gain which increases clearness to the modern reader; but on consideration I think the more mystical interpretation of the words, as *New Life* (in reference to that revulsion of his being which Dante so minutely describes as having occurred simultaneously with his first sight of Beatrice), appears the primary one, and therefore the most necessary to be given in a translation. The probability may be that both were meant, but this I cannot convey.[1]

---

1 I must hazard here (to relieve the first page of my translation from a long note) a suggestion as to the meaning of the most puzzling passage in the whole *Vita Nuova* – that sentence just at the outset which says, 'La gloriosa donna della mia mente, la quale fu chiamata da molti Beatrice, i quali non sapeano che si chiamare.' On this passage all the commentators seem helpless, turning it about and sometimes adopting alterations not to be found in any ancient manuscript of the work. The words mean literally, 'The glorious lady of my mind who was called Beatrice by many who knew not how she was called.' This presents the obvious difficulty that the lady's name really *was* Beatrice, and that Dante throughout uses that name himself. In the text of my version I have adopted, as a rendering, the one of the various compromises which seemed to give the most beauty to the meaning. But it occurs to me that a less irrational escape out of the difficulty than any I have seen suggested may possibly be found by linking this passage with the close of the sonnet at page 108 of the *Vita Nuova*, beginning, 'I felt a spirit of love begin to stir', in the last line of which sonnet Love is made to assert that the name of Beatrice is *Love*. Dante appears to have dwelt on this fancy with some pleasure, from what is said in an earlier sonnet (page 84) about 'Love in his proper form' (by which Beatrice seems to be meant) bending over a dead lady. And it is in connection with the sonnet where the name of Beatrice is said to be Love, that Dante, as if to show us that the Love he speaks of is only his own emotion, enters into an argument as to Love being merely an accident in substance – in other words, 'Amore e il cor gentil son una cosa'. This conjecture may be pronounced extravagant; but the *Vita Nuova*, when examined, proves so full of intricate and fantastic analogies, even in the mere arrangement of its parts (much more than appears on any but the closest scrutiny), that it seems admissible to suggest even a whimsical solution of a difficulty which remains unconquered.

DANTE ALIGHIERI

The New Life
(*La Vita Nuova*)

In that part of the book of my memory before the which is little that can be read, there is a rubric, saying, *Incipit Vita Nova*.[1] Under such rubric I find written many things; and among them the words which I purpose to copy into this little book; if not all of them, at the least their substance.

Nine times already since my birth had the heaven of light returned to the self-same point almost, as concerns its own revolution, when first the glorious Lady of my mind was made manifest to mine eyes; even she who was called Beatrice by many who knew not wherefore.[2] She had already been in this life for so long as that, within her time, the starry heaven had moved towards the Eastern quarter one of the twelve parts of a degree; so that she appeared to me at the beginning of her ninth year almost and I saw her almost at the end of my ninth year. Her dress, on that day, was of a most noble colour, a subdued and goodly crimson, girdled and adorned in such sort as best suited with her very tender age. At that moment, I say most truly that the spirit of life, which hath its dwelling in the secretest chamber of the heart, began to tremble so violently that the least pulses of my body shook therewith; and in trembling it said these words: *Ecce deus fortior me, qui veniens dominabitur mihi.*[3] At that moment the animate spirit, which dwelleth in the lofty chamber whither all the senses carry their perceptions, was filled with wonder, and speaking more especially unto the spirits of the eyes, said these words: *Apparuit jam beatitudo vestra.*[4] At that moment the natural spirit, which dwelleth there where our nourishment is administered, began to weep, and in weeping said these words: *Heu miser! quia frequenter impeditus ero deinceps.*[5]

1 'Here beginneth the new life.'
2 In reference to the meaning of the name, 'She who confers blessing'. We learn from Boccaccio that this first meeting took place at a May Feast, given in the year 1274 by Folco Portinari, father of Beatrice, who ranked among the principal citizens of Florence: to which feast Dante accompanied his father, Alighiero Alighieri.
3 'Here is a deity stronger than I; who, coming, shall rule over me.'
4 'Your beatitude hath now been made manifest unto you.'
5 'Alas! how often shall I be disturbed from this time forth!'

I say that, from that time forward, Love quite governed my soul; which was immediately espoused to him, and with so safe and undisputed a lordship, (by virtue of strong imagination) that I had nothing left for it but to do all his bidding continually. He oftentimes commanded me to seek if I might see this youngest of the Angels: wherefore I in my boyhood often went in search of her, and found her so noble and praiseworthy that certainly of her might have been said those words of the poet Homer, 'She seemed not to be the daughter of a mortal man, but of God.'[1] And albeit her image, that was with me always, was an exultation of Love to subdue me, it was yet of so perfect a quality that it never allowed me to be overruled by Love without the faithful counsel of reason, whensoever such counsel was useful to be heard. But seeing that were I to dwell overmuch on the passions and doings of such early youth, my words might be counted something fabulous, I will therefore put them aside; and passing many things that may be conceived by the pattern of these, I will come to such as are writ in my memory with a better distinctness.

After the lapse of so many days that nine years exactly were completed since the above-written appearance of this most gracious being, on the last of those days it happened that the same wonderful lady appeared to me dressed all in pure white, between two gentle ladies elder than she. And passing through a street, she turned her eyes thither where I stood sorely abashed: and by her unspeakable courtesy, which is now guerdoned in the Great Cycle, she saluted me with so virtuous a bearing that I seemed then and there to behold the very limits of blessedness. The hour of her most sweet salutation was certainly the ninth of that day; and because it was the first time that any words from her reached mine ears, I came into such sweetness that I parted thence as one intoxicated. And betaking me to the loneliness of mine own room, I fell to thinking of this most courteous lady, thinking of whom I was overtaken by a pleasant slumber, wherein a marvellous vision was presented to me: for there appeared to be in my room a mist of the colour of fire, within the which I discerned the figure of a lord of terrible aspect to such as should gaze upon him, but who seemed therewithal to rejoice inwardly that it was a marvel to see. Speaking he said many things, among the which I could understand but few; and of these, this: *Ego dominus tuus.*[2] In his arms it seemed to me that a person was sleeping, covered only with a bloodcoloured cloth; upon whom looking very attentively, I

---

[1]   Οὐδὲ ἐῴκει
Ἀνδρός γε θνητοῦ παῖς ἔμμεναι, ἀλλὰ θεοῖο.
                              (*Iliad,* xxiv. 58)

[2] 'I am thy master.'

knew that it was the lady of the salutation who had deigned the day before to salute me. And he who held her held also in his hand a thing that was burning in flames; and he said to me, *Vide cor tuum.*[1] But when he had remained with me a little while, I thought that he set himself to awaken her that slept; after the which he made her to eat that thing which flamed in his hand; and she ate as one fearing. Then, having waited again a space, all his joy was turned into most bitter weeping; and as he wept he gathered the lady into his arms, and it seemed to me that he went with her up towards heaven: whereby such a great anguish came upon me that my light slumber could not endure through it, but was suddenly broken. And immediately having considered, I knew that the hour wherein this vision had been made manifest to me was the fourth hour (which is to say, the first of the nine last hours) of the night.

Then, musing on what I had seen, I proposed to relate the same to many poets who were famous in that day: and for that I had myself in some sort the art of discoursing with rhyme, I resolved on making a sonnet, in the which, having saluted all such as are subject unto Love, and entreated them to expound my vision, I should write unto them those things which I had seen in my sleep. And the sonnet I made was this: —

> To every heart which the sweet pain doth move,
>   And unto which these words may now be brought
>   For true interpretation and kind thought,
> Be greeting in our Lord's name, which is Love.
> Of those long hours wherein the stars, above,
>   Wake and keep watch, the third was almost nought
>   When Love was shown me with such terrors fraught
> As may not carelessly be spoken of.
> He seem'd like one who is full of joy, and had
>   My heart within his hand, and on his arm
>   My lady, with a mantle round her, slept;
> Whom (having waken'd her) anon he made
>   To eat that heart; she ate, as fearing harm.
>   Then he went out; and as he went, he wept.

This sonnet is divided into two parts. In the first part I give greeting, and ask an answer; in the second, I signify what thing has to be answered to. The second part commences here: 'Of those long hours.'

1 'Behold thy heart.'

To this sonnet I received many answers, conveying many different opinions; of the which, one was sent by him whom I now call the first among my friends; and it began thus, 'Unto my thinking thou beheld'st all worth.'[1] And indeed, it was when he learned that I was he who had sent those rhymes to him, that our friendship commenced. But the true meaning of that vision was not then perceived by any one, though it be now evident to the least skilful.

From that night forth, the natural functions of my body began to be vexed and impeded, for I was given up wholly to thinking of this most gracious creature: whereby in short space I became so weak and so reduced that it was irksome to many of my friends to look upon me; while others, being moved by spite, went about to discover what it was my wish should be concealed. Wherefore I (perceiving the drift of their unkindly questions), by Love's will, who directed me according to the counsels of reason, told them how it was Love himself who had thus dealt with me: and I said so, because the thing was so plainly to be discerned in my countenance that there was no longer any means of concealing it. But when they went on to ask, 'And by whose help hath Love done this?' I looked in their faces smiling, and spake no word in return.

Now it fell on a day, that this most gracious creature was sitting where words were to be heard of the Queen of Glory;[2] and I was in a place whence mine eyes could behold their beatitude: and betwixt her and me, in a direct line, there sat another lady of a pleasant favour; who looked round at me many times, marvelling at my continued gaze which seemed to have *her* for its object. And many perceived that she thus looked: so that departing thence, I heard it whispered after me, 'Look you to what a pass *such a lady* hath brought him'; and in saying this they named her who had been midway between the most gentle Beatrice, and mine eyes. Therefore I was reassured, and knew that for that day my secret had not become manifest. Then immediately it came into my mind that I might make use of this lady as a screen to the truth: and so well did I play my part that the most of those who had hitherto watched and wondered at me, now imagined they had found me out. By her means I kept my secret concealed till some years were gone over; and for my better security, I even made divers rhymes in her honour; whereof I shall here write only as much as concerneth the most gentle Beatrice, which is but a

1 The friend of whom Dante here speaks was Guido Cavalcanti. For his answer, and that of Cino da Pistoia, see their poems further on [pp. 152, 175].
2 i.e. in a church.

very little. Moreover, about the same time while this lady was a screen for so much love on my part, I took the resolution to set down the name of this most gracious creature accompanied with many other women's names, and especially with hers whom I spake of. And to this end I put together the names of sixty the most beautiful ladies in that city where God had placed mine own lady; and these names I introduced in an epistle in the form of a *sirvent*, which it is not my intention to transcribe here. Neither should I have said anything of this matter, did I not wish to take note of a certain strange thing, to wit: that having written the list, I found my lady's name would not stand otherwise than ninth in order among the names of these ladies.

Now it so chanced with her by whose means I had thus long time concealed my desire, that it behoved her to leave the city I speak of, and to journey afar: wherefore I, being sorely perplexed at the loss of so excellent a defence, had more trouble than even I could before have supposed. And thinking that if I spoke not somewhat mournfully of her departure, my former counterfeiting would be the more quickly perceived, I determined that I would make a grievous sonnet[1] thereof; the which I will write here, because it hath certain words in it whereof my lady was the immediate cause, as will be plain to him that understands. And the sonnet was this:—

> All ye that pass along Love's trodden way,
> Pause ye awhile and say
>   If there be any grief like unto mine:
> I pray you that you hearken a short space
> Patiently, if my case
>   Be not a piteous marvel and a sign.
>
> Love (never, certes, for my worthless part,
> But of his own great heart,)
>   Vouchsafed to me a life so calm and sweet
> That oft I heard folk question as I went
> What such great gladness meant:—
>   They spoke of it behind me in the street.
> But now that fearless bearing is all gone
>   Which with Love's hoarded wealth was given me;
>   Till I am grown to be
> So poor that I have dread to think thereon.

1 It will be observed that this poem is not what we now call a sonnet. Its structure, however, is analogous to that of the sonnet, being two sextets followed by two quattrains, instead of two quattrains followed by two triplets. Dante applies the term sonnet to both these forms of composition, and to no other.

And thus it is that I, being like as one
  Who is ashamed and hides his poverty,
    Without seem full of glee,
And let my heart within travail and moan.

*This poem has two principal parts; for, in the first, I mean to call the
Faithful of Love in those words of Jeremias the Prophet, 'O vos omnes
qui transitis per viam, attendite et videte si est dolor sicut dolor meus,'
and to pray them to stay and hear me. In the second I tell where Love
had placed me, with a meaning other than at which the last part of the
poem shows, and I say what I have lost. The second part begins here:
'Love, (never, certes)'.*

A certain while after the departure of that lady, it pleased the
Master of the Angels to call into His glory a damsel, young and of a
gentle presence, who had been very lovely in the city I speak of: and I
saw her body lying without its soul among many ladies, who held a
pitiful weeping. Whereupon, remembering that I had seen her in the
company of excellent Beatrice, I could not hinder myself from a few
tears; and weeping, I conceived to say somewhat of her death, in
guerdon of having seen her somewhile with my lady; which thing I
spake of in the latter end of the verses that I writ in this matter, as he
will discern who understands. And I wrote two sonnets, which are
these: —

I

Weep, Lovers, sith Love's very self doth weep,
  And sith the cause for weeping is so great;
    When now so many dames, of such estate
In worth, show with their eyes a grief so deep:
For Death the churl has laid his leaden sleep
  Upon a damsel who was fair of late,
    Defacing all our earth should celebrate, –
Yea all save virtue, which the soul doth keep.
Now hearken how much Love did honour her.
  I myself saw him in his proper form
    Bending above the motionless sweet dead,
And often gazing into Heaven; for there
  The soul now sits which when her life was warm
    Dwelt with the joyful beauty that is fled.

*This first sonnet is divided into three parts. In the first, I call and
beseech the Faithful of Love to weep; and I say that their Lord weeps,*

*and that they, hearing the reason why he weeps, shall be more minded
to listen to me. In the second, I relate this reason. In the third, I speak
of honour done by Love to this Lady. The second part begins here:
'When now so many dames'; the third here: 'Now hearken'.*

II

Death, always cruel, Pity's foe in chief,
Mother who brought forth grief,
   Merciless judgement and without appeal!
   Since thou alone hast made my heart to feel
   This sadness and unweal,
My tongue upbraideth thee without relief.

And now (for I must rid thy name of ruth)
Behoves me speak the truth
   Touching thy cruelty and wickedness:
   Not that they be not known; but ne'ertheless
   I would give hate more stress
With them that feed on love in very sooth.

Out of this world thou hast driven courtesy,
   And virtue, dearly prized in womanhood;
   And out of youth's gay mood
The lovely lightness is quite gone through thee.

Whom now I mourn, no man shall learn from me
   Save by the measures of these praises given.
   Whoso deserves not Heaven
May never hope to have her company.[1]

*This poem is divided into four parts. In the first I address Death by
certain proper names of hers. In the second, speaking to her, I tell the
reason why I am moved to denounce her. In the third, I rail against
her. In the fourth, I turn to speak to a person undefined, although
defined in my own conception. The second part commences here, 'Since*

---

1 The commentators assert that the last two lines here do not allude to the dead
lady, but to Beatrice. This would make the poem very clumsy in construction; yet
there must be some covert allusion to Beatrice, as Dante himself intimates. The
only form in which I can trace it consists in the implied assertion that such
person as *had* enjoyed the dead lady's society was worthy of heaven, and that
person was Beatrice. Or indeed the allusion to Beatrice might be in the first poem,
where he says that Love '*in forma vera*' (that is, Beatrice), mourned over the
corpse; as he afterwards says of Beatrice, '*Quella ha nome Amor.*' Most probably
both allusions are intended.

thou alone'; the third here, 'And now (for I must)'; the fourth here,
'Whoso deserves not'.

Some days after the death of this lady, I had occasion to leave the
city I speak of, and to go thitherwards where she abode who had
formerly been my protection; albeit the end of my journey reached
not altogether so far. And notwithstanding that I was visibly in the
company of many, the journey was so irksome that I had scarcely
sighing enough to ease my heart's heaviness; seeing that as I went, I
left my beatitude behind me. Wherefore it came to pass that he who
ruled me by virtue of my most gentle lady was made visible to my
mind, in the light habit of a traveller, coarsely fashioned. He appeared
to me troubled, and looked always on the ground; saving only that
sometimes his eyes were turned towards a river which was clear and
rapid, and which flowed along the path I was taking. And then I
thought that Love called me and said to me these words: 'I come from
that lady who was so long thy surety; for the matter of whose return,
I know that it may not be. Wherefore I have taken that heart which I
made thee leave with her, and do bear it unto another lady, who, as
she was, shall be thy surety;' (and when he named her, I knew her
well.) 'And of these words I have spoken, if thou shouldst speak any
again, let it be in such sort as that none shall perceive thereby that thy
love was feigned for her, which thou must now feign for another.'
And when he had spoken thus, all my imagining was gone suddenly,
for it seemed to me that Love became a part of myself: so that,
changed as it were in mine aspect, I rode on full of thought the whole
of that day, and with heavy sighing. And the day being over, I wrote
this sonnet: –

A day agone, as I rode sullenly
  Upon a certain path that liked me not,
  I met Love midway while the air was hot,
Clothed lightly as a wayfarer might be.
And for the cheer he show'd, he seem'd to me
  As one who hath lost lordship he had got;
  Advancing tow'rds me full of sorrowful thought,
Bowing his forehead so that none should see.
Then as I went, he call'd me by my name,
  Saying: 'I journey since the morn was dim
    Thence where I made thy heart to be: which now
I needs must bear unto another dame.'
  Wherewith so much pass'd into me of him
    That he was gone, and I discern'd not how.

This sonnet has three parts. In the first part, I tell how I met Love, and of his aspect. In the second, I tell what he said to me, although not in full, through the fear I had of discovering my secret. In the third, I say how he disappeared. The second part commences here, 'Then as I went'; the third here, 'Wherewith so much'.

On my return, I set myself to seek out that lady whom my master had named to me while I journeyed sighing. And because I would be brief, I will now narrate that in a short while I made her my surety, in such sort that the matter was spoken of by many in terms scarcely courteous; through the which I had oftenwhiles many troublesome hours. And by this it happened (to wit: by this false and evil rumour which seemed to misfame me of vice) that she who was the destroyer of all evil and the queen of all good, coming where I was, denied me her most sweet salutation, in the which alone was my blessedness.

And here it is fitting for me to depart a little from this present matter, that it may be rightly understood of what surpassing virtue her salutation was to me. To the which end I say that when she appeared in any place, it seemed to me, by the hope of her excellent salutation, that there was no man mine enemy any longer; and such warmth of charity came upon me that most certainly in that moment I would have pardoned whosoever had done me an injury; and if one should then have questioned me concerning any matter, I could only have said unto him 'Love,' with a countenance clothed in humbleness. And what time she made ready to salute me, the spirit of Love, destroying all other perceptions, thrust forth the feeble spirits of my eyes, saying, 'Do homage unto your mistress,' and putting itself in their place to obey: so that he who would, might then have beheld Love, beholding the lids of mine eyes shake. And when this most gentle lady gave her salutation, Love, so far from being a medium beclouding mine intolerable beatitude, then bred in me such an overpowering sweetness that my body, being all subjected thereto, remained many times helpless and passive. Whereby it is made manifest that in her salutation alone was there any beatitude for me, which then very often went beyond my endurance.

And now, resuming my discourse, I will go on to relate that when, for the first time, this beatitude was denied me, I became possessed with such grief that parting myself from others, I went into a lonely place to bathe the ground with most bitter tears: and when, by this heat of weeping, I was somewhat relieved, I betook myself to my chamber, where I could lament unheard. And there, having prayed to the Lady of all Mercies, and having said also, 'O Love, aid thou thy servant'; I went suddenly asleep like a beaten sobbing child. And in my sleep, towards the middle of it, I seemed to see in the room, seated at my side, a youth in very white raiment, who kept his eyes fixed on me in deep thought. And when he had gazed some time, I thought that he sighed and called to me in these words: *'Fili mi, tempus est ut prætermittantur simulata nostra.'*[1] And thereupon I seemed to know him; for the voice was the same wherewith he had spoken at other times in my sleep. Then looking at him, I perceived that he was weeping piteously, and that he seemed to be waiting for me to speak. Wherefore, taking heart, I began thus: 'Why weepest thou, Master of all honour?' And he made answer to me: *'Ego tanquam centrum circuli, cui simili modo se habent circumferentiæ partes: tu autem non sic.'*[2] And thinking upon his words, they seemed to me obscure; so that again compelling myself unto speech, I asked of him: 'What thing is this, Master, that thou hast spoken thus darkly?' To the which he made answer in the vulgar tongue: 'Demand no more than may be useful to thee.' Whereupon I began to discourse with him concerning her salutation which she had denied me; and when I had questioned him of the cause, he said these words: 'Our Beatrice hath heard from certain persons, that the lady whom I named to thee while thou journeyedst full of sighs, is sorely disquieted by thy solicitations: and therefore this most gracious creature, who is the enemy of all disquiet, being fearful of such disquiet, refused to salute thee. For the which reason (albeit, in very sooth, thy secret must needs have become known to her by familiar observation) it is my will that thou compose certain things in rhyme, in the which thou shalt set forth how strong a mastership I have obtained over thee, through her; and how thou wast hers even from thy childhood. Also do thou call upon him that knoweth these things to bear witness to them, bidding him to speak with her thereof; the which I, who am he, will do willingly. And thus she shall be made to know thy desire; knowing which, she shall know likewise that they were deceived who spake of thee to her. And so write these things, that they shall seem rather to be spoken by a third person; and not directly by thee to her, which is scarce fitting. After

---

1 'My son, it is time for us to lay aside our counterfeiting.'
2 'I am as the centre of a circle, to the which all parts of the circumference bear an equal relation: but with thee it is not thus.' This phrase seems to have remained as obscure to commentators as Dante found it at the moment. No one, as far as I know, has even fairly tried to find a meaning for it. To me the following appears a not unlikely one. Love is weeping on Dante's account, and not on his own. He says, 'I am the centre of a circle (*Amor che nuove il sole e le altre stelle*): therefore all loveable objects, whether in heaven or earth, or any part of the circle's circumference, are equally near to me. Not so thou, who wilt one day lose Beatrice when she goes to heaven.' The phrase would thus contain an intimation of the death of Beatrice, accounting for Dante being next told not to inquire the meaning of the speech, – 'Demand no more than may be useful to thee.'

the which, send them, not without me, where she may chance to hear them; but have them fitted with a pleasant music, into the which I will pass whensoever it needeth.' With this speech he was away, and my sleep was broken up.

Whereupon, remembering me, I knew that I had beheld this vision during the ninth hour of the day; and I resolved that I would make a ditty, before I left my chamber, according to the words my master had spoken. And this is the ditty that I made: —

> Song, 'tis my will that thou do seek out Love,
>   And go with him where my dear lady is;
>   That so my cause, the which thy harmonies
> Do plead, his better speech may clearly prove.
>
> Thou goest, my Song, in such a courteous kind,
>   That even companionless
>   Thou may'st rely on thyself anywhere.
> And yet, an' thou wouldst get thee a safe mind,
>   First unto Love address
>   Thy steps; whose aid, mayhap, 'twere ill to spare:
>   Seeing that she to whom thou mak'st thy prayer
> Is, as I think, ill-minded unto me,
> And that if Love do not companion thee,
>   Thou'lt have perchance small cheer to tell me of.
>
> With a sweet accent, when thou com'st to her,
>   Begin thou in these words,
>   First having craved a gracious audience:
> 'He who hath sent me as his messenger,
>   Lady, thus much records,
>   An' thou but suffer him, in his defence.
>   Love, who comes with me, by thine influence
> Can make this man do as it liketh him:
> Wherefore, if this fault *is* or doth but *seem*
>   Do thou conceive: for his heart cannot move.'
>
> Say to her also: 'Lady, his poor heart
>   Is so confirm'd in faith
>   That all its thoughts are but of serving thee:
> 'Twas early thine, and could not swerve apart.'
>   Then, if she wavereth,
>   Bid her ask Love, who knows if these things be.
>   And in the end, beg of her modestly
> To pardon so much boldness: saying too: —

'If thou declare his death to be thy due,
  The thing shall come to pass, as doth behove.'

Then pray thou of the Master of all ruth,
  Before thou leave her there,
    That he befriend my cause and plead it well.
'In guerdon of my sweet rhymes and my truth'
  (Entreat him) 'Stay with her;
    Let not the hope of thy poor servant fail;
    And if with her thy pleading should prevail,
Let her look on him and give peace to him.'
Gentle my Song, if good to thee it seem,
  Do this: so worship shall be thine and love.

This ditty is divided into three parts. In the first, I tell it whither to go, and I encourage it, that it may go the more confidently, and I tell it whose company to join if it would go with confidence and without any danger. In the second, I say that which it behoves the ditty to set forth. In the third, I give it leave to start when it pleases, recommending its course to the arms of Fortune. The second part begins here, 'With a sweet accent'; the third here, 'Gentle my Song'. Some might contradict me, and say that they understand not whom I address in the second person, seeing that the ditty is merely the very words I am speaking. And therefore I say that this doubt I intend to solve and clear up in this little book itself, at a more difficult passage, and then let him understand who now doubts, or would now contradict as aforesaid.

After this vision I have recorded, and having written those words which Love had dictated to me, I began to be harassed with many and divers thoughts, by each of which I was sorely tempted; and in especial, there were four among them that left me no rest. The first was this: 'Certainly the lordship of Love is good; seeing that it diverts the mind from all mean things.' The second was this: 'Certainly the lordship of Love is evil; seeing that the more homage his servants pay to him, the more grievous and painful are the torments wherewith he torments them.' The third was this: 'The name of Love is so sweet in the hearing that it would not seem possible for its effects to be other than sweet; seeing that the name must needs be like unto the thing named: as it is written: *Nomina sunt consequentia rerum*.'[1] And the fourth was this: 'The lady whom Love hath chosen out to govern thee

---

1 'Names are the consequents of things.'

is not as other ladies, whose hearts are easily moved.'

And by each one of these thoughts I was so sorely assailed that I was like unto him who doubteth which path to take, and wishing to go, goeth not. And if I bethought myself to seek out some point at the which all these paths might be found to meet, I discerned but one way, and that irked me; to wit, to call upon Pity, and to commend myself unto her. And it was then that, feeling a desire to write somewhat thereof in rhyme, I wrote this sonnet: –

All my thoughts always speak to me of Love,
   Yet have between themselves such difference
   That while one bids me bow with mind and sense,
A second saith, 'Go to: look thou above;'
The third one, hoping, yields me joy enough;
   And with the last come tears, I scarce know whence:
   All of them craving pity in sore suspense,
Trembling with fears that the heart knoweth of.
And thus, being all unsure which path to take,
   Wishing to speak I know not what to say,
   And lose myself in amorous wanderings:
Until (my peace with all of them to make),
   Unto mine enemy I needs must pray,
   My lady Pity, for the help she brings.

This sonnet may be divided into four parts. In the first, I say and propound that all my thoughts are concerning Love. In the second, I say that they are diverse, and I relate their diversity. In the third, I say wherein they all seem to agree. In the fourth, I say that, wishing to speak of Love, I know not from which of these thoughts to take my argument; and that if I would take it from all, I shall have to call upon mine enemy, my Lady Pity. 'Lady' I say as in a scornful mode of speech. The second begins here, 'Yet have between themselves'; the third, 'All of then craving'; the fourth, 'And thus'.

After this battling with many thoughts, it chanced on a day that my most gracious lady was with a gathering of ladies in a certain place; to the which I was conducted by a friend of mine; he thinking to do me a great pleasure by showing me the beauty of so many women. Then I, hardly knowing whereunto he conducted me, but trusting in him (who yet was leading his friend to the last verge of life), made question: 'To what end are we come among these ladies?' and he answered: 'To the end that they may be worthily served.' And they were assembled around a gentlewoman who was given in marriage on that day; the custom of the city being that these should bear her company when she sat down for the first time at table in the house of her husband. Therefore I, as was my friend's pleasure, resolved to stay with him and do honour to those ladies.

But as soon as I had thus resolved, I began to feel a faintness and a throbbing at my left side, which soon took possession of my whole body. Whereupon I remember that I covertly leaned my back unto a painting that ran round the walls of that house; and being fearful lest my trembling should be discerned of them, I lifted mine eyes to look on those ladies, and then first perceived among them the excellent Beatrice. And when I perceived her, all my senses were overpowered by the great lordship that Love obtained, finding himself so near unto that most gracious being, until nothing but the spirits of sight remained to me; and even these remained driven out of their own instruments because Love entered in that honoured place of theirs, that so he might the better behold her. And although I was other than at first, I grieved for the spirits so expelled which kept up a sore lament, saying: 'If he had not in this wise thrust us forth, we also should behold the marvel of this lady.' By this, many of her friends, having discerned my confusion, began to wonder; and together with herself, kept whispering of me and mocking me. Whereupon my friend, who knew not what to conceive, took me by the hands, and drawing me forth from among them, required to know what ailed me. Then, having first held me at quiet for a space until my perceptions were come back to me, I made answer to my friend: 'Of a surety I have now set my feet on that point of life, beyond the which he must not pass who would return.'[1]

Afterwards, leaving him, I went back to the room where I had wept before; and again weeping and ashamed, said: 'If this lady but knew of my condition, I do not think that she would thus mock at me; nay, I am sure that she must needs feel some pity.' And in my weeping I bethought me to write certain words in the which, speaking to her, I should signify the occasion of my disfigurement, telling her also how I knew that she had no knowledge thereof: which, if it were known, I was certain must move others to pity. And then, because I hoped that peradventure it might come into her hearing, I wrote this sonnet.

1 It is difficult not to connect Dante's agony at this wedding-feast with our knowledge that in her twenty-first year Beatrice was wedded to Simone de' Bardi. That she herself was the bride on this occasion might seem out of the question from the fact of its not being in any way so stated: but on the other hand, Dante's silence throughout the *Vita Nuova* as regards her marriage (which must have brought deep sorrow even to his ideal love) is so startling, that we might almost be led to conceive in this passage the only intimation of it which he thought fit to give.

Even as the others mock, thou mockest me;
  Not dreaming, noble lady, whence it is
  That I am taken with strange semblances,
Seeing thy face which is so fair to see:
For else, compassion would not suffer thee
  To grieve my heart with such harsh scoffs as these.
  Lo! Love, when thou art present, sits at ease,
And bears his mastership so mightily,
That all my troubled senses he thrusts out,
  Sorely tormenting some, and slaying some,
    Till none but he is left and has free range
    To gaze on thee. This makes my face to change
Into another's; while I stand all dumb,
And hear my senses clamour in their rout.

This sonnet I divide not into parts, because a division is only made to open the meaning of the thing divided: and this, as it is sufficiently manifest through the reasons given, has no need of division. True it is that, amid the words whereby is shown the occasion of this sonnet, dubious words are to be found; namely, when I say that Love kills all my spirits, but that the visual remain in life, only outside of their own instruments. And this difficulty it is impossible for any to solve who is not in equal guise liege unto Love; and, to those who are so, that is manifest which would clear up the dubious words. And therefore it were not well for me to expound this difficulty, inasmuch as my speaking would be either fruitless or else superfluous.

A while after this strange disfigurement, I became possessed with a strong conception which left me but very seldom, and then to return quickly. And it was this: 'Seeing that thou comest into such scorn by the companionship of this lady, wherefore seekest thou to behold her? If she should ask thee this thing, what answer couldst thou make unto her? yea, even though thou wert master of all thy faculties, and in no way hindered from answering.' Unto the which, another very humble thought said in reply: 'If I were master of all my faculties, and in no way hindered from answering, I would tell her that no sooner do I imagine to myself her marvellous beauty than I am possessed with the desire to behold her, the which is of so great strength that it kills and destroys in my memory all those things which might oppose it; and it is therefore that the great anguish I have endured thereby is yet not enough to restrain me from seeking to behold her.' And then, because of these thoughts, I resolved to write somewhat, wherein, having pleaded mine excuse, I should tell her of what I felt in her presence. Whereupon I wrote this sonnet: –

> The thoughts are broken in my memory,
>> Thou lovely Joy, whene'er I see thy face;
>> When thou art near me, Love fills up the space,
> Often repeating, 'If death irk thee, fly.'
> My face shows my heart's colour, verily,
>> Which, fainting, seeks for any leaning-place;
>> Till, in the drunken terror of disgrace,
> The very stones seem to be shrieking, 'Die!'
> It were a grievous sin, if one should not
>> Strive then to comfort my bewilder'd mind
>> (Though merely with a simple pitying)
> For the great anguish which thy scorn has wrought
>> In the dead sight o' the eyes grown nearly blind,
>> Which look for death as for a blessed thing.

This sonnet is divided into two parts. In the first, I tell the cause why I abstain not from coming to this lady. In the second, I tell what befalls me through coming to her; and this part begins here, 'When thou art near'. And also this second part divides into five distinct statements. For, in the first, I say what Love, counselled by Reason, tells me when I am near the lady. In the second, I set forth the state of my heart by the example of the face. In the third, I say how all ground of trust fails me. In the fourth, I say that he sins who shows not pity of me, which would give me some comfort. In the last, I say why people should take pity; namely, for the piteous look which comes into mine eyes; which piteous look is destroyed, that is, appeareth not unto others, through the jeering of this lady, who draws to the like action those who peradventure would see this piteousness. The second part begins here, 'My face shows'; the third, 'Till, in the drunken terror'; the fourth, 'It were a grievous sin'; the fifth, 'For the great anguish'.

Thereafter, this sonnet bred in me desire to write down in verse four other things touching my condition, the which things it seemed to me that I had not yet made manifest. The first among these was the grief that possessed me very often, remembering the strangeness which Love wrought in me; the second was, how Love many times assailed me so suddenly and with such strength that I had no other life remaining except a thought which spake of my lady: the third was, how when Love did battle with me in this wise, I would rise up all colourless, if so I might see my lady, conceiving that the sight of her would defend me against the assault of Love, and altogether

forgetting that which her presence brought unto me; and the fourth
was, how when I saw her, the sight not only defended me not, but
took away the little life that remained to me. And I said these four
things in a sonnet, which is this: –

> At whiles (yea oftentimes) I muse over
>   The quality of anguish that is mine
>   Through Love: then pity makes my voice to pine
> Saying, 'Is any else thus, anywhere?'
> Love smiteth me, whose strength is ill to bear;
>   So that of all my life is left no sign
>   Except one thought; and that, because 'tis thine,
> Leaves not the body but abideth there.
> And then if I, whom other aid forsook,
>   Would aid myself, and innocent of art
>   Would fain have sight of thee as a last hope,
> No sooner do I lift mine eyes to look
>   Than the blood seems as shaken from my heart,
>   And all my pulses beat at once and stop.

*This sonnet is divided into four parts, four things being therein
narrated; and as these are set forth above, I only proceed to distinguish
the parts by their beginnings. Wherefore I say that the second part
begins, 'Love smiteth me'; the third, 'And then if I'; the fourth, 'No
sooner do I lift'.*

After I had written these three last sonnets, wherein I spake unto
my lady, telling her almost the whole of my condition, it seemed to
me that I should be silent, having said enough concerning myself. But
albeit I spake not to her again, yet it behoved me afterward to write of
another matter, more noble than the foregoing. And for that the
occasion of what I then wrote may be found pleasant in the hearing, I
will relate it as briefly as I may.

Through the sore change in mine aspect, the secret of my heart was
now understood of many. Which thing being thus, there came a day
when certain ladies to whom it was well known (they having been
with me at divers times in my trouble) were met together for the
pleasure of gentle company. And as I was going that way by chance,
(but I think rather by the will of fortune,) I heard one of them call
unto me, and she that called was a lady of very sweet speech. And
when I had come close up with them, and perceived that they had not
among them mine excellent lady, I was reassured; and saluted them,
asking of their pleasure. The ladies were many; divers of whom were

laughing one to another, while divers gazed at me as though I should speak anon. But when I still spake not, one of them, who before had been talking with another, addressed me by my name, saying, 'To what end lovest thou this lady, seeing that thou canst not support her presence? Now tell us this thing, that we may know it: for certainly the end of such a love must be worthy of knowledge.' And when she had spoken these words, not she only, but all they that were with her, began to observe me, waiting for my reply. Whereupon, I said thus unto them:– 'Ladies, the end and aim of my Love was but the salutation of that lady of whom I conceive that ye are speaking; wherein alone I found that beatitude which is the goal of desire. And now that it hath pleased her to deny me this, Love, my Master, of his great goodness, hath placed all my beatitude there where my hope will not fail me.' Then those ladies began to talk closely together; and as I have seen snow fall among the rain, so was their talk mingled with sighs. But after a little, that lady who had been the first to address me, addressed me again in these words: 'We pray thee that thou wilt tell us wherein abideth this thy beatitude.' And answering, I said but thus much: 'In those words that do praise my lady.' To the which she rejoined, 'If thy speech were true, those words that thou didst write concerning thy condition would have been written with another intent.'

Then I, being almost put to shame because of her answer, went out from among them; and as I walked, I said within myself: 'Seeing that there is so much beatitude in those words which do praise my lady, wherefore hath my speech of her been different?' And then I resolved that thenceforward I would choose for the theme of my writings only the praise of this most gracious being. But when I had thought exceedingly, it seemed to me that I had taken to myself a theme which was much too lofty, so that I dared not begin; and I remained during several days in the desire of speaking, and the fear of beginning. After which it happened, as I passed one day along a path which lay beside a stream of very clear water, that there came upon me a great desire to say somewhat in rhyme; but when I began thinking how I should say it, methought that to speak of her were unseemly, unless I spoke to other ladies in the second person; which is to say, not to *any* other ladies; but only to such as are so called because they are gentle, let alone for mere womanhood. Whereupon I declare that my tongue spake as though by its own impulse, and said, 'Ladies that have intelligence in love.' These words I laid up in my mind with great gladness, conceiving to take them as my commencement. Wherefore, having returned to the city I spake of, and considered thereof during certain days, I began a poem with this beginning, constructed in the

mode which will be seen below in its division. The poem begins
here: –

> Ladies that have intelligence in love,
>   Of mine own lady I would speak with you;
>   Not that I hope to count her praises through,
>   But telling what I may, to ease my mind.
> And I declare that when I speak thereof
>   Love sheds such perfect sweetness over me
>   That if my courage fail'd not, certainly
>   To him my listeners must be all resign'd.
>   Wherefore I will not speak in such large kind
> That mine own speech should foil me, which were base;
> But only will discourse of her high grace
>   In these poor words, the best that I can find,
> With you alone, dear dames and damozels:
> 'Twere ill to speak thereof with any else.
>
> An Angel, of his blessed knowledge, saith
>   To God: 'Lord, in the world that Thou hast made,
>   A miracle in action is display'd
>   By reason of a soul whose splendours fare
> Even hither: and since Heaven requireth
>   Nought saving her, for her it prayeth Thee,
>   Thy Saints crying aloud continually.'
>   Yet Pity still defends our earthly share
>   In that sweet soul; God answering thus the prayer:
> 'My well-belovèd, suffer that in peace
>   Your hope remain, while so My pleasure is,
>   There where one dwells who dreads the loss of her;
> And who in Hell unto the doom'd shall say,
> "I have look'd on that for which God's chosen pray." '
>
> My lady is desired in the high Heaven:
>   Wherefore, it now behoveth me to tell,
>   Saying: Let any maid that would be well
>   Esteem'd keep with her: for as she goes by,
> Into foul hearts a deathly chill is driven
>   By Love, that makes ill thought to perish there;
>   While any who endures to gaze on her
>   Must either be made noble, or else die.
>   When one deserving to be raised so high
> Is found, 'tis then her power attains its proof,

Making his heart strong for his soul's behoof
   With the full strength of meek humility.
Also this virtue owns she, by God's will:
Who speaks with her can never come to ill.

Love saith concerning her: 'How chanceth it
   That flesh, which is of dust, should be thus pure?'
   Then, gazing always, he makes oath: 'Forsure,
     This is a creature of God till now unknown.'
She hath that paleness of the pearl that's fit
   In a fair woman, so much and not more;
   She is as high as Nature's skill can soar;
     Beauty is tried by her comparison.
     Whatever her sweet eyes are turn'd upon,
   Spirits of love do issue thence in flame,
   Which through their eyes who then may look on them
     Pierce to the heart's deep chamber every one.
And in her smile Love's image you may see;
Whence none can gaze upon her steadfastly.

Dear Song, I know thou wilt hold gentle speech
   With many ladies, when I send thee forth:
   Wherefore (being mindful that thou hadst thy birth
     From Love, and art a modest, simple child),
Whomso thou meetest, say thou this to each:
   'Give me good speed! To her I wend along
   In whose much strength my weakness is made strong.'
     And if, i' the end, thou wouldst not be beguiled
     Of all thy labour, seek not the defiled
And common sort; but rather choose to be
Where man and woman dwell in courtesy.
     So to the road thou shalt be reconciled,
And find the lady, and with the lady, Love.
Commend thou me to each, as doth behove.

*This poem, that it may be better understood, I will divide more
subtly than the others preceeding; and therefore I will make three
parts of it. The first part is a proem to the words following. The second
is the matter treated of. The third is, as it were, a handmaid to the
preceding words. The second begins here, 'An angel'; the third here,
'Dear Song, I know'. The first part is divided into four. In the first, I
say to whom I mean to speak of my lady, and wherefore I will so
speak. In the second, I say what she appears to myself to be when I*

reflect upon her excellence, and what I would utter if I lost not courage. In the third, I say what it is I purpose to speak, so as not to be impeded by faintheartedness. In the fourth, repeating to whom I purpose speaking, I tell the reason why I speak to them. The second begins here, 'And I declare'; the third here, 'Wherefore I will not speak'; the fourth here, 'With you alone'. Then, when I say 'An Angel', I begin treating of this lady: and this part is divided into two. In the first, I tell what is understood of her in heaven. In the second, I tell what is understood of her on earth: here, 'My lady is desired'. This second part is divided into two; for, in the first, I speak of her as regards the nobleness of her soul, relating some of her virtues proceeding from her soul; in the second, I speak of her as regards the nobleness of her body, narrating some of her beauties: here, 'Love saith concerning her'. This second part is divided into two; for, in the first, I speak of certain beauties which belong to the whole person; in the second, I speak of certain beauties which belong to a distinct part of the person: here, 'Whatever her sweet eyes'. This second part is divided into two; for, in the one, I speak of the eyes, which are the beginning of love; in the second, I speak of the mouth, which is the end of love. And, that every vicious thought may be discarded herefrom, let the reader remember that it is above written that the greeting of this lady, which was an act of her mouth, was the goal of my desires, while I could receive it. Then, when I say, 'Dear Song, I know', I add a stanza as it were handmaid to the others, wherein I say what I desire from this my poem. And because this last part is easy to understand, I trouble not myself with more divisions. I say, indeed, that the further to open the meaning of this poem, more minute divisions ought to be used; but nevertheless he who is not of wit enough to understand it by these which have been already made is welcome to leave it alone; for certes I fear I have communicated its sense to too many by these present divisions, if it so happened that many should hear it.

When this song was a little gone abroad, a certain one of my friends, hearing the same, was pleased to question me, that I should tell him what thing love is; it may be, conceiving from the words thus heard a hope of me beyond my desert. Wherefore I, thinking that after such discourse it were well to say somewhat of the nature of Love, and also in accordance with my friend's desire, proposed to myself to write certain words in the which I should treat of this argument. And the sonnet that I then made is this: –

Love and the gentle heart are one same thing,
    Even as the wise man[1] in his ditty saith.
    Each, of itself, would be such life in death
As rational soul bereft of reasoning.
'Tis Nature makes them when she loves: a king
    Love is, whose palace where he sojourneth
    Is call'd the Heart; there draws he quiet breath
At first, with brief or longer slumbering.
Then beauty seen in virtuous womankind
    Will make the eyes desire, and through the heart
    Send the desiring of the eyes again;
Where often it abides so long enshrined
    That Love at length out of his sleep will start.
    And women feel the same for worthy men.

This sonnet is divided into two parts. In the first, I speak of him according to his power. In the second, I speak of him according as his power translates itself into act. The second part begins here, 'Then beauty seen'. The first is divided into two. In the first, I say in what subject this power exists. In the second, I say how this subject and this power are produced together, and how the one regards the other, as form does matter. The second begins here, ''Tis Nature'. Afterwards when I say, 'Then beauty seen in virtuous womankind', I say how this power translates itself into act; and, first, how it so translates itself in a man, then how it so translates itself in a woman: here, 'And women feel'.

Having treated of love in the foregoing, it appeared to me that I should also say something in praise of my lady, wherein it might be set forth how love manifested itself when produced by her; and how not only she could awaken it where it slept, but where it was not she could marvellously create it. To the which end I wrote another sonnet; and it is this: –

My lady carries love within her eyes;
    All that she looks on is made pleasanter;
    Upon her path men turn to gaze at her;
He whom she greeteth feels his heart to rise,
And droops his troubled visage, full of sighs,
    And of his evil heart is then aware:
    Hate loves, and pride becomes a worshipper.

1 Guido Guinicelli, in the canzone which begins, 'Within the gentle heart Love shelters him.' (See antè [p. 64])

O women, help to praise her in somewise.
Humbleness, and the hope that hopeth well,
   By speech of hers into the mind are brought,
   And who beholds is blessed oftenwhiles.
   The look she hath when she a little smiles
Cannot be said, nor holden in the thought;
   'Tis such a new and gracious miracle.

*This sonnet has three sections. In the first, I say how this lady brings
this power into action by those most noble features, her eyes: and, in
the third, I say this same as to that most noble feature, her mouth.
And between these two sections is a little section, which asks, as it
were, help for the previous section and the subsequent; and it begins
here: 'O women, help'. The third begins here, 'Humbleness'. The first
is divided into three; for, in the first, I say how she with power makes
noble that which she looks upon; and this is as much as to say that she
brings Love, in power, thither where he is not. In the second, I say
how she brings Love, in act, into the hearts of all those whom she sees.
In the third, I tell what she afterwards, with virtue, operates upon
their hearts. The second begins, 'Upon her path'; the third, 'He whom
she greeteth'. Then, when I say, 'O women, help', I intimate to whom
it is my intention to speak, calling on women to help me to honour her.
Then, when I say, 'Humbleness', I say that same which is said in the
first part, regarding two acts of her mouth, one whereof is her most
sweet speech, and the other her marvellous smile. Only, I say not of
this last how it operates upon the hearts of others, because memory
cannot retain this smile, nor its operation.*

Not many days after this (it being the will of the most High God,
who also from Himself put not away death), the father of wonderful
Beatrice, going out of this life, passed certainly into glory. Thereby it
happened, as of very sooth it might not be otherwise, that this lady
was made full of the bitterness of grief: seeing that such a parting is
very grievous unto those friends who are left, and that no other
friendship is like to that between a good parent and a good child; and
furthermore considering that this lady was good in the supreme
degree, and her father (as by many it hath been truly averred) of
exceeding goodness. And because it is the usage of that city that men
meet with men in such a grief, and women with women, certain ladies
of her companionship gathered themselves unto Beatrice, where she
kept alone in her weeping: and as they passed in and out, I could hear
them speak concerning her, how she wept. At length two of them
went by me, who said: 'Certainly she grieveth in such sort that one

might die for pity, beholding her.' Then, feeling the tears upon my
face, I put up my hands to hide them: and had it not been that I
hoped to hear more concerning her (seeing that where I sat, her
friends passed continually in and out), I should assuredly have gone
thence to be alone, when I felt the tears come. But as I still sat in that
place, certain ladies again passed near me, who were saying among
themselves: 'Which of us shall be joyful any more, who have listened
to this lady in her piteous sorrow?' And there were others who said
as they went by me: 'He that sitteth here could not weep more if he
had beheld her as we have beheld her'; and again: 'He is so altered
that he seemeth not as himself.' And still as the ladies passed to and
fro, I could hear them speak after this fashion of her and of me.

Wherefore afterwards, having considered and perceiving that there
was herein matter for poesy, I resolved that I would write certain
rhymes in the which should be contained all that those ladies had
said. And because I would willingly have spoken to them if it had not
been for discreetness, I made in my rhymes as though I had spoken
and they had answered me. And thereof I wrote two sonnets; in the
first of which I addressed them as I would fain have done; and in the
second related their answer, using the speech that I had heard from
them, as though it had been spoken unto myself. And the sonnets are
these: —

I

You that thus wear a modest countenance
   With lids weigh'd down by the heart's heaviness,
   Whence come you, that among you every face
Appears the same, for its pale troubled glance?
Have you beheld my lady's face, perchance,
   Bow'd with the grief that Love makes full of grace?
   Say now, 'This thing is thus;' as my heart says,
Marking your grave and sorrowful advance.
And if indeed you come from where she sighs
   And mourns, may it please you (for his heart's relief)
     To tell how it fares with her unto him
Who knows that you have wept, seeing your eyes,
   And is so grieved with looking on your grief
     That his heart trembles and his sight grows dim.

*This sonnet is divided into two parts. In the first, I call and ask these
ladies whether they come from her, telling them that I think they do,
because they return the nobler. In the second, I pray them to tell me of
her: and the second begins here, 'And if indeed'.*

11

Canst thou indeed be he that still would sing
  Of our dear lady unto none but us?
  For though thy voice confirms that it is thus,
Thy visage might another witness bring.
And wherefore is thy grief so sore a thing
  That grieving thou mak'st others dolorous?
  Hast thou too seen her weep, that thou from us
Canst not conceal thine inward sorrowing?
Nay, leave our woe to us: let us alone:
  'Twere sin if one should strive to soothe our woe,
  For in her weeping we have heard her speak:
Also her look's so full of her heart's moan
  That they who should behold her, looking so,
  Must fall aswoon, feeling all life grow weak.

This sonnet has four parts, as the ladies in whose person I reply had four forms of answer. And, because these are sufficiently shown above, I stay not to explain the purport of the parts, and therefore I only discriminate them. The second begins here, 'And wherefore is thy grief'; the third here, 'Nay, leave our woe'; the fourth, 'Also her look'.

A few days after this, my body became afflicted with a painful infirmity, whereby I suffered bitter anguish for many days, which at last brought me unto such weakness that I could no longer move. And I remember that on the ninth day, being overcome with intolerable pain, a thought came into my mind concerning my lady: but when it had a little nourished this thought, my mind returned to its brooding over mine enfeebled body. And then perceiving how frail a thing life is, even though health keep with it, the matter seemed to me so pitiful that I could not choose but weep; and weeping I said within myself: 'Certainly it must some time come to pass that the very gentle Beatrice will die.' Then, feeling bewildered, I closed mine eyes; and my brain began to be in travail as the brain of one frantic, and to have such imaginations as here follow.

And at the first, it seemed to me that I saw certain faces of women with their hair loosened, which called out to me, 'Thou shalt surely die;' after the which, other terrible and unknown appearances said unto me, 'Thou art dead.' At length, as my phantasy held on in its wanderings, I came to be I knew not where, and to behold a throng of dishevelled ladies wonderfully sad, who kept going hither and thither weeping. Then the sun went out, so that the stars showed themselves, and they were of such a colour that I knew they must be weeping: and it seemed to me that the birds fell dead out of the sky, and that there were great earthquakes. With that, while I wondered in my trance, and was filled with a grievous fear, I conceived that a certain friend came unto me and said: 'Hast thou not heard? She that was thine excellent lady hath been taken out of life.' Then I began to weep very piteously; and not only in mine imagination, but with mine eyes, which were wet with tears. And I seemed to look towards Heaven, and to behold a multitude of angels who were returning upwards, having before them an exceedingly white cloud: and these angels were singing together gloriously, and the words of their song were these: '*Osanna in excelsis:*' and there was no more that I heard. Then my heart that was so full of love said unto me: 'It is true that our lady lieth dead:' and it seemed to me that I went to look upon the body wherein that blessed and most noble spirit had had its abiding-place. And so strong was this idle imagining, that it made me to behold my lady in death; whose head certain ladies seemed to be covering with a white veil; and who was so humble of her aspect that it was as though she had said, 'I have attained to look on the beginning of peace.' And therewithal I came unto such humility by the sight of her, that I cried out upon Death, saying: 'Now come unto me, and be not bitter against me any longer: surely, there where thou hast been, thou hast learned gentleness. Wherefore come now unto me who do greatly desire thee: seest thou not that I wear thy colour already?' And when I had seen all those offices performed that are fitting to be done unto the dead, it seemed to me that I went back unto mine own chamber, and looked up towards heaven. And so strong was my phantasy, that I wept again in very truth, and said with my true voice: 'O excellent soul! How blessed is he that now looketh upon thee!'

And as I said these words, with a painful anguish of sobbing and another prayer unto Death, a young and gentle lady, who had been standing beside me where I lay, conceiving that I wept and cried out because of the pain of mine infirmity, was taken with trembling and began to shed tears. Whereby other ladies, who were about the room, becoming aware of my discomfort by reason of the moan that she made (who indeed was of my very near kindred), led her away from where I was, and then set themselves to awaken me, thinking that I dreamed, and saying: 'Sleep no longer, and be not disquieted.'

Then, by their words, this strong imagination was brought suddenly to an end, at the moment that I was about to say, 'O Beatrice! peace be with thee.' And already I had said, 'O Beatrice!' when being aroused, I opened mine eyes, and knew that it had been a deception. But albeit I had indeed uttered her name, yet my voice was so broken with sobs, that it was not understood by these ladies; so that in spite of the sore shame that I felt, I turned towards them by Love's counselling. And when they beheld me, they began to say, 'He seemeth as one dead,' and to whisper among themselves, 'Let us strive if we may not comfort him.' Whereupon they spake to me many soothing words, and questioned me moreover touching the cause of my fear. Then I, being somewhat reassured, and having perceived that it was a mere phantasy, said unto them, 'This thing it was that made me afeard;' and told them of all that I had seen, from the beginning even unto the end, but without once speaking the name of my lady. Also, after I had recovered from my sickness, I bethought me to write these things in rhyme; deeming it a lovely thing to be known. Whereof I wrote this poem: –

> A very pitiful lady, very young,
>   Exceeding rich in human sympathies,
>   Stood by, what time I clamour'd upon Death;
> And at the wild words wandering on my tongue
>   And at the piteous look within mine eyes
>   She was affrighted, that sobs choked her breath.
>   So by her weeping where I lay beneath,
> Some other gentle ladies came to know
> My state, and made her go:
>   Aftrward, bending themselves over me,
>   One said, 'Awaken thee!'
>   And one, 'What thing thy sleep disquieteth?'
> With that, my soul woke up from its eclipse,
> The while my lady's name rose to my lips:
>
> But utter'd in a voice so sob-broken,
>   So feeble with the agony of tears,
>   That I alone might hear it in my heart;
> And though that look was on my visage then
>   Which he who is ashamed so plainly wears,
>   Love made that I through shame held not apart,
>   But gazed upon them. And my hue was such
> That they look'd at each other and thought of death;
> Saying under their breath
>   Most tenderly, 'Oh, let us comfort him:'
>   Then unto me: 'What dream
>   Was thine, that it hath shaken thee so much?'
> And when I was a little comforted,
> 'This, ladies, was the dream I dreamt,' I said.

'I was a-thinking how life fails with us
  Suddenly after a little while;
    When Love sobb'd in my heart, which is his home.
Whereby my spirit wax'd so dolorous
  That in myself I said, with sick recoil:
    "Yea, to my lady too this Death must come."
    And therewithal such a bewilderment
Possess'd me, that I shut mine eyes for peace;
And in my brain did cease
  Order of thought, and every healthful thing.
  Afterwards, wandering
    Amid a swarm of doubts that came and went,
Some certain women's faces hurried by,
And shriek'd to me, "Thou too shalt die, shalt die!"

'Then saw I many broken hinted sights
  In the uncertain state I stepp'd into.
    Meseem'd to be I know not in what place,
Where ladies through the street, like mournful lights,
  Ran with loose hair, and eyes that frighten'd you
    By their own terror, and a pale amaze:
    The while, little by little, as I thought,
The sun ceased, and the stars began to gather,
And each wept at the other;
  And birds dropp'd in mid-flight out of the sky;
  And earth shook suddenly;
    And I was 'ware of one, hoarse and tired out,
Who ask'd of me: "Hast thou not heard it said? . . .
Thy lady, she that was so fair, is dead."

'Then lifting up mine eyes, as the tears came,
  I saw the Angels, like a rain of manna,
    In a long flight flying back Heavenward;
Having a little cloud in front of them,
  After the which they went and said, "Hosanna!"
    And if they had said more, you should have heard.
    Then Love spoke thus: "Now all shall be made clear:
Come and behold our lady where she lies."
These idle phantasies
  Then carried me to see my lady dead:
  And standing at her head
    Her ladies put a white veil over her;
And with her was such very humbleness
That she appeared to say, "I am at peace."

'And I became so humble in my grief,
　　Seeing in her such deep humility,
　　　　That I said: "Death, I hold thee passing good
Henceforth, and a most gentle sweet relief,
　　Since my dear love has chosen to dwell with thee:
　　　　Pity, not hate, is thine, well understood.
　　　　　　Lo! I do so desire to see thy face
That I am like as one who nears the tomb;
My soul entreats thee, Come."
　　Then I departed, having made my moan;
　　And when I was alone
　　　　I said, and cast my eyes to the High Place:
"Blessed is he, fair soul, who meets thy glance!"
. . . . . Just then you woke me, of your complaisaùnce.'

This poem has two parts. In the first, speaking to a person undefined, I tell how I was aroused from a vain phantasy by certain ladies, and how I promised them to tell what it was. In the second, I say how I told them. The second part begins here, 'I was a-thinking'. The first part divides into two. In the first, I tell that which certain ladies, and which one singly, did and said because of my phantasy, before I had returned into my right senses. In the second, I tell what these ladies said to me after I had left off this wandering: and it begins here, 'But uttered in a voice'. Then, when I say, 'I was a-thinking,' I say how I told them this my imagination; and concerning this I have two parts. In the first, I tell, in order, this imagination. In the second, saying at what time they called me, I covertly thank them: and this part begins here, 'Just then you woke me'.

After this empty imagining, it happened on a day, as I sat thoughtful, that I was taken with such a strong trembling at the heart, that it could not have been otherwise in the presence of my lady. Whereupon I perceived that there was an appearance of Love beside me, and I seemed to see him coming from my lady; and he said, not aloud but within my heart: 'Now take heed that thou bless the day when I entered into thee; for it is fitting that thou shouldst do so.' And with that my heart was so full of gladness, that I could hardly believe it to be of very truth mine own heart and not another.

A short while after these words which my heart spoke to me with the tongue of Love, I saw coming towards me a certain lady who was very famous for her beauty, and of whom that friend whom I have already called the first among my friends had long been enamoured. This lady's right name was Joan; but because of her comeliness (or at least it was so imagined) she was called of many *Primavera* (Spring), and went by that name among them. Then looking again, I perceived that the most noble Beatrice followed after her. And when both these ladies had passed by me, it seemed to me that Love spake again in my heart, saying: 'She that came first was called Spring, only because of that which was to happen on this day. And it was I myself who caused that name to be given her; seeing that as the Spring cometh first in the year, so should she come first on this day,[1] when Beatrice was to show herself after the vision of her servant. And even if thou go about to consider her right name, it is also as one should say, 'She shall come first;' inasmuch as her name, Joan, is taken from that John who went before the True Light, saying: '*Ego vox clamantis in deserto: "Parate viam Domini."*[2] And also it seemed to me that he added other words, to wit: 'He who should inquire delicately touching this matter, could not but call Beatrice by mine own name, which is to say, Love; beholding her so like unto me.'

Then I, having thought of this, imagined to write it with rhymes and send it unto my chief friend; but setting aside certain words[3] which seemed proper to be set aside, because I believed that his heart still regarded the beauty of her that was called Spring. And I wrote this sonnet: —

> I felt a spirit of love begin to stir
>   Within my heart, long time unfelt till then;
>   And saw Love coming towards me, fair and fain,
> (That I scarce knew him for his joyful cheer,)
> Saying, 'Be now indeed my worshipper!'
>   And in his speech he laugh'd and laugh'd again.
>   Then, while it was his pleasure to remain,
> I chanced to look the way he had drawn near,
> And saw the Ladies Joan and Beatrice
>   Approach me, this the other following,
>   One and a second marvel instantly.

---

1 There is a play in the original upon the words *Primavera* (Spring) and *prima verrà* (she shall come first), to which I have given as near an equivalent as I could.
2 'I am the voice of one crying in the wilderness: "Prepare ye the way of the Lord."'
3 That is (as I understand it), suppressing, from delicacy towards his friend, the words in which Love describes Joan as merely the forerunner of Beatrice. And perhaps in the latter part of this sentence a reproach is gently conveyed to the fickle Guido Cavalcanti, who may already have transferred his homage (though Dante had not then learned it) from Joan to Mandetta. (See his Poems.)

And even as now my memory speaketh this,
Love spake it then: 'The first is christen'd Spring;
The second Love, she is so like to me.'

*This sonnet has many parts: whereof the first tells how I felt
awakened within my heart the accustomed tremor, and how it seemed
that Love appeared to me joyful from afar. The second says how it
appeared to me that Love spake within my heart, and what was his
aspect. The third tells how, after he had in such wise been with me a
space, I saw and heard certain things. The second part begins here,
'Saying, "Be now"'; the third here, 'Then, while it was his pleasure'.
The third part divides into two. In the first, I say what I saw. In the
second, I say what I heard: and it begins here, 'Love spake it then.'*

It might be here objected unto me, (and even by one worthy of
controversy,) that I have spoken of Love as though it were a thing
outward and visible: not only a spiritual essence, but as a bodily
substance also. The which thing, in absolute truth, is a fallacy; Love
not being of itself a substance, but an accident of substance. Yet that I
speak of Love as though it were a thing tangible and even human,
appears by three things which I say thereof. And firstly, I say that I
perceived Love coming towards me; whereby, seeing that *to come*
bespeaks locomotion, and seeing also how philosophy teacheth us
that none but a corporeal substance hath locomotion, it seemeth that I
speak of Love as of a corporeal substance. And secondly, I say that
Love smiled; and thirdly, that Love spake; faculties (and especially the
risible faculty) which appear proper unto man: whereby it further
seemeth that I speak of Love as of a man. Now that this matter may
be explained (as is fitting), it must first be remembered that anciently
they who wrote poems of Love wrote not in the vulgar tongue, but
rather certain poets in the Latin tongue. I mean, among us, although
perchance the same may have been among others, and although
likewise, as among the Greeks, they were not writers of spoken
language, but men of letters, treated of these things.[1] And indeed
it is not a great number of years since poetry began to be made in
the vulgar tongue; the writing of rhymes in spoken language

---

1 On reading Dante's treatise *De Vulgari Eloquio*, it will be found that the distinction
which he intends here is not between one language, or dialect, and another; but between
'vulgar speech' (that is, the language handed down from mother to son without any
conscious use of grammar or syntax), and language as regulated by grammarians and the
laws of literary composition, and which Dante calls simply 'Grammar'. A great deal
might be said on the bearings of the present passage, but it is no part of my plan to enter
on such questions.

corresponding to the writing in metre of Latin verse, by a certain analogy. And I say that it is but a little while, because if we examine the language of *oco* and the language of *sì*[1] we shall not find in those tongues any written thing of an earlier date than the last hundred and fifty years. Also the reason why certain of a very mean sort obtained at the first some fame as poets is, that before them no man had written verses in the language of *sì*: and of these, the first was moved to the writing of such verses by the wish to make himself understood of a certain lady, unto whom Latin poetry was difficult. This thing is against such as rhyme concerning other matters than love; that mode of speech having been first used for the expression of love alone.[2] Wherefore, seeing that poets have a licence allowed them that is not allowed unto the writers of prose, and seeing also that they who write in rhyme are simply poets in the vulgar tongue, it becomes fitting and reasonable that a larger licence should be given to these than to other modern writers; and that any metaphor or rhetorical similitude which is permitted unto poets, should also be counted not unseemly in the rhymers of the vulgar tongue. Thus, if we perceive that the former have caused inanimate things to speak as though they had sense and reason, and to discourse one with another; yea, and not only actual things, but such also as have no real existence (seeing that they have made things which are not, to speak; and oftentimes written of those which are merely accidents as though they were substances and things human;) it should therefore be permitted to the latter to do the like; which is to say, not inconsiderately, but with such sufficient motive as may afterwards be set forth in prose.

That the Latin poets have done thus, appears through Virgil, where he saith that Juno (to wit, a goddess hostile to the Trojans) spake unto Æolus, master of the Winds; as it is written in the first book of the Æneid, *Æole, namque tibi, etc.*; and that this master of the Winds made reply: *Tuus, o regina, quid optes – Explorare labor, mihi jussa capessere fas est.* And through the same poet, the inanimate thing speaketh unto the animate, in the third book of the Æneid, where it is written: *Dardanidæ duri, etc.* With Lucan, the animate thing speaketh to the inanimate; as thus: *Multum, Roma, tamen debes civilibus armis.*

1 i.e. the languages of Provence and Tuscany.

2 It strikes me that this curious passage furnishes a reason, hitherto (I believe) overlooked, why Dante put such of his lyrical poems as relate to philosophy into the form of love-poems. He liked writing in Italian rhyme rather than Latin metre; he thought Italian rhyme ought to be confined to love-poems; therefore whatever he wrote (at this age) had to take the form of a love-poem. Thus any poem by Dante not concerning love is later than his twenty-seventh year (1291–2), when he wrote the prose of the *Vita Nuova*; the poetry having been written earlier, at the time of the events referred to.

In Horace man is made to speak to his own intelligence as unto another person; (and not only hath Horace done this but herein he followeth the excellent Homer), as thus in his Poetics: *Dic mihi, Musa, virum, etc.* Through Ovid, Love speaketh as a human creature, in the beginning of his discourse *De Remediis Amoris*: as thus: *Bella mihi video, bella parantur, ait.* By which ensamples this thing shall be made manifest unto such as may be offended at any part of this my book. And lest some of the common sort should be moved to jeering hereat, I will here add, that neither did these ancient poets speak thus without consideration, nor should they who are makers of rhyme in our day write after the same fashion, having no reason in what they write; for it were a shameful thing if one should rhyme under the semblance of metaphor or rhetorical similitude, and afterwards, being questioned thereof, should be unable to rid his words of such semblance, unto their right understanding. Of whom (to wit, of such as rhyme thus foolishly), myself and the first among my friends do know many.

But returning to the matter of my discourse. This excellent lady, of whom I spake in what hath gone before, came at last into such favour with all men, that when she passed anywhere folk ran to behold her; which thing was a deep joy to me: and when she drew near unto any, so much truth and simpleness entered into his heart, that he dared neither to lift his eyes nor to return her salutation: and unto this, many who have felt it can bear witness. She went along crowned and clothed with humility, showing no whit of pride in all that she heard and saw: and when she had gone by, it was said of many, 'This is not a woman, but one of the beautiful angels of Heaven', and there were some that said: 'This is surely a miracle; blessed be the Lord, who hath power to work thus marvellously.' I say, of very sooth, that she showed herself so gentle and so full of all perfection, that she bred in those who looked upon her a soothing quiet beyond any speech; neither could any look upon her without sighing immediately. These things, and things yet more wonderful, were brought to pass through her miraculous virtue. Wherefore I, considering thereof and wishing to resume the endless tale of her praises, resolved to write somewhat wherein I might dwell on her surpassing influence; to the end that not only they who had beheld her, but others also, might know as much concerning her as words could give to the understanding. And it was then that I wrote this sonnet: –

> My lady looks so gentle and so pure
>   When yielding salutation by the way,
>   That the tongue trembles and has nought to say,

And the eyes, which fain would see, may not endure.
And still, amid the praise she hears secure,
   She walks with humbleness for her array;
   Seeming a creature sent from Heaven to stay
On earth, and show a miracle made sure.
She is so pleasant in the eyes of men
That through the sight the inmost heart doth gain
   A sweetness which needs proof to know it by:
And from between her lips there seems to move
A soothing spirit that is full of love,
   Saying for ever to the soul, 'O sigh!'

This sonnet is so easy to understand, from what is afore narrated, that it needs no division: and therefore, leaving it, I say also that this excellent lady came into such favour with all men, that not only she herself was honoured and commended; but through her companionship, honour and commendation came unto others. Wherefore I, perceiving this and wishing that it should also be made manifest to those that beheld it not, wrote the sonnet here following; wherein is signified the power which her virtue had upon other ladies: –

For certain he hath seen all perfectness
   Who among other ladies hath seen mine:
   They that go with her humbly should combine
To thank their God for such peculiar grace.
So perfect is the beauty of her face
   That it begets in no wise any sign
   Of envy, but draws round her a clear line
Of love, and blessed faith, and gentleness.
Merely the sight of her makes all things bow:
   Not she herself alone is holier
   Than all; but hers, through her, are raised above.
From all her acts such lovely graces flow
   That truly one may never think of her
   Without a passion of exceeding love.

This sonnet has three parts. In the first, I say in what company this lady appeared most wondrous. In the second, I say how gracious was her society. In the third, I tell of the things which she, with power, worked upon others. The second begins here, 'They that go with her'; the third here, 'So perfect'. This last part divides into three. In the first, I tell what she operated upon women, that is, by their own faculties. In the second, I tell what she operated in them through others. In the third, I say how she not only operated in women, but in all people;

and not only while herself present, but, by memory of her, operated wondrously. The second begins here, 'Merely the sight'; the third here, 'From all her acts'.

Thereafter on a day, I began to consider that which I had said of my lady: to wit, in these two sonnets aforegone: and becoming aware that I had not spoken of her immediate effect on me at that especial time, it seemed to me that I had spoken defectively. Whereupon I resolved to write somewhat of the manner wherein I was then subject to her influence, and of what her influence then was. And conceiving that I should not be able to say these things in the small compass of a sonnet, I began therefore a poem with this beginning: –

> Love hath so long possess'd me for his own
>   And made his lordship so familiar
> That he, who at first irk'd me, is now grown
>   Unto my heart as its best secrets are.
>   And thus, when he in such sore wise doth mar
> My life that all its strength seems gone from it,
> Mine inmost being then feels throughly quit
>   Of anguish, and all evil keeps afar.
> Love also gathers to such power in me
>   That my sighs speak, each one a grievous thing,
>   Always soliciting
> My lady's salutation piteously.
> Whenever she beholds me, it is so,
> Who is more sweet than any words can show.

* * * * *
* * * * *

Quomodo sedet sola civitas plena populo! facta est quasi vidua domina gentium.[1]

I was still occupied with this poem (having composed thereof only the above-written stanza), when the Lord God of justice called my most gracious lady unto Himself, that she might be glorious under the banner of that blessed Queen Mary, whose name had always a deep reverence in the words of holy Beatrice. And because haply it might be found good that I should say somewhat concerning her

[1] How doth the city sit solitary, that was full of people! how is she become as a widow, she that was great among the nations!' – *Lamentations of Jeremiah*, C. I. V. I.

departure, I will herein declare what are the reasons which make that I shall not do so.

And the reasons are three. The first is, that such matter belongeth not of right to the present argument, if one consider the opening of this little book. The second is, that even though the present argument required it, my pen doth not suffice to write in a fit manner of this thing. And the third is, that were it both possible and of absolute necessity, it would still be unseemly for me to speak thereof, seeing that thereby it must behove me to speak also mine own praises: a thing that in whosoever doeth it is worthy of blame. For the which reasons, I will leave this matter to be treated of by some other than myself.

Nevertheless, as the number nine, which number hath often had mention in what hath gone before, (and not, as it might appear, without reason), seems also to have borne a part in the manner of her death: it is therefore right that I should say somewhat thereof. And for this cause, having first said what was the part it bore herein, I will afterwards point out a reason which made that this number was so closely allied unto my lady.

I say, then, that according to the division of time in Italy, her most noble spirit departed from among us in the first hour of the ninth day of the month; and according to the division of time in Syria, in the ninth month of the year: seeing that Tismim, which with us is October, is there the first month. Also she was taken from among us in that year of our reckoning (to wit, of the years of our Lord) in which the perfect number was nine times multiplied within that century wherein she was born into the world: which is to say, the thirteenth century of Christians.[1]

And touching the reason why this number was so closely allied unto her, it may peradventure be this. According to Ptolemy (and also to the Christian verity), the revolving heavens are nine; and according to the common opinion among astrologers, these nine heavens together have influence over the earth. Wherefore it would appear that this number was thus allied unto her for the purpose of signifying that, at her birth, all these nine heavens were at perfect unity with each other as to their influence. This is one reason that may be brought: but more narrowly considering, and according to the infallible truth, this number was her own self: that is to say by

[1] Beatrice Portinari will thus be found to have died during the first hour of the 9th of June, 1290. And from what Dante says at the commencement of this work (viz. that she was younger than himself by eight or nine months), it may also be gathered that her age, at the time of her death, was twenty-four years and three months. The 'perfect number' mentioned in the present passage is the number ten.

similitude. As thus. The number three is the root of the number nine; seeing that without the interposition of any other number, being multiplied merely by itself, it produceth nine, as we manifestly perceive that three times three are nine. Thus, three being of itself the efficient of nine, and the Great Efficient of Miracles being of Himself Three Persons (to wit: the Father, the Son, and the Holy Spirit), which, being Three, are also One: – this lady was accompanied by the number nine to the end that men might clearly perceive her to be a nine, that is, a miracle, whose only root is the Holy Trinity. It may be that a more subtile person would find for this thing a reason of greater subtilty: but such is the reason that I find, and that liketh me best.

After this most gracious creature had gone out from among us, the whole city came to be as it were widowed and despoiled of all dignity. Then I, left mourning in this desolate city, wrote unto the principal persons thereof, in an epistle, concerning its condition; taking for my commencement those words of Jeremias: *Quomodo sedet sola civitas!* *etc.* And I make mention of this, that none may marvel wherefore I set down these words before, in beginning to treat of her death. Also if any should blame me, in that I do not transcribe that epistle whereof I have spoken, I will make it mine excuse that I began this little book with the intent that it should be written altogether in the vulgar tongue; wherefore, seeing that the epistle I speak of is in Latin, it belongeth not to mine undertaking: more especially as I know that my chief friend, for whom I write this book, wished also that the whole of it should be in the vulgar tongue.

When mine eyes had wept for some while, until they were so weary with weeping that I could no longer through them give ease to my sorrow, I bethought me that a few mournful words might stand me instead of tears. And therefore I proposed to make a poem, that weeping I might speak therein of her for whom so much sorrow had destroyed my spirit; and I then began 'The eyes that weep'.

That this poem may seem to remain the more widowed at its close, I will divide it before writing it; and this method I will observe henceforward. I say that this poor little poem has three parts. The first is a prelude. In the second, I speak of her. In the third I speak pitifully to the poem. The second begins here, 'Beatrice is gone up'; the third here, 'Weep, pitiful Song of mine'. The first divides into three. In the first, I say what moves me to speak. In the second, I say to whom I mean to speak. In the third, I say of whom I mean to speak. The second begins here, 'And because often, thinking'; the third here, 'And I will say'. Then, when I say, 'Beatrice is gone up', I speak of her; and concerning this I have two parts. First, I tell the cause why she was taken away from us: afterwards, I say how one weeps her parting; and this part commences here, 'Wonderfully'. This part divides into three. In the first, I say who it is that weeps her not. In the second, I say who it is that doth weep her. In the third, I speak of my condition. The second begins here, 'But sighing comes, and grief'; the third, 'With sighs'. Then, when I say, 'Weep, pitiful Song of mine,' I speak to this my song, telling it what ladies to go to, and stay with.

The eyes that weep for pity of the heart
   Have wept so long that their grief languisheth
      And they have no more tears to weep withal:
And now, if I would ease me of a part
   Of what, little by little, leads to death,
      It must be done by speech, or not at all.
      And because often, thinking, I recall
How it was pleasant, ere she went afar,
   To talk of her with you, kind damozels,
      I talk with no one else,
But only with such hearts as women's are.
   And I will say, – still sobbing as speech fails, –
That she hath gone to Heaven suddenly,
And hath left Love below, to mourn with me.

Beatrice is gone up into high Heaven,
   The kingdom where the angels are at peace;
      And lives with them; and to her friends is dead.
Not by the frost of winter she was driven
   Away like others; nor by summer-heats;
      But through a perfect gentleness, instead.
      For from the lamp of her meek lowlihead
Such an exceeding glory went up hence
   That it woke wonder in the Eternal Sire,
      Until a sweet desire
Enter'd Him for that lovely excellence,
   So that He bade her to Himself aspire:
Counting this weary and most evil place
Unworthy of a thing so full of grace.

Wonderfully out of the beautiful form
   Soar'd her clear spirit, waxing glad the while;
      And is in its first home, there where it is.
Who speaks thereof, and feels not the tears warm

Upon his face, must have become so vile
  As to be dead to all sweet sympathies.
    Out upon him! an abject wretch like this
May not imagine anything of her, –
  He needs no bitter tears for his relief.
  But sighing comes, and grief,
And the desire to find no comforter,
  (Save only Death, who makes all sorrow brief,)
To him who for a while turns in his thought
How she hath been among us, and is not.

With sighs my bosom always laboureth
  On thinking, as I do continually,
    Of her for whom my heart now breaks apace;
And very often when I think of death,
  Such a great inward longing comes to me
    That it will change the colour of my face;
    And, if the idea settles in its place,
All my limbs shake as with an ague-fit;
  Till, starting up in wild bewilderment,
  I do become so shent
That I go forth, lest folk misdoubt of it.
  Afterward, calling with a sore lament
On Beatrice, I ask, 'Canst thou be dead?'
And calling on her, I am comforted.

Grief with its tears, and anguish with its sighs,
  Come to me now whene'er I am alone;
    So that I think the sight of me gives pain.
And what my life hath been, that living dies,
  Since for my lady the New Birth's begun,
    I have not any language to explain.
    And so, dear ladies, though my heart were fain,
I scarce could tell indeed how I am thus.
  All joy is with my bitter life at war;
  Yea, I am fallen so far
That all men seem to say, 'Go out from us,'
  Eyeing my cold white lips, how dead they are.
But she, though I be bow'd unto the dust,
Watches me; and will guerdon me, I trust.

Weep, piteous Song of mine, upon thy way,
  To the dames going, and the damozels,
  For whom, and for none else,

Thy sisters have made music many a day.
Thou, that art very sad and not as they,
   Go dwell thou with them as a mourner dwells.

After I had written this poem, I received the visit of a friend whom I counted as second unto me in the degrees of friendship, and who, moreover, had been united by the nearest kindred to that most gracious creature. And when we had a little spoken together, he began to solicit me that I would write somewhat in memory of a lady who had died; and he disguised his speech, so as to seem to be speaking of another who was but lately dead: wherefore I, perceiving that his speech was of none other than that blessed one herself, told him that it should be done as he required. Then afterwards, having thought thereof, I imagined to give vent in a sonnet to some part of my hidden lamentations: but in such sort that it might seem to be spoken by this friend of mine, to whom I was to give it. And the sonnet saith thus: 'Stay now with me,' etc.

This sonnet has two parts. In the first, I call the Faithful of Love to hear me. In the second, I relate my miserable condition. The second begins here, 'Mark how they force'.

Stay now with me, and listen to my sighs,
   Ye piteous hearts, as pity bids ye do.
   Mark how they force their way out and press through:
If they be once pent up, the whole life dies.
Seeing that now indeed my weary eyes
   Oftener refuse than I can tell to you,
   (Even though my endless grief is ever new,)
To weep, and let the smother'd anguish rise.
Also in sighing ye shall hear me call
   On her whose blessed presence doth enrich
   The only home that well befitteth her:
And ye shall hear a bitter scorn of all
   Sent from the inmost of my spirit in speech
   That mourns its joy and its joy's minister.

But when I had written this sonnet, bethinking me who he was to whom I was to give it, that it might appear to be his speech, it seemed to me that this was but a poor and barren gift for one of her so near kindred. Wherefore, before giving him this sonnet, I wrote two stanzas of a poem: the first being written in very sooth as though it were spoken by him, but the other being mine own speech, albeit, unto one who should not look closely, they would both seem to be said by the same person. Nevertheless, looking closely, one must perceive that it is not so, inasmuch as one does not call this most gracious creature *his lady*, and the other does, as is manifestly apparent. And I gave the poem and the sonnet unto my friend, saying that I had made them only for him.

The poem begins, 'Whatever while', and has two parts. In the first, that is, in the first stanza, this my dear friend, her kinsman, laments. In the second, I lament; that is, in the other stanza, which begins, 'For ever'. And thus it appears that in this poem two persons lament, of whom one laments as a brother, the other as a servant.

Whatever while the thought comes over me
   That I may not again
     Behold that lady whom I mourn for now,
About my heart my mind brings constantly
   So much of extreme pain
     That I say, Soul of mine, why stayest thou?
     Truly the anguish, soul, that we must bow
Beneath, until we win out of this life,
   Gives me full oft a fear that trembleth:
   So that I call on Death
Even as on Sleep one calleth after strife,
   Saying, Come unto me. Life showeth grim
   And bare; and if one dies, I envy him.

For ever, among all my sighs which burn,
   There is a piteous speech
     That clamours upon death continually:
Yea, unto him doth my whole spirit turn
   Since first his hand did reach
     My lady's life with most foul cruelty.
     But from the height of woman's fairness, she,
Going up from us with the joy we had,
   Grew perfectly and spiritually fair;
   That so she spreads even there
A light of Love which makes the Angels glad,
   And even unto their subtle minds can bring
   A certain awe of profound marvelling.

On that day which fulfilled the year since my lady had been made of the citizens of eternal life, remembering me of her as I sat alone, I betook myself to draw the resemblance of an angel upon certain tablets. And while I did thus, chancing to turn my head, I perceived that some were standing beside me to whom I should have given courteous welcome, and that they were observing what I did: also I learned afterwards that they had been there a while before I perceived them. Perceiving whom, I arose for salutation, and said: 'Another was with me.'[1]

Afterwards, when they had left me, I set myself again to mine occupation, to wit, to the drawing figures of angels: in doing which, I conceived to write of this matter in rhyme, as for her anniversary, and to address my rhymes unto those who had just left me. It was then that I wrote the sonnet which saith, 'That lady:' and as this sonnet hath two commencements, it behoveth me to divide it with both of them here.

I say that, according to the first, this sonnet has three parts. In the first, I say that this lady was then in my memory. In the second, I tell what Love therefore did with me. In the third, I speak of the effects of Love. The second begins here, 'Love knowing'; the third here, 'Forth went they'. This part divides into two. In the one, I say that all my sighs issued speaking. In the other, I say how some spoke certain words different from the others. The second begins here, 'And still'. In this same manner is it divided with the other beginning, save that, in the first part, I tell when this lady had thus come into my mind, and this I say not in the other.

> That lady of all gentle memories
> 　　Had lighted on my soul; – whose new abode
> 　　Lies now, as it was well ordain'd of God,
> Among the poor in heart, where Mary is.
> Love, knowing that dear image to be his,
> 　　Woke up within the sick heart sorrow-bow'd,
> 　　Unto the sighs which are its weary load,
> Saying, 'Go forth.' And they went forth, I wis;
> Forth went they from my breast that throbb'd and ached;
> 　　With such a pang as oftentimes will bathe
> 　　　　Mine eyes with tears when I am left alone.
> And still those sighs which drew the heaviest breath
> Came whispering thus: 'O noble intellect
> 　　It is a year to-day that thou art gone.'

[1] Thus according to some texts. The majority, however, add the words, 'And therefore was I in thought;' but the shorter speech is perhaps the more forcible and pathetic.

Second Commencement

That lady of all gentle memories
   Had lighted on my soul; – for whose sake flow'd
   The tears of Love; in whom the power abode
Which led you to observe while I did this.
Love, knowing that dear image to be his, etc.

Then, having sat for some space sorely in thought because of the time that was now past, I was so filled with dolorous imaginings that it became outwardly manifest in mine altered countenance. Whereupon, feeling this and being in dread lest any should have seen me, I lifted mine eyes to look; and then perceived a young and very beautiful lady, who was gazing upon me from a window with a gaze full of pity, so that the very sum of pity appeared gathered together in her. And seeing that unhappy persons, when they beget compassion in others, are then most moved unto weeping, as though they also felt pity for themselves, it came to pass that mine eyes began to be inclined unto tears. Wherefore, becoming fearful lest I should make manifest mine abject condition, I rose up, and went where I could not be seen of that lady; saying afterwards within myself: 'Certainly with her also must abide most noble Love.' And with that, I resolved upon writing a sonnet, wherein, speaking unto her, I should say all that I have just said. And as this sonnet is very evident, I will not divide it.

Mine eyes beheld the blessed pity spring
   Into thy countenance immediately
   A while agone, when thou beheld'st in me
The sickness only hidden grief can bring;
And then I knew thou wast considering
   How abject and forlorn my life must be;
   And I became afraid that thou shouldst see
My weeping, and account it a base thing.
Therefore I went out from thee; feeling how
   The tears were straightway loosen'd at my heart
     Beneath thine eyes' compassionate control.
     And afterwards I said within my soul:
'Lo! with this lady dwells the counterpart
Of the same Love who holds me weeping now.'

It happened after this, that whensoever I was seen of this lady, she became pale and of a piteous countenance, as though it had been with love; whereby she remembered me many times of my own most noble lady, who was wont to be of a like paleness. And I know that often, when I could not weep nor in any way give ease unto mine anguish, I went to look upon this lady, who seemed to bring the tears into my eyes by the mere sight of her. Of the which thing I bethought me to speak unto her in rhyme, and then made this sonnet: which begins, 'Love's pallor', and which is plain without being divided, by its exposition aforesaid.

> Love's pallor and the semblance of deep ruth
>   Were never yet shown forth so perfectly
>   In any lady's face, chancing to see
> Grief's miserable countenance uncouth,
> As in thine, lady, they have sprung to soothe,
>   When in mine anguish thou hast look'd on me;
>   Until sometimes it seems as if, through thee,
> My heart might almost wander from its truth.
> Yet so it is, I cannot hold mine eyes
>   From gazing very often upon thine
>   In the sore hope to shed those tears they keep;
> And at such time, thou mak'st the pent tears rise
>   Even to the brim, till the eyes waste and pine;
>   Yet cannot they, while thou art present, weep.

At length, by the constant sight of this lady, mine eyes began to be gladdened overmuch with her company; through which thing many times I had much unrest, and rebuked myself as a base person: also, many times I cursed the unsteadfastness of mine eyes, and said to them inwardly: 'Was not your grievous condition of weeping wont one while to make others weep? And will ye now forget this thing because a lady looketh upon you? who so looketh merely in compassion of the grief ye then showed for your own blessed lady. But whatso ye can, that do ye, accursed eyes! many a time will I make you remember it! for never, till death dry you up, should ye make an end of your weeping.' And when I had spoken thus unto mine eyes, I was taken again with extreme and grievous sighing. And to the end that this inward strife which I had undergone might not be hidden from all saving the miserable wretch who endured it, I proposed to write a sonnet, and to comprehend in it this horrible condition. And I wrote this which begins, 'The very bitter weeping.'

The sonnet has two parts. In the first, I speak to my eyes, as my heart spoke within myself. In the second, I remove a difficulty, showing who it is that speaks thus: and this part begins here, 'So far'. It well might receive other divisions also; but this would be useless, since it is manifest by the preceding exposition.

'The very bitter weeping that ye made
　　So long a time together, eyes of mine,
　　Was wont to make the tears of pity shine
In other eyes full oft, as I have said.
But now this thing were scarce rememberèd
　　If I, on my part, foully would combine
　　With you, and not recall each ancient sign
Of grief, and her for whom your tears were shed.
It is your fickleness that doth betray
　　My mind to fears, and makes me tremble thus
　　What while a lady greets me with her eyes.
Except by death, we must not any way
　　Forget our lady who is gone from us.'
　　So far doth my heart utter, and then sighs.

The sight of this lady brought me into so unwonted a condition
that I often thought of her as of one too dear unto me; and I began to
consider her thus: 'This lady is young, beautiful, gentle, and wise:
perchance it was Love himself who set her in my path, that so my life
might find peace.' And there were times when I thought yet more
fondly, until my heart consented unto its reasoning. But when it had
so consented, my thought would often turn round upon me, as
moved by reason, and cause me to say within myself: 'What hope is
this which would console me after so base a fashion, and which hath
taken the place of all other imagining?' Also there was another voice
within me, that said: 'And wilt thou, having suffered so much
tribulation through Love, not escape while yet thou mayest from so
much bitterness? Thou must surely know that this thought carries
with it the desire of Love, and drew its life from the gentle eyes of
that lady who vouchsafed thee so much pity.' Wherefore I, having
striven sorely and very often with myself, bethought me to say
somewhat thereof in rhyme. And seeing that in the battle of doubts,
the victory most often remained with such as inclined towards the
lady of whom I speak, it seemed to me that I should address this
sonnet unto her: in the first line whereof, I call that thought which
spake of her a gentle thought, only because it spoke of one who was
gentle; being of itself most vile.[1]

---

1 Boccaccio tells us that Dante was married to Gemma Donati about a year after the death
of Beatrice. Can Gemma then be 'the lady of the window', his love for whom Dante so
contemns? Such a passing conjecture (when considered together with the interpretation
of this passage in Dante's later work, the *Convito*) would of course imply an admission
of what I believe to lie at the heart of all true Dantesque commentary; that is, the
existence always of the actual events even where the allegorical superstructure has been
raised by Dante himself.

In this sonnet I make myself into two, according as my thoughts were divided one from the other. The one part I call Heart, that is, appetite; the other, Soul, that is, reason; and I tell what one saith to the other. And that it is fitting to call the appetite Heart, and the reason Soul, is manifest enough to them to whom I wish this to be open. True it is that, in the preceding sonnet, I take the part of the Heart against the Eyes; and that appears contrary to what I say in the present; and therefore I say that, there also, by the Heart I mean appetite, because yet greater was my desire to remember my most gentle lady than to see this other, although indeed I had some appetite towards her, but it appeared slight: wherefrom it appears that the one statement is not contrary to the other. This sonnet has three parts. In the first, I begin to say to this lady how my desires turn all towards her. In the second, I say how the Soul, that is, the reason, speaks to the Heart, that is, to the appetite. In the third, I say how the latter answers. The second begins here, 'And what is this?' the third here, 'And the heart answers'.

A gentle thought there is will often start,
   Within my secret self, to speech of thee;
   Also of Love it speaks so tenderly
That much in me consents and takes its part.
'And what is this,' the soul saith to the heart,
   'That cometh thus to comfort thee and me,
   And thence where it would dwell, thus potently
Can drive all other thoughts by its strange art?'
And the heart answers: 'Be no more at strife
   'Twixt doubt and doubt: this is Love's messenger
     And speaketh but his words, from him received;
And all the strength it owns and all the life
   It draweth from the gentle eyes of her
     Who, looking on our grief, hath often grieved.'

But against this adversary of reason, there rose up in me on a certain day, about the ninth hour, a strong visible phantasy, wherein I seemed to behold the most gracious Beatrice, habited in that crimson raiment which she had worn when I had first beheld her; also she appeared to me of the same tender age as then. Whereupon I fell into a deep thought of her: and my memory ran back according to the order of time, unto all those matters in the which she had borne a part; and my heart began painfully to repent of the desire by which it had so basely let itself be possessed during so many days, contrary to the constancy of reason.

And then, this evil desire being quite gone from me, all my thoughts turned again unto their excellent Beatrice. And I say most truly that from that hour I thought constantly of her with the whole humbled and ashamed heart; the which became often manifest in sighs, that had among them the name of that most gracious creature, and how she departed from us. Also it would come to pass very often, through the bitter anguish of some one thought, that I forgot both it, and myself, and where I was. By this increase of sighs, my weeping, which before had been somewhat lessened, increased in like manner; so that mine eyes seemed to long only for tears and to cherish them, and came at last to be circled about with red as though they had suffered martyrdom; neither were they able to look again upon the beauty of any face that might again bring them to shame and evil: from which things it will appear that they were fitly guerdoned for their unsteadfastness. Wherefore I, (wishing that mine abandonment of all such evil desires and vain temptations should be certified and made manifest, beyond all doubts which might have been suggested by the rhymes aforewritten), proposed to write a sonnet, wherein I should express this purport. And I then wrote, 'Woe's me!'

I said, 'Woe's me!' because I was ashamed of the trifling of mine eyes. This sonnet I do not divide, since its purport is manifest enough.

Woe's me! by dint of all these sighs that come
    Forth of my heart, its endless grief to prove,
    Mine eyes are conquer'd, so that even to move
Their lids for greeting is grown troublesome.
They wept so long that now they are grief's home
    And count their tears all laughter far above:
    They wept till they are circled now by Love
With a red circle in sign of martyrdom.
These musings, and the sighs they bring from me,
    Are grown at last so constant and so sore
        That Love swoons in my spirit with faint breath;
Hearing in those sad sounds continually
    The most sweet name that my dead lady bore,
        With many grievous words touching her death.

About this time, it happened that a great number of persons undertook a pilgrimage, to the end that they might behold that blessed portraiture bequeathed unto us by our Lord Jesus Christ as the image of his beautiful countenance,[1] (upon which countenance my dear lady now looketh continually). And certain among these pilgrims, who seemed very thoughtful, passed by a path which is wellnigh in the midst of the city where my most gracious lady was born, and abode, and at last died.

Then I, beholding them, said within myself: 'These pilgrims seem to be come from very far; and I think they cannot have heard speak of this lady, or know anything concerning her. Their thoughts are not of her, but of other things; it may be, of their friends who are far distant, and whom we, in our turn, know not.' And I went on to say: 'I know that if they were of a country near unto us, they would in some wise seem disturbed, passing through this city which is so full of grief.' And I said also: 'If I could speak with them a space, I am certain that I should make them weep before they went forth of this city; for those things that they would hear from me must needs beget weeping in any.'

And when the last of them had gone by me, I bethought me to write a sonnet, showing forth mine inward speech; and that it might seem the more pitiful, I made as though I had spoken it indeed unto them. And I wrote this sonnet, which beginneth: 'Ye pilgrim-folk'. I made use of the word *pilgrim* for its general signification; for 'pilgrim' may be understood in two senses, one general, and one special. General, so far as any man may be called a pilgrim who leaveth the place of his birth; whereas, more narrowly speaking, he only is a pilgrim who goeth towards or frowards the House of St James. For there are three separate denominations proper unto those who undertake journeys to the glory of God. They are called Palmers who go beyond the seas eastward, whence often they bring palm-branches. And Pilgrims, as I have said, are they who journey unto the holy House of Gallicia; seeing that no other apostle was buried so far from his birth-place as was the blessed Saint James. And there is a third sort who are called Romers; in that they go whither these whom I have called pilgrims went: which is to say, unto Rome.

This sonnet is not divided, because its own words sufficiently declare it.

1 The Veronica (*Vera icon*, or true image); that is, the napkin with which a woman was said to have wiped our Saviour's face on his way to the cross, and which miraculously retained its likeness. Dante makes mention of it also in the *Commedia* (*Paradiso*, xxi. 103), where he says: –

'Qual è colui che forse di Croazia
    Viene a veder la Veronica nostra,
Che per l'antica fama non si sazia
    Ma dice nel pensier fin che si mostra:
Signor mio Gesù Cristo, Iddio verace,
    Or fu sì fatta la sembianza vostra?' etc.

Ye pilgrim-folk, advancing pensively
   As if in thought of distant things, I pray,
   Is your own land indeed so far away
As by your aspect it would seem to be, —
That nothing of our grief comes over ye
   Though passing through the mournful town mid-way;
   Like unto men that understand to-day
Nothing at all of her great misery?
Yet if ye will but stay, whom I accost,
   And listen to my words a little space,
    At going ye shall mourn with a loud voice.
It is her Beatrice that she hath lost;
   Of whom the least word spoken holds such grace
    That men weep hearing it, and have no choice.

A while after these things, two gentle ladies sent unto me, praying that I would bestow upon them certain of these my rhymes. And I (taking into account their worthiness and consideration), resolved that I would write also a new thing, and send it them together with those others, to the end that their wishes might be more honourably fulfilled. Therefore I made a sonnet, which narrates my condition, and which I caused to be conveyed to them, accompanied with the one preceding, and with that other which begins, 'Stay now with me and listen to my sighs.' And the new sonnet is, 'Beyond the sphere'.

This sonnet comprises five parts. In the first, I tell whither my thought goeth, naming the place by the name of one of its effects. In the second, I say wherefore it goeth up, and who makes it go thus. In the third, I tell what it saw, namely, a lady honoured. And I then call it a 'Pilgrim Spirit', because it goes up spiritually, and like a pilgrim who is out of his known country. In the fourth, I say how the spirit sees her such (that is, in such quality) that I cannot understand her; that is to say, my thought rises into the quality of her in a degree that my intellect cannot comprehend, seeing that our intellect is, towards those blessed souls, like our eyes weak against the sun; and this the Philosopher says in the Second of the Metaphysics. In the fifth, I say that, although I cannot see there whither my thought carries me — that is, to her admirable essence — I at least understand this, namely, that it is a thought of my lady, because I often hear her name therein. And, at the end of this fifth part, I say, 'Ladies mine', to show that they are ladies to whom I speak. The second part begins, 'A new perception'; the third, 'When it hath reached'; the fourth, 'It sees her such'; the fifth, 'And yet I know'. It might be divided yet more nicely, and made yet clearer; but this division may pass, and therefore I stay not to divide it further.

Beyond the sphere which spreads to widest space
   Now soars the sigh that my heart sends above:
   A new perception born of grieving Love
Guideth it upward the untrodden ways.
When it hath reach'd unto the end, and stays,
   It sees a lady round whom splendours move
   In homage; till, by the great light thereof
Abash'd, the pilgrim spirit stands at gaze.
It sees her such, that when it tells me this
   Which it hath seen, I understand it not,
     It hath a speech so subtile and so fine.
And yet I know its voice within my thought
   Often remembereth me of Beatrice:
     So that I understand it, ladies mine.

After writing this sonnet, it was given unto me to behold a very wonderful vision;[1] wherein I saw things which determined me that I would say nothing further of this most blessed one, until such time as I could discourse more worthily concerning her. And to this end I labour all I can; as she well knoweth. Wherefore if it be His pleasure through whom is the life of all things, that my life continue with me a few years, it is my hope that I shall yet write concerning her what hath not before been written of any woman. After the which, may it seem good unto Him who is the Master of Grace, that my spirit should go hence to behold the glory of its lady: to wit, of that blessed Beatrice who now gazeth continually on His countenance *qui est per omnia sæcula benedictus*.[2] *Laus Deo.*

---

1 This we may believe to have been the Vision of Hell, Purgatory, and Paradise, which furnished the triple argument of the *Divina Commedia*. The Latin words ending the *Vita Nuova* are almost identical with those at the close of the letter in which Dante, on concluding the *Paradise*, and accomplishing the hope here expressed, dedicates his great work to Can Grande della Scala.
2 'Who is blessed throughout all ages.'

POEMS BY DANTE ALIGHIERI, GUIDO CAVALCANTI AND CINO DA PISTOIA

from Introduction to Part II

Among the poets of Dante's circle, the first in order, the first in power, and the one whom Dante has styled his 'first friend', is GUIDO CAVALCANTI, born about 1250, and thus Dante's senior by some fifteen years. It is therefore probable that there is some inaccuracy about the statement, often repeated, that he was Dante's fellow-pupil under Brunetto Latini; though it seems certain that they both studied, probably Guido before Dante, with the same teacher. The Cavalcanti family was among the most ancient in Florence; and its importance may be judged by the fact that in 1280, on the occasion of one of the various missions sent from Rome with the view of pacifying the Florentine factions, the name of 'Guido the son of Messer Cavalcante de' Cavalcanti' appears as one of the sureties offered by the city for the quarter of San Piero Scheraggio. His father must have been notoriously a sceptic in matters of religion, since we find him placed by Dante in the sixth circle of Hell, in one of the fiery tombs of the unbelievers. That Guido shared this heresy was the popular belief, as is plain from an anecdote in Boccaccio which I shall give; and some corroboration of such reports, at any rate as applied to Guido's youth, seems capable of being gathered from an extremely obscure poem, which I have translated on that account (at p. 170) as clearly as I found possible. It must be admitted, however, that there is to the full as much devotional as sceptical tendency implied here and there in his writings; while the presence of either is very rare. We may also set against such a charge the fact that Dino Compagni refers, as will be seen, to his having undertaken a religious pilgrimage. But indeed he seems to have been in all things of that fitful and vehement nature which would impress others always strongly, but often in opposite ways. Self-reliant pride gave its colour to all his moods; making his exploits as a soldier frequently abortive through the headstrong ardour of partisanship, and causing the perversity of a logician to prevail in much of his amorous poetry. The writings of his contemporaries, as well as his own, tend to show him rash in war, fickle in love, and presumptuous in belief; but also, by the same concurrent testimony, he was distinguished by great personal beauty, high accomplishments of all kinds, and daring nobility of soul. Not unworthy, for all the weakness of his strength, to have been the object of Dante's early emulation, the first friend of his youth, and his precursor and fellow-labourer in the creation of Italian Poetry.

In the year 1267, when Guido cannot have been much more than seventeen years of age, a last attempt was made in Florence to reconcile the Guelfs and Ghibellines. With this view several alliances were formed between the leading families of the two factions; and among others, the Guelf Cavalcante de' Cavalcanti wedded his son Guido to a daughter of the Ghibelline Farinata degli Uberti. The peace was of short duration; the utter expulsion of the Ghibellines (through French intervention solicited by the Guelfs) following almost immediately. In the subdivision, which afterwards took place, of the victorious Guelfs into so-called 'Blacks' and 'Whites', Guido embraced the White party, which tended strongly to Ghibellinism, and whose chief was Vieri de' Cerchi, while Corso Donati headed the opposite faction. Whether his wife was still living at the time when the events of the *Vita Nuova* occurred is probably not ascertainable; but about that time Dante tells us that Guido was enamoured of a lady named *Giovanna* or Joan, and whose Christian name is absolutely all that we know of her. However, on the occasion of his pilgrimage to Thoulouse, recorded by Dino Compagni, he seems to have conceived a fresh passion for a lady of that city named Mandetta, who first attracted him by a striking resemblance to his Florentine mistress. Thoulouse had become a place of pilgrimage from its laying claim to the possession of the body, or part of the body, of St James the Greater; though the same supposed distinction had already made the shrine of Compostella in Galicia one of the most famous throughout all Christendom. That this devout journey of Guido's had other results besides a new love will be seen by the passage from Compagni's Chronicle. He says: –

'A young and noble knight named Guido, son of Messer Cavalcante Cavalcanti, – full of courage and courtesy, but disdainful, solitary, and devoted to study, – was a foe to Messer Corso (Donati), and had many times cast about to do him hurt. Messer Corso feared him exceedingly, as knowing him to be of a great spirit, and sought to assassinate him on a pilgrimage which Guido made to the shrine of St James; but he might not compass it. Wherefore, having returned to Florence and being made aware of this, Guido incited many youths against Messer Corso, and these promised to stand by him. Who being one day on horseback with certain of the house of the Cerchi, and having a javelin in his hand, spurred his horse against Messer

Corso, thinking to be followed by the Cerchi that so their companies might engage each other; and he running in on his horse cast the javelin, which missed its aim. And with Messer Corso were Simon, his son, a strong and daring youth, and Cecchino de' Bardi, who with many others pursued Guido with drawn swords; but not overtaking him they threw stones after him, and also others were thrown at him from the windows, whereby he was wounded in the hand. And by this matter hate was increased. And Messer Corso spoke great scorn of Messer Vieri, calling him the Ass of the Gate; because, albeit a very handsome man, he was but of blunt wit and no great speaker. And therefore Messer Corso would say often, "To-day the Ass of the Gate has brayed," and so greatly disparage him; and Guido he called Cavicchia.[1] And thus it was spread abroad of the *jongleurs*; and especially one named Scampolino reported worse things than were said, that so the Cerchi might be provoked to engage the Donati.'

The praise which Compagni, his contemporary, awards to Guido at the commencement of the foregoing extract, receives additional value when viewed in connection with the sonnet addressed to him by the same writer [omitted], where we find that he could tell him of his faults.

Such scenes as the one related above had become common things in Florence, which kept on its course from bad to worse till Pope Boniface VII resolved on sending a legate to propose certain amendments in its scheme of government by *Priori*, or representatives of the various arts and companies. These proposals, however, were so ill received, that the legate, who arrived in Florence in the month of June 1300, departed shortly afterwards greatly incensed, leaving the city under a papal interdict. In the ill-considered tumults which ensued we again hear of Guido Cavalcanti.

'It happened' (says Giovanni Villani in his *History of Florence*) 'that in the month of December (1300) Messer Corso Donati with his followers, and also those of the house of the Cerchi and their followers, going armed to the funeral of a lady of the Frescobaldi family, this party defying that by their looks would have assailed the

---

1 A nickname chiefly chosen, no doubt, for its resemblance to *Cavalcanti*. The word *cavicchia*, *cavicchio*, or *caviglia*, means a wooden peg or pin. A passage in Boccaccio says, 'He had tied his ass to a strong wooden pin' (*caviglia*). Thus Guido, from his mental superiority, might be said to be the Pin to which the Ass, Messer Vieri, was tethered at the Gate (that is, the gate of San Pietro, near which he lived). However, it seems quite as likely that the nickname was founded on a popular phrase by which one who fails in any undertaking is said 'to run his rear on a peg' (*dare del culo in un cavicchio*). The haughty Corso Donati himself went by the name of *Malefammi* or 'Do-me-harm'. For an account of his death in 1307, which proved in keeping with his turbulent life, see Dino Compagni's *Chronicle*, or the *Pecorone* of Giovanni Fiorentin.

one the other; whereby all those who were at the funeral having risen up tumultuously and fled each to his house, the whole city got under arms, both factions assembling in great numbers, at their respective houses. Messer Gentile de' Cerchi, Guido Cavalcanti, Baldinuccio and Corso Adimari, Baschiero della Tosa and Naldo Gherardini, with their comrades and adherents on horse and on foot, hastened to St Peter's Gate to the house of the Donati. Not finding them there they went on to San Pier Maggiore, where Messer Corso was with his friends and followers; by whom they were encountered and put to flight, with many wounds and with much shame to the party of the Cerchi and to their adherents.'

By this time we may conjecture as probable that Dante, in the arduous position which he then filled as chief of the nine *Priori* on whom the Government of Florence devolved, had resigned for far other cares the sweet intercourse of thought and poetry which he once held with that first friend of his who had now become so factious a citizen. Yet it is impossible to say how much of the old feeling may still have survived in Dante's mind when, at the close of the year 1300 or beginning of 1301, it became his duty, as a faithful magistrate of the republic, to add his voice to those of his colleagues in pronouncing a sentence of banishment on the heads of both the Black and White factions, Guido Cavalcanti being included among the latter. The Florentines had been at last provoked almost to demand this course from their governors, by the discovery of a conspiracy, at the head of which was Corso Donati (while among its leading members was Simone de' Bardi, once the husband of Beatrice Portinari), for the purpose of inducing the Pope to subject the republic to a French peace-maker (*Paciere*), and so shamefully free it from its intestine broils. It appears therefore that the immediate cause of the exile to which both sides were subjected lay entirely with the 'Black' party, the leaders of which were banished to the Castello della Pieve in the wild district of Massa Traberia, while those of the 'White' faction were sent to Sarzana, probably (for more than one place bears the name) in the Genovesato. 'But this party' (writes Villani) 'remained a less time in exile, being recalled on account of the unhealthiness of the place, which made that Guido Cavalcanti returned with a sickness, whereof he died. And of him was a great loss; seeing that he was a man, as in philosophy, so in many things deeply versed; but therewithal too fastidious and prone to take offence.' His death apparently took place in 1301.

When the discords of Florence ceased, for Guido, in death, Dante also had seen their native city for the last time. Before Guido's return he had undertaken that embassy to Rome which bore him the bitter fruit of unjust and perpetual exile: and it will be remembered that a chief accusation against him was that of favour shown to the White party on the banishment of the factions.

Besides the various affectionate allusions to Guido in the *Vita Nuova*, Dante has unmistakably referred to him in at least two passages of the *Commedia*. One of these references is to be found in those famous lines of the *Purgatory* (C. xi) where he awards him the palm of poetry over Guido Guinicelli (though also of the latter he speaks elsewhere with high praise), and implies at the same time, it would seem, a consciousness of his own supremacy over both.

'Lo, Cimabue thought alone to tread
    The lists of painting; now doth Giotto gain
The praise, and darkness on his glory shed.
    Thus hath one Guido from another ta'en
The praise of speech, and haply one hath pass'd
    Through birth, who from their nest will chase the twain.'

(Cayley's Translation)

The other mention of Guido is in that pathetic passage of the *Hell* (C. x) where Dante meets among the lost souls Cavalcante de' Cavalcanti: —

All roundabout he looks, as though he had
Desire to see if one was with me else.
But after his surmise was all extinct,
He weeping said: 'If through this dungeon blind
Thou guest by loftiness of intellect, —
Where is my son, and wherefore not with thee?'
And I to him: 'Of myself come I not:
He who there waiteth leads me thoro' here,
Whom haply in disdain your Guido had.'[1]

*   *   *   *   *

Raised upright of a sudden, cried he: 'How
Didst say *He had*? Is he not living still?
Doth not the sweet light strike upon his eyes?'
When he perceived a certain hesitance
Which I was making ere I should reply,
He fell supine, and forth appeared no more.

1 Virgil, Dante's guide through Hell. Any prejudice which Guido entertained against Virgil depended, no doubt, only on his strong desire to see the Latin language give place, in poetry and literature, to a perfected Italian idiom.

Dante, however, conveys his answer afterwards to the spirit of Guido's father, through another of the condemned also related to Guido, Farinata degli Uberti, with whom he has been speaking meanwhile: –

> Then I, as in compunction for my fault,
> Said: 'Now then shall ye tell that fallen one
> His son is still united with the quick.
> And, if I erst was dumb to the response,
> I did it, make him know, because I thought
> Yet on the error you have solved for me.'

(Translated by W. M. Rossetti)[1]

The date which Dante fixed for his vision is Good Friday of the year 1300. A year later, his answer must have been different. The love and friendship of his *Vita Nuova* had then both left him. For ten years Beatrice Portinari had been dead, or (as Dante says in the *Convito*) 'lived in heaven with the angels and on earth with his soul'. And now, distant and probably estranged from him, Guido Cavalcanti was gone too.

Among the Tales from Franco Sacchetti, and in the Decameron of Boccaccio, are two anecdotes relating to Guido. Sacchetti tells us how, one day that he was intent on a game at chess, Guido (who is described as 'one who perhaps had not his equal in Florence') was disturbed by a child playing about, and threatened punishment if the

---

1 These passages are extracted from a literal blank verse translation of the *Inferno* made by my brother, which is as yet in MS, but which I trust may before long see the light; as I believe such a work not to be superfluous even now, notwithstanding the many existing versions of the *Commedia*. It is long since Mr Cary led the way with a good but rather free rendering, more perhaps in the spirit of that day than of this, and accompanied by notes and other editorial matter which are among the clearest and most complete that Dante's work has ever received. Mr Cayley's version, of much more recent date, seems to me to have now occupied (and that without much likelihood of its being superseded) the post which is the first in all such cases, – that of a fine English poem rendering a great foreign one in its own metre, with all essential fidelity, for the use of English readers who read for the sake of poetry. Dr Carlyle's prose translation takes other ground, that of word-for-word literality, for which it presupposes prose to be indispensable. I will venture to assert that my brother's work yields nothing to his, however, in minute precision of this kind; and if so, it can hardly be doubtful that its being in blank verse is a great gain, even as adding the last refinement to exactness by showing the division of the lines; but of course also on the higher poetic ground. I do not forget that a version already exists, by Mr Pollock, professing a like aim with my brother's; and must again express a hope that publicity will shortly afford to all an opportunity of judging the claims of the new attempt. I may here also acknowledge my obligations to my brother for valuable suggestions and assistance in the course of my present work.

noise continued. The child, however, managed slily to nail Guido's coat to the chair on which he sat, and so had the laugh against him when he rose soon afterwards to fulfil his threat. This may serve as an amusing instance of Guido's hasty temper, but is rather a disappointment after its magniloquent heading, which sets forth how 'Guido Cavalcanti, being a man of great valour and a philosopher, is defeated by the cunning of a child'.

The ninth Tale of the sixth Day of the Decameron relates a repartee of Guido's, which has all the profound platitude of mediaeval wit. As the anecdote, however, is interesting on other grounds, I translate it here.

You must know that in past times there were in our city certain goodly and praiseworthy customs no one of which is now left, thanks to avarice, which has so increased with riches that it has driven them all away. Among the which was one whereby the gentlemen of the outskirts were wont to assemble together in divers places throughout Florence, and to limit their fellowships to a certain number, having heed to compose them of such as could fitly discharge the expense. Of whom to-day one, and to-morrow another, and so all in turn, laid tables each on his own day for all the fellowship. And in such wise often they did honour to strangers of worship and also to citizens. They all dressed alike at least once in the year, and the most notable among them rode together through the city; also at seasons they held passages of arms, and specially on the principal feast-days, or whenever any news of victory or other glad tidings had reached the city. And among these fellowships was one headed by Messer Betto Brunelleschi, into the which Messer Betto and his companions had often intrigued to draw Guido di Messer Cavalcante de' Cavalcanti; and this not without cause, seeing that not only he was one of the best logicians that the world held, and a surpassing natural philosopher (for the which things the fellowship cared little), but also he exceeded in beauty and courtesy, and was of great gifts as a speaker; and everything that it pleased him to do, and that best became a gentleman, he did better than any other; and was exceeding rich and knew well to solicit with honourable words whomsoever he deemed worthy. But Messer Betto had never been able to succeed in enlisting him; and he and his companions believed that this was through Guido's much pondering which divided him from other men. Also because he held somewhat of the opinion of the Epicureans, it was said among the vulgar sort that his speculations were only to cast about whether he might find that there was no God. Now on a certain day Guido having left Or San Michele, and held along the Corso degli Adimari as far as San Giovanni (which oftentimes was his walk); and coming to the great marble tombs which now are in the Church of Santa Reparata, but were then with many others in San Giovanni; he being between the porphyry columns which are there among those tombs, and the gate of San Giovanni which was locked; – it so chanced that Messer Betto and his fellowship came riding up by the Piazza di Santa Reparata, and seeing Guido among the sepulchres, said, 'Let us go and engage him.' Whereupon, spurring their horses in the fashion of a pleasant assault, they were on him almost before he was aware, and began to say to him, 'Thou, Guido, wilt none of our fellowship; but lo now! when thou shalt have found that there is no God, what wilt thou have done?' To whom Guido, seeing himself hemmed in among them, readily replied, 'Gentlemen, ye are at home here, and may say what ye please to me.' Wherewith, setting his hand on one of those high tombs, being very light of his person, he took a leap and was over on the other side; and so having freed himself from them, went his way. And they all remained bewildered, looking on one another; and began to say that he was but a shallow-witted fellow, and that the answer he made was as though one should say nothing; seeing that where they were, they had not more to do than other citizens, and Guido not less than they. To whom Messer Betto turned and said thus: 'Ye yourselves are shallow-witted if ye have not understood him. He has civilly and in a few words said to us the most uncivil thing in the world; for if ye look well to it, these tombs are the homes of the dead, seeing that in them the dead are set to dwell; and here he says that we are at home; giving us to know that we and all other simple unlettered men, in comparison of him and the learned, are even as dead men; wherefore, being here, we are at home.' Thereupon each of them understood what Guido had meant, and was ashamed; nor ever again did they set themselves to engage him. Also from that day forth they held Messer Betto to be a subtle and understanding knight.

In the above story mention is made of Guido Cavalcanti's wealth, and there seems no doubt that at that time the family was very rich and powerful. On this account I am disposed to question whether the Canzone at page 168 (where the author speaks of his poverty) can really be Guido's work, though I have included it as being interesting if rightly attributed to him; and it is possible that, when exiled, he may have suffered for the time in purse as well as person. About three years after his death, on the 10th June, 1304, the Black party plotted together and set fire to the quarter of Florence chiefly held by their adversaries. In this conflagration the houses and possessions of the Cavalcanti were almost entirely destroyed; the flames in that neighbourhood (as Dino Compagni records) gaining rapidly in consequence of the great number of waxen images in the Virgin's shrine at Or San Michele; one of which, no doubt, was the very image resembling his lady to which Guido refers in a sonnet. After this, their enemies succeeded in finally expelling from Florence the Cavalcanti family,[1] greatly impoverished by this monstrous fire, in which nearly two thousand houses were consumed.

Guido appears, by various evidence, to have written, besides his poems, a treatise on Philosophy, and another on Oratory, but his poems only have survived to our day. As a poet, he has more individual life of his own than belongs to any of his predecessors; by far the best of his pieces being those which relate to himself, his loves and hates. The best known, however, and perhaps the one for whose sake the rest have been preserved, is the metaphysical canzone on the Nature of Love, beginning 'Donna mi priega', and intended, it is said, as an answer to a sonnet by Guido Orlandi, written as though coming from a lady, and beginning, 'Onde si muove e donde nasce Amore?' On this canzone of Guido's there are known to exist no fewer than eight commentaries, some of them very elaborate, and written by prominent learned men of the middle ages and *renaissance*; the earliest being that by Egidio Colonna, a beatified churchman who died in 1316; while most of the too numerous Academic writers on Italian literature speak of this performance with great admiration as Guido's crowning work. A love-song which acts as such a fly-catcher for priests and pedants looks very suspicious; and accordingly, on examination, it proves to be a poem beside the purpose of poetry, filled with metaphysical jargon, and perhaps the very worst of Guido's productions. Its having been written by a man whose life and works include so much that is impulsive and real, is easily accounted for by scholastic pride in those early days of learning. I have not translated it, as being of little true interest; but was pleased lately, nevertheless, to meet with a remarkably complete translation of it by

1 With them were expelled the still more powerful Gherardini, also great sufferers by the conflagration; who, on being driven from their own country, became the founders of the ancient Geraldine family in Ireland. The Cavalcanti reappear now and then in later European history; and especially we hear of a second Guido Cavalcanti, who also cultivated poetry, and travelled to collect books for the Ambrosian Library; and who, in 1563, visited England as Ambassador to the court of Elizabeth from Charles IX of France.

the Rev. Charles T. Brooks, of Cambridge, United States.[1] The stiffness and cold conceits which prevail in this poem may be found disfiguring much of what Guido Cavalcanti has left, while much besides is blunt, obscure, and abrupt: nevertheless, if it need hardly be said how far he falls short of Dante in variety and personal directness, it may be admitted that he worked worthily at his side, and perhaps before him, in adding those qualities to Italian poetry. That Guido's poems dwelt in the mind of Dante is evident by his having appropriated lines from them (as well as from those of Guincelli) with little alteration, more than once, in the *Commedia*.

Towards the close of his life, Dante, in his Latin treatise *De Vulgari Eloquio*, again speaks of himself as the friend of a poet – this time of CINO DA PISTOIA. In an early passage of that work he says that 'those who have most sweetly and subtly written poems in modern Italian are Cino da Pistoia and a friend of his'. This friend we afterwards find to be Dante himself; as among the various poetical examples quoted are several by Cino followed in three instances by lines from Dante's own lyrics, the author of the latter being again described merely as 'Amicus ejus'. In immediate proximity to these, or coupled in two instances with examples from Dante alone, are various quotations taken from Guido Cavalcanti; but in none of these cases is anything said to connect Dante with him who was once 'the first of his friends'. As commonly between old and new, the change of Guido's friendship for Cino's seems doubtful gain. Cino's poetry, like his career, is for the most part smoother than that of Guido, and in some instances it rises into truth and warmth of expression; but it conveys no idea of such powers, for life or for work, as seem to have distinguished the 'Cavicchia' of Messer Corso Donati. However, his one talent (reversing the parable) appears generally to be made the most of, while Guido's two or three remain uncertain through the manner of their use.

Cino's Canzone addressed to Dante on the death of Beatrice, as well as his answer to the first sonnet of the *Vita Nuova*, indicate that the two poets must have become acquainted in youth, though there is no earlier mention of Cino in Dante's writings than those which occur in his treatise on the Vulgar Tongue. It might perhaps be inferred with some plausibility that their acquaintance was revived

---

1 This translation occurs in the Appendix to an Essay on the *Vita Nuova* of Dante, including extracts, by my friend Mr Charles E. Norton, of Cambridge, U.S.A. – a work of high delicacy and appreciation, which originally appeared by portions in the *Atlantic Monthly*, but has since been augmented by the author and privately printed in a volume which is a beautiful specimen of American typography.

after an interruption by the sonnet and answer at p. 148, and that they afterwards corresponded as friends till the period of Dante's death, when Cino wrote his elegy. Of the two sonnets in which Cino expresses disapprobation of what he thinks the partial judgements of Dante's *Commedia*, the first seems written before the great poet's death, but I should think that the second dated after that event, as the *Paradise*, to which it refers, cannot have become fully known in its author's lifetime. Another sonnet sent to Dante elicited a Latin epistle in reply, where we find Cino addressed as 'frater carissime'. Among Cino's lyrical poems are a few more written in correspondence with Dante, which I have not translated as being of little personal interest.

Guittoncino de' Sinibuldi (for such was Cino's full name) was born in Pistoia, of a distinguished family, in the year 1270. He devoted himself early to the study of law, and in 1307 was Assessor of Civil Causes in his native city. In this year, and in Pistoia, the endless contest of the 'Black' and 'White' factions again sprang into activity; the 'Blacks' and Guelfs of Florence and Lucca driving out the 'Whites' and Ghibellines, who had ruled in the city since 1300. With their accession to power came many iniquitous laws in favour of their own party; so that Cino, as a lawyer of Ghibelline opinions, soon found it necessary or advisable to leave Pistoia, for it seems uncertain whether his removal was voluntary or by proscription. He directed his course towards Lombardy, on whose confines the chief of the 'White' party, in Pistoia, Filippo Vergiolesi, still held the fortress of Pitecchio. Hither Vergiolesi had retreated with his family and adherents when resistance in the city became no longer possible; and it may be supposed that Cino came to join him not on account of political sympathy alone; as Selvaggia Vergiolesi, his daughter, is the lady celebrated throughout the poet's compositions. Three years later, the Vergiolesi and their followers, finding Pitecchio untenable, fortified themselves on the Monte della Sambuca, a lofty peak on the Apennines; which again they were finally obliged to abandon, yielding it to the Guelfs of Pistoia at the price of eleven thousand *lire*. Meanwhile the bleak air of the Sambuca had proved fatal to the lady Selvaggia, who remained buried there, or, as Cino expresses it in one of his poems,

> Cast out upon the steep path of the mountains,
> Where Death had shut her in between hard stones.

Over her cheerless tomb Cino bent and mourned, as he has told us, when, after a prolonged absence spent partly in France, he returned through Tuscany on his way to Rome. He had not been with

Selvaggia's family at the time of her death; and it is probable that, on his return to the Sambuca, the fortress was already surrendered, and her grave almost the only record left there of the Vergiolesi.

Cino's journey to Rome was on account of his having received a high office under Louis of Savoy, who preceded the Emperor Henry VII when he went thither to be crowned in 1310. In another three years the last blow was dealt to the hopes of the exiled and persecuted Ghibellines, by the death of the Emperor, caused almost surely by poison. This death Cina has lamented in a canzone. It probably determined him to abandon a cause which seemed dead, and return, when possible, to his native city. This he succeeded in doing before 1319, as in that year we find him deputed, together with six other citizens, by the government of Pistoia to take possession of a stronghold recently yielded to them. He had now been for some time married to Margherita degli Ughi, of a very noble Pistoiese family, who bore him a son named Mino, and four daughters, Diamante, Beatrice, Giovanna, and Lombarduccia. Indeed, this marriage must have taken place before the death of Selvaggia in 1310, as in 1325–6 his son Mino was one of those by whose aid from within the Ghibelline Castruccio Antelminelli obtained possession of Pistoia, which he held in spite of revolts till his death some two or three years afterwards, when it again reverted to the Guelfs.

After returning to Pistoia, Cino's whole life was devoted to the attainment of legal and literary fame. In these pursuits he reaped the highest honours, and taught at the universities of Siena, Perugia, and Florence; having for his disciples men who afterwards became celebrated, among whom rumour has placed Petrarch, though on examination this seems very doubtful. A sonnet by Petrarch exits, however, commencing 'Piangete donne e con voi pianga Amore', written as a lament on Cino's death, and bestowing the highest praise on him. He and his Selvaggia are also coupled with Dante and Beatrice in the same poet's *Trionfi d'Amore* (cap. 4).

Though established again in Pistoia, Cino resided there but little till about the time of his death, which occurred in 1336–7. His monument, where he is represented as a professor among his disciples, still exists in the Cathedral of Pistoia, and is a mediaeval work of great interest. Messer Cino de' Sinibuldi was a prosperous man, of whom we have ample records, from the details of his examinations as a student, to the inventory of his effects after death, and the curious items of his funeral expenses. Of his claims of a poet it may be said that he filled creditably the interval which elapsed between the death of Dante and the full blaze of Petrarch's success. Most of his poems in honour of Selvaggia are full of an elaborate and mechanical tone of complaint which hardly reads like the expression of a real love; nevertheless there are some, and especially the sonnet on her tomb (at p. 180), which display feeling and power. The finest, as well as the most interesting, of all his pieces, is the very beautiful canzone in which he attempts to console Dante for the death of Beatrice. Though I have found much fewer among Cino's poems than among Guido's which seem to call for translation, the collection of the former is a larger one. Cino produced legal writings also, of which the chief one that has survived is a Commentary on the Statutes of Pistoia, said to have great merit, and whose production in the short space of two years was accounted an extraordinary achievement.

DANTE ALIGHIERI

SONNET

To Brunetto Latini
SENT WITH THE VITA NUOVA

Master Brunetto, this my little maid
  Is come to spend her Easter-tide with you;
  Not that she reckons feasting as her due, –
Whose need is hardly to be fed, but read.
Not in a hurry can her sense be weigh'd,   5
  Nor mid the jests of any noisy crew:
  Ah! and she wants a little coaxing too
Before she'll get into another's head.
But if you do not find her meaning clear,
  You've many Brother Alberts[1] hard at hand,   10
  Whose wisdom will respond to any call.
Consult with them and do not laugh at her;
  And if she still is hard to understand,
  Apply to Master Giano last of all.

1 Probably in allusion to Albert of Cologne. Giano (Janus), which follows, was in
use as an Italian name, as for instance Giano della Bella; but it seems possible that
Dante is merely playfully advising his preceptor to avail himself of the two-fold
insight of Janus the double-faced.

SONNET[1]

Of Beatrice de' Portinari, on All Saints' Day

Last All Saints' holy-day, even now gone by,
  I met a gathering of damozels:
  She that came first, as one doth who excels,
Had Love with her, bearing her company:
A flame burn'd forward through her steadfast eye,   5
  As when in living fire a spirit dwells:
  So, gazing with the boldness which prevails
O'er doubt, I saw an angel visibly.
As she pass'd on, she bow'd her mild approof
  And salutation to all men of worth,   10
Lifting the soul to solemn thoughts aloof.

In Heaven itself that lady had her birth,
I think, and is with us for our behoof:
Blessed are they who meet her on the earth.

1 This and the five following pieces seem so certainly to have been written at the
same time as the poetry of the *Vita Nuova*, that it becomes difficult to guess why
they were omitted from that work. Other poems in Dante's *Canzoniere* refer in a
more general manner to his love for Beatrice, but each among those I have selected
bears the impress of some special occasion.

SONNET

To certain Ladies; when Beatrice was lamenting her Father's Death[1]

Whence come you, all of you so sorrowful?
    An' it may please you, speak for courtesy.
    I fear for my dear lady's sake, least she
Have made you to return thus fill'd with dule.
O gentle ladies, be not hard to school   5
    In gentleness, but to some pause agree,
    And something of my lady say to me,
For with a little my desire is full.
Howbeit it be a heavy thing to hear:
    For love now utterly has thrust me forth,   10
With hand for ever lifted, striking fear.
    See if I be not worn unto the earth:
Yea, and my spirit must fail from me here,
    If, when you speak, your words are of no worth.

1 See the *Vita Nuova*, at page 101.

SONNET

To the same Ladies; with their Answer

'Ye ladies, walking past me piteous-eyed,
    Who is the lady that lies prostrate here?
    Can this be even she my heart holds dear?
Nay, if it be so, speak, and nothing hide.
Her very aspect seems itself beside,   5
    And all her features of such alter'd cheer
    That to my thinking they do not appear
Hers who makes others seem beatified.'

'If thou forget to know our lady thus,
   Whom grief o'ercomes, we wonder in no wise,   10
For also the same thing befalleth us.
   Yet if thou watch the movement of her eyes,
Of her thou shalt be straightway conscious.
   O weep no more! thou art all wan with sighs.'

BALLATA

He will gaze upon Beatrice

Because mine eyes can never have their fill
   Of looking at my lady's lovely face,
     I will so fix my gaze
That I may become bless'd, beholding her.

Even as an angel, up at his great height   5
Standing amid the light,
   Becometh bless'd by only seeing God: –
So, though I be a simple earthly wight,
Yet none the less I might,
   Beholding her who is my heart's dear load,   10
   Be bless'd, and in the spirit soar abroad.
Such power abideth in that gracious one;
Albeit felt of none
   Save of him who, desiring, honours her.

CANZONE

He beseeches Death for the Life of Beatrice

Death, since I find not one with whom to grieve,
   Nor whom this grief of mine may move to tears,
     Whereso I be or whitherso I turn:
Since it is thou who in my soul wilt leave
   No single joy, but chill'st it with just fears   5
     And makest it in fruitless hopes to burn:
     Since thou, Death, and thou only canst discern
Wealth to my life, or want, at thy free choice: –
It is to thee that I lift up my voice,
   Bowing my face that's like a face just dead.   10
I come to thee, as to one pitying,
   In grief for that sweet rest which nought can bring

Again, if thou but once be enterèd
Into her life whom my heart cherishes
Even as the only portal of its peace. –   15

Death, how most sweet the peace is that thy grace
    Can grant to me, and that I pray thee for,
        Thou easily mayst know by a sure sign,
If in mine eyes thou look a little space
    And read in them the hidden dread they store, –   20
        If upon all thou look which proves me thine.
        Since the fear only maketh me to pine
After this sort, – what will mine anguish be
When her eyes close, of dreadful verity,
    In whose light is the light of mine own eyes?   25
But now I know that thou wouldst have my life
As hers, and joy'st thee in my fruitless strife.
    Yet I do think this which I feel implies
That soon, when I would die to flee from pain,
I shall find none by whom I may be slain.   30

Death, if indeed thou smite this gentle one,
    Whose outward worth but tells the intellect
        How wondrous is the miracle within, –
Thou biddest Virtue rise up and begone,
    Thou dost away with Mercy's best effect,   35
        Thou spoil'st the mansion of God's sojourning;
        Yea, unto naught her beauty thou dost bring
Which is above all other beauties, even
In so much as befitteth one whom Heaven
    Sent upon earth in token of its own.   40
Thou dost break through the perfect trust which hath
Been alway her companion in Love's path:
    The light once darken'd which was hers alone,
Love needs must say to them he ruleth o'er,
'I have lost the noble banner that I bore.'   45

Death, have some pity then for all the ill
    Which cannot choose but happen if she die,
    And which will be the sorest ever known.
Slacken the string, if so it be thy will,
    That the sharp arrow leave it not, – thereby   50
        Sparing her life, which if it flies is flown.
        O Death, for God's sake, be some pity shown!
Restrain within thyself, even at its height,

The cruel wrath which moveth thee to smite
   Her in whom God hath set so much of grace.   55
Show now some ruth if 'tis a thing thou hast!
I seem to see Heaven's gate, that is shut fast,
   Open, and angels filling all the space
About me, – come to fetch her soul whose laud
Is sung by saints and angels before God.   60

Song, thou must surely see how fine a thread
   This is that my last hope is holden by,
     And what I should be brought to without her.
Therefore for thy plain speech and lowlihead
   Make thou no pause; but go immediately,   65
     (Knowing thyself for my heart's minister,)
     And with that very meek and piteous air
Thou hast, stand up before the face of Death,
To wrench away the bar that prisoneth
   And win unto the place of the good fruit.   70
And if indeed thou shake by thy soft voice
Death's mortal purpose, – haste thee and rejoice
   Our lady with the issue of thy suit.
So yet awhile our earthly nights and days
Shall keep the blessed spirit that I praise.   75

SONNET

On the 9th of June, 1290

Upon a day, came Sorrow in to me,
   Saying, 'I've come to stay with thee a while;'
   And I perceived that she had usher'd Bile
And Pain into my house for company.
Wherefore I said, 'Go forth, – away with thee!'   5
   But like a Greek she answer'd, full of guile,
   And went on arguing in an easy style.
Then, looking, I saw Love come silently,
Habited in black raiment, smooth and new,
   Having a black hat set upon his hair;   10
And certainly the tears he shed were true.
   So that I ask'd, 'What ails thee, trifler?'
Answering he said; 'A grief to be gone through;
   For our own lady's dying, brother dear.'

TO CINA DA PISTOIA

SONNET

He rebukes Cino for Fickleness

I thought to be for ever separate,
 Fair Master Cino, from these rhymes of yours;
 Since further from the coast, another course,
My vessel now must journey with her freight.[1]
Yet still, because I hear men name your state   5
 As his whom every lure doth straight beguile,
 I pray you lend a very little while
Unto my voice your ear grown obdurate.
The man after this measure amorous,
 Who still at his own will is bound and loosed,   10
 How slightly Love him wounds is lightly known.
If on this wise your heart in homage bows,
 I pray you for God's sake it be disused,
 So that the deed and the sweet words be one.

1 This might seem to suggest that the present sonnet was written about the same time as the close of the *Vita Nuova,* and that an allusion may also here be intended to the first conception of Dante's great work.

CINO DA PISTOIA TO DANTE ALIGHIERI

SONNET

He answers Dante, confessing his unsteadfast Heart

Dante, since I from my own native place
 In heavy exile have turn'd wanderer,
 Far distant from the purest joy which e'er
Had issued from the Fount of joy and grace,
I have gone weeping through the world's dull space,   5
 And me proud Death, as one too mean, doth spare;

Yet meeting Love, Death's neighbour, I declare
That still his arrows hold my heart in chase.
Nor from his pitiless aim can I get free,
   Nor from the hope which comforts my weak will,   10
      Though no true aid exists which I could share.
One pleasure ever binds and looses me;
   That so, by one same Beauty lured, I still
      Delight in many women here and there.

DANTE ALIGHIERI TO CINO DA PISTOIA

SONNET
Written in Exile

Because I find not whom to speak withal
   Anent that lord whose I am as thou art,
   Behoves that in thine ear I tell some part
Of this whereof I gladly would say all.
And deem thou nothing else occasional   5
   Of my long silence while I kept apart,
   Except this place, so guilty at the heart
That the right has not who will give it stall.
Love comes not here to any woman's face,
   Nor any man here for his sake will sigh,   10
      For unto such 'thou fool' were straightway said.
Ah! Master Cino, how the time turns base,
   And mocks at us, and on our rhymes says fie,
      Since truth has been thus thinly harvested.

CINO DA PISTOIA TO DANTE ALIGHIERI

SONNET

He answers the foregoing Sonnet, and prays Dante, in the name of Beatrice, to continue his great Poem

I know not, Dante, in what refuge dwells
  The truth, which with all men is out of mind;
  For long ago it left this place behind,
Till in its stead at last God's thunder swells.
Yet if our shifting life too clearly tells   5
  That here the truth has no reward assign'd, –
  'Twas God, remember, taught it to mankind,
And even among the fiends preach'd nothing else.
Then, though the kingdoms of the earth be torn,
  Where'er thou set thy feet, from Truth's control,   10
  Yet unto me thy friend this prayer accord: –
Beloved, O my brother, sorrow-worn,
  Even in that lady's name who is thy goal,
  Sing on till thou redeem thy plighted word!¹

1 That is, the pledge given at the end of the *Vita Nuova*. This may perhaps have been written in the early days of Dante's exile, before his resumption of the interrupted *Commedia*.

DANTE ALIGHIERI

SONNET

Of Beauty and Duty

Two ladies to the summit of my mind
  Have clomb, to hold an argument of love.
  The one has wisdom with her from above,
For every noblest virtue well design'd:
The other, beauty's tempting power refined   5
  And the high charm of perfect grace approve:
  And I, as my sweet Master's will doth move,
At feet of both their favours am reclined.

Beauty and Duty in my soul keep strife,
  At question if the heart such course can take   10
    And 'twixt two ladies hold its love complete.
    The font of gentle speech yields answer meet,
  That Beauty may be loved for gladness' sake,
And Duty in the lofty ends of life.

SESTINA

Of the Lady Pietra degli Scrovigni

To the dim light and the large circle of shade
I have clomb, and to the whitening of the hills
There where we see no colour in the grass.
Natheless my longing loses not its green,
It has so taken root in the hard stone   5
Which talks and hears as though it were a lady.

Utterly frozen is this youthful lady
Even as the snow that lies within the shade:
For she is no more moved than is a stone
By the sweet season which makes warm the hills   10
And alters them afresh from white to green,
Covering their sides again with flowers and grass.

When on her hair she sets a crown of grass
The thought has no more room for other lady;
Because she weaves the yellow with the green   15
So well that Love sits down there in the shade, –
Love who has shut me in among low hills
Faster than between walls of granite-stone.

She is more bright than is a precious stone;
The wound she gives may not be heal'd with grass: 20
I therefore have fled far o'er plains and hills
For refuge from so dangerous a lady;
But from her sunshine nothing can give shade, –
Not any hill, nor wall, nor summer-green.

A while ago, I saw her dress'd in green, –   25
So fair, she might have waken'd in a stone
This love which I do feel even for her shade;
And therefore, as one woos a graceful lady,
I wooed her in a field that was all grass
Girdled about with very lofty hills.   30

Yet shall the streams turn back and climb the hills
Before Love's flame in this damp wood and green
Burn, as it burns within a youthful lady,
For my sake, who would sleep away in stone
My life, or feed like beasts upon the grass, 35
Only to see her garments cast a shade.

How dark soe'er the hills throw out their shade,
Under her summer-green the beautiful lady
Covers it, like a stone cover'd in grass.

1 I have translated this piece both on account of its great and peculiar beauty, and also because it affords an example of a form of composition which I have met with in no Italian writer before Dante's time, though it is not uncommon among the Provençal poets (see Dante, *de Vulg. Eloq.*). I have headed it with the name of a Paduan lady to whom it is surmised by some to have been addressed during Dante's exile; but this must be looked upon as a rather doubtful conjecture. I have adopted the name chiefly to mark it at once as not referring to Beatrice; and have ventured for the same reason to give a like heading to the sonnet which follows it.

SONNET

To the Lady Pietra degli Scrovigni

My curse be on the day when first I saw
 The brightness in those treacherous eyes of thine, –
The hour when from my heart thou cam'st to draw
 My soul away, that both might fail and pine –
 My curse be on the skill that smooth'd each line 5
Of my vain songs, – the music and just law
 Of art, by which it was my dear design
That the whole world should yield thee love and awe.
Yea, let me curse mine own obduracy,
 Which firmly holds what doth itself confound – 10
 To wit, thy fair perverted face of scorn:
 For whose sake Love is oftentimes forsworn
So that men mock at him; but most at me
 Who would hold fortune's wheel and turn it round.

GUIDO CAVALCANTI

SONNET TO DANTE ALIGHIERI

He interprets Dante's Dream,
related in the first Sonnet
of the Vita Nuova[1]

Unto my thinking, thou beheld'st all worth,
   All joy, as much of good as man may know,
   If thou wert in his power who here below
Is honour's righteous lord throughout this earth.
Where evil dies, even there he has his birth,   5
   Whose justice out of pity's self doth grow.
   Softly to sleeping persons he will go,
And, with no pain to them, their hearts draw forth.
Thy heart he took, as knowing well, alas!
   That Death had claim'd thy lady for her prey: 10
   In fear whereof, he fed her with thy heart.
   But when he seem'd in sorrow to depart,
   Sweet was thy dream; for by that sign, I say,
Surely the opposite shall come to pass.[2]

1 See the *Vita Nuova*, at page 81.
2 This may refer to the belief that, towards morning, dreams go by contraries.

SONNET

To his Lady Joan, of Florence

Flowers hast thou in thyself, and foliage,
   And what is good, and what is glad to see;
The sun is not so bright as thy visàge;
   All is stark naught when one hath look'd on thee;
There is not such a beautiful personage   5
   Anywhere on the green earth verily;
If one fear love, thy bearing sweet and sage
   Comforteth him, and no more fear hath he.
Thy lady friends and maidens ministering
   Are all, for love of thee, much to my taste: 10

And much I pray them that in everything
  They honour thee even as thou meritest,
And have thee in their gentle harbouring:
  Because among them all thou art the best.

SONNET

He compares all Things with his Lady, and finds them wanting

Beauty in woman; the high will's decree;
  Fair knighthood arm'd for manly exercise;
  The pleasant song of birds; love's soft replies;
The strength of rapid ships upon the sea;
The serene air when light begins to be;   5
  The white snow, without wind that falls and lies;
  Fields of all flower; the place where waters rise;
Silver and gold; azure in jewellery: —
Weigh'd against these, the sweet and quiet worth
  Which my dear lady cherishes at heart   10
    Might seem a little matter to be shown;
  Being truly, over these, as much apart
As the whole heaven is greater than this earth.
    All good to kindred natures cleaveth soon.

SONNET

A Rapture concerning his Lady

Who is she coming, whom all gaze upon,
  Who makes the air all tremulous with light,
And at whose side is Love himself? that none
  Dare speak, but each man's sighs are infinite.
Ah me! how she looks round from left to right,   5
  Let Love discourse: I may not speak thereon.
  Lady she seems of such high benison
As makes all others graceless in men's sight.
The honour which is hers cannot be said;
  To whom are subject all things virtuous,   10
    While all things beauteous own her deity.
Ne'er was the mind of man so nobly led
  Nor yet was such redemption granted us
    That we should ever know her perfectly.

BALLATA
Of his Lady among other Ladies

With other women I beheld my love; –
  Not that the rest were women to mine eyes,
Who only as her shadows seem'd to move.

I do not praise her more than with the truth,
  Nor blame I these if it be rightly read.   5

But while I speak, a thought I may not soothe
  Says to my senses: 'Soon shall ye be dead,
  If for my sake your tears ye will not shed.'

And then the eyes yield passage, at that thought,
To the heart's weeping, which forgets her not.   10

SONNET
Of the Eyes of a certain Mandetta, of Thoulouse, which resemble those of his Lady Joan, of Florence

A certain youthful lady in Thoulouse,
  Gentle and fair, of cheerful modesty,
  Is in her eyes, with such exact degree,
Of likeness unto mine own lady, whose
I am, that through the heart she doth abuse   5
  The soul to sweet desire. It goes from me
  To her; yet, fearing, saith not who is she
That of a truth its essence thus subdues.
This lady looks on it with the sweet eyes
  Whose glance did erst the wounds of Love anoint   10
    Through its true lady's eyes which are as they.
Then to the heart returns it, full of sighs,
  Wounded to death by a sharp arrow's point
    Wherewith this lady speeds it on its way.

BALLATA
He reveals, in a Dialogue, his increasing Love for Mandetta

Being in thought of love, I chanced to see
    Two youthful damozels.
  One sang: 'Our life inhales
    All love continually.'

Their aspect was so utterly serene,   5
    So courteous, of such quiet nobleness,
That I said to them: 'Yours, I well may ween,
    'Tis of all virtue to unlock the place.
    Ah! damozels, do not account him base
      Whom thus his wound subdues: 10
      Since I was at Thoulouse,
        My heart is dead in me.'

They turn'd their eyes upon me in so much
    As to perceive how wounded was my heart;
While, of the spirits born of tears, one such   15
    Had been begotten through the constant smart.
    Then seeing me, abash'd, to turn apart,
      One of them said, and laugh'd:
      'Love, look you, by his craft
        Holds this man thoroughly.'   20

But with grave sweetness, after a brief while,
    She who at first had laugh'd on me replied,
Saying: 'This lady, who by Love's great guile
    Her countenance in thy heart has glorified,
    Look'd thee so deep within the eyes, Love sigh'd   25
      And was awaken'd there.
      If it seem ill to bear,
        In him thy hope must be.'

The second piteous maiden, of all ruth,
    Fashion'd for sport in Love's own image, said: 30
'This stroke, whereof thy heart bears trace in sooth,
    From eyes of too much püissance was shed,
    Whence in thy heart such brightness enterèd,
      Thou may'st not look thereon.

Say, of those eyes that shone   35
  Canst thou remember thee?'

Then said I, yielding answer therewithal
  Unto this virgin's difficult behest:
'A lady of Thoulouse, whom Love doth call
  Mandetta, sweetly kirtled and enlaced,   40
  I do remember to my sore unrest.
    Yea, by her eyes indeed
    My life has been decreed
      To death inevitably.'

Go, Ballad, to the city, even Thoulouse,   45
  And softly entering the Dauràde,[1] look round
  And softly call, that so there may be found
Some lady who for compleasaunce may choose
To show thee her who can my life confuse.
    And if she yield thee way,   50
    Lift thou thy voice and say:
      'For grace I come to thee.'

1 The ancient church of the Daurade still exists at Thoulouse. It was so called from
the golden effect of the mosaics adorning it.

DANTE ALIGHIERI TO GUIDO CAVALCANTI

SONNET

He imagines a pleasant Voyage for Guido, Lapo Gianni, and himself, with their three Ladies

Guido, I wish that Lapo, thou, and I,
  Could be by spells convey'd, as it were now,
  Upon a barque, with all the winds that blow
Across all seas at our good will to hie
So no mischance nor temper of the sky   5
  Should mar our course with spite or cruel slip;
  But we, observing old companionship,
To be companions still should long thereby.
And Lady Joan, and Lady Beatrice,
  And her the thirtieth on my roll,[1] with us   10
    Should our good wizard set, o'er seas to move
    And not to talk of anything but love:

And they three ever to be well at ease
As we should be, I think, if this were thus.

1 That is, his list of the sixty most beautiful ladies of Florence, referred to in the *Vita Nuova*; among whom Lapo Gianni's lady, Lagia, would seem to have stood thirtieth.

GUIDO CAVALCANTI TO DANTE ALIGHIERI

SONNET

Guido answers the foregoing Sonnet, speaking with shame of his changed Love

If I were still that man, worthy to love,
  Of whom I have but the remembrance now,
  Or if the lady bore another brow,
To hear this thing might bring me joy thereof.
But thou, who in Love's proper court dost move,   5
  Even there where hope is born of grace, – see how
  My very soul within me is brought low:
For a swift archer, whom his feats approve,
Now bends the bow, which Love to him did yield,
  In such mere sport against me, it would seem   10
  As though he held his lordship for a jest.
  Then hear the marvel which is sorriest: –
My sorely wounded soul forgiveth him,
Yet knows that in his act her strength is kill'd.

TO DANTE ALIGHIERI

SONNET

He reports, in a feigned Vision, the successful Issue of Lapo Gianni's Love

Dante, a sigh that rose from the heart's core
  Assail'd me, while I slumber'd, suddenly;
So that I woke o' the instant, fearing sore
  Lest it came thither in Love's company:
Till, turning, I beheld the servitor   5
  Of lady Lagia: 'Help me,' so said he,

'O help me, Pity.' Though he said no more,
  So much of Pity's essence enter'd me,
That I was ware of Love, those shafts he wields
  A-whetting, and preferr'd the mourner's quest   10
  To him, who straightway answer'd on this wise:
'Go tell my servant that the lady yields,
  And that I hold her now at his behest:
  If he believe not, let him note her eyes.'

TO DANTE ALIGHIERI

SONNET
He mistrusts the Love of Lapo Gianni

I pray thee, Dante, shouldst thou meet with Love
  In any place where Lapo then may be,
  That there thou fail not to mark heedfully
If Love with lover's name that man approve;
If to our Master's will his lady move   5
  Aright, and if himself show fealty:
  For ofttimes, by ill custom, ye may see
This sort profess the semblance of true love.
Thou know'st that in the court where Love holds sway,
  A law subsists, that no man who is vile   10
  Can service yield to a lost woman there.
  If suffering aught avail the sufferer,
  Thou straightway shalt discern our lofty style,
Which needs the badge of honour must display.

SONNET
On the Detection of a false Friend[1]

Love and the lady Lagia, Guido and I,
  Unto a certain lord are bounden all,
  Who has released us – know ye from whose thrall?
Yet I'll not speak, but let the matter die:
Since now these three no more are held thereby,   5
  Who in such homage at his feet did fall
  That I myself was not more whimsical,
In him conceiving godship from on high.

Let Love be thank'd the first, who first discern'd
   The truth; and that wise lady afterward,   10
Who in fit time took back her heart again;
And Guido next, from worship wholly turn'd;
And I, as he. But if ye have not heard,
   I shall not tell how much I loved him then.

1 I should think, from the mention of lady Lagia, that this might refer again to Lapo
Gianni, who seems (one knows not why) to have fallen into disgrace with his
friends. The Guido mentioned is probably Guido Orlandi.

BALLATA
Of a continual Death in Love

Though thou, indeed, hast quite forgotten ruth,
Its steadfast truth my heart abandons not;
But still its thought yields service in good part
   To that hard heart in thee.

Alas! who hears believes not I am so.   5
Yet who can know? of very surety, none.
From Love is won a spirit, in some wise,
   Which dies perpetually:

And, when at length in that strange ecstasy
   The heavy sigh will start,   10
   There rains upon my heart
   A love so pure and fine,
That I say: 'Lady, I am wholly thine.'1

1 I may take this opportunity of mentioning that, in every case where an abrupt
change of metre occurs in one of my translations, it is so also in the original poem.

SONNET
To a Friend who does not pity his Love

If I entreat this lady that all grace
   Seem not unto her heart an enemy,
   Foolish and evil thou declarest me,
And desperate in idle stubbornness.
Whence is such cruel judgment thine, whose face,   5
   To him that looks thereon, professeth thee
   Faithful, and wise, and of all courtesy,
And made after the way of gentleness.

Alas! my soul within my heart doth find
  Sighs, and its grief by weeping doth enhance,   10
    That, drown'd in bitter tears, those sighs depart:
And then there seems a presence in the mind,
  As of a lady's thoughtful countenance
    Come to behold the death of the poor heart.

BALLATA
He perceives that his highest Love is gone from him

Through this my strong and new misaventure,
  All now is lost to me
Which most was sweet in Love's supremacy.

So much of life is dead in its control,
  That she, my pleasant lady of all grace,   5
Is gone out of the devastated soul:
  I see her not, nor do I know her place;
  Nor even enough of virtue with me stays
    To understand, ah me!
The flower of her exceeding purity.   10

Because there comes – to kill that gentle thought
  With saying that I shall not see her more –
This constant pain wherewith I am distraught,
  Which is a burning torment very sore,
  Wherein I know not whom I should implore.   15
    Thrice thank'd the Master be
Who turns the grinding wheel of misery!

Full of great anguish in a place of fear
  The spirit of my heart lies sorrowing,
Through Fortune's bitter craft. She lured it here,   20
  And gave it o'er to Death, and barb'd the sting;
  She wrought that hope which was a treacherous thing;
    In Time, which dies from me,
She made me lose mine hour of ecstasy.

For ye, perturb'd and fearful words of mine,   25
  Whither it like yourselves, even thither go;
But always burthen'd with shame's troublous sign,
  And on my lady's name still calling low:

For me, I must abide in such deep woe
   That all who look shall see   30
Death's shadow on my face assuredly.

SONNET

Of his Pain from a new Love

Why from the danger did not mine eyes start, –
   Why not become even blind, – ere through my sight
   Within my soul thou ever couldst alight
To say: 'Dost thou not hear me in thy heart?'
New torment then, the old torment's counterpart,   5
   Fill'd me at once with such a sore affright,
   That, Lady, lady, (I said,) destroy not quite
Mine eyes and me! O help us where thou art!
Thou hast so left mine eyes, that Love is fain –
   Even Love himself – with pity uncontroll'd   10
   To bend above them, weeping for their loss:
Saying: If any man feel heavy pain,
   This man's more painful heart let him behold:
   Death has it in her hand, cut like a cross.[1]

1 Death (*la* Morte), being feminine in Italian, is naturally personified as a female. I
have endeavoured to bear this in mind throughout my translations, but possibly
some instances might be found in which habit has prevailed, and I have made
Death masculine.

GUIDO ORLANDI TO GUIDO CAVALCANTI

PROLONGED SONNET

He finds fault with the Conceits of the foregoing Sonnet

Friend, well I know thou knowest well to bear
   Thy sword's-point, that it pierce the close-lock'd mail:
   And like a bird to flit from perch to pale:
And out of difficult ways to find the air:
Largely to take and generously to share: 5
   Thrice to secure advantage: to regale
   Greatly the great, and over lands prevail.
In all thou art, one only fault is there: –

For still among the wise of wit thou say'st
   That Love himself doth weep for thine estate;   10
      And yet, no eyes no tears: lo now, thy whim!
Soft, rather say: This is not held in haste;
   But bitter are the hours and passionate,
      To him that loves, and love is not for him.

For me, (by usage strengthen'd to forbear   15
From carnal love,) I fall not in such snare.

GUIDO CAVALCANTI TO DANTE ALIGHIERI

SONNET

He rebukes Dante for his way of Life, after the death of Beatrice[1]

I come to thee by daytime constantly,
   But in thy thoughts too much of baseness find:
   Greatly it grieves me for thy gentle mind,
And for thy many virtues gone from thee.
It was thy wont to shun much company,   5
   Unto all sorry concourse ill inclined:
   And still thy speech of me, heartfelt and kind,
Had made me treasure up thy poetry.
But now I dare not, for thine abject life,
   Make manifest that I approve thy rhymes;   10
      Nor come I in such sort that thou may'st know.
Ah! prythee read this sonnet many times:
So shall that evil one who bred this strife
   Be thrust from thy dishonour'd soul and go.

1 This interesting sonnet must refer to the same period of Dante's life regarding
which he has made Beatrice address him in words of noble reproach when he
meets her in Eden (*Purgatorio* C. xxx).

SONNET

Of an ill-favoured Lady

Just look, Manetto, at that wry-mouth'd minx;
    Merely take notice what a wretch it is;
    How well contrived in her deformities,
How beastly favour'd when she scowls and blinks.
Why, with a hood on (if one only thinks)   5
    Or muffle of prim veils and scapularies, –
    And set together, on a day like this,
Some pretty lady with the odious sphinx; –
Why, then thy sins could hardly have such weight,
    Nor thou be so subdued from Love's attack,   10
        Nor so possess'd in Melancholy's sway,
But that perforce thy peril must be great
    Of laughing till the very heart-strings crack:
        Either thou'dst die, or thou must run away.

BALLATA

Concerning a Shepherd-maid

Within a copse I met a shepherd-maid,
More fair, I said, than any star to see.

She came with waving tresses pale and bright,
    With rosy cheer, and loving eyes of flame,
Guilding the lambs beneath her wand aright.   5
    Her naked feet still had the dews on them,
    As, singing like a lover, so she came;
Joyful, and fashion'd for all ecstasy.

I greeted her at once, and question made
    What escort had she through the woods in spring?   10
But with soft accents she replied and said
    That she was all alone there, wandering;
    Moreover: 'Do you know, when the birds sing,
My heart's desire is for a mate,' said she.

While she was telling me this wish of hers,   15
    The birds were all in song throughout the wood.
'Even now then,' said my thought, 'the time recurs,
    With mine own longing to assuage her mood.'
    And so, in her sweet favour's name, I sued

That she would kiss there and embrace with me.   20

She took my hand to her with amorous will,
   And answer'd that she gave me all her heart,
And drew me where the leaf is fresh and still,
   Where spring the wood-flowers in the shade apart.
   And on that day, by Joy's enchanted art,   25
There Love in very presence seem'd to be.[1]

[1] The glossary to Barberino, already mentioned, refers to the existence, among the Strozzi MSS, of a poem by Lapo di Farinata degli Uberti, written in answer to the above ballata of Cavalcanti. As this respondent was no other than Guido's brother-in-law, one feels curious to know what he said to the peccadilloes of his sister's husband. But I fear the poem cannot yet have been published, as I have sought for it in vain at all my printed sources of information.

SONNET

To a newly enriched Man; reminding him of the Wants of the Poor

As thou wert loth to see, before thy feet,
   The dear broad coin roll all thy hill-slope down,
   Till, 'twixt the cracks of the hard glebe, some clown
Should find, rub oft, and scarcely render it; –
Tell me, I charge thee, if by generous heat   5
   Or clutching frost the fruits of earth be grown,
   And by what wind the blight is o'er them strown,
And with what gloom the tempest is replete.
Moreover (an' it please thee,) when at morn
   Thou hear'st the voice of the poor husbandman,   10
   And those loud herds, his other family, –
I feel quite sure that if Bettina's born
   With a kind heart, she does the best she can
   To wheedle some of thy new wealth from thee.

BALLATA

In Exile at Sarzana

Because I think not ever to return,
   Ballad, to Tuscany, –
   Go therefore thou for me
   Straight to my lady's face,

Who, of her noble grace,   5
    Shall show thee courtesy.

Thou seekest her in charge of many sighs,
    Full of much grief and of exceeding fear.
But have good heed thou come not to the eyes
    Of such as are sworn foes to gentle cheer: 10
    For, certes, if this thing should chance, – from her
            Thou then couldst only look
            For scorn, and such rebuke
            As needs must bring me pain; –
            Yea, after death again   15
            Tears and fresh agony.

Surely thou knowest, Ballad, how that Death
    Assails me, till my life is almost sped:
Thou knowest how my heart still travaileth
    Through the sore pangs which in my soul are bred: –   20
    My body being now so nearly dead,
            It cannot suffer more.
            Then, going, I implore
            That this my soul thou take
            (Nay, do so for my sake,)   25
            When my heart sets it free.

Ah! Ballad, unto thy dear offices
    I do commend my soul, thus trembling;
That thou may'st lead it, for pure piteousness,
    Even to that lady's presence whom I sing.   30
    Ah! Ballad, say thou to her, sorrowing,
            Whereso thou meet her then: –
            'This thy poor handmaiden
            Is come, nor will be gone,
            Being parted now from one   35
            Who served Love painfully.'

Thou also, thou bewilder'd voice and weak
    That goest forth in tears from my grieved heart,
Shalt, with my soul and with this ballad, speak
    Of my dead mind, when thou dost hence depart,   40
    Unto that lady (piteous as thou art!)
            Who is so calm and bright
            It shall be deep delight
            To feel her presence there.

And thou, Soul, worship her   45
Still in her purity.

CANZONE[1]
A Song of Fortune

Lo! I am she who makes the wheel to turn;
  Lo! I am she who gives and takes away;
    Blamed idly, day by day,
  In all mine acts by you, ye humankind.
For whoso smites his visage and doth mourn,   5
  What time he renders back my gifts to me,
    Learns then that I decree
  No state which mine own arrows may not find.
  Who clomb must fall: – this bear ye well in mind,
Nor say, because he fell, I did him wrong.   10
    Yet mine is a vain song:
For truly ye may find out wisdom when
King Arthur's resting-place is found of men.

Ye make great marvel and astonishment
  What time ye see the sluggard lifted up   15
    And the just man to drop,
  And ye complain on God and on my sway.
O humankind, ye sin in your complaint:
  For He, that Lord who made the world to live,
    Lets me not take or give   20
  By mine own act, but as he wills I may.
  Yet is the mind of man so castaway,
That it discerns not the supreme behest.
    Alas! ye wretchedest,
And chide ye at God also? Shall not He   25
Judge between good and evil righteously?

Ah! had ye knowledge how God evermore,
  With agonies of soul and grievous heats,
    As on an anvil beats
  On them that in this earth hold high estate, –   30
Ye would choose little rather than much store,
  And solitude than spacious palaces;
    Such is the sore disease
Of anguish that on all their days doth wait.
Behold if they be not unfortunate,   35

When oft the father dares not trust the son!
        O wealth, with thee is won
A worm to gnaw for ever on his soul
Whose abject life is laid in thy control!

If also ye take note what piteous death   40
    They ofttimes make, whose hoards were manifold,
        Who cities had and gold
    And multitudes of men beneath their hand;
Then he among you that most angereth
    Shall bless me saying, 'Lo! I worship thee   45
        That I was not as he
    Whose death is thus accurst throughout the land.'
But now your living souls are held in band
Of avarice, shutting you from the true light
        Which shows how sad and slight   50
Are this world's treasured riches and array
That still change hands a hundred times a-day.

For me, – could envy enter in my sphere,
    Which of all human taint is clean and quit, –
        I well might harbour it   55
    When I behold the peasant at his toil.
Guiding his team, untroubled, free from fear,
    He leaves his perfect furrow as he goes,
        And gives his field repose
    From thorns and tares and weeds that vex the soil: 60
    Thereto he labours, and without turmoil
Entrusts his work to God, content if so
        Such guerdon from it grow
That in that year his family shall live:
Nor care nor thought to other things will give.   65

But now ye may no more have speech of me,
    For this mine office craves continual use:
        Ye therefore deeply muse
    Upon those things which ye have heard the while:
Yea, and even yet remember heedfully   70
    How this my wheel a motion hath so fleet,
        That in an eyelid's beat
    Him whom it raised it maketh low and vile.
    None was, nor is, nor shall be of such guile,
Who could, or can, or shall, I say, at length   75
        Prevail against my strength.

But still those men that are my questioners
In bitter torment own their hearts perverse.

Song, that wast made to carry high intent
    Dissembled in the garb of humbleness, –   80
        With fair and open face
To Master Thomas let thy course be bent.
Say that a great thing scarcely may be pent
    In little room: yet always pray that he
        Commend us, thee and me,   85
To them that are more apt in lofty speech:
For truly one must learn ere he can teach.

1 This and the three following Canzoni are only to be found in the later collections
of Guido Cavalcanti's poems. I have included them on account of their interest if
really his, and especially for the beauty of the last among them; but must confess
to some doubts of their authenticity.

CANZONE
A Song against Poverty

O poverty, by thee the soul is wrapp'd
    With hate, with envy, dolefulness, and doubt.
        Even so be thou cast out,
    And even so he that speaks thee otherwise.
I name thee now, because my mood is apt   5
To curse thee, bride of every lost estate,
        Through whom are desolate
    On earth all honourable things and wise.
    Within thy power, each blessed condition dies:
By thee, men's minds with sore mistrust are made   10
        Fantastic and afraid: –
Thou, hated worse than Death, by just accord,
And with the loathing of all hearts abhorr'd.

Yea, rightly art thou hated worse than Death,
    For he at length is long'd for in the breast.   15
        But not with thee, wild beast,
    Was ever aught found beautiful or good.
For life is all that man can lose by death,
Not fame, and the fair summits of applause;
        His glory shall not pause.   20
    But live in men's perpetual gratitude.
    While he who on thy naked sill has stood,

Though of great heart and worthy everso,
   He shall be counted low.
Then let the man thou troublest never hope   25
To spread his wings in any lofty scope.

Hereby my mind is laden with a fear,
   And I will take some thought to shelter me.
      For this I plainly see: –
   Through thee, to fraud the honest man is led;   30
To tyranny the just lord turneth here,
And the magnanimous soul to avarice.
      Of every bitter vice
   Thou, to my thinking, art the fount and head.
   From thee no light in any wise is shed,   35
Who bringest to the paths of dusky hell.
      I therefore see full well,
That death, the dungeon, sickness, and old age,
Weigh'd against thee, are blessed heritage.

And what though many a goodly hypocrite,   40
   Lifting to thee his veritable prayer,
      Call God to witness there
   How this thy burden moved not Him to wrath.
Why, who may call (of them that muse aright)
Him poor, who of the whole can say, 'Tis Mine?   45
      Methinks I well divine
   That want, to such, should seem an easy path.
   God, who made all things, all things had and hath;
Nor any tongue may say that He was poor,
      What while He did endure   50
For man's best succour among men to dwell:
Since to have all, with Him, was possible.

Song, thou shalt wend upon thy journey now:
   And, if thou meet with folk who rail at thee,
      Saying that poverty   55
   Is not even sharper than thy words allow, –
Unto such brawlers briefly answer thou,
To tell them they are hypocrites; and then
      Say mildly, once again,
That I, who am nearly in a beggar's case,   60
Might not presume to sing my proper praise.

CANZONE

He laments the Presumption and Incontinence of his Youth

The devastating flame of that fierce plague,
  The foe of virtue, fed with others' peace
    More than itself foresees,
  Being still shut in to gnaw its own desire;
Its strength not weaken'd, nor its hues more vague,   5
  For all the benison that virtue sheds,
    But which for ever spreads
  To be a living curse that shall not tire:
  Or yet again, that other idle fire
Which flickers with all change as winds may please: 10
    One whichsoe'er of these
  At length has hidden the true path from me
    Which twice man may not see,
And quench'd the intelligence of joy, till now
All solace but abides in perfect woe.   15

Alas! the more my painful spirit grieves,
  The more confused with miserable strife
    Is that delicious life
  Which sighing it recalls perpetually:
But its worst anguish, whence it still receives   20
  More pain than death, is sent, to yield the sting
    Of perfect suffering,
  By him who is my lord and governs me;
  Who holds all gracious truth in fealty,
Being nursed in those four sisters' fond caress   25
    Through whom comes happiness.
  He now has left me; and I draw my breath
    Wound in the arms of Death,
Desirous of her: she is cried upon
In all the prayers my heart puts up alone.   30

How fierce aforetime and how absolute
  That wheel of flame which turn'd within my head,
    May never quite be said,
  Because there are not words to speak the whole.
It slew my hope whereof I lack the fruit,   35
  And stung the blood within my living flesh

To be an intricate mesh
Of pain beyond endurance or control;
Withdrawing me from God, who gave my soul
To know the sign where honour has its seat   40
    From honour's counterfeit.
So in its longing my heart finds not hope,
    Nor knows what door to ope;
Since, parting me from God, this foe took thought
To shut those paths wherein He may be sought.   45

My second enemy, thrice arm'd in guile,
    As wise and cunning to mine overthrow
    As her smooth face doth show,
    With yet more shameless strength holds mastery.
My spirit, naked of its light and vile,   50
    If lit by her with her own deadly gleam,
    Which makes all anguish seem
    As nothing to her scourges that I see.
O thou the body of grace, abide with me
As thou wert once in the once joyful time;   55
    And though thou hate my crime,
Fill not my life with torture to the end;
    But in thy mercy, bend
My steps, and for thine honour, back again;
Till finding joy through thee, I bless my pain.   60

Since that first frantic devil without faith
    Fell, in thy name, upon the stairs that mount
    Unto the limpid fount
    Of thine intelligence, – withhold not now
Thy grace, nor spare my second foe from death.   65
    For lo! on this my soul has set her trust;
    And failing this, thou must
    Prove false to truth and honour, seest thou!
    Then, saving light and throne of strength, allow
My prayer, and vanquish both my foes at last;   70
    That so I be not cast
Into that woe wherein I fear to end.
    Yet if it is ordain'd
That I must die ere this be perfected, –
Ah! yield me comfort after I am dead.   75

Ye unadornèd words obscure of sense,
    Go weeping, and these sighs along with ye,

    And bear mine agony
(Not to be told by words, being too intense,)
    To His intelligence   80
Who moved by virtue shall fulfil my breath
In human life or compensating death.

CANZONE

A Dispute with Death

'O sluggish, hard, ingrate, what doest thou?
    Poor sinner, folded round with heavy sin,
        Whose life to find out joy alone is bent.
I call thee, and thou fall'st to deafness now;
    And, deeming that my path whereby to win   5
        Thy seat is lost, there sitt'st thee down content,
        And hold'st me to thy will subservient.
But I into thy heart have crept disguised:
    Among thy senses and thy sins I went,
By roads thou didst not guess, unrecognized.   10
Tears will not now suffice to bid me go,
Nor countenance abased, nor words of woe.'

Now, when I heard the sudden dreadful voice
    Wake thus within to cruel utterance,
        Whereby the very heart of hearts did fail,   15
My spirit might not any more rejoice,
    But fell from its courageous pride at once,
        And turn'd to fly, where flight may not avail.
        Then slowly 'gan some strength to re-inhale
The trembling life which heard that whisper speak,   20
    And had conceived the sense with sore travail;
Till in the mouth it murmur'd, very weak,
Saying: 'Youth, wealth, and beauty, these have I:
O Death! remit thy claim, – I would not die.'

Small sign of pity in that aspect dwells   25
    Which then had scatter'd all my life abroad
        Till there was comfort with no single sense:
And yet almost in piteous syllables,
    When I had ceased to speak, this answer flow'd:
        'Behold what path is spread before thee hence;   30
        Thy life has all but a day's permanence.
And is it for the sake of youth there seems

In loss of human years such sore offence?
Nay, look unto the end of youthful dreams.
What present glory does thy hope possess,   35
That shall not yield ashes and bitterness?'

But, when I look'd on Death made visible,
    From my heart's sojourn brought before mine eyes,
    And holding in her hand my grievous sin,
I seem'd to see my countenance, that fell,   40
    Shake like a shadow: my heart utter'd cries,
    And my soul wept the curse that lay therein.
    Then Death: 'Thus much thine urgent prayer shall win: –
I grant thee the brief interval of youth
    At natural pity's strong soliciting.'   45
And I (because I knew that moment's ruth
But left my life to groan for a frail space)
Fell in the dust upon my weeping face.

So, when she saw me thus abash'd and dumb,
    In loftier words she weigh'd her argument,   50
    That new and strange it was to hear her speak;
Saying: 'The path thy fears withhold thee from
    Is thy best path. To folly be not shent,
    Nor shrink from me because thy flesh is weak.
    Thou seest how man is sore confused, and eke   55
How ruinous Chance makes havoc of his life,
    And grief is in the joys that he doth seek;
Nor ever pauses the perpetual strife
'Twixt fear and rage; until beneath the sun
His perfect anguish be fulfill'd and done.'   60

'O Death! thou art so dark and difficult,
    That never human creature might attain
    By his own will to pierce thy secret sense;
Because, foreshadowing thy dread result,
    He may not put his trust in heart or brain,   65
    Nor power avails him, nor intelligence.
    Behold how cruelly thou takest hence
These forms so beautiful and dignified,
    And chain'st them in thy shadow chill and dense,
And forcest them in narrow graves to hide;   70
With pitiless hate subduing still to thee
The strength of man and woman's delicacy.'

'Not for thy fear the less I come at last,
  For this thy tremor, for thy painful sweat.
    Take therefore thought to leave (for lo! I call:)   75
Kinsfolk and comrades, all thou didst hold fast, –
  Thy father and thy mother, – to forget
    All these thy brethren, sisters, children, all
    Cast sight and hearing from thee; let hope fall;
Leave every sense and thy whole intellect,   80
    These things wherein thy life made festival:
For I have wrought thee to such strange effect
That thou hast no more power to dwell with these
As living man. Let pass thy soul in peace.'

Yea, Lord. O thou, the Builder of the spheres,   85
  Who, making me, didst shape me, of thy grace,
    In thine own image and high counterpart;
Do thou subdue my spirit, long perverse,
  To weep within thy will a certain space,
    Ere yet thy thunder come to rive my heart.   90
    Set in my hand some sign of what thou art,
Lord God, and suffer me to seek out Christ, –
    Weeping, to seek him in thy ways apart;
Until my sorrow have at length sufficed
In some accepted instant to atone   95
For sins of thought, for stubborn evil done.

Dishevell'd and in tears, go, song of mine,
  To break the hardness of the heart of man:
    Say how his life began
From dust, and in that dust doth sink supine: 100
  Yet, say, the unerring spirit of grief shall guide
    His soul, being purified,
To seek its Maker at the heavenly shrine.

CINO DA PISTOIA

TO DANTE ALIGHIERI

SONNET

He interprets Dante's Dream, related in the first Sonnet of the Vita Nuova[1]

Each lover's longing leads him naturally
  Unto his lady's heart his heart to show;
  And this it is that Love would have thee know
By the strange vision which he sent to thee.
With thy heart therefore, flaming outwardly,   5
  In humble guise he fed thy lady so,
  Who long had lain in slumber, from all woe
Folded within a mantle silently.
Also, in coming, Love might not repress
  His joy, to yield thee thy desire achieved,   10
    Whence heart should unto heart true service bring.
But understanding the great love-sickness
  Which in thy lady's bosom was conceived,
    He pitied her, and wept in vanishing.

1 See antè, page 81.

TO DANTE ALIGHIERI

SONNET

He conceives of some Compensation in Death[1]

Dante, whenever this thing happeneth, –
  That Love's desire is quite bereft of Hope,
  (Seeking in vain at ladies' eyes some scope
Of joy, through what the heart for ever saith,) –
I ask thee, can amends be made by Death?   5
  Is such sad pass the last extremity? –
  Or may the Soul that never fear'd to die
Then in another body draw new breath?

Lo! thus it is through her who governs all
   Below, – that I, who enter'd at her door,   10
     Now at her dreadful window must fare forth.
Yea, and I think through her it doth befall
   That even ere yet the road is travell'd o'er
     My bones are weary and life is nothing worth.

1 Among Dante's Epistles, there is a Latin letter to Cino, which I should judge was
written in reply to this Sonnet.

TO DANTE ALIGHIERI

CANZONE
On the Death of Beatrice Portinari

Albeit my prayers have not so long delay'd,
   But craved for thee, ere this, that Pity and Love
     Which only bring our heavy life some rest;
Yet is not now the time so much o'erstay'd
   But that these words of mine which tow'rds thee move   5
     Must find thee still with spirit dispossess'd,
     And say to thee: 'In Heaven she now is bless'd
Even as the blessed name men call'd her by;
     While thou dost ever cry,
   "Alas! the blessing of mine eyes is flown!"'   10
     Behold, these words set down
Are needed still, for still thou sorrowest.
Then hearken; I would yield advisedly
Some comfort: Stay these sighs: give ear to me.

We know for certain that in this blind world   15
   Each man's subsistence is of grief and pain,
     Still trail'd by fortune through all bitterness:
At last the flesh within a shroud is furl'd,
   And into Heaven's rejoicing doth attain
     The joyful soul made free of earthly stress.   20
     Then wherefore sighs thy heart in abjectness,
Which for her triumph should exult aloud?
     For He the Lord our God
Hath call'd her, hearkening what her Angel said,
     To have Heaven perfected.   25
   Each saint for a new thing beholds her face,

And she the face of our Redemption sees,
Discoursing with immortal substances.

Why now do pangs of torment clutch thy heart
　　Which with thy love should make thee overjoy'd, 　　30
　　　As him whose intellect hath pass'd the skies?
Behold, the spirits of thy life depart
　　Daily to Heaven with her, they so are buoy'd
　　　With their desire, and Love so bids them rise.
　　　O God! and thou, a man whom God made wise, 　　35
To nurse a charge of care, and love the same!
　　　　I tell thee in His Name
From sin of sighing grief to hold thy breath,
　　　　Nor let thy heart to death,
　　　Nor harbour death's resemblance in thine eyes. 　　40
God hath her with Himself eternally,
Yet she inhabits every hour with thee.

Be comforted, Love cries, be comforted!
　　Devotion pleads, Peace, for the love of God!
　　　O yield thyself to prayers so full of grace; 　　45
And make thee naked now of this dull weed
　　Which 'neath thy foot were better to be trod;
　　　For man through grief despairs and ends his days.
　　　How ever shouldst thou see the lovely face
If any desperate death should once be thine? 　　50
　　　　From justice so condign
Withdraw thyself even now; that in the end
　　　　Thy heart may not offend
　　　Against thy soul, which in the holy place,
In Heaven, still hopes to see her and to be 　　55
Within her arms. Let this hope comfort thee.

Look thou into the pleasure wherein dwells
　　Thy lovely lady who is in Heaven crown'd,
　　　Who is herself thy rope in Heaven, the while
To make thy memory hallow'd she avails; 　　60
　　Being a soul within the deep Heaven bound,
　　　A face on thy heart painted, to beguile
　　　Thy heart of grief which else should turn it vile.
Even as she seem'd a wonder here below,
　　　　On high she seemeth so, – 　　65
Yea, better known, is there more wondrous yet.
　　　　And even as she was met

First by the angels with sweet song and smile,
Thy spirit bears her back upon the wing,
Which often in those ways is journeying.   70

Of thee she entertains the blessed throngs,
    And says to them: 'While yet my body thrave
    On earth, I gat much honour which he gave,
Commending me in his commended songs.'
    Also she asks alway of God our Lord   75
    To give thee peace according to His word.

MADRIGAL
To his Lady Selvaggia Vergiolesi; likening his Love to a search for Gold

I am all bent to glean the golden ore
    Little by little from the river-bed;
        Hoping the day to see
When Crœsus shall be conquer'd in my store.
    Therefore, still sifting where the sands are spread,   5
        I labour patiently:
Till, thus intent on this thing and no more, –
    If to a vein of silver I were led,
        It scarce could gladden me.
And, seeing that no joy's so warm i' the core   10
    As this whereby the heart is comforted
        And the desire set free, –
Therefore thy bitter love is still my scope,
    Lady, from whom it is my life's sore theme
More painfully to sift the grains of hope   15
        Than gold out of that stream.

SONNET
To Love, in great Bitterness

O Love, O thou that, for my fealty,
    Only in torment dost thy power employ,
    Give me, for God's sake, something of thy joy,
That I may learn what good there is in thee.
Yea, for, if thou art glad with grieving me,   5
    Surely my very life thou shalt destroy

When thou renew'st my pain, because the joy
Must then be wept for with the misery.
He that had never sense of good, nor sight,
  Esteems his ill estate but natural,   10
    Which so is lightlier borne: his case is mine.
    But, if thou wouldst uplift me for a sign,
  Bidding me drain the curse and know it all,
I must a little taste its opposite.

SONNET
Death is not without but within him

This fairest lady, who, as well I wot,
  Found entrance by her beauty to my soul,
  Pierced through mine eyes my heart, which erst was whole,
Sorely, yet, makes as though she knew it not;
Nay, turns upon me now, to anger wrought,   5
  Dealing me harshness for my pain's best dole,
  And is so changed by her own wrath's control,
That I go thence, in my distracted thought
Content to die; and, mourning, cry abroad
  On Death, as upon one afar from me;   10
    But Death makes answer from within my heart.
  Then, hearing her so hard at hand to be,
I do commend my spirit unto God;
  Saying to her too, 'Ease and peace thou art.'

SONNET
A Trance of Love

Vanquish'd and weary was my soul in me,
  And my heart gasp'd after its much lament,
  When sleep at length the painful languor sent.
And, as I slept (and wept incessantly), –
Through the keen fixedness of memory   5
  Which I had cherish'd ere my tears were spent,
  I pass'd to a new trance of wonderment;
Wherein a visible spirit I could see,
Which caught me up, and bore me to a place
  Where my most gentle lady was alone;   10
    And still before us a fire seem'd to move,

Out of the which methought there came a moan,
Uttering, 'Grace, a little season, grace!
I am of one that hath the wings of Love.'

SONNET

Of the grave of Selvaggia, on the Monte della Sambuca

I was upon the high and blessed mound,
  And kiss'd, long worshipping, the stones and grass,
  There on the hard stones prostrate, where, alas!
That pure one laid her forehead in the ground.
Then were the springs of gladness seal'd and bound,   5
  The day that unto Death's most bitter pass
  My sick heart's lady turn'd her feet, who was
Already in her gracious life renown'd.
So in that place I spake to Love, and cried:
  'O sweet my god, I am one whom Death may claim   10
  Hence to be his; for lo! my heart lies here.'
  Anon, because my Master lent no ear,
  Departing, still I call'd Selvaggia's name.
So with my moan I left the mountain-side.

CANZONE

His Lament for Selvaggia

Ay me, alas! the beautiful bright hair
  That shed reflected gold
    O'er the green growths on either side the way;
Ay me! the lovely look, open and fair,
  Which my heart's core doth hold
    With all else of that best-remember'd day;   5
    Ay me! the face made gay
With joy that Love confers;
Ay me! that smile of hers
  Where whiteness as of snow was visible   10
Among the roses at all seasons red!
  Ay me! and was this well,
O Death, to let me live when she is dead?

Ay me! the calm, erect, dignified walk;

Ay me! the sweet salute, –   15
  The thoughtful mind, – the wit discreetly worn;
Ay me! the clearness of her noble talk,
  Which made the good take root
    In me, and for the evil woke my scorn;
    Ay me! the longing born   20
Of so much loveliness, –
The hope, whose eager stress
  Made other hopes fall back to let it pass,
Even till my load of love grew light thereby!
  These thou hast broken, as glass,   25
O Death, who makest me, alive, to die!

Ay me! Lady, the lady of all worth; –
  Saint, for whose single shrine
    All other shrines I left, even as Love will'd; –
Ay me! what precious stone in the whole earth,   30
  For that pure fame of thine
    Worthy the marble statue's base to yield?
    Ay me! fair vase fullfill'd
With more than this world's good, –
By cruel chance and rude   35
  Cast out upon the steep path of the mountains
Where Death has shut thee in between hard stones!
  Ay me! two languid fountains
Of weeping are these eyes, which joy disowns.

Ay me, sharp Death! till what I ask is done   40
  And my whole life is ended utterly, –
Answer – must I weep on
  Even thus, and never cease to moan Ay me?

TO GUIDO CAVALCANTI

SONNET
He owes nothing to Guido as a Poet

What rhymes are thine which I have ta'en from thee,
  Thou Guido, that thou ever say'st I thieve?[1]
    'Tis true, fine fancies gladly I receive,
But when was aught found beautiful in thee?
Nay, I have search'd my pages diligently,   5

And tell the truth, and lie not, by your leave.
From whose rich store of web of songs I weave
Love knoweth well, well knowing them and me.
No artist I, – all men may gather it;
   Nor do I work in ignorance of pride,   10
(Though the world reach alone the coarser sense:)
But am a certain man of humble wit
   Who journeys with his sorrow at his side,
      For a heart's sake, alas! that is gone hence.

1 I have not examined Cino's poetry with special reference to this accusation; but there is a Canzone of his in which he speaks of having conceived an affection for another lady from her resemblance to Selvaggia. Perhaps Guido considered this as a sort of plagiarism *de facto* on his own change of love through Mandetta's likeness to Giovanna.

SONNET
He impugns the verdicts of Dante's Commedia

This book of Dante's, very sooth to say,
   Is just a poet's lovely heresy,
   Which by a lure as sweet as sweet can be
Draws other men's concerns beneath its sway;
While, among stars' and comets' dazzling play,   5
   It beats the right down, lets the wrong go free,
   Shows some abased, and others in great glee,
Much as with lovers is Love's ancient way.
Therefore his vain decrees, wherein he lied,
   Fixing folks' nearness to the Fiend their foe,   10
Must be like empty nutshells flung aside.
   Yet through the rash false witness set to grow,
French and Italian vengeance on such pride
   May fall, like Antony's on Cicero.

Poems
first published
1870

(excluding *The House of Life*)

The Portrait

This is her picture as she was:
   It seems a thing to wonder on,
As though mine image in the glass
   Should tarry when myself am gone.
I gaze until she seems to stir, –   5
Until mine eyes almost aver
   That now, even now, the sweet lips part
   To breathe the words of the sweet heart: –
And yet the earth is over her.

Alas! even such the thin-drawn ray   10
   That makes the prison-depths more rude, –
The drip of water night and day
   Giving a tongue to solitude.
Yet this, of all love's perfect prize,
Remains; save what in mournful guise   15
   Takes counsel with my soul alone, –
   Save what is secret and unknown,
Below the earth, above the skies.

In painting her I shrined her face
   Mid mystic trees, where light falls in   20
Hardly at all; a covert place
   Where you might think to find a din
Of doubtful talk, and a live flame
Wandering, and many a shape whose name
   Not itself knoweth, and old dew,   25
   And your own footsteps meeting you,
And all things going as they came.

A deep dim wood; and there she stands
   As in that wood that day: for so
Was the still movement of her hands   30
   And such the pure line's gracious flow.
And passing fair the type must seem,
Unknown the presence and the dream.
   'Tis she: though of herself, alas!
   Less than her shadow on the grass   35
Or than her image in the stream.

That day we met there, I and she
  One with the other all alone;
And we were blithe; yet memory
  Saddens those hours, as when the moon   40
Looks upon daylight. And with her
I stooped to drink the spring-water,
  Athirst where other waters sprang;
  And where the echo is, she sang, –
My soul another echo there.   45

But when that hour my soul won strength
  For words whose silence wastes and kills,
Dull raindrops smote us, and at length
  Thundered the heat within the hills.
That eve I spoke those words again   50
Beside the pelted window-pane;
  And there she hearkened what I said,
  With under-glances that surveyed
The empty pastures blind with rain.

Next day the memories of these things,   55
  Like leaves through which a bird has flown,
Still vibrated with Love's warm wings;
  Till I must make them all my own
And paint this picture. So, 'twixt ease
Of talk and sweet long silences,   60
  She stood among the plants in bloom
  At windows of a summer room,
To feign the shadow of the trees.

And as I wrought, while all above
  And all around was fragrant air,   65
In the sick burthen of my love
  It seemed each sun-thrilled blossom there
Beat like a heart among the leaves.
O heart that never beats nor heaves,
  In that one darkness lying still,   70
  What now to thee my love's great will
Or the fine web the sunshine weaves?

For now doth daylight disavow
  Those days, – naught left to see or hear.
Only in solemn whispers now   75
  At night-time these things reach mine ear,
When the leaf-shadows at a breath

Shrink in the road, and all the heath,
   Forest and water, far and wide,
    In limpid starlight glorified,   80
Lie like the mystery of death.

Last night at last I could have slept,
   And yet delayed my sleep till dawn,
Still wandering. Then it was I wept:
   For unawares I came upon   85
Those glades where once she walked with me:
And as I stood there suddenly,
   All wan with traversing the night,
    Upon the desolate verge of light
Yearned loud the iron-bosomed sea.   90

Even so, where Heaven holds breath and hears
   The beating heart of Love's own breast, –
Where round the secret of all spheres
   All angels lay their wings to rest, –
How shall my soul stand rapt and awed,   95
When, by the new birth borne abroad
   Throughout the music of the suns,
    It enters in her soul at once
And knows the silence there for God!

Here with her face doth memory sit   100
   Meanwhile, and wait the day's decline,
Till other eyes shall look from it,
   Eyes of the spirit's Palestine,
Even than the old gaze tenderer:
While hopes and aims long lost with her   105
   Stand round her image side by side,
    Like tombs of pilgrims that have died
About the Holy Sepulchre.

Ave

Mother of the Fair Delight,
Thou handmaid perfect in God's sight,
Now sitting fourth beside the Three,
Thyself a woman-Trinity, –
Being a daughter borne to God,   5

Mother of Christ from stall to rood,
And wife unto the Holy Ghost: –
Oh when our need is uttermost,
Think that to such as death may strike
Thou once wert sister sisterlike!   10
Thou headstone of humanity
Groundstone of the great Mystery,
Fashioned like us, yet more than we!

Mind'st thou not (when June's heavy breath
Warmed the long days in Nazareth,)   15
That eve thou didst go forth to give
Thy flowers some drink that they might live
One faint night more amid the sands?
Far off the trees were as pale wands
Against the fervid sky: the sea   20
Sighed further off eternally
As human sorrow sighs in sleep.
Then suddenly the awe grew deep,
As of a day to which all days
Were footsteps in God's secret ways: 25
Until a folding sense, like prayer,
Which is, as God is, everywhere
Gathered about thee; and a voice
Spake to thee without any noise,
Being of the silence: – 'Hail,' it said,   30
'Thou that art highly favourèd;
The Lord is with thee here and now;
Blessed among all women thou.'

'Ah! knew'st thou of the end, when first
That Babe was on thy bosom nurs'd? –   35
Or when He tottered round thy knee
Did thy great sorrow dawn on thee? –
And through His boyhood, year by year
Eating with Him the Passover,
Didst thou discern confusedly   40
That holier sacrament, when He,
The bitter cup about to quaff,
Should break the bread and eat thereof? –
Or came not yet the knowledge, even
Till on some day forecast in Heaven   45
His feet passed through thy door to press

Upon His Father's business? –
Or still was God's high secret kept?

    Nay, but I think the whisper crept
Like growth through childhood. Work and play,   50
Things common to the course of day,
Awed thee with meanings unfulfill'd;
And all through girlhood, something still'd
Thy senses like the birth of light,
When thou hast trimmed thy lamp at night   55
Or washed thy garments in the stream;
To whose white bed had come the dream
That He was thine and thou wast His
Who feeds among the field-lilies.
O solemn shadow of the end   60
In that wise spirit long contain'd!
O awful end! and those unsaid
Long years when It was Finishèd!

    Mind'st thou not (when the twilight gone
Left darkness in the house of John,)   65
Between the naked window-bars
That spacious vigil of the stars? –
For thou, a watcher even as they,
Wouldst rise from where throughout the day
Thou wroughtest raiment for His poor;   70
And, finding the fixed terms endure
Of day and night which never brought
Sounds of His coming chariot,
Wouldst lift through cloud-waste unexplor'd
Those eyes which said, 'How long, O Lord?'   75
Then that disciple whom He loved,
Well heeding, haply would be moved
To ask thy blessing in His name;
And that one thought in both, the same
Though silent, then would clasp ye round   80
To weep together, – tears long bound,
Sick tears of patience, dumb and slow.
Yet, 'Surely I come quickly,' – so
He said, from life and death gone home.
Amen: even so, Lord Jesus, come!   85

    But oh! what human tongue can speak
That day when death was sent to break

From the tir'd spirit, like a veil,
Its covenant with Gabriel
Endured at length unto the end?   90
What human thought can apprehend
That mystery of motherhood
When thy Beloved at length renew'd
The sweet communion severèd, –
His left hand underneath thine head   95
And His right hand embracing thee? –
Lo! He was thine, and this is He!

   Soul, is it Faith, or Love, or Hope,
That lets me see her standing up
Where the light of the Throne is bright?   100
Unto the left, unto the right,
The cherubim, arrayed, conjoint,
Float inward to a golden point,
And from between the seraphim
The glory issues for a hymn.   105
O Mary Mother, be not loth
To listen, – thou whom the stars clothe,
Who seëst and mayst not be seen!
Hear us at last, O Mary Queen!
Into our shadow bend thy face,   110
Bowing thee from the secret place,
O Mary Virgin, full of grace!

A Last Confession
(Regno Lombardo-Veneto, 1848)

Our Lombard country-girls along the coast
Wear daggers in their garters; for they know
That they might hate another girl to death
Or meet a German lover. Such a knife
I bought her, with a hilt of horn and pearl.   5

   Father, you cannot know of all my thoughts
That day in going to meet her, – that last day
For the last time, she said; – of all the love
And all the hopeless hope that she might change
And go back with me. Ah! and everywhere,   10

At places we both knew along the road,
Some fresh shape of herself as once she was
Grew present at my side; until it seemed –
So close they gathered round me – they would all
Be with me when I reached the spot at last,   15
To plead my cause with her against herself
So changed. O Father, if you knew all this
You cannot know, then you would know too, Father,
And only then, if God can pardon me.
What can be told I'll tell, if you will hear.   20

    I passed a village-fair upon my road,
And thought, being empty-handed, I would take
Some little present: such might prove, I said,
Either a pledge between us, or (God help me!)
A parting gift. And there it was I bought   25
The knife I spoke of such as women wear.

    That day, some three hours afterwards, I found
For certain, it must be a parting gift.
And, standing silent now at last, I looked
Into her scornful face; and heard the sea   30
Still trying hard to din into my ears
Some speech it knew which still might change her heart
If only it could make me understand.
One moment thus. Another, and her face
Seemed further off than the last line of sea,   35
So that I thought, if now she were to speak
I could not hear her. Then again I knew
All, as we stood together on the sand
At Iglio, in the first thin shade o' the hills.

    'Take it,' I said, and held it out to her,   40
While the hilt glanced within my trembling hold;
'Take it and keep it for my sake,' I said.
Her neck unbent not, neither did her eyes
Move, nor her foot left beating of the sand;
Only she put it by from her and laughed.   45

    Father, you hear my speech and not her laugh;
But God heard that. Will God remember all?

    It was another laugh than the sweet sound
Which rose from her sweet childish heart, that day
Eleven years before, when first I found her   50

Alone upon the hill-side; and her curls
Shook down in the warm grass as she looked up
Out of her curls in my eyes bent to hers.
She might have served a painter to pourtray
That heavenly child which in the latter days   55
Shall walk between the lion and the lamb.
I had been for nights in hiding, worn and sick
And hardly fed; and so her words at first
Seemed fitful like the talking of the trees
And voices in the air that knew my name.   60
And I remember that I sat me down
Upon the slope with her, and thought the world
Must be all over or had never been,
We seemed there so alone. And soon she told me
Her parents both were gone away from her.   65
I thought perhaps she meant that they had died;
But when I asked her this, she looked again
Into my face, and said that yestereve
They kissed her long, and wept and made her weep,
And gave her all the bread they had with them,   70
And then had gone together up the hill
Where we were sitting now, and had walked on
Into the great red light: 'and so,' she said,
'I have come up here too; and when this evening
They step out of the light as they stepped in,   75
I shall be here to kiss them.' And she laughed.

   Then I bethought me suddenly of the famine;
And how the church-steps throughout all the town,
When last I had been there a month ago,
Swarmed with starved folk; and how the bread was weighed 80
By Austrians armed; and women that I knew
For wives and mothers walked the public street,
Saying aloud that if their husbands feared
To snatch the children's food, themselves would stay
Till they had earned it there. So then this child   85
Was piteous to me; for all told me then
Her parents must have left her to God's chance,
To man's or to the Church's charity,
Because of the great famine, rather than
To watch her growing thin between their knees.   90
With that, God took my mother's voice and spoke,
And sights and sounds came back and things long since,

And all my childhood found me on the hills;
And so I took her with me.

                    I was young,
Scarce man then, Father; but the cause which gave   95
The wounds I die of now had brought me then
Some wounds already; and I lived alone,
As any hiding hunted man must live.
It was no easy thing to keep a child
In safety; for herself it was not safe,   100
And doubled my own danger: but I knew
That God would help me.

               Yet a little while
Pardon me, Father, if I pause. I think
I have been speaking to you of some matters
There was no need to speak of, have I not?   105
You do not know how clearly those things stood
Within my mind, which I have spoken of,
Nor how they strove for utterance. Life all past
Is like the sky when the sun sets in it,
Clearest where furthest off.

               I told you how   110
She scorned my parting gift and laughed. And yet
A woman's laugh's another thing sometimes:
I think they laugh in Heaven. I know last night
I dreamed I saw into the garden of God,
Where women walked whose painted images   115
I have seen with candles round them in the church.
They bent this way and that, one to another,
Playing: and over the long golden hair
Of each there floated like a ring of fire
Which when she stooped stooped with her, and when she rose 120
Rose with her. Then a breeze flew in among them,
As if a window had been opened in heaven
For God to give his blessing from, before
This world of ours should set; (for in my dream
I thought our world was setting, and the sun   125
Flared, a spent taper;) and beneath that gust
The rings of light quivered like forest-leaves.
Then all the blessed maidens who were there
Stood up together, as it were a voice
That called them; and they threw their tresses back 130
And smote their palms, and all laughed up at once,
For the strong heavenly joy they had in them

To hear God bless the world. Wherewith I woke:
And looking round, I saw as usual
That she was standing there with her long locks   135
Pressed to her side; and her laugh ended theirs.

For always when I see her now, she laughs.
And yet her childish laughter haunts me too,
The life of this dead terror; as in days
When she, a child, dwelt with me. I must tell   140
Something of those days yet before the end.

I brought her from the city – one such day
When she was still a merry loving child, –
The earliest gift I mind my giving her;
A little image of a flying Love   145
Made of our coloured glass-ware, in his hands
A dart of gilded metal and a torch.
And him she kissed and me, and fain would know
Why were his poor eyes blindfold, why the wings
And why the arrow. What I knew I told   150
Of Venus and of Cupid, – strange old tales.
And when she heard that he could rule the loves
Of men and women, still she shook her head
And wondered; and, 'Nay, nay,' she murmured still,
'So strong, and he a younger child than I!'   155
And then she'd have me fix him on the wall
Fronting her little bed; and then again
She needs must fix him there herself, because
I gave him to her and she loved him so,
And he should make her love me better yet,   160
If women loved the more, the more they grew.
But the fit place upon the wall was high
For her, and so I held her in my arms:
And each time that the heavy pruning-hook
I gave her for a hammer slipped away   165
As it would often, still she laughed and laughed
And kissed and kissed me. But amid her mirth,
Just as she hung the image on the nail,
It slipped and all its fragments strewed the ground:
And as it fell she screamed, for in her hand   170
The dart had entered deeply and drawn blood.
And so her laughter turned to tears: and 'Oh!'
I said, the while I bandaged the small hand, –

'That I should be the first to make you bleed,
Who love and love and love you!' – kissing still   175
The fingers till I got her safe to bed.
And still she sobbed, – 'not for the pain at all,'
She said, 'but for the Love, the poor good Love
You gave me.' So she cried herself to sleep.

    Another later thing comes back to me.   180
'Twas in those hardest foulest days of all,
When still from his shut palace, sitting clean
Above the splash of blood, old Metternich
(May his soul die, and never-dying worms
Feast on its pain for ever!) used to thin   185
His year's doomed hundreds daintily, each month
Thirties and fifties. This time, as I think,
Was when his thrift forbad the poor to take
That evil brackish salt which the dry rocks
Keep all through winter when the sea draws in.   190
The first I heard of it was a chance shot
In the street here and there, and on the stones
A stumbling clatter as of horse hemmed round.
Then, when she saw me hurry out of doors,
My gun slung at my shoulder and my knife   195
Stuck in my girdle, she smoothed down my hair
And laughed to see me look so brave, and leaped
Up to my neck and kissed me. She was still
A child; and yet that kiss was on my lips
So hot all day where the smoke shut us in.   200

    For now, being always with her, the first love
I had – the father's, brother's love – was changed,
I think, in somewise; like a holy thought
Which is a prayer before one knows of it.
The first time I perceived this, I remember,   205
Was once when after hunting I came home
Weary, and she brought food and fruit for me,
And sat down at my feet upon the floor
Leaning against my side. But when I felt
Her sweet head reach from that low seat of hers   210
So high as to be laid upon my heart,
I turned and looked upon my darling there
And marked for the first time how tall she was;
And my heart beat with so much violence

Under her cheek, I thought she could not choose   215
But wonder at it soon and ask me why;
And so I bade her rise and eat with me.
And when, remembering all and counting back
The time, I made out fourteen years for her
And told her so, she gazed at me with eyes   220
As of the sky and sea on a grey day,
And drew her long hands through her hair, and asked me
If she was not a woman; and then laughed:
And as she stooped in laughing, I could see
Beneath the growing throat the breasts half globed   225
Like folded lilies deepset in the stream.

   Yes, let me think of her as then; for so
Her image, Father, is not like the sights
Which come when you are gone. She had a mouth
Made to bring death to life, – the underlip   230
Sucked in, as if it strove to kiss itself.
Her face was ever pale, as when one stoops
Over wan water; and the dark crisped hair
And the hair's shadow made it paler still: –
Deep-serried locks, the darkness of the cloud   235
Where the moon's gaze is set in eddying gloom.
Her body bore her neck as the tree's stem
Bears the top branch; and as the branch sustains
The flower of the year's pride, her high neck bore
That face made wonderful with night and day.   240
Her voice was swift, yet ever the last words
Fell lingeringly; and rounded finger-tips
She had, that clung a little where they touched
And then were gone o' the instant. Her great eyes,
That sometimes turned half dizzily beneath   245
The passionate lids, as faint, when she would speak,
Had also in them hidden springs of mirth,
Which under the dark lashes evermore
Shook to her laugh, as when a bird flies low
Between the water and the willow-leaves,   250
And the shade quivers till he wins the light.

   I was a moody comrade to her then,
For all the love I bore her. Italy,
The weeping desolate mother, long has claimed
Her son's strong arms to lean on, and their hands   255

To lop the poisonous thicket from her path,
Cleaving her way to light. And from her need
Had grown the fashion of my whole poor life
Which I was proud to yield her, as my father
Had yielded his. And this had come to be   260
A game to play, a love to clasp, a hate
To wreak, all things together that a man
Needs for his blood to ripen: till at times
All else seemed shadows, and I wondered still
To see such life pass muster and be deemed   265
Time's bodily substance. In those hours, no doubt,
To the young girl my eyes were like my soul, –
Dark wells of death-in-life that yearned for day.
And though she ruled me always, I remember
That once when I was thus and she still kept   270
Leaping about the place and laughing, I
Did almost chide her; whereupon she knelt
And putting her two hands into my breast
Sang me a song. Are these tears in my eyes?
'Tis long since I have wept for anything.   275
I thought that song forgotten out of mind,
And now, just as I spoke of it, it came
All back. It is but a rude thing, ill rhymed,
Such as a blind man chaunts and his dog hears
Holding the platter, when the children run   280
To merrier sport and leave him. Thus it goes: –

      La bella donna[1]
      Piangendo disse:
      'Come son fisse
      Le stelle in cielo!   285
      Quel fiato anelo
      Dello stanco sole,
      Quanto m'assonna!
      E la luna, macchiata
      Come uno specchio   290
      Logoro e vecchio, –

[1] She wept, sweet lady,   Of the sun's noon-hour
And said in weeping: To sleep so move me?
'What spell is keeping   And the moon in heaven,
The stars so steady?   Stained where she passes
Why does the power   As a worn-out glass is, –

Faccia affannata,
Che cosa vuole?

'Chè stelle, luna, e sole,
Ciascun m'annoja   295
E m'annojano insieme;
Non me ne preme
Nè ci prendo gioja.
E veramente,
Che le spalle sien franche   300
E le braccia bianche
E il seno caldo e tondo,
Non mi fa niente.
Chè cosa al mondo
Posso più far di questi   305
Se non piacciono a te, come dicesti?'

La donna rise
E riprese ridendo: –
'Questa mano che prendo
È dunque mia?   310
Tu m'ami dunque?
Dimmelo ancora,
Non in modo qualunque,
Ma le parole
Belle e precise   315
Che dicesti pria.
'Siccome suole
La state talora

Wearily driven,
Why walks she above me?

  'Stars, moon, and sun too,
I'm tired of either
And all together!
Whom speak they unto
That I should listen?
For very surely,
Though my arms and shoulders
Dazzle beholders,
And my eyes glisten,
All's nothing purely!
What are words said for
At all about them,

If he they are made for
Can do without them?'

  She laughed, sweet lady,
And said in laughing:
'His hand clings half in
My own already!
Oh! do you love me?
Oh! speak of passion
In no new fashion
No loud inveighings,
But the old sayings
You once said of me.
  'You said: "As summer,
Through boughs grown brittle,

(Dicesti) *un qualche istante*
Tornare innanzi inverno,　　　　　　　　　320
Così tu fai ch' io scerno
Le foglie tutte quante,
Ben ch' io certo tenessi
Per passato l'autunno.

'Eccolo il mio alunno!　　　　　　　　　　325
Io debbo insegnargli
Quei cari detti istessi
Ch' ei mi disse una volta!
Oimè! Che cosa, dargli,'
(Ma ridea piano piano　　　　　　　　　　330
Dei baci in sulla mano,)
'Ch' ei non m' abbia da lungo tempo tolta?'

Comes back a little	He then spoke of me?
Ere frosts benumb her, –	Alas! what flavour
So bring'st thou to me	Still with me lingers?'
All leaves and flowers,	(But she laughed as my kisses
Though autumn's gloomy	Glowed in her fingers
To-day in the bowers."	With love's old blisses.)
	'Oh! what one favour
'Oh! does he love me,	Remains to woo him,
When my voice teaches	Whose whole poor savour
The very speeches	Belongs not to him?'

That I should sing upon this bed! – with you
To listen, and such words still left to say!
Yet was it I that sang? The voice seemed hers,　　335
As on the very day she sang to me;
When, having done, she took out of my hand
Something that I had played with all the while
And laid it down beyond my reach; and so
Turning my face round till it fronted hers, –　　340
'Weeping or laughing, which was best?' she said.

But these are foolish tales. How should I show
The heart that glowed then with love's heat, each day
More and more brightly? – when for long years now
The very flame that flew about the heart,　　　345
And gave it fiery wings, has come to be

The lapping blaze of hell's environment
Whose tongues all bid the molten heart despair.

Yet one more thing comes back on me to-night
Which I may tell you: for it bore my soul   350
Dread firstlings of the brood that rend it now.
It chanced that in our last year's wanderings
We dwelt at Monza, far away from home,
If home we had: and in the Duomo there
I sometimes entered with her when she prayed.   355
An image of Our Lady stands there, wrought
In marble by some great Italian hand
In the great days when she and Italy
Sat on one throne together: and to her
And to none else my loved one told her heart.   360
She was a woman then; and as she knelt, –
Her sweet brow in the sweet brow's shadow there, –
They seemed two kindred forms whereby our land
(Whose work still serves the world for miracle)
Made manifest herself in womanhood.   365
Father, the day I speak of was the first
For weeks that I had borne her company
Into the Duomo; and those weeks had been
Much troubled, for then first the glimpses came
Of some impenetrable restlessness   370
Growing in her to make her changed and cold.
And as we entered there that day, I bent
My eyes on the fair Image, and I said
Within my heart, 'Oh turn her heart to me!'
And so I left her to her prayers, and went   375
To gaze upon the pride of Monza's shrine,
Where in the sacristy the light still falls
Upon the Iron Crown of Italy,
On whose crowned heads the day has closed, nor yet
The daybreak gilds another head to crown.   380
But coming back, I wondered when I saw
That the sweet Lady of her prayers now stood
Alone without her; until further off,
Before some new Madonna gaily decked,
Tinselled and gewgawed, a slight German toy,   385
I saw her kneel, still praying. At my step
She rose, and side by side we left the church.
I was much moved, and sharply questioned her

Of her transferred devotion; but she seemed
Stubborn and heedless; till she lightly laughed   390
And said: 'The old Madonna? Aye indeed,
She had my old thoughts, – this one has my new.'
Then silent to the soul I held my way:
And from the fountains of the public place
Unto the pigeon-haunted pinnacles,   395
Bright wings and water winnowed the bright air;
And stately with her laugh's subsiding smile
She went, with clear-swayed waist and towering neck
And hands held light before her; and the face
Which long had made a day in my life's night   400
Was night in day to me; as all men's eyes
Turned on her beauty, and she seemed to tread
Beyond my heart to the world made for her.

Ah there! my wounds will snatch my sense again:
The pain comes billowing on like a full cloud   405
Of thunder, and the flash that breaks from it
Leaves my brain burning. That's the wound he gave,
The Austrian whose white coat I still made match
With his white face, only the two were red
As suits his trade. The devil makes them wear   410
White for a livery, that the blood may show
Braver that brings them to him. So he looks
Sheer o'er the field and knows his own at once.

Give me a draught of water in that cup;
My voice feels thick; perhaps you do not hear;   415
But you *must* hear. If you mistake my words
And so absolve me, I am sure the blessing
Will burn my soul. If you mistake my words
And so absolve me, Father, the great sin
Is yours, not mine: mark this: your soul shall burn   420
With mine for it. I have seen pictures where
Souls burned with Latin shriekings in their mouths:
Shall my end be as theirs? Nay, but I know
'Tis you shall shriek in Latin. Some bell rings,
Rings through my brain: it strikes the hour in hell.   425

You see I cannot, Father; I have tried,
But cannot, as you see. These twenty times
Beginning, I have come to the same point
And stopped. Beyond, there are but broken words

Which will not let you understand my tale.   430
It is that when we have her with us here,
As when she wrung her hair out in my dream
To-night, till all the darkness reeked of it.
Her hair is always wet, for she has kept
Its tresses wrapped about her side for years;   435
And when she wrung them round over the floor,
I heard the blood between her fingers hiss;
So that I sat up in my bed and screamed
Once and again; and once to once, she laughed.
Look that you turn not now, – she's at your back: 440
Gather your robe up, Father, and keep close,
Or she'll sit down on it and send you mad.

  At Iglio in the first thin shade o' the hills
The sand is black and red. The black was black
When what was spilt that day sank into it,   445
And the red scarcely darkened. There I stood
This night with her, and saw the sand the same.

                    .   .   .   .   .   .

  What would you have me tell you? Father, father,
How shall I make you know? You have not known
The dreadful soul of woman, who one day   450
Forgets the old and takes the new to heart,
Forgets what man remembers, and therewith
Forgets the man. Nor can I clearly tell
How the change happened between her and me.
Her eyes looked on me from an emptied heart   455
When most my heart was full of her; and still
In every corner of myself I sought
To find what service failed her; and no less
Than in the good time past, there all was hers.
What do you love? Your Heaven? Conceive it spread   460
For one first year of all eternity
All round you with all joys and gifts of God;
And then when most your soul is blent with it
And all yields song together, – then it stands
O' the sudden like a pool that once gave back   465
Your image, but now drowns it and is clear
Again, – or like a sun bewitched, that burns
Your shadow from you, and still shines in sight.
How could you bear it? Would you not cry out,

Among those eyes grown blind to you, those ears   470
That hear no more your voice you hear the same, –
'God! what is left but hell for company,
But hell, hell, hell?' – until the name so breathed
Whirled with hot wind and sucked you down in fire?
Even so I stood the day her empty heart   475
Left her place empty in our home, while yet
I knew not why she went nor where she went
Nor how to reach her: so I stood the day
When to my prayers at last one sight of her
Was granted, and I looked on heaven made pale   480
With scorn, and heard heaven mock me in that laugh.

    O sweet, long sweet! Was that some ghost of you
Even as your ghost that haunts me now, – twin shapes
Of fear and hatred? May I find you yet
Mine when death wakes? Ah! be it even in flame,   485
We may have sweetness yet, if you but say
As once in childish sorrow: 'Not my pain,
My pain was nothing: oh your poor poor love,
Your broken love!'
                My Father, have I not
Yet told you the last things of that last day   490
On which I went to meet her by the sea?
O God, O God! but I must tell you all.

    Midway upon my journey, when I stopped
To buy the dagger at the village fair,
I saw two cursed rats about the place   495
I knew for spies – blood-sellers both. That day
Was not yet over; for three hours to come
I prized my life: and so I looked around
For safety. A poor painted mountebank
Was playing tricks and shouting in a crowd.   500
I knew he must have heard my name, so I
Pushed past and whispered to him who I was,
And of my danger. Straight he hustled me
Into his booth, as it were in the trick,
And brought me out next minute with my face   505
All smeared in patches, and a zany's gown;
And there I handed him his cups and balls
And swung the sand-bags round to clear the ring
For half an hour. The spies came once and looked;

And while they stopped, and made all sights and sounds   510
Sharp to my startled senses, I remember
A woman laughed above me. I looked up
And saw where a brown-shouldered harlot leaned
Half through a tavern window thick with vine.
Some man had come behind her in the room   515
And caught her by her arms, and she had turned
With that coarse empty laugh on him, as now
He munched her neck with kisses, while the vine
Crawled in her back.
              And three hours afterwards,
When she that I had run all risks to meet   520
Laughed as I told you, my life burned to death
Within me, for I thought it like the laugh
Heard at the fair. She had not left me long;
But all she might have changed to, or might change to,
(I know naught since – she never speaks a word –)   525
Seemed in that laugh. Have I not told you yet,
Not told you all this time what happened, Father,
When I had offered her the little knife,
And bade her keep it for my sake that loved her,
And she had laughed? Have I not told you yet?   530

   'Take it,' I said to her the second time,
'Take it and keep it.' And then came a fire
That burnt my hand; and then the fire was blood,
And sea and sky were blood and fire, and all
The day was one red blindness; till it seemed   535
Within the whirling brain's entanglement
That she or I or all things bled to death.
And then I found her laid against my feet
And knew that I had stabbed her, and saw still
Her look in falling. For she took the knife   540
Deep in her heart, even as I bade her then,
And fell; and her stiff bodice scooped the sand
Into her bosom.
             And she keeps it, see,
Do you not see she keeps it? – there, beneath
Wet fingers and wet tresses, in her heart.   545
For look you, when she stirs her hand, it shows
The little hilt of horn and pearl, – even such
A dagger as our women of the coast
Twist in their garters.

Father, I have done:
And from her side now she unwinds the thick   550
Dark hair; all round her side it is wet through,
But like the sand at Iglio does not change.
Now you may see the dagger clearly. Father,
I have told all: tell me at once what hope
Can reach me still. For now she draws it out   555
Slowly, and only smiles as yet: look, Father,
She scarcely smiles: but I shall hear her laugh
Soon, when she shows the crimson blade to God.

Dante at Verona

Yea, thou shalt learn how salt his food who fares
   Upon another's bread, – how steep his path
Who treadeth up and down another's stairs
                  (*Divine Comedy Paradise* xvii)

Behold, even I, even I am Beatrice.
                  (*Divine Comedy Purgatory* xxx)

Of Florence and of Beatrice
   Servant and singer from of old,
   O'er Dante's heart in youth had toll'd
The knell that gave his Lady peace;
   And now in manhood flew the dart   5
   Wherewith his City pierced his heart.

Yet if his Lady's home above
   Was Heaven, on earth she filled his soul;
   And if his City held control
To cast the body forth to rove,   10
   The soul could soar from earth's vain throng,
   And Heaven and Hell fulfil the song.

Follow his feet's appointed way; –
   But little light we find that clears
   The darkness of the exiled years.
Follow his spirit's journey: – nay,   15
   What fires are blent, what winds are blown
   On paths his feet may tread alone?

Yet of the twofold life he led
   In chainless thought and fettered will   20

Some glimpses reach us, – somewhat still
Of the steep stairs and bitter bread, –
   Of the soul's quest whose stern avow
   For years had made him haggard now.

Alas! the Sacred Song whereto   25
   Both heaven and earth had set their hand
   Not only at Fame's gate did stand
Knocking to claim the passage through,
   But toiled to ope that heavier door
   Which Florence shut for evermore.   30

Shall not his birth's baptismal Town
   One last high presage yet fulfil,
   And at that font in Florence still
His forehead take the laurel-crown?
   O God! or shall dead souls deny   35
   The undying soul its prophecy?

Aye, 'tis their hour. Not yet forgot
   The bitter words he spoke that day
   When for some great charge far away
Her rulers his acceptance sought.   40
   'And if I go, who stays?' – so rose
   His scorn: – 'and if I stay, who goes?'

'Lo! thou art gone now, and we stay:'
   (The curled lips mutter): 'and no star
   Is from thy mortal path so far   45
As streets where childhood knew the way.
   To Heaven and Hell thy feet may win,
   But thine own house they come not in.'

Therefore, the loftier rose the song
   To touch the secret things of God,   50
   The deeper pierced the hate that trod
On base men's track who wrought the wrong;
   Till the soul's effluence came to be
   Its own exceeding agony.

Arriving only to depart,   55
   From court to court, from land to land,
   Like flame within the naked hand
His body bore his burning heart
   That still on Florence strove to bring
   God's fire for a burnt offering.   60

Even such was Dante's mood, when now,
  Mocked for long years with Fortune's sport,
  He dwelt at yet another court,
There where Verona's knee did bow
  And her voice hailed with all acclaim   65
  Can Grande della Scala's name.

As that lord's kingly guest awhile
  His life we follow; through the days
  Which walked in exile's barren ways, –
The nights which still beneath one smile   70
  Heard through all spheres one song increase, –
  'Even I, even I am Beatrice.'

At Can La Scala's court, no doubt,
  Due reverence did his steps attend;
  The ushers on his path would bend   75
At ingoing as at going out;
  The penmen waited on his call
  At council-board, the grooms in hall.

And pages hushed their laughter down,
  And gay squires stilled the merry stir,   80
  When he passed up the dais-chamber
With set brows lordlier than a frown;
  And tire-maids hidden among these
  Drew close their loosened bodices.

Perhaps the priests, (exact to span   85
  All God's circumference,) if at whiles
  They found him wandering in their aisles,
Grudged ghostly greeting to the man
  By whom, though not of ghostly guild,
  With Heaven and Hell men's hearts were fill'd. 90

And the court-poets (he, forsooth,
  A whole world's poet strayed to court!)
  Had for his scorn their hate's retort.
He'd meet them flushed with easy youth,
  Hot on their errands. Like noon-flies   95
  They vexed him in the ears and eyes.

But at this court, peace still must wrench
  Her chaplet from the teeth of war:

By day they held high watch afar,
At night they cried across the trench;   100
    And still, in Dante's path, the fierce
    Gaunt soldiers wrangled o'er their spears.

But vain seemed all the strength to him,
    As golden convoys sunk at sea
    Whose wealth might root out penury: 105
Because it was not, limb with limb,
    Knit like his heart-strings round the wall
    Of Florence, that ill pride might fall.

Yet in the tiltyard, when the dust
    Cleared from the sundered press of knights   110
    Ere yet again it swoops and smites,
He almost deemed his longing must
    Find force to wield that multitude
    And hurl that strength the way he would.

How should he move them, – fame and gain   115
    On all hands calling them at strife?
    He still might find but his one life
To give, by Florence counted vain;
    One heart the false hearts made her doubt;
    One voice she heard once and cast out.   120

Oh! if his Florence could but come,
    A lily-sceptred damsel fair,
    As her own Giotto painted her
On many shields and gates at home, –
    A lady crowned, at a soft pace   125
    Riding the lists round to the dais:

Till where Can Grande rules the lists,
    As young as Truth, as calm as Force,
    She draws her rein now, while her horse
Bows at the turn of the white wrists;   130
    And when each knight within his stall
    Gives ear, she speaks and tells them all:

All the foul tale, – truth sworn untrue
    And falsehood's triumph. All the tale?
    Great God! and must she not prevail   135
To fire them ere they heard it through, –
    And hand achieve ere heart could rest
    That high adventure of her quest?

How would his Florence lead them forth,
   Her bridle ringing as she went;   140
   And at the last within her tent,
'Neath golden lilies worship-worth,
   How queenly would she bend the while
   And thank the victors with her smile!

Also her lips should turn his way   145
   And murmur: 'O thou tried and true,
   With whom I wept the long years through!
What shall it profit if I say,
   Thee I remember? Nay, through thee
   All ages shall remember me.'   150

Peace, Dante, peace! The task is long,
   The time wears short to compass it.
   Within thine heart such hopes may flit
And find a voice in deathless song:
   But lo! as children of man's earth,   155
   Those hopes are dead before their birth.

Fame tells us that Verona's court
   Was a fair place. The feet might still
   Wander for ever at their will
In many ways of sweet resort;   160
   And still in many a heart around
   The Poet's name due honour found.

Watch we his steps. He comes upon
   The women at their palm-playing.
   The conduits round the gardens sing   165
And meet in scoops of milk-white stone,
   Where wearied damsels rest and hold
   Their hands in the wet spurt of gold.

One of whom, knowing well that he,
   By some found stern, was mild with them,   170
   Would run and pluck his garment's hem,
Saying, 'Messer Dante, pardon me,' –
   Praying that they might hear the song
   Which first of all he made, when young.

'Donne che avete'[1] ... Thereunto   175
  Thus would he murmur, having first
  Drawn near the fountain, while she nurs'd
His hand against her side: a few
  Sweet words, and scarcely those, half said:
  Then turned, and changed, and bowed his head.   180

For then the voice said in his heart,
  'Even I, even I am Beatrice;'
  And his whole life would yearn to cease:
Till having reached his room, apart
  Beyond vast lengths of palace-floor,   185
  He drew the arras round his door.

At such times, Dante, thou hast set
  Thy forehead to the painted pane
  Full oft, I know; and if the rain
Smote it outside, her fingers met   190
  Thy brow; and if the sun fell there,
  Her breath was on thy face and hair.

Then, weeping, I think certainly
  Thou hast beheld, past sight of eyne, –
  Within another room of thine   195
Where now thy body may not be
  But where in thought thou still remain'st, –
  A window often wept against:

The window thou, a youth, hast sought,
  Flushed in the limpid eventime,   200
  Ending with daylight the day's rhyme
Of her: where oftenwhiles her thought
  Held thee – the lamp untrimmed to write –
  In joy through the blue lapse of night.

At Can La Scala's court, no doubt,   205
  Guests seldom wept. It was brave sport,
  No doubt, at Can La Scala's court,
Within the palace and without;
  Where music, set to madrigals,
  Loitered all day through groves and halls.   210

Because Can Grande of his life
  Had not had six-and-twenty years

---

1 'Donne che avete intelletto d'amore:' – the first canzone of the *Vita Nuova*.

As yet. And when the chroniclers
Tell you of that Vicenza strife
    And of strifes elsewhere, – you must not   215
    Conceive for church-sooth he had got

Just nothing in his wits but war:
    Though doubtless 'twas the young man's joy
    (Grown with his growth from a mere boy,)
To mark his 'Viva Cane!' scare   220
    The foe's shut front, till it would reel
    All blind with shaken points of steel.

But there were places – held too sweet
    For eyes that had not the due veil
    Of lashes and clear lids – as well   225
In favour as his saddle-seat:
    Breath of low speech he scorned not there
    Nor light cool fingers in his hair.

Yet if the child whom the sire's plan
    Made free of a deep treasure-chest   230
    Scoffed it with ill-conditioned jest, –
We may be sure too that the man
    Was not mere thews, nor all content
    With lewdness swathed in sentiment.

So you may read and marvel not   235
    That such a man as Dante – one
    Who, while Can Grande's deeds were done,
Had drawn his robe round him and thought –
    Now at the same guest-table far'd
    Where keen Uguccio wiped his beard.[1]   240

Through leaves and trellis-work the sun
    Left the wine cool within the glass, –
    They feasting where no sun could pass:
And when the women, all as one,
    Rose up with brightened cheeks to go,   245
    It was a comely thing, we know.

But Dante recked not of the wine;
    Whether the women stayed or went,
    His visage held one stern intent:

1 Uguccione della Faggiuola, Dante's former protector, was now his fellow-guest at Verona.

And when the music had its sign   250
　　To breathe upon them for more ease,
　　Sometimes he turned and bade it cease.

And as he spared not to rebuke
　　The mirth, so oft in council he
　　To bitter truth bore testimony: 255
And when the crafty balance shook
　　Well poised to make the wrong prevail
　　Then Dante's hand would turn the scale.

And if some envoy from afar
　　Sailed to Verona's sovereign port   260
　　For aid or peace, and all the court
Fawned on its lord, 'the Mars of war,
　　Sole arbiter of life and death,' –
　　Be sure that Dante saved his breath.

And Can La Scala marked askance   265
　　These things, accepting them for shame
　　And scorn, till Dante's guestship came
To be a peevish sufferance:
　　His host sought ways to make his days
　　Hateful; and such have many ways.   270

There was a Jester, a foul lout
　　Whom the court loved for graceless arts;
　　Sworn scholiast of the bestial parts
Of speech; a ribald mouth to shout
　　In Folly's horny tympanum   275
　　Such things as make the wise man dumb.

Much loved, him Dante loathed. And so,
　　One day when Dante felt perplex'd
　　If any day that could come next
Were worth the waiting for or no,   280
　　And mute he sat amid their din, –
　　Can Grande called the Jester in.

Rank words, with such, are wit's best wealth.
　　Lords mouthed approval; ladies kept
　　Twittering with clustered heads, except   285
Some few that took their trains by stealth
　　And went. Can Grande shook his hair
　　And smote his thighs and laughed i' the air.

Then, facing on his guest, he cried, –
   'Say, Messer Dante, how it is   290
   I get out of a clown like this
More than your wisdom can provide.'
   And Dante: ''Tis man's ancient whim
   That still his like seems good to him.'

Also a tale is told, how once,   295
   At clearing tables after meat,
   Piled for a jest at Dante's feet
Were found the dinner's well-picked bones;
   So laid, to please the banquet's lord,
   By one who crouched beneath the board.   300

Then smiled Can Grande to the rest: –
   'Our Dante's tuneful mouth indeed
   Lacks not the gift on flesh to feed!'
'Fair host of mine,' replied the guest,
   'So many bones you'd not descry   305
   If so it chanced the *dog* were I.'[1]

But wherefore should we turn the grout
   In a drained cup, or be at strife
   From the worn garment of a life
To rip the twisted ravel out?   310
   Good needs expounding; but of ill
   Each hath enough to guess his fill.

They named him Justicer-at-Law:
   Each month to bear the tale in mind
   Of hues a wench might wear unfin'd   315
And of the load an ox might draw;
   To cavil in the weight of bread
   And to see purse-thieves gibbeted.

And when his spirit wove the spell
   (From under even to over-noon   320
   In converse with itself alone,)
As high as Heaven, as low as Hell, –
   He would be summoned and must go:
   For had not Gian stabbed Giacomo?

Therefore the bread he had to eat   325

---

1 '*Messere, voi non vedreste tant 'ossa se cane io fossi.*' The point of the reproach is difficult to render, depending as it does on the literal meaning of the name *Cane*.

Seemed brackish, less like corn than tares;
  And the rush-strown accustomed stairs
Each day were steeper to his feet;
  And when the night-vigil was done,
  His brows would ache to feel the sun.   330

Nevertheless, when from his kin
  There came the tidings how at last
  In Florence a decree was pass'd
Whereby all banished folk might win
  Free pardon, so a fine were paid   335
  And act of public penance made, –

This Dante writ in answer thus,
  Words such as these: 'That clearly they
  In Florence must not have to say, –
The man abode aloof from us   340
  Nigh fifteen years, yet lastly skulk'd
  Hither to candleshrift and mulct.

'That he was one the Heavens forbid
  To traffic in God's justice sold
  By market-weight of earthly gold,   345
Or to bow down over the lid
  Of steaming censers, and so be
  Made clean of manhood's obloquy.

'That since no gate led, by God's will,
  To Florence, but the one whereat   350
  The priests and money-changers sat,
He still would wander; for that still,
  Even through the body's prison-bars,
  His soul possessed the sun and stars.'

Such were his words. It is indeed   355
  For ever well our singers should
  Utter good words and know them good
Not through song only; with close heed
  Lest, having spent for the work's sake
  Six days, the man be left to make.   360

Months o'er Verona, till the feast
  Was come for Florence the Free Town:
  And at the shrine of Baptist John
The exiles, girt with many a priest

And carrying candles as they went,   365
    Were held to mercy of the saint.

On the high seats in sober state, –
    Gold neck-chains range o'er range below
    Gold screen-work where the lilies grow, –
The Heads of the Republic sate,   370
    Marking the humbled face go by
    Each one of his house-enemy.

And as each proscript rose and stood
    From kneeling in the ashen dust
    On the shrine-steps, some magnate thrust   375
A beard into the velvet hood
    Of his front colleague's gown, to see
    The cinders stuck in the bare knee.

Tosinghi passed, Manelli passed,
    Rinucci passed, each in his place;   380
    But not an Alighieri's face
Went by that day from first to last
    In the Republic's triumph; nor
    A foot came home to Dante's door.

(RESPUBLICA – a public thing: 385
    A shameful shameless prostitute,
    Whose lust with one lord may not suit,
So takes by turns its revelling
    A night with each, till each at morn
    Is stripped and beaten forth forlorn,   390

And leaves her, cursing her. If she,
    Indeed, have not some spice-draught, hid
    In scent under a silver lid,
To drench his open throat with – he
    Once hard asleep; and thrust him not   395
    At dawn beneath the boards to rot.)

Years filled out their twelve moons, and ceased
    One in another; and alway
    There were the whole twelve hours each day
And each night as the years increased;   400
    And rising moon and setting sun
    Beheld that Dante's work was done.

What of his work for Florence? Well
    It was, he knew, and well must be.
    Yet evermore her hate's decree   405
Dwelt in his thought intolerable: –
    His body to be burned,[1] – his soul
    To beat its wings at hope's vain goal.

What of his work for Beatrice?
    Now well-nigh was the third song writ, –   410
    The stars a third time sealing it
With sudden music of pure peace:
    For echoing thrice the threefold song,
    The unnumbered stars the tone prolong.[2]

Each hour, as then the Vision pass'd,   415
    He heard the utter harmony
    Of the nine trembling spheres, till she
Bowed her eyes towards him in the last,
    So that all ended with her eyes,
    Hell, Purgatory, Paradise.   420

'It is my trust, as the years fall,
    To write more worthily of her
    Who now, being made God's minister,
Looks on His visage and knows all.'
    Such was the hope that love did blend   425
    With grief's slow fires, to make an end

Of the 'New Life', his youth's dear book:
    Adding thereunto: 'In such trust
    I labour, and believe I must
Accomplish this which my soul took   430
    In charge, if God, my Lord and hers,
    Leave my life with me a few years.'

The trust which he had borne in youth
    Was all at length accomplished. He
    At length had written worthily –   435
Yea even of her; no rhymes uncouth
    'Twixt tongue and tongue; but by God's aid
    The first words Italy had said.

---

1 Such was the last sentence passed by Florence against Dante, as a recalcitrant exile.
2 'E quindi escimmo a riveder le *stelle*.' – *Inferno*.
  'Puro e disposto a salire alle *stelle*.' – *Purgatorio*.
  'L'amor che muove il sole e l'altre *stelle*.' – *Paradiso*.

Ah! haply now the heavenly guide
    Was not the last form seen by him: 440
    But there that Beatrice stood slim
And bowed in passing at his side,
    For whom in youth his heart made moan
    Then when the city sat alone.[1]

Clearly herself; the same whom he   445
    Met, not past girlhood, in the street,
    Low-bosomed and with hidden feet;
And then as woman perfectly,
    In years that followed, many an once, –
    And now at last among the suns   450

In that high vision. But indeed
    It may be memory did recall
    Last to him then the first of all, –
The child his boyhood bore in heed
    Nine years. At length the voice brought peace, –   455
    'Even I, even I am Beatrice.'

All this, being there, we had not seen.
    Seen only was the shadow wrought
    On the strong features bound in thought;
The vagueness gaining gait and mien;   460
    The white streaks gathering clear to view
    In the burnt beard the women knew.

For a tale tells that on his track,
    As through Verona's streets he went,
    This saying certain women sent: –   465
'Lo, he that strolls to Hell and back
    At will! Behold him, how Hell's reek
    Has crisped his beard and singed his cheek.'

'Whereat' (Boccaccio's words) 'he smil'd
    For pride in fame.' It might be so: 470
    Nevertheless we cannot know
If haply he were not beguil'd
    To bitterer mirth, who scarce could tell
    If he indeed were back from Hell.

So the day came, after a space,   475
    When Dante felt assured that there

---

1 '*Quomodo sedet sola civitas!*' – the words quoted by Dante in the *Vita Nuova* when he speaks of the death of Beatrice.

The sunshine must lie sicklier
Even than in any other place,
   Save only Florence. When that day
   Had come, he rose and went his way.   480

He went and turned not. From his shoes
   It may be that he shook the dust,
   As every righteous dealer must
Once and again ere life can close:
   And unaccomplished destiny   485
   Struck cold his forehead, it may be.

No book keeps record how the Prince
   Sunned himself out of Dante's reach,
   Nor how the Jester stank in speech;
While courtiers, used to smile and wince,   490
   Poets and harlots, all the throng,
   Let loose their scandal and their song.

No book keeps record if the seat
   Which Dante held at his host's board
   Were sat in next by clerk or lord, –   495
If leman lolled with dainty feet
   At ease, or hostage brooded there,
   Or priest lacked silence for his prayer.

Eat and wash hands, Can Grande; – scarce
   We know their deeds now; hands which fed   500
   Our Dante with that bitter bread;
And thou the watch-dog of those stairs
   Which, of all paths his feet knew well,
   Were steeper found than Heaven or Hell.

On Refusal of Aid Between Nations

Not that the earth is changing, O my God!
   Nor that the seasons totter in their walk, –
   Not that the virulent ill of act and talk
Seethes ever as a winepress ever trod, –
Not therefore are we certain that the rod   5
   Weighs in thine hand to smite thy world; though now
   Beneath thine hand so many nations bow,
So many kings: – not therefore, O my God! –

But because Man is parcelled out in men
  To-day; because, for any wrongful blow   10
    No man not stricken asks, 'I would be told
Why thou dost thus;' but his heart whispers then,
  'He is he, I am I.' By this we know
    That our earth falls asunder, being old.

A Young Fir-Wood

These little firs to-day are things
  To clasp into a giant's cap,
  Or fans to suit his lady's lap.
From many winters many springs
  Shall cherish them in strength and sap   5
  Till they be marked upon the map,
A wood for the wind's wanderings.

All seed is in the sower's hands:
  And what at first was trained to spread
  Its shelter for some single head, –   10
Yea, even such fellowship of wands, –
  May hide the sunset, and the shade
  Of its great multitude be laid
Upon the earth and elder sands.

For
'Our Lady of the Rocks' by Leonardo da Vinci

Mother, is this the darkness of the end,
  The Shadow of Death? and is that outer sea
    Infinite imminent Eternity?
And does the death-pang by man's seed sustain'd
In Time's each instant cause thy face to bend   5
  Its silent prayer upon the Son, while he
    Blesses the dead with his hand so silently
To his long day which hours no more offend?

Mother of grace, the pass is difficult,
  Keen as these rocks and the bewildered souls   10

Throng it like echoes, blindly shuddering through.
Thy name, O Lord, each spirit's voice extols,
   Whose peace abides in the dark avenue
Amid the bitterness of things occult.

On the 'Vita Nuova' of Dante

As he that loves oft looks on the dear form
   And guesses how it grew to womanhood,
   And gladly would have watched the beauties bud
And the mild fire of precious life wax warm:
So I, long bound within the threefold charm   5
   Of Dante's love sublimed to heavenly mood,
   Had marvelled, touching his Beatitude,
How grew such presence from man's shameful swarm.

At length within this book I found pourtrayed
   Newborn that Paradisal Love of his,   10
And simple like a child; with whose clear aid
   I understood. To such a child as this,
Christ, charging well His chosen ones, forbade
   Offence: 'for lo! of such my kingdom is.'

Penumbra

I did not look upon her eyes,
(Though scarcely seen, with no surprise,
'Mid many eyes a single look,)
Because they should not gaze rebuke,
At night, from stars in sky and brook.   5

I did not take her by the hand,
(Though little was to understand
From touch of hand all friends might take,)
Because it should not prove a flake
Burnt in my palm to boil and ache.   10

I did not listen to her voice,
(Though none had noted, where at choice

All might rejoice in listening,)
Because no such a thing should cling
In the wood's moan at evening.   15

I did not cross her shadow once,
(Though from the hollow west the sun's
Last shadow runs along so far,)
Because in June it should not bar
My ways, at noon when fevers are.   20

They told me she was sad that day,
(Though wherefore tell what love's soothsay,
Sooner than they, did register?)
And my heart leapt and wept to her,
And yet I did not speak nor stir.   25

So shall the tongues of the sea's foam
(Though many voices therewith come
From drowned hope's home to cry to me,)
Bewail one hour the more, when sea
And wind are one with memory.   30

The Honeysuckle

I plucked a honeysuckle where
    The hedge on high is quick with thorn,
    And climbing for the prize, was torn,
And fouled my feet in quag-water;
    And by the thorns and by the wind   5
    The blossom that I took was thinn'd,
And yet I found it sweet and fair.

Thence to a richer growth I came,
    Where, nursed in mellow intercourse,
    The honeysuckles sprang by scores,   10
Not harried like my single stem,
    All virgin lamps of scent and dew.
    So from my hand that first I threw,
Yet plucked not any more of them.

A Match with the Moon

Weary already, weary miles to-night
   I walked for bed: and so, to get some ease,
   I dogged the flying moon with similes.
And like a wisp she doubled on my sight
In ponds; and caught in tree-tops like a kite: 5
   And in a globe of film all liquorish
   Swam full-faced like a silly silver fish; –
Last like a bubble shot the welkin's height
Where my road turned, and got behind me, and sent
   My wizened shadow craning round at me,   10
   And jeered, 'So, step the measure, – one two three!' –
And if I faced on her, looked innocent.
But just at parting, halfway down a dell,
She kissed me for good-night. So you'll not tell.

Stratton Water

   'O have you seen the Stratton flood
      That's great with rain to-day?
   It runs beneath your wall, Lord Sands,
      Full of the new-mown hay.

   'I led your hounds to Hutton bank   5
      To bathe at early morn:
   They got their bath by Borrowbrake
      Above the standing corn.'

   Out from the castle-stair Lord Sands
      Looked up the western lea;   10
   The rook was grieving on her nest,
      The flood was round her tree.

   Over the castle-wall Lord Sands
      Looked down the eastern hill:
   The stakes swam free among the boats,   15
      The flood was rising still.

'What's yonder far below that lies
  So white against the slope?'
'O it's a sail o' your bonny barks
  The waters have washed up.'   20

'But I have never a sail so white,
  And the water's not yet there.'
'O it's the swans o' your bonny lake
  The rising flood doth scare.'

'The swans they would not hold so still,'   25
  So high they would not win.'
'O it's Joyce my wife has spread her smock
  And fears to fetch it in.'

'Nay, knave, it's neither sail nor swans,
  Nor aught that you can say;   30
For though your wife might leave her smock,
  Herself she'd bring away.'

Lord Sands has passed the turret-stair,
  The court, and yard, and all;
The kine were in the byre that day,   35
  The nags were in the stall.

Lord Sands has won the weltering slope
  Whereon the white shape lay:
The clouds were still above the hill,
  And the shape was still as they.   40

Oh pleasant is the gaze of life
  And sad is death's blind head;
But awful are the living eyes
  In the face of one thought dead!

'In God's name, Janet, is it me   45
  Thy ghost has come to seek?'
'Nay, wait another hour, Lord Sands, –
  Be sure my ghost shall speak.'

A moment stood he as a stone,
  Then grovelled to his knee.   50
'O Janet, O my love, my love,
  Rise up and come with me!'
'O once before you bade me come,
  And it's here you have brought me!'

'O many's the sweet word, Lord Sands,   55
    You've spoken oft to me;
But all that I have from you to-day
    Is the rain on my body.

'And many's the good gift, Lord Sands,
    You've promised oft to me;   60
But the gift of yours I keep to-day
    Is the babe in my body.

'O it's not in any earthly bed
    That first my babe I'll see;
For I have brought my body here   65
    That the flood may cover me.'

His face was close against her face,
    His hands of hers were fain:
O her wet cheeks were hot with tears,
    Her wet hands cold with rain.   70

'They told me you were dead, Janet, –
    How could I guess the lie?'
'They told me you were false, Lord Sands, –
    What could I do but die?'

'Now keep you well, my brother Giles, –   75
    Through you I deemed her dead!
As wan as your towers be to-day
    To-morrow they'll be red.

'Look down, look down, my false mother,
    That bade me not to grieve: 80
You'll look up when our marriage fires
    Are lit to-morrow eve.

'O more than one and more than two
    The sorrow of this shall see:
But it's to-morrow, love, for them, –   85
    To-day's for thee and me.'

He's drawn her face between his hands
    And her pale mouth to his:
No bird that was so still that day
    Chirps sweeter than his kiss.   90

The flood was creeping round their feet.
    'O Janet, come away!

The hall is warm for the marriage-rite,
  The bed for the birthday.'

'Nay, but I hear your mother cry,   95
  "Go bring this bride to bed!
And would she christen her babe unborn
  So wet she comes to wed?"

'I'll be your wife to cross your door
  And meet your mother's e'e.   100
We plighted troth to wed i' the kirk,
  And it's there I'll wed with ye.'

He's ta'en her by the short girdle
  And by the dripping sleeve:
'Go fetch Sir Jock my mother's priest, –   105
  You'll ask of him no leave.

'O it's one half-hour to reach the kirk
  And one for the marriage-rite;
And kirk and castle and castle-lands
  Shall be our babe's to-night.'   110

'The flood's in the kirkyard, Lord Sands,
  And round the belfry-stair.'
'I bade ye fetch the priest,' he said,
  'Myself shall bring him there.

'It's for the lilt of wedding bells   115
  We'll have the hail to pour,
And for the clink of bridle-reins
  The plashing of the oar.'

Beneath them on the nether hill
  A boat was floating wide: 120
Lord Sands swam out and caught the oars
  And rowed to the hill-side.

He's wrapped her in a green mantle
  And set her softly in;
Her hair was wet upon her face,   125
  Her face was grey and thin;
And 'Oh!' she said, 'lie still, my babe,
  It's out you must not win!'

But woe's my heart for Father John!
  As hard as he might pray,   130

There seemed no help but Noah's ark
   Or Jonah's fish that day.

The first strokes that the oars struck
   Were over the broad leas;
The next strokes that the oars struck   135
   They pushed beneath the trees;

The last stroke that the oars struck,
   The good boat's head was met,
And there the gate of the kirkyard
   Stood like a ferry-gate.   140

He's set his hand upon the bar
   And lightly leaped within:
He's lifted her to his left shoulder,
   Her knees beside his chin.

The graves lay deep beneath the flood   145
   Under the rain alone;
And when the foot-stone made him slip,
   He held by the head-stone.

The empty boat thrawed i' the wind
   Against the postern tied.   150
'Hold still, you've brought my love with me,
   You shall take back my bride.'

But woe's my heart for Father John
   And the saints he clamoured to!
There's never a saint but Christopher   155
   Might hale such buttocks through!

And 'Oh!' she said, 'on men's shoulders
   I well had thought to wend,
And well to travel with a priest,
   But not to have cared or ken'd.   160

'And oh!' she said, 'it's well this way
   That I thought to have fared, –
Not to have lighted at the kirk
   But stopped in the kirkyard.

'For it's oh and oh I prayed to God,   165
   Whose rest I hoped to win,
That when to-night at your board-head
   You'd bid the feast begin,

This water past your window-sill
  Might bear my body in.'   170

Now make the white bed warm and soft
  And greet the merry morn.
The night the mother should have died
  The young son shall be born.

Love's Nocturn

Master of the murmuring courts
  Where the shapes of sleep convene! –
Lo! my spirit here exhorts
  All the powers of thy demesne
  For their aid to woo my queen.   5
      What reports
  Yield thy jealous courts unseen?

Vaporous, unaccountable,
  Dreamland lies forlorn of light,
Hollow like a breathing shell.   10
  Ah! that from all dreams I might
  Choose one dream and guide its flight!
      I know well
  What her sleep should tell to-night.

There the dreams are multitudes: 15
  Some whose buoyance waits not sleep,
Deep within the August woods;
  Some that hum while rest may steep
  Weary labour laid a-heap;
      Interludes,   20
  Some, of grievous moods that weep.

Poets' fancies all are there:
  There the elf-girls flood with wings
Valleys full of plaintive air;
  There breathe perfumes; there in rings   25
  Whirl the foam-bewildered springs;
      Siren there
  Winds her dizzy hair and sings.

Thence the one dream mutually
  Dreamed in bridal unison,   30

Less than waking ecstasy;
   Half-formed visions that make moan
   In the house of birth alone;
      And what we
   At death's wicket see, unknown.   35

But for mine own sleep, it lies
   In one gracious form's control,
Fair with honourable eyes,
   Lamps of an auspicious soul:
   O their glance is loftiest dole,   40
      Sweet and wise,
   Wherein Love descries his goal.

Reft of her, my dreams are all
   Clammy trance that fears the sky:
Changing footpaths shift and fall;   45
   From polluted coverts nigh,
   Miserable phantoms sigh;
      Quakes the pall,
   And the funeral goes by.

Master, is it soothly said   50
   That, as echoes of man's speech
Far in secret clefts are made,
   So do all men's bodies reach
   Shadows o'er thy sunken beach, –
      Shape or shade   55
   In those halls pourtrayed of each?

Ah! might I, by thy good grace
   Groping in the windy stair,
(Darkness and the breath of space
   Like loud waters everywhere,)   60
   Meeting mine own image there
      Face to face,
   Send it from that place to her!

Nay, not I; but oh! do thou,
   Master, from thy shadowkind   65
Call my body's phantom now:
   Bid it bear its face declin'd
   Till its flight her slumbers find,
      And her brow
   Feel its presence bow like wind.   70

Where in groves the gracile Spring
  Trembles, with mute orison
Confidently strengthening,
    Water's voice and wind's as one
    Shed an echo in the sun.   75
          Soft as Spring,
    Master, bid it sing and moan.

Song shall tell how glad and strong
  Is the night she soothes away;
Moan shall grieve with that parched tongue   80
    Of the brazen hours of day:
    Sounds as of the springtide they,
          Moan and song,
    While the chill months long for May.

Not the prayers which with all leave   85
  The world's fluent woes prefer, –
Not the praise the world doth give,
    Dulcet fulsome whisperer; –
    Let it yield my love to her,
          And achieve   90
Strength that shall not grieve or err.

Wheresoe'er my dreams befall,
  Both at night-watch, (let it say,)
And where round the sundial
    The reluctant hours of day,   95
    Heartless, hopeless of their way,
          Rest and call; –
    There her glance doth fall and stay.

Suddenly her face is there:
  So do mounting vapours wreathe   100
Subtle-scented transports where
    The black firwood sets its teeth.
    Part the boughs and look beneath, –
          Lilies share
    Secret waters there, and breathe.   105

Master, bid my shadow bend
  Whispering thus till birth of light,
Lest new shapes that sleep may send

Scatter all its work to flight; –
Master, master of the night,
    Bid it spend
Speech, song, prayer, and end aright.   110

Yet, ah me! if her head
There another phantom lean
Murmuring o'er the fragrant bed, –   115
    Ah! and if my spirit's queen
    Smile those alien words between, –
        Ah! poor shade!
    Shall it strive, or fade unseen?

How should love's own messenger   120
    Strive with love and be love's foe?
Master, nay! If thus, in her,
    Sleep a wedded heart should show, –
    Silent let mine image go,
        Its old share   125
    Of thy spell-bound air to know.

Like a vapour wan and mute,
    Like a flame, so let it pass;
One low sigh across her lute,
    One dull breath against her glass;   130
    And to my sad soul, alas!
        One salute
    Cold as when death's foot shall pass.

Then, too, let all hopes of mine,
    All vain hopes by night and day,   135
Slowly at thy summoning sign
    Rise up pallid and obey.
    Dreams, if this is thus, were they: –
        Be they thine.
    And to dreamland pine away.   140

Yet from old time, life, not death,
    Master, in thy rule is rife:
Lo! through thee, with mingling breath,
    Adam woke beside his wife.
    O Love bring me so, for strife,   145
        Force and faith,
    Bring me so not death but life!

Yea, to Love himself is pour'd
This frail song of hope and fear.
Thou art Love, of one accord 150
With kind Sleep to bring her near,
Still-eyed, deep-eyed, ah how dear!
Master, Lord,
In her name implor'd, O hear!

The Woodspurge

The wind flapped loose, the wind was still,
Shaken out dead from tree and hill:
I had walked on at the wind's will, –
I sat now, for the wind was still.

Between my knees my forehead was, – 5
My lips, drawn in, said not Alas!
My hair was over in the grass,
My naked ears heard the day pass.

My eyes, wide open, had the run
Of some ten weeds to fix upon; 10
Among those few, out of the sun,
The woodspurge flowered, three cups in one.

From perfect grief there need not be
Wisdom or even memory:
One thing then learnt remains to me, – 15
The woodspurge has a cup of three.

Beauty and the Bird

She fluted with her mouth as when one sips,
And gently waved her golden head, inclin'd
Outside his cage close to the window-blind;
Till her fond bird, with little turns and dips,
Piped low to her of sweet companionships. 5
And when he made an end, some seed took she
And fed him from her tongue, which rosily
Peeped as a piercing bud between her lips.

And like the child in Chaucer, on whose tongue
  The Blessed Mary laid, when he was dead,   10
A grain, – who straightway praised her name in song:
  Even so, when she, a little lightly red,
Now turned on me and laughed, I heard the throng
  Of inner voices praise her golden head.

Jenny

'Vengeance of Jenny's case! Fie on her! Never name her, child!'
                                        – (Mistress Quickly)

    Lazy laughing languid Jenny,
    Fond of a kiss and fond of a guinea,
    Whose head upon my knee to-night
    Rests for a while, as if grown light
    With all our dances and the sound   5
    To which the wild tunes spun you round:
    Fair Jenny mine, the thoughtless queen
    Of kisses which the blush between
    Could hardly make much daintier;
    Whose eyes are as blue skies, whose hair   10
    Is countless gold incomparable:
    Fresh flower, scarce touched with signs that tell
    Of Love's exuberant hotbed: – Nay,
    Poor flower left torn since yesterday
    Until to-morrow leave you bare;   15
    Poor handful of bright spring-water
    Flung in the whirlpool's shrieking face;
    Poor shameful Jenny, full of grace
    Thus with your head upon my knee; –
    Whose person or whose purse may be   20
    The lodestar of your reverie?

      This room of yours, my Jenny, looks
    A change from mine so full of books,
    Whose serried ranks hold fast, forsooth,
    So many captive hours of youth, –   25
    The hours they thieve from day and night
    To make one's cherished work come right,
    And leave it wrong for all their theft,

Even as to-night my work was left:
Until I vowed that since my brain 30
And eyes of dancing seemed so fain,
My feet should have some dancing too: –
And thus it was I met with you.
Well, I suppose 'twas hard to part,
For here I am. And now, sweetheart, 35
You seem too tired to get to bed.

It was a careless life I led
When rooms like this were scarce so strange
Not long ago. What breeds the change, –
The many aims or the few years? 40
Because to-night it all appears
Something I do not know again.

The cloud's not danced out of my brain, –
The cloud that made it turn and swim
While hour by hour the books grew dim. 45
Why, Jenny, as I watch you there, –
For all your wealth of loosened hair,
Your silk ungirdled and unlac'd
And warm sweets open to the waist,
All golden in the lamplight's gleam, – 50
You know not what a book you seem,
Half-read by lightning in a dream!
How should you know, my Jenny? Nay,
And I should be ashamed to say: –
Poor beauty, so well worth a kiss! 55
But while my thought runs on like this
With wasteful whims more than enough,
I wonder what you're thinking of.

If of myself you think at all,
What is the thought? – conjectural 60
On sorry matters best unsolved? –
Or inly is each grace revolved
To fit me with a lure? – or (sad
To think!) perhaps you're merely glad
That I'm not drunk or ruffianly 65
And let you rest upon my knee.

For sometimes, were the truth confess'd,
You're thankful for a little rest, –

Glad from the crush to rest within,
From the heart-sickness and the din   70
Where envy's voice at virtue's pitch
Mocks you because your gown is rich;
And from the pale girl's dumb rebuke,
Whose ill-clad grace and toil-worn look
Proclaim the strength that keeps her weak   75
And other nights than yours bespeak;
And from the wise unchildish elf
To schoolmate lesser than himself
Pointing you out, what thing you are: –
Yes, from the daily jeer and jar,   80
From shame and shame's outbraving too,
Is rest not sometimes sweet to you? –
But most from the hatefulness of man
Who spares not to end what he began.
Whose acts are ill and his speech ill,   85
Who, having used you at his will,
Thrusts you aside as when I dine
I serve the dishes and the wine.

Well, handsome Jenny mine, sit up,
I've filled our glasses, let us sup,   90
And do not let me think of you,
Lest shame of yours suffice for two.
What, still so tired? Well, well then, keep
Your head there, so you do not sleep;
But that the weariness may pass   95
And leave you merry, take this glass.
Ah! lazy lily hand, more bless'd
If ne'er in rings it had been dress'd
Nor ever by a glove conceal'd!

Behold the lilies of the field,   100
They toil not neither do they spin;
(So doth the ancient text begin, –
Not of such rest as one of these
Can share.) Another rest and ease
Along each summer-sated path   105
From its new lord the garden hath,
Than that whose spring in blessings ran
Which praised the bounteous husbandman,
Ere yet, in days of hankering breath,
The lilies sickened unto death.   110

What, Jenny, are your lilies dead?
Aye, and the snow-white leaves are spread
Like winter on the garden-bed.
But you had roses left in May, –
They were not gone too. Jenny, nay,   115
But must your roses die, and those
Their purfled buds that should unclose?
Even so; the leaves are curled apart,
Still red as from the broken heart,
And here's the naked stem of thorns.   120

    Nay, nay, mere words. Here nothing warns
As yet of winter. Sickness here
Or want alone could waken fear, –
Nothing but passion wrings a tear.
Except when there may rise unsought   125
Haply at times a passing thought
Of the old days which seem to be
Much older than any history
That is written in any book;
When she would lie in fields and look   130
Along the ground through the blown grass,
And wonder where the city was,
Far out of sight, whose broil and bale
They told her then for a child's tale.

    Jenny, you know the city now.   135
A child can tell the tale there, how
Some things which are not yet enroll'd
In market-lists are bought and sold
Even till the early Sunday light,
When Saturday night is market-night   140
Everywhere, be it dry or wet,
And market-night in the Haymarket.
Our learned London children know,
Poor Jenny, all your pride and woe;
Have seen your lifted silken skirt   145
Advertise dainties through the dirt;
Have seen your coach-wheels splash rebuke
On virtue; and have learned your look
When, wealth and health slipped past, you stare
Along the streets alone, and there,   150

Round the long park, across the bridge,
The cold lamps at the pavement's edge
Wind on together and apart,
A fiery serpent for your heart.

    Let the thoughts pass, an empty cloud!   155
Suppose I were to think aloud, –
What if to her all this were said?
Why, as a volume seldom read
Being opened halfway shuts again,
So might the pages of her brain   160
Be parted at such words, and thence
Close back upon the dusty sense.
For is there hue or shape defin'd
In Jenny's desecrated mind,
Where all contagious currents meet,   165
A Lethe of the middle street?
Nay, it reflects not any face,
Nor sound is in its sluggish pace,
But as they coil those eddies clot,
And night and day remember not.   170

    Why, Jenny, you're asleep at last! –
Asleep, poor Jenny, hard and fast, –
So young and soft and tired; so fair,
With chin thus nestled in your hair,
Mouth quiet, eyelids almost blue   175
As if some sky of dreams shone through!

    Just as another woman sleeps!
Enough to throw one's thoughts in heaps
Of doubt and horror, – what to say
Or think, – this awful secret sway,   180
The potter's power over the clay!
Of the same lump (it has been said)
For honour and dishonour made,
Two sister vessels. Here is one.

    My cousin Nell is fond of fun,   185
And fond of dress, and change, and praise,
So mere a woman in her ways:
And if her sweet eyes rich in youth
Are like her lips that tell the truth,
My cousin Nell is fond of love.   190

And she's the girl I'm proudest of.
Who does not prize her, guard her well?
The love of change, in cousin Nell,
Shall find the best and hold it dear:
The unconquered mirth turn quieter   195
Not through her own, through others' woe:
The conscious pride of beauty glow
Beside another's pride in her,
One little part of all they share.
For Love himself shall ripen these   200
In a kind soil to just increase
Through years of fertilizing peace.

Of the same lump (as it is said)
For honour and dishonour made,
Two sister vessels. Here is one.   205

It makes a goblin of the sun.

So pure, – so fall'n! How dare to think
Of the first common kindred link?
Yet, Jenny, till the world shall burn
It seems that all things take their turn;   210
And who shall say but this fair tree
May need, in changes that may be,
Your children's children's charity?
Scorned then, no doubt, as you are scorn'd!
Shall no man hold his pride forewarn'd   215
Till in the end, the Day of Days,
At Judgement, one of his own race,
As frail and lost as you, shall rise, –
His daughter, with his mother's eyes?

How Jenny's clock ticks on the shelf!   220
Might not the dial scorn itself
That has such hours to register?
Yet as to me, even so to her
Are golden sun and silver moon,
In daily largesse of earth's boon,   225
Counted for life-coins to one tune.
And if, as blindfold fates are toss'd,
Through some one man this life be lost,
Shall soul not somehow pay for soul?

Fair shines the gilded aureole   230
In which our highest painters place
Some living woman's simple face.
And the stilled features thus descried
As Jenny's long throat droops aside, –
The shadows where the cheeks are thin,   235
And pure wide curve from ear to chin, –
With Raffael's or Da Vinci's hand
To show them to men's souls, might stand,
Whole ages long, the whole world through,
For preachings of what God can do.   240
What has man done here? How atone,
Great God, for this which man has done?
And for the body and soul which by
Man's pitiless doom must now comply
With lifelong hell, what lullaby   245
Of sweet forgetful second birth
Remains? All dark. No sign on earth
What measure of God's rest endows
The many mansions of his house.

    If but a woman's heart might see   250
Such erring heart unerringly
For once! But that can never be.

    Like a rose shut in a book
In which pure women may not look,
For its base pages claim control   255
To crush the flower within the soul;
Where through each dead rose-leaf that clings,
Pale as transparent psyche-wings,
To the vile text, are traced such things
As might make lady's cheek indeed   260
More than a living rose to read;
So nought save foolish foulness may
Watch with hard eyes the sure decay;
And so the life-blood of this rose,
Puddled with shameful knowledge, flows   265
Through leaves no chaste hand may unclose:
Yet still it keeps such faded show
Of when 'twas gathered long ago,
That the crushed petals' lovely grain,
The sweetness of the sanguine stain,   270
Seen of a woman's eyes, must make

Her pitiful heart, so prone to ache,
Love roses better for its sake: –
Only that this can never be: –
Even so unto her sex is she.   275

Yet, Jenny, looking long at you,
The woman almost fades from view.
A cipher of man's changeless sum
Of lust, past, present, and to come,
Is left. A riddle that one shrinks   280
To challenge from the scornful sphinx.

Like a toad within a stone
Seated while Time crumbles on;
Which sits there since the earth was curs'd
For Man's transgression at the first;   285
Which, living through all centuries,
Not once has seen the sun arise;
Whose life, to its cold circle charmed,
The earth's whole summers have not warmed;
Which always – whitherso the stone   290
Be flung – sits there, deaf, blind, alone; –
Aye, and shall not be driven out
Till that which shuts him round about
Break at the very Master's stroke,
And the dust thereof vanish as smoke,   295
And the seed of Man vanish as dust: –
Even so within this world is Lust.

Come, come, what use in thoughts like this?
Poor little Jenny, good to kiss, –
You'd not believe by what strange roads   300
Thought travels, when your beauty goads
A man to-night to think of toads!
Jenny, wake up.... Why, there's the dawn!

And there's an early waggon drawn
To market, and some sheep that jog   305
Bleating before a barking dog;
And the old streets come peering through
Another night that London knew;
And all as ghostlike as the lamps.

So on the wings of day decamps   310
My last night's frolic. Glooms begin

To shiver off as lights creep in
Past the gauze curtains half drawn-to,
And the lamp's doubled shade grows blue, –
Your lamp, my Jenny, kept alight,   315
Like a wise virgin's, all one night!
And in the alcove coolly spread
Glimmers with dawn your empty bed;
And yonder your fair face I see
Reflected lying on my knee,   320
Where teems with first foreshadowings
Your pier-glass scrawled with diamond rings.

    And now without, as if some word
Had called upon them that they heard,
The London sparrows far and nigh   325
Clamour together suddenly;
And Jenny's cage-bird grown awake
Here in their song his part must take,
Because here too the day doth break.

    And somehow in myself the dawn   330
Among stirred clouds and veils withdrawn
Strikes greyly on her. Let her sleep.
But will it wake her if I heap
These cushions thus beneath her head
Where my knee was? No, – there's your bed,   335
My Jenny, while you dream. And there
I lay among your golden hair
Perhaps the subject of your dreams,
These golden coins.
                For still one deems
That Jenny's flattering sleep confers   340
New magic on the magic purse, –
Grim web, how clogged with shrivelled flies!
Between the threads fine fumes arise
And shape their pictures in the brain.
There roll no streets in glare and rain,   345
Nor flagrant man-swine whets his tusk;
But delicately sighs in musk
The homage of the dim boudoir;
Or like a palpitating star
Thrilled into song, the opera-night   350
Breathes faint in the quick pulse of light;

Or at the carriage-window shine
Rich wares for choice; or, free to dine,
Whirls through its hour of health (divine
For her) the concourse of the Park.   355
And though in the discounted dark
Her functions there and here are one,
Beneath the lamps and in the sun
There reigns at least the acknowledged belle
Apparelled beyond parallel.   360
Ah Jenny, yes, we know your dreams.

    For even the Paphian Venus seems
A goddess o'er the realms of love,
When silver-shrined in shadowy grove:
Aye, or let offerings nicely placed   365
But hide Priapus to the waist,
And whoso looks on him shall see
An eligible deity.

    Why, Jenny, waking here alone
May help you to remember one,   370
Though all the memory's long outworn
Of many a double-pillowed morn.
I think I see you when you wake,
And rub your eyes for me, and shake
My gold, in rising, from your hair,   375
A Danaë for a moment there.

    Jenny, my love rang true! for still
Love at first sight is vague, until
That tinkling makes him audible.

    And must I mock you to the last,   380
Ashamed of my own shame, – aghast
Because some thoughts not born amiss
Rose at a poor fair face like this?
Well, of such thoughts so much I know:
In my life, as in hers, they show,   385
By a far gleam which I may near,
A dark path I can strive to clear.

    Only one kiss. Good-bye, my dear.

Even So

So it is, my dear.
All such things touch secret strings
    For heavy hearts to hear.
    So it is, my dear.

    Very like indeed: 5
Sea and sky, afar, on high,
    Sand and strewn seaweed, –
    Very like indeed.

    But the sea stands spread
As one wall with the flat skies,   10
Where the lean black craft like flies
    Seem well-nigh stagnated,
    Soon to drop off dead.

    Seemed it so to us
When I was thine and thou wast mine,   15
    And all these things were thus,
    But all our world in us?

    Could we be so now?
Not if all beneath heaven's pall
    Lay dead but I and thou,   20
    Could we be so now!

A New Year's Burden

Along the grass sweet airs are blown
    Our way this day in Spring.
Of all the songs that we have known
    Now which one shall we sing?
        Not that, my love, ah no! –   5
        Not this, my love? why, so! –
Yet both were ours, but hours will come and go.

The grove is all a pale frail mist,
    The new year sucks the sun.
Of all the kisses that we kissed   10
    Now which shall be the one?

Not that, my love, ah no! –
Not this, my love? – heigh-ho
For all the sweets that all the winds can blow!

The branches cross above our eyes,   15
  The skies are in a net:
And what's the thing beneath the skies
  We two would most forget?
        Not birth, my love, no, no –
        Not death, my love, no, no, –   20
The love once ours, but ours long hours ago.

A Little While

A little while a little love
  The hour yet bears for thee and me
  Who have not drawn the veil to see
If still our heaven be lit above.
Thou merely, at the day's last sigh,   5
  Hast felt thy soul prolong the tone;
And I have heard the night-wind cry
  And deemed its speech mine own.

A little while a little love
  The scattering autumn hoards for us   10
  Whose bower is not yet ruinous
Nor quite unleaved our songless grove.
Only across the shaken boughs
  We hear the flood-tides seek the sea,
And deep in both our hearts they rouse   15
  One wail for thee and me.

A little while a little love
  May yet be ours who have not said
  The word it makes our eyes afraid
To know that each is thinking of.
Not yet the end: be our lips dumb   20
  In smiles a little season yet:
I'll tell thee, when the end is come,
  How we may best forget.

An Old Song Ended

'How should I your true love know
  From another one?'
'By his cockle-hat and staff
  And his sandal-shoon.'

'And what signs have told you now   5
  That he hastens home?'
'Lo! the spring is nearly gone,
  He is nearly come.'

'For a token is there nought,
  Say, that he should bring?   10
'He will bear a ring I gave
  And another ring.'

'How may I, when he shall ask,
  Tell him who lies there?'
'Nay, but leave my face unveiled   15
  And unbound my hair.'

'Can you say to me some word
  I shall say to him?'
'Say I'm looking in his eyes
  Though my eyes are dim.'   20

The Song of the Bower

Say, is it day, is it dusk in thy bower,
  Thou whom I long for, who longest for me?
Oh! be it light, be it night, 'tis Love's hour,
  Love's that is fettered as Love's that is free.
Free Love has leaped to that innermost chamber,   5
  Oh! the last time, and the hundred before:
Fettered Love, motionless, can but remember,
  Yet something that sighs from him passes the door.

Nay, but my heart when it flies to thy bower,
  What does it find there that knows it again?   10
There it must droop like a shower-beaten flower,
  Red at the rent core and dark with the rain.

Ah! yet what shelter is still shed above it, –
    What waters still image its leaves torn apart?
Thy soul is the shade that clings round it to love it,   15
    And tears are its mirror deep down in thy heart.

What were my prize, could I enter thy bower,
    This day, to-morrow, at eve or at morn?
Large lovely arms and a neck like a tower,
    Bosom then heaving that now lies forlorn.   20
Kindled with love-breath, (the sun's kiss is colder!)
    Thy sweetness all near me, so distant to-day;
My hand round thy neck and thy hand on my shoulder,
    My mouth to thy mouth as the world melts away.

What is it keeps me afar from thy bower, –   25
    My spirit, my body, so fain to be there?
Waters engulfing or fires that devour? –
    Earth heaped against me or death in the air?
Nay, but in day-dreams, for terror, for pity,
    The trees wave their heads with an omen to tell;   30
Nay, but in night-dreams, throughout the dark city,
    The hours, clashed together, lose count in the bell.

Shall I not one day remember thy bower,
    One day when all days are one day to me? –
Thinking, 'I stirred not, and yet had the power,' –   35
    Yearning, 'Ah God, if again it might be!'
Peace, peace! such a small lamp illumes, on this highway,
    So dimly so few steps in front of my feet, –
Yet shows me that her way is parted from my way....
    Out of sight, beyond light, at what goal may we meet?   40

John of Tours
(Old French)

John of Tours is back with peace,
But he comes home ill at ease.

'Good-morrow, mother.' 'Good-morrow, son;
Your wife has borne you a little one.'

'Go now, mother, go before,   5
Make me a bed upon the floor;

'Very low your foot must fall,
That my wife hear not at all.'

As it neared the midnight toll,
John of Tours gave up his soul.   10

'Tell me now, my mother my dear,
What's the crying that I hear?'

'Daughter, it's the children wake
Crying with their teeth that ache.'

'Tell me though, my mother my dear,   15
What's the knocking that I hear?'

'Daughter, it's the carpenter
Mending planks upon the stair.'

'Tell me too, my mother my dear,
What's the singing that I hear?'   20

'Daughter, it's the priests in rows
Going round about our house.'

'Tell me then, my mother my dear,
What's the dress that I should wear?'

'Daughter, any reds or blues,   25
But the black is most in use.'

'Nay, but say, my mother my dear,
Why do you fall weeping here?'

'Oh! the truth must be said, –
It's that John of Tours is dead.'   30

'Mother, let the sexton know
That the grave must be for two;

'Aye, and still have room to spare,
For you must shut the baby there.'

My Father's Close
(Old French)

Inside my father's close,
   (Fly away O my heart away!)
Sweet apple-blossom blows
    So sweet.

Three kings' daughters fair,   5
   (Fly away O my heart away!)
They lie below it there
    So sweet.

'Ah!' says the eldest one,
   (Fly away O my heart away!)   10
'I think the day's begun
    So sweet.'

'Ah!' says the second one,
   (Fly away O my heart away!)
'Far off I hear the drum   15
    So sweet.

'Ah!' says the youngest one,
   (Fly away O my heart away!)
'It's my true love, my own,
    So sweet.   20

'Oh! if he fight and win,'
   (Fly away O my heart away!)
'I keep my love for him,
    So sweet:
Oh! let him lose or win,
    He hath it still complete.'   25

Dantis Tenebræ
(*In Memory of my Father*)

And didst thou know indeed, when at the font
  Together with thy name thou gav'st me his,
  That also on thy son must Beatrice
Decline her eyes according to her wont,
Accepting me to be of those that haunt   5
  The vale of magical dark mysteries
  Where to the hills her poet's foot-track lies
And wisdom's living fountain to his chaunt
Trembles in music? This is that steep land
  Where he that holds his journey stands at gaze   10
    Tow'rd sunset, when the clouds like a new height
Seem piled to climb. These things I understand:
  For here, where day still soothes my lifted face,
  On thy bowed head, my father, fell the night.

Aspecta Medusa

Andromeda, by Perseus saved and wed,
Hankered each day to see the Gorgon's head:
Till o'er a fount he held it, bade her lean,
And mirrored in the wave was safely seen
That death she lived by.

              Let not thine eyes know   5
Any forbidden thing itself, although
It once should save as well as kill: but be
Its shadow upon life enough for thee.

Plighted Promise

In a soft-complexioned sky,
  Fleeting rose and kindling grey,
Have you seen Aurora fly
  At the break of day?
So my maiden, so my plighted may   5

Blushing cheek and gleaming eye
   Lifts to look my way.

Where the inmost leaf is stirred
   With the heart-beat of the grove,
Have you heard a hidden bird   10
   Cast her note above?
So my lady, so my lovely love,
   Echoing Cupid's prompted word,
   Makes a tune thereof.

Have you seen, at heaven's mid-height,   15
   In the moon-rack's ebb and tide,
Venus leap forth burning white,
   Dian pale and hide?
So my bright breast-jewel, so my bride,
   One sweet night, when fear takes flight,   20
   Shall leap against my side.

Venus Verticordia

(FOR A PICTURE)

She hath the apple in her hand for thee,
   Yet almost in her heart would hold it back;
   She muses, with her eyes upon the track
Of that which in thy spirit they can see.
Haply, 'Behold, he is at peace,' saith she;   5
   'Alas! the apple for his lips, – the dart
   That follows its brief sweetness to his heart, –
The wandering of his feet perpetually!'

A little space her glance is still and coy;
   But if she give the fruit that works her spell,   10
Those eyes shall flame as for her Phrygian boy.
   Then shall her bird's strained throat the woe foretell,
   And her far seas moan as a single shell,
And her grove glow with love-lit fires of Troy.

The Passover in the Holy Family

(FOR A DRAWING)[1]

Here meet together the prefiguring day
   And day prefigured. 'Eating, thou shalt stand,
   Feet shod, loins girt, thy road-staff in thine hand,
With blood-stained door and lintel,' – did God say
By Moses' mouth in ages passed away.   5
   And now, where this poor household doth comprise
   At Pashcal-Feast two kindred families, –
Lo! the slain lamb confronts the Lamb to slay.

The pyre is piled. What agony's crown attained,
   What shadow of death the Boy's fair brow subdues   10
Who holds that blood wherewith the porch is stained
   By Zachary the priest? John binds the shoes
   He deemed himself not worthy to unloose;
And Mary culls the bitter herbs ordained.

1 The scene is in the house-porch, where Christ holds a bowl of blood from which
Zacharias is sprinkling the posts and lintel. Joseph has brought the lamb and
Elisabeth lights the pyre. The shoes which John fastens and the bitter herbs which
Mary is gathering form part of the ritual.

Mary Magdalene at the Door of Simon the Pharisee

(FOR A DRAWING)[1]

'Why wilt thou cast the roses from thine hair?
   Nay, be thou all a rose, – wreath, lips, and cheek.
   Nay, not this house, – that banquet-house we seek;
See how they kiss and enter; come thou there.
This delicate day of love we two will share   5
   Till at our ear love's whispering night shall speak.
   What, sweet one, – hold'st thou still the foolish freak?
Nay, when I kiss thy feet they'll leave the stair.'

'Oh loose me! See'st thou not my Bridegroom's face
   That draws me to Him? For His feet my kiss,   10
   My hair, my tears He craves to-day: – and oh!
What words can tell what other day and place
   Shall see me clasp those blood-stained feet of His?
   He needs me, calls me, loves me: let me go!'

1 In the drawing Mary has left a festal procession, and is ascending by a sudden impulse the steps of the house where she sees Christ. Her lover has followed her and is trying to turn her back.

Cassandra

(FOR A DRAWING)[1]

I

Rend, rend thine hair, Cassandra: he will go
  Yea, rend thy garments, wring thine hands, and cry
  From Troy still towered to the unreddened sky.
See, all but she that bore thee mock thy woe: –
He most whom that fair woman arms, with show   5
  Of wrath on her bent brows; for in this place
  This hour thou bad'st all men in Helen's face
The ravished ravishing prize of Death to know.

What eyes, what ears hath sweet Andromache,
  Save for her Hector's form and step; as tear   10
    On tear make salt the warm last kiss he gave?
He goes. Cassandra's words beat heavily
  Like crows above his crest, and at his ear
    Ring hollow in the shield that shall not save.

II

'O Hector, gone, gone, gone! O Hector, thee   15
  Two chariots wait, in Troy long bless'd and curs'd;
  And Grecian spear and Phrygian sand athirst
Crave from thy veins the blood of victory.
Lo! long upon our hearth the brand had we,
  Lit for the roof-tree's ruin: and to-day   20
  The ground-stone quits the wall, – the wind hath way, –
And higher and higher the wings of fire are free.

O Paris, Paris! O thou burning brand,
  Thou beacon of the sea whence Venus rose,
Lighting thy race to shipwreck! Even that hand   25
  Wherewith she took thine apple let her close
  Within thy curls at last, and while Troy glows
Lift thee her trophy to the sea and land.'

1 The subject shows Cassandra prophesying among her kindred, as Hector leaves them for his last battle. They are on the platform of a fortress, from which the

Trojan troops are marching out. Helen is arming Paris; Priam soothes Hecuba; and Andromache holds the child to her bosom.

Pandora

(FOR A PICTURE)

What of the end, Pandora? Was it thine,
  The deed that set these fiery pinions free?
  Ah! wherefore did the Olympian consistory
In its own likeness make thee half divine?
Was it that Juno's brow might stand a sign   5
  For ever? and the mien of Pallas be
  A deadly thing? and that all men might see
In Venus' eyes the gaze of Proserpine?

What of the end? These beat their wings at will,
The ill-born things, the good things turned to ill, –   10
  Powers of the impassioned hours prohibited.
Aye, hug the casket now! Whither they go
Thou mayst not dare to think: nor canst thou know
  If Hope still pent there be alive or dead.

For
'The Wine of Circe'
by Edward Burne Jones

Dusk-haired and gold-robed o'er the golden wine
  She stoops, wherein, distilled of death and shame,
  Sink the black drops; while, lit with fragrant flame,
Round her spread board the golden sunflowers shine.
Doth Helios here with Hecatè combine   5
  (O Circe, thou their votaress!) to proclaim
  For these thy guests all rapture in Love's name,
Till pitiless Night gave Day the countersign?

Lords of their hour, they come. And by her knee
  Those cowering beasts, their equals heretofore,   10
Wait; who with them in new equality
  To-night shall echo back the unchanging roar
  Which sounds for ever from the tide-strown shore
Where the dishevelled seaweed hates the sea.

Three Translations from François Villon, 1450

I

THE BALLAD OF DEAD LADIES

Tell me now in what hidden way is
  Lady Flora the lovely Roman?
Where's Hipparchia, and where is Thais,
  Neither of them the fairer woman?
  Where is Echo, beheld of no man,   5
Only heard on river and mere, –
  She whose beauty was more than human? . . .
But where are the snows of yester-year?

Where's Héloise, the learned nun,
  For whose sake Abeillard, I ween,   10
Lost manhood and put priesthood on?
  (From Love he won such dule and teen!)
  And where, I pray you, is the Queen
Who willed that Buridan should steer
  Sewed in a sack's mouth down the Seine? . . .   15
But where are the snows of yester-year?

White Queen Blanche, like a queen of lilies,
  With a voice like any mermaiden –
Bertha Broadfoot, Beatrice, Alice,
  And Ermengarde the lady of Maine, –   20
  And that good Joan whom Englishmen
At Rouen doomed and burned her there, –
  Mother of God, where are they then? . . .
But where are the snows of yester-year?

Nay, never ask this week, fair lord,   25
  Where they are gone, nor yet this year,
Except with this for an overword, –
  But where are the snows of yester-year?

II

TO DEATH, OF HIS LADY

Death, of thee do I make my moan,
  Who hadst my lady away from me,
  Nor wilt assuage thine enmity
Till with her life thou hast mine own;

For since that hour my strength has flown.   5
   Lo! what wrong was her life to thee,
         Death?

Two we were, and the heart was one;
   Which now being dead, dead I must be,
   Or seem alive as lifelessly   10
As in the choir the painted stone,
         Death!

III

HIS MOTHER'S SERVICE TO OUR LADY

Lady of Heaven and earth, and therewithal
   Crowned Empress of the nether clefts of Hell, –
I, thy poor Christian, on thy name do call,
   Commending me to thee, with thee to dwell,
   Albeit in nought I be commendable.   5
But all mine undeserving may not mar
Such mercies as thy sovereign mercies are;
   Without the which (as true words testify)
No soul can reach thy Heaven so fair and far.
   Even in this faith I choose to live and die.   10

Unto thy Son say thou that I am His,
   And to me graceless make Him gracious.
Sad Mary of Egypt lacked not of that bliss,
   Nor yet the sorrowful clerk Theophilus,
   Whose bitter sins were set aside even thus   15
Though to the Fiend his bounden service was.
Oh help me, lest in vain for me should pass
   (Sweet Virgin that shalt have no loss thereby!)
The blessed Host and sacring of the Mass.
   Even in this faith I choose to live and die.   20

A pitiful poor woman, shrunk and old,
   I am, and nothing learn'd in letter-lore.
Within my parish-cloister I behold
   A painted Heaven where harps and lutes adore,
   And eke an Hell whose damned folk seethe full sore: 25
One bringeth fear, the other joy to me.
That joy, great Goddess, make thou mine to be, –
   Thou of whom all must ask it even as I;
And that which faith desires, that let it see.
   For in this faith I choose to live and die.   30

O excellent Virgin Princess! thou didst bear
King Jesus, the most excellent comforter,
Who even of this our weakness craved a share
    And for our sake stooped to us from on high,
Offering to death His young life sweet and fair.   35
Such as He is, Our Lord, I Him declare,
    And in this faith I choose to live and die.

One Girl
(A combination from Sappho)

I

Like the sweet apple which reddens upon the topmost bough,
A-top on the topmost twig, – which the pluckers forgot,
  somehow, –
Forgot it not, nay, but got it not, for none could get it till
  now.

II

Like the wild hyacinth flower which on the hills is found,
Which the passing feet of the shepherds for ever tear and
  wound,
Until the purple blossom is trodden into the ground.   5

Love-Lily

Between the hands, between the brows,
    Between the lips of Love-Lily,
A spirit is born whose birth endows
    My blood with fire to burn through me;
Who breathes upon my gazing eyes,   5
    Who laughs and murmurs in mine ear,
At whose least touch my colour flies,
    And whom my life grows faint to hear.

Within the voice, within the heart,
    Within the mind of Love-Lily,   10
A spirit is born who lifts apart
    His tremulous wings and looks at me;

Who on my mouth his finger lays,
   And shows, while whispering lutes confer,
That Eden of Love's watered ways   15
   Whose winds and spirits worship her.

Brows, hands, and lips, heart, mind, and voice,
   Kisses and words of Love-Lily, –
Oh! bid me with your joy rejoice
   Till riotous longing rest in me!   20
Ah! let not hope be still distraught,
   But find in her its gracious goal,
Whose speech Truth knows not from her thought
   Nor Love her body from her soul.

First Love Remembered

Peace in her chamber, wheresoe'er
   It be, a holy place:
The thought still brings my soul such grace
   As morning meadows wear.

Whether it still be small and light,   5
   A maid's who dreams alone,
As from her orchard-gate the moon
   Its ceiling showed at night:

Or whether, in a shadow dense
   As nuptial hymns invoke,   10
Innocent maidenhood awoke
   To married innocence:

There still the thanks unheard await
   The unconscious gift bequeathed;
For there my soul this hour has breathed   15
   An air inviolate.

Troy Town

Heavenborn Helen, Sparta's queen,
    (O Troy Town!)
Had two breasts of heavenly sheen,
The sun and moon of the heart's desire:
All Love's lordship lay between.   5
    (O Troy's down,
    Tall Troy's on fire!)

Helen knelt at Venus' shrine,
    (O Troy Town!)
Saying, 'A little gift is mine,   10
A little gift for a heart's desire.
Hear me speak and make me a sign!
    (O Troy's down,
    Tall Troy's on fire!)

'Look, I bring thee a carven cup;   15
    (O Troy Town!)
See it here as I hold it up, –
Shaped it is to the heart's desire,
Fit to fill when the gods would sup.
    (O Troy's down,   20
    Tall Troy's on fire!)

'It was moulded like my breast
    (O Troy Town!)
He that sees it may not rest,
Rest at all for his heart's desire.
O give ear to my heart's behest!   25
    (O Troy's down,
    Tall Troy's on fire!)

'See my breast, how like it is;
    (O Troy Town!)   30
See it bare for the air to kiss!
Is the cup to thy heart's desire?
O for the breast, O make it his!
    (O Troy's down,
    Tall Troy's on fire!)   35

'Yea, for my bosom here I sue;
    (O Troy Town!)

Thou must give it where 'tis due,
Give it there to the heart's desire.
Whom do I give my bosom to?　　　　　40
　　　(*O Troy's down,*
　　　Tall Troy's on fire!)

'Each twin breast is an apple sweet
　　　(*O Troy Town!*)
Once an apple stirred the beat　　　　45
Of thy heart with the heart's desire: –
Say, who brought it then to thy feet?
　　　(*O Troy's down,*
　　　Tall Troy's on fire!)

'They that claimed it then were three:　　50
　　　(*O Troy Town!*)
For thy sake two hearts did he
Make forlorn of the heart's desire.
Do for him as he did for thee!
　　　(*O Troy's down,*　　　　55
　　　Tall Troy's on fire!)

'Mine are apples grown to the south,
　　　(*O Troy Town!*)
Grown to taste in the days of drouth,
Taste and waste to the heart's desire:　　60
Mine are apples meet for his mouth.'
　　　(*O Troy's down,*
　　　Tall Troy's on fire!)

Venus looked on Helen's gift,
　　　(*O Troy Town!*)　　　　65
Looked and smiled with subtle drift,
Saw the work of her heart's desire: –
'There thou kneel'st for Love to lift!'
　　　(*O Troy's down,*
　　　Tall Troy's on fire!)　　　　70

Venus looked in Helen's face,
　　　(*O Troy Town!*)
Knew far off an hour and place,
And fire lit from the heart's desire;
Laughed and said, 'Thy gift hath grace!'　　75
　　　(*O Troy's down,*
　　　Tall Troy's on fire!)

Cupid looked on Helen's breast,
　　　(*O Troy Town!*)
Saw the heart within its nest,
Saw the flame of the heart's desire, –
Marked his arrow's burning crest.
　　　(*O Troy's down,*
　　　Tall Troy's on fire!)

Cupid took another dart,
　　　(*O Troy Town!*)
Fledged it for another heart,
Winged the shaft with the heart's desire,
Drew the string and said, 'Depart!'
　　　(*O Troy's down,*
　　　Tall Troy's on fire!)

Paris turned upon his bed,
　　　(*O Troy Town!*)
Turned upon his bed and said,
Dead at heart with the heart's desire, –
'O to clasp her golden head!'
　　　(*O Troy's down,*
　　　Tall Troy's on fire!)

Eden Bower

It was Lilith the wife of Adam:
　　　(*Eden bower's in flower.*)
Not a drop of her blood was human,
But she was made like a soft sweet woman.

Lilith stood on the skirts of Eden;
　　　(*And O the bower and the hour!*)
She was the first that thence was driven;
With her was hell and with Eve was heaven.

In the ear of the Snake said Lilith: –
　　　(*Eden bower's in flower.*)
'To thee I come when the rest is over;
A snake was I when thou wast my lover.

'I was the fairest snake in Eden:
　　　(*And O the bower and the hour!*)

By the earth's will, new form and feature   15
Made me a wife for the earth's new creature.

'Take me thou as I come from Adam:
     (*Eden bower's in flower.*)
Once again shall my love subdue thee;
The past is past and I am come to thee.   20

'O but Adam was thrall to Lilith!
     (*And O the bower and the hour!*)
All the threads of my hair are golden,
And there in a net his heart was holden.

'O and Lilith was queen of Adam!   25
     (*Eden bower's in flower.*)
All the day and the night together
My breath could shake his soul like a feather.

'What great joys had Adam and Lilith! –
     (*And O the bower and the hour!*)   30
Sweet close rings of the serpent's twining,
As heart in heart lay sighing and pining.

'What bright babes had Lilith and Adam! –
     (*Eden bower's in flower.*)
Shapes that coiled in the woods and waters,   35
Glittering sons and radiant daughters.

'O thou God, the Lord God of Eden!
     (*And O the bower and the hour!*)
Say, was this fair body for no man,
That of Adam's flesh thou mak'st him a woman?   40

'O thou Snake, the King-snake of Eden!
     (*Eden bower's in flower.*)
God's strong will our necks are under,
But thou and I may cleave it in sunder.

'Help, sweet Snake, sweet lover of Lilith!   45
     (*And O the bower and the hour!*)
And let God learn how I loved and hated
Man in the image of God created.

'Help me once against Eve and Adam!
     (*Eden bower's in flower.*)   50
Help me once for this one endeavour,
And then my love shall be thine for ever!

'Strong is God, the fell foe of Lilith:
          (*And O the bower and the hour!*)
Nought in heaven or earth may affright him;   55
But join thou with me and we will smite him.

'Strong is God, the great God of Eden:
          (*Eden bower's in flower.*)
Over all He made He hath power;
But lend me thou thy shape for an hour!   60

'Lend thy shape for the love of Lilith!
          (*And O the bower and the hour!*)
Look, my mouth and my cheek are ruddy,
And thou art cold, and fire is my body.

'Lend thy shape for the hate of Adam!   65
          (*Eden bower's in flower.*)
That he may wail my joy that forsook him,
And curse the day when the bride-sleep took him.

'Lend thy shape for the shame of Eden!
          (*And O the bower and the hour!*)   70
Is not the foe-God weak as the foeman
When love grows hate in the heart of a woman?

'Would'st thou know the heart's hope of Lilith?
          (*Eden bower's in flower.*)
Then bring thou close thine head till it glisten   75
Along my breast, and lip me and listen.

'Am I sweet, O sweet Snake of Eden?
          (*And O the bower and the hour!*)
Then ope thine ear to my warm mouth's cooing
And learn what deed remains for our doing.   80

'Thou didst hear when God said to Adam: –
          (*Eden bower's in flower.*)
"Of all this wealth I have made thee warden;
Thou'rt free to eat of the trees of the garden:

' "Only of one tree eat not in Eden;   85
          (*And O the bower and the hour!*)
All save one I give to thy freewill, –
The Tree of the Knowledge of Good and Evil."

'O my love, come nearer to Lilith!
          (*Eden bower's in flower.*)   90

In thy sweet folds bind me and bend me,
And let me feel the shape thou shalt lend me!

'In thy shape I'll go back to Eden;
    (And O the bower and the hour!)
In these coils that Tree will I grapple,   95
And stretch this crowned head forth by the apple.

'Lo, Eve bends to the breath of Lilith!
    (Eden bower's in flower.)
O how then shall my heart desire
All her blood as food to its fire!   100

'Lo, Eve bends to the words of Lilith! –
    (And O the bower and the hour!)
"Nay, this Tree's fruit, – why should ye hate it,
Or Death be born the day that ye ate it?

' "Nay, but on that great day in Eden.   105
    (Eden bower's in flower.)
By the help that in this wise Tree is,
God knows well ye shall be as He is."

'Then Eve shall eat and give unto Adam;
    (And O the bower and the hour!)
And then they both shall know they are naked,   110
And their hearts ache as my heart hath achèd.

'Aye, let them hide in the trees of Eden,
    (Eden bower's in flower.)
As in the cool of the day in the garden   115
God shall walk without pity or pardon.

'Hear, thou Eve, the man's heart in Adam!
    (And O the bower and the hour!)
Of his brave words hark to the bravest: –
"This the woman gave that thou gavest."   120

'Hear Eve speak, yea, list to her, Lilith!
    (Eden bower's in flower.)
Feast thine heart with words that shall sate it –
"This the serpent gave and I ate it."

'O proud Eve, cling close to thine Adam,   125
    (And O the bower and the hour!)
Driven forth as the beasts of his naming
By the sword that for ever is flaming.

'Know, thy path is known unto Lilith!
  (*Eden bower's in flower.*)   130
While the blithe birds sang at thy wedding,
There her tears grew thorns for thy treading.

'O my love, thou Love-snake of Eden!
  (*And O the bower and the hour!*)
O to-day and the day to come after!   135
Loose me, love, – give breath to my laughter!

'O bright Snake, the Death-worm of Adam!
  (*Eden bower's in flower.*)
Wreathe thy neck with my hair's bright tether,
And wear my gold and thy gold together! 140

'On that day on the skirts of Eden,
  (*And O the bower and the hour!*)
In thy shape shall I glide back to thee,
And in my shape for an instant view thee.

'But when thou'rt thou and Lilith is Lilith, 145
  (*Eden bower's in flower.*)
In what bliss past hearing or seeing
Shall each one drink of the other's being!

With cries of "Eve!" and "Eden!" and "Adam!"
  (*And O the bower and the hour!*)   150
How shall we mingle our love's caresses,
I in thy coils, and thou in my tresses!

'With those names, ye echoes of Eden,
  (*Eden bower's in flower.*)
Fire shall cry from my heart that burneth, – 155
"Dust he is and to dust returneth!"

'Yet to-day, thou master of Lilith, –
  (*And O the bower and the hour!*)
Wrap me round in the form I'll borrow
And let me tell thee of sweet to-morrow. 160

'In the planted garden eastward in Eden,
  (*Eden bower's in flower.*)
Where the river goes forth to water the garden,
The springs shall dry and the soil shall harden.

'Yea, where the bride-sleep fell upon Adam, 165
  (*And O the bower and the hour!*)

None shall hear when the storm-wind whistles
Through roses choked among thorns and thistles.

'Yea, beside the east-gate of Eden,
      (Eden bower's in flower.)   170
Where God joined them and none might sever,
The sword turns this way and that for ever.

'What of Adam cast out of Eden?
      (And O the bower and the hour!)
Lo! with care like a shadow shaken,   175
He tills the hard earth whence he was taken.

'What of Eve too, cast out of Eden?
      (Eden bower's in flower.)
Nay, but she, the bride of God's giving,
Must yet be mother of all men living.   180

'Lo, God's grace, by the grace of Lilith!
      (And O the bower and the hour!)
To Eve's womb, from our sweet to-morrow,
God shall greatly multiply sorrow.

'Fold me fast, O God-snake of Eden!   185
      (Eden bower's in flower.)
What more prize than love to impel thee?
Grip and lip my limbs as I tell thee!

'Lo! two babes for Eve and for Adam!
      (And O the bower and the hour!)
Lo! sweet Snake, the travail and treasure, – 190
Two men-children born for their pleasure!

'The first is Cain and the second Abel:
      (Eden bower's in flower.)
The soul of one shall be made thy brother,   195
And thy tongue shall lap the blood of the other.'
      (And O the bower and the hour!)

The Stream's Secret

What thing unto mine ear
Wouldst thou convey, – what secret thing,
O wandering water ever whispering?
Surely thy speech shall be of her.
Thou water, O thou whispering wanderer,   5
What message dost thou bring?

Say, hath not Love leaned low
This hour beside thy far well-head,
And there through jealous hollowed fingers said
The thing that most I long to know, –   10
Murmuring with curls all dabbled in thy flow
And washed lips rosy red?

He told it to thee there
Where thy voice hath a louder tone;
But where it welters to this little moan   15
His will decrees that I should hear.
Now speak: for with the silence is no fear,
And I am all alone.

Shall Time not still endow
One hour with life, and I and she   20
Slake in one kiss the thirst of memory?
Say stream; lest Love should disavow
Thy service, and the bird upon the bough
Sing first to tell it me.

What whisperest thou? Nay, why   25
Name the dead hours? I mind them well:
Their ghosts in many darkened doorways dwell
With desolate eyes to know them by.
The hour that must be born ere it can die, –
Of that I'd have thee tell.   30

But hear, before thou speak!
Withhold, I pray, the vain behest
That while the maze hath still its bower for quest
My burning heart should cease to seek.
Be sure that Love ordained for souls more meek   35
His roadside dells of rest.

Stream, when this silver thread
In flood-time is a torrent brown,
May any bulwark bind thy foaming crown?
Shall not the waters surge and spread   40
And to the crannied boulders of their bed
Still shoot the dead leaves down?

Let no rebuke find place
In speech of thine: or it shall prove
That thou dost ill expound the words of Love,   45
Even as thine eddy's rippling race
Would blur the perfect image of his face.
I will have none thereof.

O learn and understand
That 'gainst the wrongs himself did wreak   50
Love sought her aid; until her shadowy cheek
And eyes beseeching gave command;
And compassed in her close compassionate hand
My heart must burn and speak.

For then at last we spoke   55
What eyes so oft had told to eyes
Through that long-lingering silence whose half-sighs
Alone the buried secret broke
Which with snatched hands and lips' reverberate stroke
Then from the heart did rise.   60

But she is far away
Now; nor the hours of night grown hoar
Bring yet to me, long gazing from the door,
The wind-stirred robe of roseate grey
And rose-crown of the hour that leads the day   65
When we shall meet once more.

Dark as thy blinded wave
When brimming midnight floods the glen, –
Bright as the laughter of thy runnels when
The dawn yields all the light they crave;   70
Even so these hours to wound and that to save
Are sisters in Love's ken.

Oh sweet her bending grace
Then when I kneel beside her feet;
And sweet her eyes' o'erhanging heaven; and sweet   75

The gathering folds of her embrace;
And her fall'n hair at last shed round my face
    When breaths and tears shall meet.

    Beneath her sheltering hair,
In the warm silence near her breast,   80
Our kisses and our sobs shall sink to rest;
    As in some still trance made aware
That day and night have wrought to fulness there
    And Love has built our nest.

    And as in the dim grove,   85
When the rains cease that hushed them long,
'Mid glistening boughs the song-birds wake to song, –
    So from our hearts deep-shrined in love,
While the leaves throb beneath, around, above,
    The quivering notes shall throng.   90

    Till tenderest words found vain
Draw back to wonder mute and deep,
And closed lips in closed arms a silence keep,
    Subdued by memory's circling strain, –
The wind-rapt sound that the wind brings again   95
    While all the willows weep.

    Then by her summoning art
Shall memory conjure back the sere
Autumnal Springs, from many a dying year
    Born dead; and, bitter to the heart,   100
The very ways where now we walk apart
    Who then shall cling so near.

    And with each thought new-grown,
Some sweet caress or some sweet name
Low-breathed shall let me know her thought the same; 105
    Making me rich with every tone
And touch of the dear heaven so long unknown
    That filled my dreams with flame.

    Pity and love shall burn
In her pressed cheek and cherishing hands;   110
And from the living spirit of love that stands
    Between her lips to soothe and yearn,
Each separate breath shall clasp me round in turn
    And loose my spirit's bands.

Oh passing sweet and dear,   115
Then when the worshipped form and face
Are felt at length in darkling close embrace;
Round which so oft the sun shone clear,
With mocking light and pitiless atmosphere,
    In many an hour and place.   120

Ah me! with what proud growth
Shall that hour's thirsting race be run;
While, for each several sweetness still begun
Afresh, endures love's endless drouth:
Sweet hands, sweet hair, sweet cheeks, sweet eyes, sweet mouth, 125
    Each singly wooed and won.

Yet most with the sweet soul
Shall love's espousals then be knit;
For very passion of peace shall breathe from it
    O'er tremulous wings that touch the goal,   130
As on the unmeasured height of Love's control
    The lustral fires are lit.

Therefore, when breast and cheek
Now part, from long embraces free, –
Each on the other gazing shall but see   135
    A self that has no need to speak:
All things unsought, yet nothing more to seek, –
    One love in unity.

O water wandering past, –
    Albeit to thee I speak this thing,   140
O water, thou that wanderest whispering,
    Thou keep'st thy counsel to the last.
What spell upon thy bosom should Love cast,
    His message thence to wring?

Nay, must thou hear the tale   145
    Of the past days, – the heavy debt
Of life that obdurate time withholds, – ere yet
    To win thine ear these prayers prevail,
And by thy voice Love's self with high All-hail
    Yield up the love-secret?   150

How should all this be told? –
    All the sad sum of wayworn days; –
Heart's anguish in the impenetrable maze;

And on the waste uncoloured wold
The visible burthen of the sun grown cold   155
   And the moon's labouring gaze?

   Alas! shall hope be nurs'd
On life's all-succouring breast in vain,
And made so perfect only to be slain?
   Or shall not rather the sweet thirst   160
Even yet rejoice the heart with warmth dispers'd
   And strength grown fair again?

   Stands it not by the door –
Love's Hour – till she and I shall meet;
With bodiless form and unapparent feet   165
   That cast no shadow yet before,
Though round its head the dawn begins to pour
   The breath that makes day sweet?

   Its eyes invisible
Watch till the dial's thin-thrown shade   170
Be born, – yea, till the journeying line be laid
   Upon the point that wakes the spell,
And there in lovelier light than tongue can tell
   Its presence stand array'd.

   Its soul remembers yet   175
Those sunless hours that passed it by;
And still it hears the night's disconsolate cry,
   And feels the branches wringing wet
Cast on its brow, that may not once forget,
   Dumb tears from the blind sky.   180

   But oh! when now her foot
Draws near, for whose sake night and day
Were long in weary longing sighed away, –
   The Hour of Love, 'mid airs grown mute,
Shall sing beside the door, and Love's own lute   185
   Thrill to the passionate lay.

   Thou know'st, for Love has told
Within thine ear, O stream, how soon
That song shall lift its sweet appointed tune.
   O tell me, for my lips are cold,   190
And in my veins the blood is waxing old
   Even while I beg the boon.

So, in that hour of sighs
    Assuaged, shall we beside this stone
Yield thanks for grace; while in thy mirror shown   195
    The twofold image softly lies,
Until we kiss, and each in other's eyes
    Is imaged all alone.

    Still silent? Can no art
Of Love's then move thy pity? Nay,   200
To thee let nothing come that owns his sway:
    Let happy lovers have no part
With thee; nor even so sad and poor a heart
    As thou hast spurned to-day.

    To-day? Lo! night is here.   205
The glen grows heavy with some veil
Risen from the earth or fall'n to make earth pale;
    And all stands hushed to eye and ear,
Until the night-wind shake the shade like fear
    And every covert quail.   210

    Ah! by a colder wave
On deathlier airs the hour must come
Which to thy heart, my love, shall call me home.
    Between the lips of the low cave
Against that night the lapping waters lave,   215
    And the dark lips are dumb.

    But there Love's self doth stand,
And with Life's weary wings far-flown,
And with Death's eyes that make the water moan,
    Gathers the water in his hand: 220
And they that drink know nought of sky or land
    But only love alone.

    O soul-sequestered face
Far off, – O were that night but now!
So even beside that stream even I and thou   225
    Through thirsting lips should draw Love's grace,
And in the zone of that supreme embrace
    Bind aching breast and brow.

    O water whispering
Still through the dark into mine ears, –   230
As with mine eyes, is it not now with hers? –

Mine eyes that add to thy cold spring,
Wan water, wandering water weltering,
This hidden tide of tears.

The House of Life,
1881

The House of Life:

A SONNET SEQUENCE

Part I

YOUTH AND CHANGE

Part II

CHANGE AND FATE

A Sonnet is a moment's monument, –
Memorial from the Soul's eternity
To one dead deathless hour. Look that it be,
Whether for lustral rite or dire portent,
Of its own arduous fulness reverent:
  Carve it in ivory or in ebony,
   As Day or Night may rule; and let Time see
Its flowering crest impearled and orient.

A Sonnet is a coin: its face reveals
  The soul, – its converse, to what Power 'tis due: –
Whether for tribute to the august appeals
  Of Life, or dower in Love's high retinue,
It serve; or, 'mid the dark wharf's cavernous breath,
In Charon's palm it pay the toll to Death.

(The present full series of *The House of Life* consists of sonnets only. It will be evident that many among those now first added are still the work of earlier years. – 1881.)

PART I – YOUTH AND CHANGE

I

Love Enthroned

I marked all kindred Powers the heart finds fair: –
  Truth, with awed lips; and Hope, with eyes upcast;
  And Fame, whose loud wings fan the ashen Past
To signal-fires, Oblivion's flight to scare;
And Youth, with still some single golden hair   5
  Unto his shoulder clinging, since the last
  Embrace wherein two sweet arms held him fast;
And Life, still wreathing flowers for Death to wear.

Love's throne was not with these; but far above
  All passionate wind of welcome and farewell   10
He sat in breathless bowers they dream not of;
  Though Truth foreknow Love's heart, and Hope foretell,
  And Fame be for Love's sake desirable,
And Youth be dear, and Life be sweet to Love.

II

Bridal Birth

As when desire, long darkling, dawns, and first
  The mother looks upon the newborn child,
  Even so my Lady stood at gaze and smiled
When her soul knew at length the Love it nurs'd.
Born with her life, creature of poignant thirst   5
  And exquisite hunger, at her heart Love lay
  Quickening in darkness, till a voice that day
Cried on him, and the bonds of birth were burst.

Now, shadowed by his wings, our faces yearn
  Together, as his full-grown feet now range   10
    The grove, and his warm hands our couch prepare;
Till to his song our bodiless souls in turn
  Be born his children, when Death's nuptial change
  Leaves us for light the halo of his hair.

III
Love's Testament

O thou who at Love's hour ecstatically
  Unto my heart dost evermore present,
  Clothed with his fire, thy heart his testament;
Whom I have neared and felt thy breath to be
The inmost incense of his sanctuary;   5
  Who without speech hast owned him, and, intent
  Upon his will, thy life with mine hast blent,
And murmured, 'I am thine, thou'rt one with me!'

O what from thee the grace, to me the prize,
  And what to Love the glory, – when the whole   10
  Of the deep stair thou tread'st to the dim shoal
And weary water of the place of sighs,
And there dost work deliverance, as thine eyes
  Draw up my prisoned spirit to thy soul!

IV
Lovesight

When do I see thee most, beloved one?
  When in the light the spirits of mine eyes
  Before thy face, their altar, solemnize
The worship of that Love through thee made known?
Or when in the dusk hours, (we two alone,)   5
  Close-kissed and eloquent of still replies
  Thy twilight-hidden glimmering visage lies,
And my soul only sees thy soul its own?

O love, my love! if I no more should see
Thyself, nor on the earth the shadow of thee,   10
  Nor image of thine eyes in any spring, –
How then should sound upon Life's darkening slope
The ground-whirl of the perished leaves of Hope,
  The wind of Death's imperishable wing?

V

Heart's Hope

By what word's power, the key of paths untrod,
  Shall I the difficult deeps of Love explore,
  Till parted waves of Song yield up the shore
Even as that sea which Israel crossed dryshod?
For lo! in some poor rhythmic period,   5
  Lady, I fain would tell how evermore
  Thy soul I know not from thy body, nor
Thee from myself, neither our love from God.

Yea, in God's name, and Love's, and thine, would I
  Draw from one loving heart such evidence   10
As to all hearts all things shall signify;
  Tender as dawn's first hill-fire, and intense
  As instantaneous penetrating sense,
In Spring's birth-hour, of other Springs gone by.

VI

The Kiss

What smouldering senses in death's sick delay
  Or seizure of malign vicissitude
  Can rob this body of honour, or denude
This soul of wedding-raiment worn to-day?
For lo! even now my lady's lips did play   5
  With these my lips such consonant interlude
  As laurelled Orpheus longed for when he wooed
The half-drawn hungering face with that last lay.

I was a child beneath her touch, – a man
  When breast to breast we clung, even I and she, –   10
  A spirit when her spirit looked through me, –
A god when all our life-breath met to fan
Our life-blood, till love's emulous ardours ran,
  Fire within fire, desire in deity.

(VIa)
Nuptial Sleep

At length their long kiss severed, with sweet smart:
   And as the last slow sudden drops are shed
   From sparkling eaves when all the storm has fled,
So singly flagged the pulses of each heart.
Their bosoms sundered, with the opening start   5
   Of married flowers to either side outspread
   From the knit stem; yet still their mouths, burnt red,
Fawned on each other where they lay apart.

Sleep sank them lower than the tide of dreams,
   And their dreams watched them sink, and slid away.   10
Slowly their souls swam up again, through gleams
   Of watered light and dull drowned waifs of day;
Till from some wonder of new woods and streams
   He woke, and wondered more: for there she lay.

VII
Supreme Surrender

To all the spirits of Love that wander by
   Along the love-sown harvest-field of sleep
   My lady lies apparent; and the deep
Calls to the deep; and no man sees but I.
The bliss so long afar, at length so nigh,   5
   Rests there attained. Methinks proud Love must weep
   When Fate's control doth from his harvest reap
The sacred hour for which the years did sigh.

First touched, the hand now warm around my neck
   Taught memory long to mock desire: and lo!   10
   Across my breast the abandoned hair doth flow,
Where one shorn tress long stirred the longing ache:
And next the heart that trembled for its sake
   Lies the queen-heart in sovereign overthrow.

VIII

Love's Lovers

Some ladies love the jewels in Love's zone
  And gold-tipped darts he hath for painless play
  In idle scornful hours he flings away;
And some that listen to his lute's soft tone
Do love to vaunt the silver praise their own;   5
  Some prize his blindfold sight; and there be they
  Who kissed his wings which brought him yesterday
And thank his wings to-day that he is flown.

My lady only loves the heart of Love:
  Therefore Love's heart, my lady, hath for thee   10
  His bower of unimagined flower and tree:
There kneels he now, and all-anhungered of
Thine eyes grey-lit in shadowing hair above,
  Seals with thy mouth his immortality.

IX

Passion and Worship

One flame-winged brought a white-winged harp-player
  Even where my lady and I lay all alone;
  Saying: 'Behold, this minstrel is unknown;
Bid him depart, for I am minstrel here:
Only my strains are to Love's dear ones dear.'   5
  Then said I: 'Through thine hautboy's rapturous tone
  Unto my lady still this harp makes moan,
And still she deems the cadence deep and clear.'

Then said my lady: 'Thou art Passion of Love,
  And this Love's Worship: both he plights to me.   10
  Thy mastering music walks the sunlit sea:
But where wan water trembles in the grove
And the wan moon is all the light thereof,
  This harp still makes my name its voluntary.'

X

The Portrait

O Lord of all compassionate control,
   O Love! let this my lady's picture glow
   Under my hand to praise her name, and show
Even of her inner self the perfect whole:
That he who seeks her beauty's furthest goal,   5
   Beyond the light that the sweet glances throw
   And refluent wave of the sweet smile, may know
The very sky and sea-line of her soul.

Lo! it is done. Above the long lithe throat
   The mouth's mould testifies of voice and kiss,   10
     The shadowed eyes remember and foresee.
Her face is made her shrine. Let all men note
   That in all years (O Love, thy gift is this!)
     They that would look on her must come to me.

XI

The Love-Letter

Warmed by her hand and shadowed by her hair
   As close she leaned and poured her heart through thee,
   Whereof the articulate throbs accompany
The smooth black stream that makes thy whiteness fair, –
Sweet fluttering sheet, even of her breath aware, –   5
   Oh let thy silent song disclose to me
   That soul wherewith her lips and eyes agree
Like married music in Love's answering air.

Fain had I watched her when, at some fond thought,
   Her bosom to the writing closelier press'd,
   And her breast's secrets peered into her breast;   10
When, through eyes raised an instant, her soul sought
My soul, and from the sudden confluence caught
   The words that made her love the loveliest.

XII
The Lovers' Walk

Sweet twining hedgeflowers wind-stirred in no wise
  On this June day; and hand that clings in hand:
  Still glades; and meeting faces scarcely fann'd: –
An osier-odoured stream that draws the skies
Deep to its heart; and mirrored eyes in eyes: –   5
  Fresh hourly wonder o'er the Summer land
  Of light and cloud; and two souls softly spann'd
With one o'erarching heaven of smiles and sighs: –

Even such their path, whose bodies lean unto
  Each other's visible sweetness amorously, –   10
  Whose passionate hearts lean by Love's high decree
Together on his heart for ever true,
As the cloud-foaming firmamental blue
  Rests on the blue line of a foamless sea.

XIII
Youth's Antiphony

'I love you, sweet: how can you ever learn
  How much I love you?' 'You I love even so,
  And so I learn it.' 'Sweet, you cannot know
How fair you are.' 'If fair enough to earn
Your love, so much is all my love's concern.'   5
  'My love grows hourly, sweet.' 'Mine too doth grow,
  Yet love seemed full so many hours ago!'
Thus lovers speak, till kisses claim their turn.

Ah! happy they to whom such words as these
  In youth have served for speech the whole day long,   10
  Hour after hour, remote from the world's throng,
Work, contest, fame, all life's confederate pleas, –
What while Love breathed in sighs and silences
  Through two blent souls one rapturous undersong.

XIV
Youth's Spring-Tribute

On this sweet bank your head thrice sweet and dear
  I lay, and spread your hair on either side,
  And see the newborn woodflowers bashful-eyed
Look through the golden tresses here and there.
On these debateable borders of the year   5
  Spring's foot half falters; scarce she yet may know
  The leafless blackthorn-blossom from the snow;
And through her bowers the wind's way still is clear.

But April's sun strikes down the glades to-day;
  So shut your eyes upturned, and feel my kiss   10
Creep, as the Spring now thrills through every spray,
  Up your warm throat to your warm lips: for this
  Is even the hour of Love's sworn suitservice,
With whom cold hearts are counted castaway.

XV
The Birth-Bond

Have you not noted, in some family
  Where two were born of a first marriage-bed,
  How still they own their gracious bond, though fed
And nursed on the forgotten breast and knee? —
How to their father's children they shall be   5
  In act and thought of one goodwill; but each
  Shall for the other have, in silence speech,
And in a word complete community?

Even so, when first I saw you, seemed it, love,
  That among souls allied to mine was yet   10
One nearer kindred than life hinted of.
  O born with me somewhere that men forget,
  And though in years of sight and sound unmet,
Known for my soul's birth-partner well enough!

XVI

A Day of Love

Those envied places which do know her well,
   And are so scornful of this lonely place,
   Even now for once are emptied of her grace:
Nowhere but here she is: and while Love's spell
From his predominant presence doth compel   5
   All alien hours, an outworn populace,
   The hours of Love fill full the echoing space
With sweet confederate music favourable.

Now many memories make solicitous
   The delicate love-lines of her mouth, till, lit   10
   With quivering fire, the words take wing from it;
As here between our kisses we sit thus
   Speaking of things remembered, and so sit
Speechless while things forgotten call to us.

XVII

Beauty's Pageant

What dawn-pulse at the heart of heaven, or last
   Incarnate flower of culminating day, –
   What marshalled marvels on the skirts of May,
Or song full-quired, sweet June's encomiast;
What glory of change by Nature's hand amass'd   5
   Can vie with all those moods of varying grace
   Which o'er one loveliest woman's form and face
Within this hour, within this room, have pass'd?

Love's very vesture and elect disguise
   Was each fine movement, – wonder new-begot   10
   Of lily or swan or swan-stemmed galiot;
Joy to his sight who now the sadlier sighs,
Parted again; and sorrow yet for eyes
   Unborn that read these words and saw her not.

XVIII

Genius in Beauty

Beauty like hers is genius. Not the call
  Of Homer's or of Dante's heart sublime, –
  Not Michael's hand furrowing the zones of time, –
Is more with compassed mysteries musical;
Nay, not in Spring's or Summer's sweet footfall   5
  More gathered gifts exuberant Life bequeathes
  Than doth this sovereign face, whose love-spell breathes
Even from its shadowed contour on the wall.

As many men are poets in their youth,
  But for one sweet-strung soul the wires prolong   10
  Even through all change the indomitable song;
So in like wise the envenomed years, whose tooth
Rends shallower grace with ruin void of ruth,
  Upon this beauty's power shall wreak no wrong.

XIX

Silent Noon

Your hands lie open in the long fresh grass, –
  The finger-points look through like rosy blooms:
  Your eyes smile peace. The pasture gleams and glooms
'Neath billowing skies that scatter and amass.
All round our nest, far as the eye can pass,   5
  Are golden kingcup-fields with silver edge
  Where the cow-parsley skirts the hawthorn-hedge.
'Tis visible silence, still as the hour-glass.

Deep in the sun-searched growths the dragon-fly
Hangs like a blue thread loosened from the sky: –   10
  So this wing'd hour is dropt to us from above.
Oh! clasp we to our hearts, for deathless dower,
This close-companioned inarticulate hour
  When twofold silence was the song of love.

XX
Gracious Moonlight

Even as the moon grows queenlier in mid-space
   When the sky darkens, and her cloud-rapt car
   Thrills with intenser radiance from afar, –
So lambent, lady, beams thy sovereign grace
When the drear soul desires thee. Of that face   5
   What shall be said, – which, like a governing star,
   Gathers and garners from all things that are
Their silent penetrative loveliness?

O'er water-daisies and wild waifs of Spring,
   There where the iris rears its gold-crowned sheaf   10
   With flowering rush and sceptred arrow-leaf,
So have I marked Queen Dian, in bright ring
Of cloud above and wave below, take wing
   And chase night's gloom, as thou the spirit's grief.

XXI
Love-Sweetness

Sweet dimness of her loosened hair's downfall
   About thy face; her sweet hands round thy head
   In gracious fostering union garlanded;
Her tremulous smiles; her glances' sweet recall
Of love; her murmuring sighs memorial;   5
   Her mouth's culled sweetness by thy kisses shed
   On cheeks and neck and eyelids, and so led
Back to her mouth which answers there for all: –

What sweeter than these things, except the thing
   In lacking which all these would lose their sweet: –   10
   The confident heart's still fervour: the swift beat
And soft subsidence of the spirit's wing,
Then when it feels, in cloud-girt wayfaring,
   The breath of kindred plumes against its feet?

XXII

Heart's Haven

Sometimes she is a child within mine arms,
  Cowering beneath dark wings that love must chase,
  With still tears showering and averted face,
Inexplicably filled with faint alarms:
And oft from mine own spirit's hurtling harms   5
  I crave the refuge of her deep embrace, –
  Against all ills the fortified strong place
And sweet reserve of sovereign counter-charms.

And Love, our light at night and shade at noon,
  Lulls us to rest with songs, and turns away   10
  All shafts of shelterless tumultuous day.
Like the moon's growth, his face gleams through his tune;
And as soft waters warble to the moon,
  Our answering spirits chime one roundelay.

XXIII

Love's Baubles

I stood where Love in brimming armfuls bore
  Slight wanton flowers and foolish toys of fruit:
  And round him ladies thronged in warm pursuit,
Fingered and lipped and proffered the strange shore.
And from one hand the petal and the core   5
  Savoured of sleep; and cluster and curled shoot
  Seemed from another hand like shame's salute, –
Gifts that I felt my cheek was blushing for.

At last Love bade my Lady give the same:
  And as I looked, the dew was light thereon;   10
  And as I took them, at her touch they shone
With inmost heaven-hue of the heart of flame.
And then Love said: 'Lo! when the hand is hers,
Follies of love are love's true ministers.'

XXIV
Pride of Youth

Even as a child, of sorrow that we give
  The dead, but little in his heart can find,
  Since without need of thought to his clear mind
Their turn it is to die and his to live: –
Even so the winged New Love smiles to receive   5
  Along his eddying plumes the auroral wind,
  Nor, forward glorying, casts one look behind
Where night-rack shrouds the Old Love fugitive.

There is a change in every hour's recall,
  And the last cowslip in the fields we see   10
  On the same day with the first corn-poppy.
Alas for hourly change! Alas for all
The loves that from his hand proud Youth lets fall,
  Even as the beads of a told rosary!

XXV
Winged Hours

Each hour until we meet is as a bird
  That wings from far his gradual way along
  The rustling covert of my soul, – his song
Still loudlier trilled through leaves more deeply stirr'd, –
But at the hour of meeting, a clear word   5
  Is every note he sings, in Love's own tongue;
  Yet, Love, thou know'st the sweet strain suffers wrong
Full oft through our contending joys unheard.

What of that hour at last, when for her sake
  No wing may fly to me nor song may flow;   10
  When, wandering round my life unleaved, I know
The bloodied feathers scattered in the brake,
And think how she, far from me, with like eyes
Sees through the untuneful bough the wingless skies?

XXVI
Mid-Rapture

Thou lovely and beloved, thou my love;
  Whose kiss seems still the first; whose summoning eyes,
  Even now, as for our love-world's new sunrise,
Shed very dawn; whose voice, attuned above
All modulation of the deep-bowered dove, 5
  Is like a hand laid softly on the soul;
  Whose hand is like a sweet voice to control
Those worn tired brows it hath the keeping of: –

What word can answer to thy word, – what gaze
  To thine, which now absorbs within its sphere 10
  My worshipping face, till I am mirrored there
Light-circled in a heaven of deep-drawn rays?
What clasp, what kiss mine inmost heart can prove,
O lovely and beloved, O my love?

XXVII
Heart's Compass

Sometimes thou seem'st not as thyself alone,
  But as the meaning of all things that are;
  A breathless wonder, shadowing forth afar
Some heavenly solstice hushed and halcyon;
Whose unstirred lips are music's visible tone; 5
  Whose eyes the sun-gate of the soul unbar,
  Being of its furthest fires oracular; –
The evident heart of all life sown and mown.

Even such Love is; and is not thy name Love?
  Yea, by thy hand the Love-god rends apart 10
  All gathering clouds of Night's ambiguous art;
Flings them far down, and sets thine eyes above;
And simply, as some gage of flower or glove,
  Stakes with a smile the world against thy heart.

XXVIII
Soul-Light

What other woman could be loved like you,
  Or how of you should love possess his fill?
  After the fulness of all rapture, still, –
As at the end of some deep avenue
A tender glamour of day, – there comes to view   5
  Far in your eyes a yet more hungering thrill, –
  Such fire as Love's soul-winnowing hands distil
Even from his inmost arc of light and dew.

And as the traveller triumphs with the sun,
  Glorying in heat's mid-height, yet startide brings   10
  Wonder new-born, and still fresh transport springs
From limpid lambent hours of day begun; –
Even so, through eyes and voice, your soul doth move
My soul with changeful light of infinite love.

XXIX
The Moonstar

Lady, I thank thee for thy loveliness,
  Because my lady is more lovely still.
  Glorying I gaze, and yield with glad goodwill
To thee thy tribute; by whose sweet-spun dress
Of delicate life Love labours to assess   5
  My lady's absolute queendom; saying, 'Lo!
  How high this beauty is, which yet doth show
But as that beauty's sovereign votaress.'

Lady, I saw thee with her, side by side;
  And as, when night's fair fires their queen surround,   10
An emulous star too near the moon will ride, –
  Even so thy rays within her luminous bound
  Were traced no more; and by the light so drown'd,
Lady, not thou but she was glorified.

XXX
Last Fire

Love, through your spirit and mine what summer eve
  Now glows with glory of all things possess'd,
  Since this day's sun of rapture filled the west
And the light sweetened as the fire took leave?
Awhile now softlier let your bosom heave,   5
  As in Love's harbour, even that loving breast,
  All care takes refuge while we sink to rest,
And mutual dreams the bygone bliss retrieve.

Many the days that Winter keeps in store,
  Sunless throughout, or whose brief sun-glimpses   10
  Scarce shed the heaped snow through the naked trees.
This day at least was Summer's paramour,
Sun-coloured to the imperishable core
  With sweet well-being of love and full heart's ease.

XXXI
Her Gifts

High grace, the dower of queens; and therewithal
  Some wood-born wonder's sweet simplicity
  A glance like water brimming with the sky
Or hyacinth-light where forest-shadows fall;
Such thrilling pallor of cheek as doth enthral   5
  The heart; a mouth whose passionate forms imply
  All music and all silence held thereby;
Deep golden locks, her sovereign coronal;
A round reared neck, meet column of Love's shrine
  To cling to when the heart takes sanctuary;   10
  Hands which for ever at Love's bidding be,
And soft-stirred feet still answering to his sign: –
These are her gifts, as tongue may tell them o'er.
Breathe low her name, my soul; for that means more.

XXXII
Equal Troth

Not by one measure mayst thou mete our love;
  For how should I be loved as I love thee? –
  I, graceless, joyless, lacking absolutely
All gifts that with thy queenship best behove; –
Thou, throned in every heart's elect alcove,   5
  And crowned with garlands culled from every tree,
  Which for no head but thine, by Love's decree,
All beauties and all mysteries interwove.

But here thine eyes and lips yield soft rebuke: –
  'Then only' (say'st thou) 'could I love thee less,   10
  When thou couldst doubt my love's equality.'
Peace, sweet! If not to sum but worth we look, –
  Thy heart's transcendence, not my heart's excess, –
  Then more a thousandfold thou lov'st than I.

XXXIII
Venus Victrix

Could Juno's self more sovereign presence wear
  Than thou, 'mid other ladies throned in grace? –
  Or Pallas, when thou bend'st with soul-stilled face
O'er poet's page gold-shadowed in thy hair?
Dost thou than Venus seem less heavenly fair   5
  When o'er the sea of love's tumultuous trance
  Hovers thy smile, and mingles with thy glance
That sweet voice like the last wave murmuring there?

Before such triune loveliness divine
  Awestruck I ask, which goddess here most claims   10
The prize that, howsoe'er adjudged, is thine?
  Then Love breathes low and sweetest of thy names;
And Venus Victrix to my heart doth bring
Herself, the Helen of her guerdoning.

XXXIV
The Dark Glass

Not I myself know all my love for thee:
　　How should I reach so far, who cannot weigh
　　To-morrow's dower by gage of yesterday?
Shall birth and death, and all dark names that be
As doors and windows bared to some loud sea,　　　　5
　　Lash deaf mine ears and blind my face with spray;
　　And shall my sense pierce love, – the last relay
And ultimate outpost of eternity?

Lo! what am I to Love, the lord of all?
　　One murmuring shell he gathers from the sand, –　　10
　　One little heart-flame sheltered in his hand.
Yet through thine eyes he grants me clearest call
And veriest touch of powers primordial
　　That any hour-girt life may understand.

XXXV
The Lamp's Shrine

Sometimes I fain would find in thee some fault,
　　That I might love thee still in spite of it:
　　Yet how should our Lord Love curtail one whit
Thy perfect praise whom most he would exalt?
Alas! he can but make my heart's low vault　　　　5
　　Even in men's sight unworthier, being lit
　　By thee, who thereby show'st more exquisite
Like fiery chrysoprase in deep basalt.

Yet will I nowise shrink; but at Love's shrine
　　Myself within the beams his brow doth dart　　　10
　　Will set the flashing jewel of thy heart
In that dull chamber where it deigns to shine:
For lo! in honour of thine excellencies
My heart takes pride to show how poor it is.

XXXVI

Life-in-Love

Not in thy body is thy life at all,
    But in this lady's lips and hands and eyes;
    Through these she yields thee life that vivifies
What else were sorrow's servant and death's thrall.
Look on thyself without her, and recall   5
    The waste remembrance and forlorn surmise
    That lived but in a dead-drawn breath of sighs
O'er vanished hours and hours eventual.

Even so much life hath the poor tress of hair
    Which, stored apart, is all love hath to show   10
    For heart-beats and for fire-heats long ago;
Even so much life endures unknown, even where,
'Mid change the changeless night environeth,
Lies all that golden hair undimmed in death.

XXXVII

The Love-Moon

'When that dead face, bowered in the furthest years,
    Which once was all the life years held for thee,
    Can now scarce bid the tides of memory
Cast on thy soul a little spray of tears, –
How canst thou gaze into these eyes of hers   5
    Whom now thy heart delights in, and not see
    Within each orb Love's philtred euphrasy
Make them of buried troth remembrancers?'

'Nay, pitiful Love, nay, loving Pity! Well
    Thou knowest that in these twain I have confess'd   10
Two very voices of thy summoning bell.
    Nay, Master, shall not Death make manifest
In these the culminant changes which approve
The love-moon that must light my soul to Love?'

XXXVIII
The Morrow's Message

'Thou Ghost,' I said, 'and is thy name To-day? –
   Yesterday's son, with such an abject brow! –
   And can To-morrow be more pale than thou?'
While yet I spoke, the silence answered: 'Yea,
Henceforth our issue is all grieved and grey,   5
   And each beforehand makes such poor avow
   As of old leaves beneath the budding bough
Or night-drift that the sundawn shreds away.'

Then cried I: 'Mother of many malisons,
   O Earth, receive me to thy dusty bed!'   10
   But therewithal the tremulous silence said:
'Lo! Love yet bids thy lady greet thee once: –
Yea, twice, – whereby thy life is still the sun's;
   And thrice, – whereby the shadow of death is dead.'

XXXIX
Sleepless Dreams

Girt in dark growths, yet glimmering with one star,
   O night desirous as the nights of youth!
   Why should my heart within thy spell, forsooth,
Now beat, as the bride's finger-pulses are
Quickened within the girdling golden bar?   5
   What wings are these that fan my pillow smooth?
   And why does Sleep, waved back by Joy and Ruth,
Tread softly round and gaze at me from far?

Nay, night deep-leaved! And would Love feign in thee
   Some shadowy palpitating grove that bears   10
   Rest for man's eyes and music for his ears?
O lonely night! art thou not known to me,
A thicket hung with masks of mockery
   And watered with the wasteful warmth of tears?

XL

Severed Selves

Two separate divided silences,
    Which, brought together, would find loving voice;
    Two glances which together would rejoice
In love, now lost like stars beyond dark trees;
Two hands apart whose touch alone gives ease;   5
    Two bosoms which, heart-shrined with mutual flame,
    Would, meeting in one clasp, be made the same;
Two souls, the shores wave-mocked of sundering seas: –

Such are we now. Ah! may our hope forecast
    Indeed one hour again, when on this stream   10
    Of darkened love once more the light shall gleam? –
An hour how slow to come, how quickly past, –
Which blooms and fades, and only leaves at last,
    Faint as shed flowers, the attenuated dream.

XLI

Through Death to Love

Like labour-laden moonclouds fain to flee
    From winds that sweep the winter-bitten wold –
    Like multiform circumfluence manifold
Of night's flood-tide, – like terrors that agree
Of hoarse-tongued fire and inarticulate sea, –   5
    Even such, within some glass dimmed by our breath,
    Our hearts discern wild images of Death,
Shadows and shoals that edge eternity.

Howbeit athwart Death's imminent shade doth soar
    One Power, than flow of stream or flight of dove   10
    Sweeter to glide around, to brood above.
Tell me, my heart, – what angel-greeted door
Or threshold of wing-winnowed threshing-floor
    Hath guest fire-fledged as thine, whose lord is Love?

XLII
Hope Overtaken

I deemed thy garments, O my Hope, were grey,
  So far I viewed thee. Now the space between
  Is passed at length; and garmented in green
Even as in days of yore thou stand'st to-day.
Ah God! and but for lingering dull dismay,   5
  On all that road our footsteps erst had been
  Even thus commingled, and our shadows seen
Blent on the hedgerows and the water-way.

O Hope of mine whose eyes are living love,
  No eyes but hers, – O Love and Hope the same! –   10
    Lean close to me, for now the sinking sun
That warmed our feet scarce gilds our hair above.
    O hers thy voice and very hers thy name!
    Alas, cling round me, for the day is done!

XLIII
Love and Hope

Bless love and hope. Full many a withered year
  Whirled past us, eddying to its chill doomsday;
  And clasped together where the blown leaves lay
We long have knelt and wept full many a tear.
Yet lo! one hour at last, the Spring's compeer,   5
  Flutes softly to us from some green byeway:
  Those years, those tears are dead, but only they: –
Bless love and hope, true soul; for we are here.

Cling heart to heart; nor of this hour demand
  Whether in very truth, when we are dead,   10
  Our hearts shall wake to know Love's golden head
Sole sunshine of the imperishable land;
Or but discern, through night's unfeatured scope,
Scorn-fired at length the illusive eyes of Hope.

XLIV
Cloud and Wind

Love, should I fear death most for you or me?
  Yet if you die, can I not follow you,
  Forcing the straits of change? Alas! but who
Shall wrest a bond from night's inveteracy,
Ere yet my hazardous soul put forth, to be   5
  Her warrant against all her haste might rue? —
  Ah! in your eyes so reached what dumb adieu,
What unsunned gyres of waste eternity?

And if I die the first, shall death be then
  A lampless watchtower whence I see you weep? —   10
  Or (woe is me!) a bed wherein my sleep
Ne'er notes (as death's dear cup at last you drain)
The hour when you too learn that all is vain
  And that Hope sows what Love shall never reap?

XLV
Secret Parting

Because our talk was of the cloud-control
  And moon-track of the journeying face of Fate,
  Her tremulous kisses faltered at love's gate
And her eyes dreamed against a distant goal:
But soon, remembering her how brief the whole   5
  Of joy, which its own hours annihilate,
  Her set gaze gathered, thirstier than of late,
And as she kissed, her mouth became her soul.

Thence in what ways we wandered, and how strove
  To build with fire-tried vows the piteous home   10
  Which memory haunts and whither sleep may roam, —
They only know for whom the roof of Love
Is the still-seated secret of the grove,
  Nor spire may rise nor bell be heard therefrom.

XLVI
Parted Love

What shall be said of this embattled day
   And armèd occupation of this night
   By all thy foes beleaguered, – now when sight
Nor sound denotes the loved one far away?
Of these thy vanquished hours what shalt thou say, –   5
   As every sense to which she dealt delight
   Now labours lonely o'er the stark noon-height
To reach the sunset's desolate disarray?

Stand still, fond fettered wretch! while Memory's art
   Parades the Past before thy face, and lures   10
   Thy spirit to her passionate portraitures:
Till the tempestuous tide-gates flung apart
Flood with wild will the hollows of thy heart,
   And thy heart rends thee, and thy body endures.

XLVII
Broken Music

The mother will not turn, who thinks she hears
   Her nursling's speech first grow articulate;
   But breathless with averted eyes elate
She sits, with open lips and open ears,
That it may call her twice. 'Mid doubts and fears   5
   Thus oft my soul has hearkened; till the song,
   A central moan for days, at length found tongue,
And the sweet music welled and the sweet tears.

But now, whatever while the soul is fain
   To list that wonted murmur, as it were   10
The speech-bound sea-shell's low importunate strain, –
   No breath of song, thy voice alone is there,
O bitterly beloved! and all her gain
   Is but the pang of unpermitted prayer.

XLVIII
Death-in-Love

There came an image in Life's retinue
   That had Love's wings and bore his gonfalon:
   Fair was the web, and nobly wrought thereon,
O soul-sequestered face, thy form and hue!
Bewildering sounds, such as Spring wakens to,   5
   Shook in its folds; and through my heart its power
   Sped trackless as the immemorable hour
When birth's dark portal groaned and all was new.

But a veiled woman followed, and she caught
   The banner round its staff, to furl and cling, –   10
   Then plucked a feather from the bearer's wing,
And held it to his lips that stirred it not,
And said to me, 'Behold, there is no breath:
I and this Love are one, and I am Death.'

XLIX, L, LI, LII
Willowwood

I

I sat with Love upon a woodside well,
   Leaning across the water, I and he;
   Nor ever did he speak nor looked at me,
But touched his lute wherein was audible
The certain secret thing he had to tell: 5
   Only our mirrored eyes met silently
   In the low wave; and that sound came to be
The passionate voice I knew; and my tears fell.

And at their fall, his eyes beneath grew hers;
And with his foot and with his wing-feathers   10
   He swept the spring that watered my heart's drouth.
Then the dark ripples spread to waving hair,
And as I stooped, her own lips rising there
   Bubbled with brimming kisses at my mouth.

II

And now Love sang: but his was such a song
   So meshed with half-remembrance hard to free,

As souls disused in death's sterility
May sing when the new birthday tarries long.
And I was made aware of a dumb throng   5
   That stood aloof, one form by every tree,
   All mournful forms, for each was I or she,
The shades of those our days that had no tongue.

They looked on us, and knew us and were known;
   While fast together, alive from the abyss,   10
   Clung the soul-wrung implacable close kiss;
And pity of self through all made broken moan
Which said, 'For once, for once, for once alone!'
   And still Love sang, and what he sang was this: –

III

'O ye, all ye that walk in Willowwood,
   That walk with hollow faces burning white;
What fathom-depth of soul-struck widowhood,
   What long, what longer hours, one lifelong night,
Ere ye again, who so in vain have wooed   5
   Your last hope lost, who so in vain invite
Your lips to that their unforgotten food,
   Ere ye, ere ye again shall see the light!

Alas! the bitter banks in Willowwood,
   With tear-spurge wan, with blood-wort burning red: 10
Alas! if ever such a pillow could
   Steep deep the soul in sleep till she were dead, –
Better all life forget her than this thing,
That Willowwood should hold her wandering!'

IV

So sang he: and as meeting rose and rose
   Together cling through the wind's wellaway
   Nor change at once, yet near the end of day
The leaves drop loosened where the heart-stain glows, –
So when the song died did the kiss unclose;   5
   And her face fell back drowned, and was as grey
   As its grey eyes; and if it ever may
Meet mine again I know not if Love knows.

Only I know that I leaned low and drank
A long draught from the water where she sank,   10
   Her breath and all her tears and all her soul:
And as I leaned, I know I felt Love's face

Pressed on my neck with moan of pity and grace,
Till both our heads were in his aureole.

LIII

Without Her

What of her glass without her? The blank grey
   There where the pool is blind of the moon's face.
   Her dress without her? The tossed empty space
Of cloud-rack whence the moon has passed away.
Her paths without her? Day's appointed sway   5
   Usurped by desolate night. Her pillowed place
   Without her? Tears, ah me! for love's good grace,
And cold forgetfulness of night or day.

What of the heart without her? Nay, poor heart,
   Of thee what word remains ere speech be still?   10
   A wayfarer by barren ways and chill,
Steep ways and weary, without her thou art,
Where the long cloud, the long wood's counterpart,
   Sheds doubled darkness up the labouring hill.

LIV

Love's Fatality

Sweet Love, – but oh! most dread Desire of Love
   Life-thwarted. Linked in gyves I saw them stand,
   Love shackled with Vain-longing, hand to hand:
And one was eyed as the blue vault above:
But hope tempestuous like a fire-cloud hove   5
   I' the other's gaze, even as in his whose wand
   Vainly all night with spell-wrought power has spann'd
The unyielding caves of some deep treasure-trove.

Also his lips, two writhen flakes of flame,
   Made moan: 'Alas O Love, thus leashed with me!   10
   Wing-footed thou, wing-shouldered, once born free:
And I, thy cowering self, in chains grown tame, –
Bound to thy body and soul, named with thy name, –
   Life's iron heart, even Love's Fatality.'

LV
Stillborn Love

The hour which might have been yet might not be,
    Which man's and woman's heart conceived and bore
    Yet whereof life was barren, – on what shore
Bides it the breaking of Time's weary sea?
Bondchild of all consummate joys set free,   5
    It somewhere sighs and serves, and mute before
    The house of Love, hears through the echoing door
His hours elect in choral consonancy.

But lo! what wedded souls now hand in hand
Together tread at last the immortal strand   10
    With eyes where burning memory lights love home?
Lo! how the little outcast hour has turned
And leaped to them and in their faces yearned: –
    'I am your child: O parents, ye have come!'

LVI, LVII, LVIII
True Woman
I HERSELF

To be a sweetness more desired than Spring;
    A bodily beauty more acceptable
    Than the wild rose-tree's arch that crowns the fell;
To be an essence more environing
Than wine's drained juice; a music ravishing   5
    More than the passionate pulse of Philomel; –
    To be all this 'neath one soft bosom's swell
That is the flower of life: – how strange a thing!

How strange a thing to be what Man can know
    But as a sacred secret! Heaven's own screen   10
Hides her soul's purest depth and loveliest glow;
    Closely withheld, as all things most unseen, –
    The wave-bowered pearl, – the heart-shaped seal of green
That flecks the snowdrop underneath the snow.

II HER LOVE

She loves him; for her infinite soul is Love,
    And he her lodestar. Passion in her is

A glass facing his fire, where the bright bliss
Is mirrored, and the heat returned. Yet move
That glass, a stranger's amorous flame to prove   5
    And it shall turn, by instant contraries,
    Ice to the moon; while her pure fire to his
For whom it burns, clings close i' the heart's alcove.

Lo! they are one. With wifely breast to breast
    And circling arms, she welcomes all command   10
    Of love, – her soul to answering ardours fann'd:
Yet as morn springs or twilight sinks to rest,
Ah! who shall say she deems not loveliest
    The hour of sisterly sweet hand-in-hand?

III HER HEAVEN

If to grow old in Heaven is to grow young,
    (As the Seer saw and said,) then blest were he
    With youth for evermore, whose heaven should be
True Woman, she whom these weak notes have sung.
Here and hereafter, – choir-strains of her tongue, –   5
    Sky-spaces of her eyes, – sweet signs that flee
    About her soul's immediate sanctuary, –
Were Paradise all uttermost worlds among.

The sunrise blooms and withers on the hill
    Like any hillflower; and the noblest troth   10
    Dies here to dust. Yet shall Heaven's promise clothe
Even yet those lovers who have cherished still
This test for love: – in every kiss sealed fast
To feel the first kiss and forebode the last.

LIX

Love's Last Gift

Love to his singer held a glistening leaf,
    And said: 'The rose-tree and the apple-tree
    Have fruits to vaunt or flowers to lure the bee;
And golden shafts are in the feathered sheaf
Of the great harvest-marshal, the year's chief,   5
    Victorious Summer; aye and 'neath warm sea
    Strange secret grasses lurk inviolably
Between the filtering channels of sunk reef.

All are my blooms; and all sweet blooms of love
   To thee I gave while Spring and Summer sang;   10
   But Autumn stops to listen, with some pang
From those worse things the wind is moaning of.
Only this laurel dreads no winter days:
Take my last gift; thy heart hath sung my praise.'

PART II – CHANGE AND FATE

LX

Transfigured Life

As growth of form or momentary glance
   In a child's features will recall to mind
   The father's with the mother's face combin'd, –
Sweet interchange that memories still enhance:
And yet, as childhood's years and youth's advance,   5
   The gradual mouldings leave one stamp behind,
   Till in the blended likeness now we find
A separate man's or woman's countenance: –

So in the Song, the singer's Joy and Pain,
   Its very parents, evermore expand   10
To bid the passion's fullgrown birth remain,
   By Art's transfiguring essence subtly spann'd;
   And from that song-cloud shaped as a man's hand
There comes the sound as of abundant rain.

LXI

The Song-Throe

By thine own tears thy song must tears beget,
   O Singer! Magic mirror thou hast none
   Except thy manifest heart; and save thine own
Anguish or ardour, else no amulet.
Cisterned in Pride, verse is the feathery jet   5
   Of soulless air-flung fountains; nay, more dry
   Than the Dead Sea for throats that thirst and sigh,
That song o'er which no singer's lids grew wet.

The Song-god – He the Sun-god – is no slave
   Of thine: thy Hunter he, who for thy soul   10
   Fledges his shaft: to no august control
Of thy skilled hand his quivered store he gave:
But if thy lips' loud cry leap to his smart,
The inspir'd recoil shall pierce thy brother's heart.

LXII

The Soul's Sphere

Some prisoned moon in steep cloud-fastnesses, –
　　Throned queen and thralled; some dying sun whose pyre
　　Blazed with momentous memorable fire; –
Who hath not yearned and fed his heart with these?
Who, sleepless, hath not anguished to appease　　　　5
　　Tragical shadow's realm of sound and sight
　　Conjectured in the lamentable night? . . .
Lo! the soul's sphere of infinite images!

What sense shall count them? Whether it forecast
　　The rose-winged hours that flutter in the van　　　10
　　Of Love's unquestioning unrevealèd span, –
Visions of golden futures: or that last
Wild pageant of the accumulated past
　　That clangs and flashes for a drowning man.

LXIII

Inclusiveness

The changing guests, each in a different mood,
　　Sit at the roadside table and arise:
　　And every life among them in likewise
Is a soul's board set daily with new food.
What man has bent o'er his son's sleep, to brood　　5
　　How that face shall watch his when cold it lies? –
　　Or thought, as his own mother kissed his eyes,
Of what her kiss was when his father wooed?

May not this ancient room thou sitt'st in dwell
　　In separate living souls for joy or pain?　　　　10
　　Nay, all its corners may be painted plain
Where Heaven shows pictures of some life spent well,
　　And may be stamped, a memory all in vain,
Upon the sight of lidless eyes in Hell.

LXIV

Ardour and Memory

The cuckoo-throb, the heartbeat of the Spring;
   The rosebud's blush that leaves it as it grows
   Into the full-eyed fair unblushing rose;
The summer clouds that visit every wing
With fires of sunrise and of sunsetting;   5
   The furtive flickering streams to light re-born
   'Mid airs new-fledged and valorous lusts of morn,
While all the daughters of the daybreak sing: –

These ardour loves, and memory: and when flown
   All joys, and through dark forest-boughs in flight   10
   The wind swoops onward brandishing the light,
Even yet the rose-tree's verdure left alone
Will flush all ruddy though the rose be gone;
   With ditties and with dirges infinite.

LXV

Known in Vain

As two whose love, first foolish, widening scope,
   Knows suddenly, to music high and soft,
   The Holy of holies; who because they scoff'd
Are now amazed with shame, nor dare to cope
With the whole truth aloud, lest heaven should ope;   5
   Yet, at their meetings, laugh not as they laugh'd
   In speech; nor speak, at length; but sitting oft
Together, within hopeless sight of hope
For hours are silent: – So it happeneth
   When Work and Will awake too late, to gaze   10
After their life sailed by, and hold their breath.
   Ah! who shall dare to search through what sad maze
   Thenceforth their uncommunicable ways
Follow the desultory feet of Death?

LXVI

The Heart of the Night

From child to youth; from youth to arduous man;
  From lethargy to fever of the heart;
  From faithful life to dream-dowered days apart;
From trust to doubt; from doubt to brink of ban; –
Thus much of change in one swift cycle ran   5
  Till now. Alas, the soul! – how soon must she
  Accept her primal immortality, –
The flesh resume its dust whence it began?

O Lord of work and peace! O Lord of life!
  O Lord, the awful Lord of will! though late,   10
    Even yet renew this soul with duteous breath:
That when the peace is garnered in from strife,
  The work retrieved, the will regenerate,
    This soul may see thy face, O Lord of death!

LXVII

The Landmark

Was *that* the landmark? What, – the foolish well
  Whose wave, low down, I did not stoop to drink
  But sat and flung the pebbles from its brink
In sport to send its imaged skies pell-mell,
(And mine own image, had I noted well!) –   5
  Was that my point of turning? – I had thought
  The stations of my course should rise unsought,
As altar-stone or ensigned citadel.

But lo! the path is missed, I must go back,
  And thirst to drink when next I reach the spring   10
Which once I stained, which since may have grown black.
  Yet though no light be left nor bird now sing
  As here I turn, I'll thank God, hastening,
That the same goal is still on the same track.

LXVIII
A Dark Day

The gloom that breathes upon me with these airs
  Is like the drops which strike the traveller's brow
  Who knows not, darkling, if they bring him now
Fresh storm, or be old rain the covert bears.
Ah! bodes this hour some harvest of new tares,   5
  Or hath but memory of the day whose plough
  Sowed hunger once, – the night at length when thou,
O prayer found vain, didst fall from out my prayers?

How prickly were the growths which yet how smooth,
  Along the hedgerows of this journey shed,   10
Lie by Time's grace till night and sleep may soothe!
  Even as the thistledown from pathsides dead
Gleaned by a girl in autumns of her youth,
  Which one new year makes soft her marriage-bed.

LXIX
Autumn Idleness

This sunlight shames November where he grieves
  In dead red leaves, and will not let him shun
  The day, though bough with bough be over-run.
But with a blessing every glade receives
High salutation; while from hillock-eaves   5
  The deer gaze calling, dappled white and dun,
  As if, being foresters of old, the sun
Had marked them with the shade of forest-leaves.

Here dawn to-day unveiled her magic glass;
  Here noon now gives the thirst and takes the dew;   10
Till eve bring rest when other good things pass.
  And here the lost hours the lost hours renew
While I still lead my shadow o'er the grass,
  Nor know, for longing, that which I should do.

LXX
The Hill Summit

This feast-day of the sun, his altar there
  In the broad west has blazed for vesper-song;
  And I have loitered in the vale too long
And gaze now a belated worshipper.
Yet may I not forget that I was 'ware,   5
  So journeying, of his face at intervals
  Transfigured where the fringed horizon falls, –
A fiery bush with coruscating hair.

And now that I have climbed and won this height,
  I must tread downward through the sloping shade   10
And travel the bewildered tracks till night.
  Yet for this hour I still may here be stayed
  And see the gold air and the silver fade
And the last bird fly into the last light.

LXXI, LXXII, LXXIII
The Choice

I

Eat thou and drink; to-morrow thou shalt die.
  Surely the earth, that's wise being very old,
  Needs not our help. Then loose me, love, and hold
Thy sultry hair up from my face; that I
May pour for thee this golden wine, brim-high,   5
  Till round the glass thy fingers glow like gold.
  We'll drown all hours: thy song, while hours are toll'd,
Shall leap, as fountains veil the changing sky.

Now kiss, and think that there are really those,
  My own high-bosomed beauty, who increase   10
    Vain gold, vain lore, and yet might choose our way!
    Through many years they toil; then on a day
  They die not, – for their life was death, – but cease;
And round their narrow lips the mould falls close.

II

Watch thou and fear; to-morrow thou shalt die.
  Or art thou sure thou shalt have time for death?
  Is not the day which God's word promiseth
To come man knows not when? In yonder sky,
Now while we speak, the sun speeds forth: can I   5
  Or thou assure him of his goal? God's breath
  Even at this moment haply quickeneth
The air to a flame; till spirits, always nigh
Though screened and hid, shall walk the daylight here.
  And dost thou prate of all that man shall do?   10
    Canst thou, who hast but plagues, presume to be
    Glad in his gladness that comes after thee?
  Will *his* strength slay *thy* worm in Hell? Go to:
Cover thy countenance, and watch, and fear.

III

Think thou and act; to-morrow thou shalt die.
  Outstretched in the sun's warmth upon the shore,
  Thou say'st: 'Man's measured path is all gone o'er:
Up all his years, steeply, with strain and sigh,
Man clomb until he touched the truth; and I,   5
  Even I, am he whom it was destined for.'
  How should this be? Art thou then so much more
Than they who sowed, that thou shouldst reap thereby?

Nay, come up hither. From this wave-washed mound
  Unto the furthest flood-brim look with me;   10
Then reach on with thy thought till it be drown'd.
  Miles and miles distant though the last line be,
And though thy soul sail leagues and leagues beyond, –
  Still, leagues beyond those leagues, there is more sea.

LXXIV, LXXV, LXXVI
Old and New Art
I ST LUKE THE PAINTER

Give honour unto Luke Evangelist;
  For he it was (the aged legends say)
  Who first taught Art to fold her hands and pray.
Scarcely at once she dared to rend the mist
Of devious symbols: but soon having wist   5

How sky-breadth and field-silence and this day
  Are symbols also in some deeper way,
She looked through these to God and was God's priest.

And if, past noon, her toil began to irk,
  And she sought talismans, and turned in vain   10
    To soulless self-reflections of man's skill, –
    Yet now, in this the twilight, she might still
  Kneel in the latter grass to pray again,
Ere the night cometh and she may not work.

II NOT AS THESE

'I am not as these are,' the poet saith
  In youth's pride, and the painter, among men
  At bay, where never pencil comes nor pen,
And shut about with his own frozen breath.
To others, for whom only rhyme wins faith   5
  As poets, – only paint as painters, – then
  He turns in the cold silence; and again
Shrinking, 'I am not as these are,' he saith.

And say that this is so, what follows it?
  For were thine eyes set backwards in thine head,   10
    Such words were well; but they see on, and far.
Unto the lights of the great Past, new-lit
  Fair for the Future's track, look thou instead, –
    Say thou instead, 'I am not as *these* are.'

III THE HUSBANDMEN

Though God, as one that is an householder,
  Called these to labour in His vineyard first,
  Before the husk of darkness was well burst
Bidding them grope their way out and bestir,
(Who, questioned of their wages, answered, 'Sir,   5
  Unto each man a penny':) though the worst
  Burthen of heat was theirs and the dry thirst:
Though God has since found none such as these were
To do their work like them: – Because of this
  Stand not ye idle in the market-place.   10
    Which of ye knoweth *he* is not that last
Who may be first by faith and will? – yea, his
  The hand which after the appointed days
    And hours shall give a Future to their Past?

LXXVII

Soul's Beauty

Under the arch of Life, where love and death,
  Terror and mystery, guard her shrine, I saw
  Beauty enthroned; and though her gaze struck awe,
I drew it in as simply as my breath.
Hers are the eyes which, over and beneath,   5
  The sky and sea bend on thee, – which can draw,
  By sea or sky or woman, to one law,
The allotted bondman of her palm and wreath.

This is that Lady Beauty, in whose praise
  Thy voice and hand shake still, – long known to thee   10
    By flying hair and fluttering hem, – the beat
    Following her daily of thy heart and feet,
  How passionately and irretrievably,
In what fond flight, how many ways and days!

LXXVIII

Body's Beauty

Of Adam's first wife, Lilith, it is told
  (The witch he loved before the gift of Eve,)
  That, ere the snake's, her sweet tongue could deceive,
And her enchanted hair was the first gold.
And still she sits, young while the earth is old,   5
  And, subtly of herself contemplative,
  Draws men to watch the bright web she can weave,
Till heart and body and life are in its hold.

The rose and poppy are her flowers; for where
  Is he not found, O Lilith, whom shed scent   10
And soft-shed kisses and soft sleep shall snare?
  Lo! as that youth's eyes burned at thine, so went
  Thy spell through him, and left his straight neck bent
And round his heart one strangling golden hair.

LXXIX
The Monochord

Is it this sky's vast vault or ocean's sound
  That is Life's self and draws my life from me,
  And by instinct ineffable decree
Holds my breath quailing on the bitter bound?
Nay, is it Life or Death, thus thunder-crown'd,   5
  That 'mid the tide of all emergency
  Now notes my separate wave, and to what sea
Its difficult eddies labour in the ground?

Oh! what is this that knows the road I came,
The flame turned cloud, the cloud returned to flame,   10
  The lifted shifted steeps and all the way? –
That draws round me at last this wind-warm space,
And in regenerate rapture turns my face
  Upon the devious coverts of dismay?

LXXX
From Dawn to Noon

As the child knows not if his mother's face
  Be fair; nor of his elders yet can deem
  What each most is; but as of hill or stream
At dawn, all glimmering life surrounds his place:
Who yet, tow'rd noon of his half-weary race,   5
  Pausing awhile beneath the high sun-beam
  And gazing steadily back, – as through a dream,
In things long past new features now can trace: –

Even so the thought that is at length fullgrown
  Turns back to note the sun-smit paths, all grey   10
And marvellous once, where first it walked alone;
  And haply doubts, amid the unblenching day,
  Which most or least impelled its onward way, –
Those unknown things or these things overknown.

LXXXI
Memorial Thresholds

What place so strange, – though unrevealèd snow
  With unimaginable fires arise
  At the earth's end, – what passion of surprise
Like frost-bound fire-girt scenes of long ago?
Lo! this is none but I this hour; and lo!   5
  This is the very place which to mine eyes
  Those mortal hours in vain immortalize,
'Mid hurrying crowds, with what alone I know.

City, of thine a single simple door,
  By some new Power reduplicate, must be   10
  Even yet my life-porch in eternity,
Even with one presence filled, as once of yore:
Or mocking winds whirl round a chaff-strown floor
  Thee and thy years and these my words and me.

LXXXII
Hoarded Joy

I said: 'Nay, pluck not, – let the first fruit be:
  Even as thou sayest, it is sweet and red,
  But let it ripen still. The tree's bent head
Sees in the stream its own fecundity
And bides the day of fulness. Shall not we   5
  At the sun's hour that day possess the shade,
  And claim our fruit before its ripeness fade,
And eat it from the branch and praise the tree?'

I say: 'Alas! our fruit hath wooed the sun
  Too long, – 'tis fallen and floats adown the stream.   10
Lo, the last clusters! Pluck them every one,
  And let us sup with summer; ere the gleam
Of autumn set the year's pent sorrow free,
And the woods wail like echoes from the sea.'

LXXXIII

Barren Spring

Once more the changed year's turning wheel returns:
   And as a girl sails balanced in the wind,
   And now before and now again behind
Stoops as it swoops, with cheek that laughs and burns, –
So Spring comes merry towards me here, but earns   5
   No answering smile from me, whose life is twin'd
   With the dead boughs that winter still must bind,
And whom to-day the Spring no more concerns.

Behold, this crocus is a withering flame;
   This snowdrop, snow; this apple-blossom's part   10
   To breed the fruit that breeds the serpent's art.
Nay, for these Spring-flowers, turn thy face from them,
Nor stay till on the year's last lily-stem
   The white cup shrivels round the golden heart.

LXXXIV

Farewell to the Glen

Sweet stream-fed glen, why say 'farewell' to thee
   Who far'st so well and find'st for ever smooth
   The brow of Time where man may read no ruth?
Nay, do thou rather say 'farewell' to me,
Who now fare forth in bitterer fantasy   5
   Than erst was mine where other shade might soothe
   By other streams, what while in fragrant youth
The bliss of being sad made melancholy.

And yet, farewell! For better shalt thou fare
   When children bathe sweet faces in thy flow   10
And happy lovers blend sweet shadows there
   In hours to come, than when an hour ago
Thine echoes had but one man's sighs to bear
   And thy trees whispered what he feared to know.

LXXXV
Vain Virtues

What is the sorriest thing that enters Hell?
  None of the sins, – but this and that fair deed
  Which a soul's sin at length could supersede.
These yet are virgins, whom death's timely knell
Might once have sainted; whom the fiends compel   5
  Together now, in snake-bound shuddering sheaves
  Of anguish, while the pit's pollution leaves
Their refuse maidenhood abominable.

Night sucks them down, the tribute of the pit,
  Whose names, half entered in the book of Life,   10
    Were God's desire at noon. And as their hair
And eyes sink last, the Torturer deigns no whit
  To gaze, but, yearning, waits his destined wife,
    The Sin still blithe on earth that sent them there.

LXXXVI
Lost Days

The lost days of my life until to-day,
  What were they, could I see them on the street
  Lie as they fell? Would they be ears of wheat
Sown once for food but trodden into clay?
Or golden coins squandered and still to pay?   5
  Or drops of blood dabbling the guilty feet?
  Or such spilt water as in dreams must cheat
The undying throats of Hell, athirst alway?

I do not see them here; but after death
  God knows I know the faces I shall see,   10
Each one a murdered self, with low last breath.
  'I am thyself, – what hast thou done to me?'
'And I – and I – thyself,' (lo! each one saith,)
  'And thou thyself to all eternity!'

LXXXVII
Death's Songsters

When first that horse, within whose populous womb
  The birth was death, o'ershadowed Troy with fate,
  Her elders, dubious of its Grecian freight,
Brought Helen there to sing the songs of home;
She whispered, 'Friends, I am alone; come, come!'   5
  Then, crouched within, Ulysses waxed afraid,
  And on his comrades' quivering mouths he laid
His hands, and held them till the voice was dumb.

The same was he who, lashed to his own mast,
  There where the sea-flowers screen the charnel-caves,   10
Beside the sirens' singing island pass'd,
  Till sweetness failed along the inveterate waves.
Say, soul, – are songs of Death no heaven to thee,
Nor shames her lip the cheek of Victory?

LXXXVIII
Hero's Lamp[1]

That lamp thou fill'st in Eros' name to-night,
  O Hero, shall the Sestian augurs take
  To-morrow, and for drowned Leander's sake
To Anteros its fireless lip shall plight.
Aye, waft the unspoken vow: yet dawn's first light   5
  On ebbing storm and life twice ebb'd must break;
  While 'neath no sunrise, by the Avernian Lake,
Lo where Love walks, Death's pallid neophyte.

That lamp within Anteros' shadowy shrine
  Shall stand unlit (for so the gods decree)   10
  Till some one man the happy issue see
Of a life's love, and bid its flame to shine:
Which still may rest unfir'd; for, theirs or thine,
  O brother, what brought love to them or thee?

1 After the deaths of Leander and of Hero, the signal-lamp was dedicated to Anteros, with the edict that no man should light it unless his love had proved fortunate.

LXXXIX
The Trees of the Garden

Ye who have passed Death's haggard hills; and ye
  Whom trees that knew your sires shall cease to know
  And still stand silent: – is it all a show, –
A wisp that laughs upon the wall? – decree
Of some inexorable supremacy   5
  Which ever, as man strains his blind surmise
  From depth to ominous depth, looks past his eyes,
Sphinx-faced with unabashèd augury?

Nay, rather question the Earth's self. Invoke
  The storm-felled forest-trees moss-grown to-day   10
  Whose roots are hillocks where the children play;
Or ask the silver sapling 'neath what yoke
Those stars, his spray-crown's clustering gems, shall wage
Their journey still when his boughs shrink with age.

XC
'Retro me, Sathana!'

Get thee behind me. Even as, heavy-curled,
  Stooping against the wind, a charioteer
  Is snatched from out his chariot by the hair,
So shall Time be; and as the void car, hurled
Abroad by reinless steeds, even so the world: 5
  Yea, even as chariot-dust upon the air,
  It shall be sought and not found anywhere.
Get thee behind me, Satan. Oft unfurled,
  Thy perilous wings can beat and break like lath
  Much mightiness of men to win thee praise.   10
  Leave these weak feet to tread in narrow ways.
Thou still, upon the broad vine-sheltered path,
Mayst wait the turning of the phials of wrath
  For certain years, for certain months and days.

XCI

Lost on Both Sides

As when two men have loved a woman well,
  Each hating each, through Love's and Death's deceit;
  Since not for either this stark marriage-sheet
And the long pauses of this wedding-bell;
Yet o'er her grave the night and day dispel   5
  At last their feud forlorn, with cold and heat;
  Nor other than dear friends to death may fleet
The two lives left that most of her can tell: –

So separate hopes, which in a soul had wooed
  The one same Peace, strove with each other long,   10
  And Peace before their faces perished since:
So through that soul, in restless brotherhood,
  They roam together now, and wind among
  Its bye-streets, knocking at the dusty inns.

XCII, XCIII

The Sun's Shame

I

Beholding youth and hope in mockery caught
  From life; and mocking pulses that remain
  When the soul's death of bodily death is fain;
Honour unknown, and honour known unsought;
And penury's sedulous self-torturing thought   5
  On gold, whose master therewith buys his bane;
  And longed-for woman longing all in vain
For lonely man with love's desire distraught;
And wealth, and strength, and power, and pleasantness,
  Given unto bodies of whose souls men say,   10
  None poor and weak, slavish and foul, as they: –
Beholding these things, I behold no less
The blushing morn and blushing eve confess
  The shame that loads the intolerable day.

II

As some true chief of men, bowed down with stress
  Of life's disastrous eld, on blossoming youth
  May gaze, and murmur with self-pity and ruth, –

'Might I thy fruitless treasure but possess,
Such blessing of mine all coming years should bless;' –   5
    Then sends one sigh forth to the unknown goal,
    And bitterly feels breathe against his soul
The hour swift-winged of nearer nothingness: –

Even so the World's grey Soul to the green World
    Perchance one hour must cry: 'Woe's me, for whom   10
    Inveteracy of ill portends the doom, –
Whose heart's old fire in shadow of shame is furl'd:
While thou even as of yore art journeying,
All soulless now, yet merry with the Spring!'

XCIV
Michelangelo's Kiss

Great Michelangelo, with age grown bleak
    And uttermost labours, having once o'ersaid
    All grievous memories on his long life shed,
This worst regret to one true heart could speak: –
That when, with sorrowing love and reverence meek,   5
    He stooped o'er sweet Colonna's dying bed,
    His Muse and dominant Lady, spirit-wed, –
Her hand he kissed, but not her brow or cheek.

O Buonarruoti, – good at Art's fire-wheels
    To urge her chariot! – even thus the Soul,   10
    Touching at length some sorely-chastened goal,
Earns oftenest but a little: her appeals
Were deep and mute, – lowly her claim. Let be:
What holds for her Death's garner? And for thee?

XCV
The Vase of Life

Around the vase of Life at your slow pace
    He has not crept, but turned it with his hands,
    And all its sides already understands.
There, girt, one breathes alert for some great race;
Whose road runs far by sands and fruitful space;   5
    Who laughs, yet through the jolly throng has pass'd;

Who weeps, nor stays for weeping; who at last,
A youth, stands somewhere crowned, with silent face.

And he has filled this vase with wine for blood,
　　With blood for tears, with spice for burning vow,　　10
　　　With watered flowers for buried love most fit;
And would have cast it shattered to the flood,
　　Yet in Fate's name has kept it whole; which now
　　　Stands empty till his ashes fall in it.

XCVI
Life the Beloved

As thy friend's face, with shadow of soul o'erspread,
　　Somewhile unto thy sight perchance hath been
　　Ghastly and strange, yet never so is seen
In thought, but to all fortunate favour wed;
As thy love's death-bound features never dead　　5
　　To memory's glass return, but contravene
　　Frail fugitive days, and alway keep, I ween,
Than all new life a livelier lovelihead: –

So Life herself, thy spirit's friend and love,
　　Even still as Spring's authentic harbinger　　10
　　　Glows with fresh hours for hope to glorify;
Though pale she lay when in the winter grove
　　Her funeral flowers were snow-flakes shed on her
　　　And the red wings of frost-fire rent the sky.

XCVII
A Superscription

Look in my face; my name is Might-have-been;
　　I am also called No-more, Too-late, Farewell;
　　Unto thine ear I hold the dead-sea shell
Cast up thy Life's foam-fretted feet between;
Unto thine eyes the glass where that is seen　　5
　　Which had Life's form and Love's, but by my spell
　　Is now a shaken shadow intolerable,
Of ultimate things unuttered the frail screen.

Mark me, how still I am! But should there dart
　　One moment through thy soul the soft surprise　　10

Of that winged Peace which lulls the breath of sighs, –
Then shalt thou see me smile, and turn apart
Thy visage to mine ambush at thy heart
Sleepless with cold commemorative eyes.

XCVIII
He and I

Whence came his feet into my field, and why?
  How is it that he sees it all so drear?
  How do I see his seeing, and how hear
The name his bitter silence knows it by?
This was the little fold of separate sky   5
  Whose pasturing clouds in the soul's atmosphere
  Drew living light from one continual year:
How should he find it lifeless? He, or I?

Lo! this new Self now wanders round my field,
  With plaints for every flower, and for each tree   10
  A moan, the sighing wind's auxiliary:
And o'er sweet waters of my life, that yield
Unto his lips no draught but tears unseal'd,
  Even in my place he weeps. Even I, not he.

XCIX, C
Newborn Death

I

To-day Death seems to me an infant child
  Which her worn mother Life upon my knee
  Has set to grow my friend and play with me;
If haply so my heart might be beguil'd
To find no terrors in a face so mild, –   5
  If haply so my weary heart might be
  Unto the newborn milky eyes of thee,
O Death, before resentment reconcil'd.

How long, O Death? And shall thy feet depart
  Still a young child's with mine, or wilt thou stand   10
Fullgrown the helpful daughter of my heart,
  What time with thee indeed I reach the strand

Of the pale wave which knows thee what thou art,
    And drink it in the hollow of thy hand?

II

And thou, O Life, the lady of all bliss,
    With whom, when our first heart beat full and fast,
    I wandered till the haunts of men were pass'd,
And in fair places found all bowers amiss
Till only woods and waves might hear our kiss,   5
    While to the winds all thought of Death we cast: –
    Ah, Life! and must I have from thee at last
No smile to greet me and no babe but this?

Lo! Love, the child once ours; and Song, whose hair
    Blew like a flame and blossomed like a wreath;   10
And Art, whose eyes were worlds by God found fair:
    These o'er the book of Nature mixed their breath
With neck-twined arms, as oft we watched them there;
    And did these die that thou mightst bear me Death?

CI

The One Hope

When vain desire at last and vain regret
    Go hand in hand to death, and all is vain,
    What shall assuage the unforgotten pain
And teach the unforgetful to forget?
Shall Peace be still a sunk stream long unmet, –   5
    Or may the soul at once in a green plain
    Stoop through the spray of some sweet life-fountain
And cull the dew-drenched flowering amulet?

Ah! when the wan soul in that golden air
    Between the scriptured petals softly blown   10
    Peers breathless for the gift of grace unknown, –
Ah! let none other alien spell soe'er
But only the one Hope's one name be there, –
    Not less nor more, but even that word alone.

Prose,
published
1871

The Stealthy School of Criticism
from The Athenæum, *16 December 1871*

Your paragraph, a fortnight ago, relating to the pseudonymous authorship of an article, violently assailing myself and other writers of poetry, in the *Contemporary Review* for October last, reveals a species of critical masquerade which I have expressed in the heading given to this letter. Since then, Mr Sidney Colvin's note, qualifying the report that he intends to 'answer' that article, has appeared in your pages; and my own view as to the absolute forfeit, under such conditions, of all claim to honourable reply, is precisely the same as Mr Colvin's. For here a critical organ, professedly adopting the principle of open signature, would seem, in reality, to assert (by silent practice, however, not by enunciation,) that if the anonymous in criticism was – as itself originally inculcated – but an early caterpillar stage, the nominate too is found to be no better than a homely transitional chrysalis, and that the ultimate butterfly form for a critic who likes to sport in sunlight and yet to elude the grasp, is after all the pseudonymous. But, indeed, what I may call the 'Siamese' aspect of the entertainment provided by the *Review* will elicit but one verdict. Yet I may, perhaps, as the individual chiefly attacked, be excused for asking your assistance now in giving a specific denial to specific charges which, if unrefuted, may still continue, in spite of their author's strategic *fiasco*, to serve his purpose against me to some extent.

The primary accusation, on which this writer grounds all the rest, seems to be that others and myself 'extol fleshliness as the distinct and supreme end of poetic and pictorial art; aver that poetic expression is greater than poetic thought; and, by inference, that the body is greater than the soul, and sound superior to sense.'

As my own writings are alone formally dealt with in the article, I shall confine my answer to myself; and this must first take unavoidably the form of a challenge to prove so broad a statement. It is true, some fragmentary pretence at proof is put in here and there throughout the attack, and thus far an opportunity is given of contesting the assertion.

A Sonnet entitled *Nuptial Sleep* is quoted and abused at page 338 of the *Review*, and is there dwelt upon as a 'whole poem,' describing 'merely animal sensations.' It is no more a whole poem, in reality, than is any single stanza of any poem throughout the book. The poem, written chiefly in sonnets, and of which this is one sonnet-stanza, is entitled *The House of Life*; and even in my first published instalment of the whole work (as contained in the volume under notice) ample evidence is included that no such passing phase of description as the one headed *Nuptial Sleep* could possibly be put forward by the author of *The House of Life* as his own representative view of the subject of love. In proof of this, I will direct attention (among the love-sonnets of this poem) to Nos. 2, 8, 11, 17, 28, and more especially 13, which, indeed, I had better print here.

LOVE-SWEETNESS

'Sweet dimness of her loosened hair's downfall
   About thy face; her sweet hands round thy head
   In gracious fostering union garlanded;
Her tremulous smiles; her glances' sweet recall
Of love; her murmuring sighs memorial;
   Her mouth's culled sweetness by thy kisses shed
   On cheeks and neck and eyelids, and so led
Back to her mouth which answers there for all: –

'What sweeter than these things, except the thing
   In lacking which all these would lose their sweet: –
   The confident heart's still fervour; the swift beat
And soft subsidence of the spirit's wing
Then when it feels, in cloud-girt wayfaring,
   The breath of kindred plumes against its feet?'

Any reader may bring any artistic charge he pleases against the above sonnet; but one charge it would be impossible to maintain against the writer of the series in which it occurs and that is, the wish on his part to assert that the body is greater than the soul. For here all the passionate and just delights of the body are declared – somewhat figuratively, it is true, but unmistakably – to be as naught if not ennobled by the concurrence of the soul at all times. Moreover, nearly one half of this series of sonnets has nothing to do with love, but treats of quite other life-influences. I would defy any one to couple with fair quotation of Sonnets 29, 30, 31, 39, 40, 41, 43, or others, the slander that their author was not impressed, like all other thinking men, with the responsibilities and higher mysteries of life; while Sonnets 35, 36, and 37, entitled *The Choice*, sum up the general view taken in a manner only to be evaded by conscious insincerity.

Thus much for *The House of Life*, of which the sonnet *Nuptial Sleep* is one stanza, embodying, for its small constituent share, a beauty of natural universal function, only to be reprobated in art if dwelt on (as I have shown that it is not here) to the exclusion of those other highest things of which it is the harmonious concomitant.

At page 342, an attempt is made to stigmatize four short quotations as being specially 'my own property,' that is, (for the context shows the meaning,) as being grossly sensual; though all guiding reference to any precise page or poem in my book is avoided here. The first of these unspecified quotations is from the *Last Confession*; and is the description referring to the harlot's laugh, the hideous character of which, together with its real or imagined resemblance to the laugh heard soon afterwards from the lips of one long cherished as an ideal, is the immediate cause which makes the maddened hero of the poem a murderer. Assailants may say what they please; but no poet or poetic reader will blame me for making the incident recorded in these seven lines as repulsive to the reader as it was to the hearer and beholder. Without this, the chain of motive and result would remain obviously incomplete. Observe also that these are but seven lines in a poem of some five hundred, not one other of which could be classed with them.

A second quotation gives the last two lines *only* of the following sonnet, which is the first of four sonnets in *The House of Life* jointly entitled *Willowwood*: –

'I sat with Love upon a woodside well,
    Leaning across the water, I and he;
    Nor ever did he speak nor looked at me,
But touched his lute wherein was audible
The certain secret thing he had to tell:
    Only our mirrored eyes met silently
    In the low wave; and that sound seemed to be
The passionate voice I knew; and my tears fell.

'And at their fall, his eyes beneath grew hers;
And with his foot and with his wing-feathers
    He swept the spring that watered my heart's drouth.
Then the dark ripples spread to waving hair,
And as I stooped, her own lips rising there
    Bubbled with brimming kisses at my mouth.'

The critic has quoted (as I said) only the last two lines, and he has italicized the second as something unbearable and ridiculous. Of course the inference would be that this was really my own absurd bubble-and-squeak notion of an actual kiss. The reader will perceive at once, from the whole sonnet transcribed above, how untrue such an inference would be. The sonnet describes a dream or trance of divided love momentarily re-united by the longing fancy; and in the imagery of the dream, the face of the beloved rises through deep dark waters to kiss the lover. Thus the phrase, 'Bubbled with brimming kisses,' etc., bears purely on the special symbolism employed, and from that point of view will be found, I believe, perfectly simple and just.

A third quotation is from *Eden Bower*, and says,

> 'What more prize than love to impel thee?
> Grip and lip my limbs as I tell thee!'

Here again no reference is given, and naturally the reader would suppose that a human embrace is described. The embrace, on the contrary, is that of a fabled snake-woman and a snake. It would be possible still, no doubt, to object on other grounds to this conception; but the ground inferred and relied on for full effect by the critic is none the less an absolute misrepresentation. These three extracts, it will be admitted, are virtually, though not verbally, garbled with malicious intention; and the same is the case, as I have shown, with the sonnet called *Nuptial Sleep* when purposely treated as a 'whole poem.'

The last of the four quotations grouped by the critic as conclusive examples consists of two lines from *Jenny*. Neither some thirteen years ago, when I wrote this poem, nor last year when I published it, did I fail to foresee impending charges of recklessness and aggressiveness, or to perceive that even some among those who could really *read* the poem, and acquit me on these grounds, might still hold that the thought in it had better have dispensed with the situation which serves it for framework. Nor did I omit to consider how far a treatment from without might here be possible. But the motive powers of art reverse the requirement of science, and demand first of all an *inner* standing-point. The heart of such a mystery as this must be plucked from the very world in which it beats or bleeds; and the beauty and pity, the self-questionings and all-questionings which it brings with it, can come with full force only from the mouth of one alive to its whole appeal, such as the speaker put forward in the poem, – that is, of a young and thoughtful man of the world. To such a speaker, many half-cynical revulsions of feeling and reverie, and a recurrent presence of the impressions of beauty (however artificial) which first brought him within such a circle of influence, would be inevitable features of the dramatic relations portrayed. Here again I can give the lie, in hearing of honest readers, to the base or trivial ideas which my critic labours to connect with the poem. There is another little charge, however, which this minstrel in mufti brings against *Jenny*, namely, one of plagiarism from that very poetic self of his which the tutelary prose does but enshroud for the moment. This question can, fortunately, be settled with ease by others who have read my critic's poems; and thus I need the less regret that, not happening myself to be in that position, I must be content to rank with those who cannot pretend to an opinion on the subject.

It would be humiliating, need one come to serious detail, to have to refute such an accusation as that of 'binding oneself by solemn league and covenant to extol fleshliness as the distinct and supreme end of poetic and pictorial art'; and one cannot but feel that here every one will think it allowable merely to pass by with a smile the foolish fellow who has brought a charge thus framed against any reasonable man. Indeed, what I have said already is substantially enough to refute it, even did I not feel sure that a fair balance of my poetry must, of itself, do so in the eyes of every candid reader. I say nothing of my pictures; but those who know them will laugh at the idea. That I may, nevertheless, take a wider view than some poets or critics, of how much, in the material conditions absolutely given to man to deal with as distinct from his spiritual aspirations, is admissible within the limits of Art, – this, I say, is possible enough; nor do I wish to shrink from such responsibility. But to state that I do so to the ignoring or overshadowing of spiritual beauty, is an absolute falsehood, impossible to be put forward except in the indulgence of prejudice or rancour.

I have selected, amid much railing on my critic's part, what seemed the most representative indictment against me, and have, so far, answered it. Its remaining clauses set forth how others and myself 'aver that poetic expression is greater than poetic thought ... and sound superior to sense' – an accusation elsewhere, I observe, expressed by saying that we 'wish to create form for its own sake.' If writers of verse are to be listened to in such arraignment of each other, it might be quite competent to me to prove, from the works of my friends in question, that no such thing is the case with them; but my present function is to confine myself to my own defence. This, again, it is difficult to do quite seriously. It is no part of my undertaking to dispute the verdict of any 'contemporary,' however contemptuous or contemptible, on my own measure of executive success; but the accusation cited above is not against the poetic value of certain work, but against its primary and (by assumption) its admitted aim. And to this I must reply that so far, assuredly, not even Shakspeare himself could desire more arduous human tragedy for development in Art than belongs to the themes I venture to embody, however incalculably higher might be his power of dealing with them. What more inspiring for poetic effort than the terrible Love turned to Hate, – perhaps the deadliest of all passion-woven complexities, – which is the theme of *Sister Helen*, and in a more fantastic form, of *Eden Bower* – the surroundings of both poems being the mere machinery of a central universal meaning? What, again, more so than the savage penalty exacted for a lost ideal, as expressed in the *Last Confession*; – than the outraged love for man and burning compensations in art and memory of *Dante at Verona*; – than the baffling problems which the face of *Jenny* conjures up; – or than the analysis of passion and feeling attempted in *The House of Life*, and others among the more purely lyrical poems? I speak here, as does my critic in the clause adduced, of *aim*, not of *achievement*; and so far, the mere summary is instantly subversive of the preposterous imputation. To assert that the poet whose matter is such as this aims chiefly at 'creating form for its own sake,' is, in fact, almost an ingenuous kind of dishonesty; for surely it delivers up the asserter at once, bound hand and foot, to the tender mercies of contradictory proof. Yet this may fairly be taken as an example of the spirit in which a constant effort is here made against me to appeal to those who either are ignorant of what I write, or else belong to the large class too easily influenced by an assumption of authority in addressing them. The false name appended to the article must, as is evident, aid this position vastly; for who, after all, would not be apt to laugh at seeing one poet confessedly come forward as aggressor against another in the field of criticism?

It would not be worth while to lose time and patience in noticing minutely how the system of misrepresentation is carried into points of artistic detail, – giving us, for example, such statements as that the burthen employed in the ballad of *Sister Helen* 'is repeated with little or no alteration through thirty-four verses,' whereas the fact is, that the alteration of it in every verse is the very scheme of the poem. But these are minor matters quite thrown into the shade by the critic's more daring sallies. In addition to the class of attack I have answered above, the article contains, of course, an immense amount of personal paltriness; as, for instance, attributions of my work to this, that, or the other absurd derivative source; or again, pure nonsense (which can have no real meaning even to the writer) about 'one art getting hold of another, and imposing on it its conditions and limitations'; or, indeed, what not besides? However, to such antics as this, no more attention is possible than that which Virgil enjoined Dante to bestow on the meaner phenomena of his pilgrimage.

Thus far, then, let me thank you for the opportunity afforded me to join issue with the Stealthy School of Criticism. As for any literary justice to be done on this particular Mr Robert-Thomas, I will merely ask the reader whether, once identified, he does not become manifestly his own best 'sworn tormentor'? For who will then fail to discern all the palpitations which preceded his final resolve in the great question whether to be or not to be his acknowledged self when he became an assailant? And yet this is he who, from behind his mask, ventures to charge another with 'bad blood,' with 'insincerity,' and the rest of it (and that where poetic fancies are alone in question); while every word on his own tongue is covert rancour, and every stroke from his pen perversion of truth. Yet, after all, there is nothing wonderful in the lengths to which a fretful poet-critic will carry such grudges as he may bear, while publisher and editor can both be found who are willing to consider such means admissible, even to the clear subversion of first professed tenets in the *Review* which they conduct.

In many phases of outward nature, the principle of chaff and grain holds good, – the base enveloping the precious continually; but an untruth was never yet the husk of a truth. Thresh and riddle and winnow it as you may, – let it fly in shreds to the four winds, – falsehood only will be that which flies and that which stays. And thus the sheath of deceit which this pseudonymous undertaking presents at the outset insures in fact what will be found to be its real character to the core.

Poems
published
1871–82

On the Site of a Mulberry-Tree

Planted by Wm. Shakspeare; felled by the Rev. F. Gastrell

This tree, here fall'n, no common birth or death
  Shared with its kind. The world's enfranchised son,
  Who found the trees of Life and Knowledge one,
Here set it, frailer than his laurel-wreath.
Shall not the wretch whose hand it fell beneath   5
  Rank also singly – the supreme unhung?
  Lo! Sheppard, Turpin, pleading with black tongue
This viler thief's unsuffocated breath!

We'll search thy glossary, Shakspeare! whence almost,
  And whence alone, some name shall be reveal'd   10
    For this deaf drudge, to whom no length of ears
    Sufficed to catch the music of the spheres;
  Whose soul is carrion now, – too mean to yield
Some tailor's ninth allotment of a ghost.

Down Stream

Between Holmscote and Hurstcote
  The river-reaches wind,
The whispering trees accept the breeze,
  The ripple's cool and kind:
With love low-whispered 'twixt the shores,   5
  With rippling laughters gay,
With white arms bared to ply the oars,
  On last year's first of May.

Between Holmscote and Hurstcote
  The river's brimmed with rain,   10
Through close-met banks and parted banks
  Now near, now far again:
With parting tears caressed to smiles,
  With meeting promised soon,
With every sweet vow that beguiles,   15
  On last year's first of June.

Between Holmscote and Hurstcote
  The river's flecked with foam,

'Neath shuddering clouds that hang in shrouds
   And lost winds wild for home: 20
With infant wailings at the breast,
   With homeless steps astray,
With wanderings shuddering tow'rds one rest
   On this year's first of May.

Between Holmscote and Hurstcote   25
   The summer river flows
With doubled flight of moons by night
   And lilies' deep repose:
With lo! beneath the moon's white stare
   A white face not the moon,   30
With lilies meshed in tangled hair,
   On this year's first of June.

Between Holmscote and Hurstcote
   A troth was given and riven,
From heart's trust grew one life to two,   35
   Two lost lives cry to Heaven:
With banks spread calm to meet the sky,
   With meadows newly mowed,
The harvest-paths of glad July,
   The sweet school-children's road.   40

The Cloud Confines

The day is dark and the night
   To him that would search their heart;
   No lips of cloud that will part
Nor morning song in the light:
   Only, gazing alone,   5
   To him wild shadows are shown,
   Deep under deep unknown
And height above unknown height.
      Still we say as we go, –
       'Strange to think by the way,   10
      Whatever there is to know,
       That shall we know one day.'

  The Past is over and fled;
   Named new, we name it the old;

Thereof some tale hath been told, 15
But no word comes from the dead;
  Whether at all they be,
  Or whether as bond or free,
  Or whether they too were we,
Or by what spell they have sped. 20
    Still we say as we go, –
      'Strange to think by the way,
    Whatever there is to know,
      That shall we know one day.'

What of the heart of hate 25
  That beats in thy breast, O Time? –
  Red strife from the furthest prime,
And anguish of fierce debate;
  War that shatters her slain,
  And peace that grinds them as grain, 30
  And eyes fixed ever in vain
On the pitiless eyes of Fate.
    Still we say as we go, –
      'Strange to think by the way,
    Whatever there is to know, 35
      That shall we know one day.'

What of the heart of love
  That bleeds in thy breast, O Man? –
  Thy kisses snatched 'neath the ban
Of fangs that mock them above; 40
  Thy bells prolonged unto knells,
  Thy hope that a breath dispels,
  Thy bitter forlorn farewells
And the empty echoes thereof?
    Still we say as we go, – 45
      'Strange to think by the way,
    Whatever there is to know,
      That shall we know one day.'

The sky leans dumb on the sea,
  Aweary with all its wings; 50
  And oh! the song the sea sings
Is dark everlastingly.
  Our past is clean forgot,
  Our present is and is not,
  Our future's a sealed seedplot, 55

And what betwixt them are we? –
We who say as we go, –
'Strange to think by the way,
Whatever there is to know,
That shall we know one day.'   60

Sunset Wings

To-night this sunset spreads two golden wings
Cleaving the western sky;
Winged too with wind it is, and winnowings
Of birds; as if the day's last hour in rings
Of strenuous flight must die.   5

Sun-steeped in fire, the homeward pinions sway
Above the dovecote-tops;
And clouds of starlings, ere they rest with day,
Sink, clamorous like mill-waters, at wild play,
By turns in every copse: 10

Each tree heart-deep the wrangling rout receives, –
Save for the whirr within,
You could not tell the starlings from the leaves;
Then one great puff of wings, and the swarm heaves
Away with all its din.   15

Even thus Hope's hours, in ever-eddying flight,
To many a refuge tend;
With the first light she laughed, and the last light
Glows round her still; who natheless in the night
At length must make an end.   20

And now the mustering rooks innumerable
Together sail and soar,
While for the day's death, like a tolling knell,
Unto the heart they seem to cry, Farewell,
No more, farewell, no more!   25

Is Hope not plumed, as 'twere a fiery dart?
And oh! thou dying day,
Even as thou goest must she too depart,
And Sorrow fold such pinions on the heart
As will not fly away?   30

Two Lyrics from Niccolò Tommaseo

I – THE YOUNG GIRL

Even as a child that weeps,
Lulled by the love it keeps,
My grief lies back and sleeps.

Yes, it is Love bears up
　My soul on his spread wings,   5
Which the days would else chafe out
　With their infinite harassings.
　To quicken it, he brings
The inward look and mild
That thy face wears, my child.   10

As in a gilded room
　Shines 'mid the braveries
Some wild-flower, by the bloom
　Of its delicate quietness
　Recalling the forest-trees   15
In whose shadow it was,
And the water and the green grass: –

Even so, 'mid the stale loves
　The city prisoneth,
Thou touchest me gratefully,   20
　Like Nature's wholesome breath:
　Thy heart nor hardeneth
In pride, nor putteth on
Obeisance not its own.

Not thine the skill to shut   25
　The love up in thine heart,
Neither to seem more tender,
　Less tender than thou art.
　Thou dost not hold apart
In silence when thy joys   30
Most long to find a voice.

Let the proud river-course,
　That shakes its mane and champs,
Run between marble shores
　By the light of many lamps,   35
　While all the ooze and the damps

Of the city's choked-up ways
Make it their draining-place.

Rather the little stream
  For me; which, hardly heard,   40
Unto the flower, its friend,
  Whispers as with a word.
  The timid journeying bird
Of the pure drink that flows
Takes but one drop, and goes.   45

II A FAREWELL

I soothed and pitied thee: and for thy lips, –
  A smile, a word (sure guide
  To love that's ill to hide!)
    Was all I had thereof.

Even as an orphan boy, who, sore distress'd,   5
  A gentle woman meets beside the road
And takes him home with her, – so to thy breast
  Thou didst take home my image: pure abode!
  'Twas but a virgin's dream. This heart bestow'd
    Respect and piety   10
    And friendliness on thee:
    But it is poor in love.

No, I am not for thee. Thou art too new,
  I am too old, to the old beaten way.
The griefs are not the same which grieve us two: 15
  Less than I wish, more than I hope, alway
    Are heart and soul in thee.
    Thou art too much for me
    Sister, and not enough.

A better and a fresher heart than mine   20
  Perchance may meet thee ere thy youth be told;
Or, cheated by the longing that is thine,
  Waiting for life perchance thou shalt wax old.
  Perchance the time may come when I may hold
    It had been best for me   25
    To have had thy ministry
    On the steep path and rough.

The Leaf

LEOPARDI

'Torn from your parent bough,
Poor leaf all withered now,
    Where go you?' 'I cannot tell.
Storm-stricken is the oak-tree
    Where I grew, whence I fell.   5
Changeful continually,
    The zephyr and hurricane
Since that day bid me flee
From deepest woods to the lea,
    From highest hills to the plain.   10
Where the wind carries me
    I go without fear or grief:
I go whither each one goes, –
Thither the leaf of the rose
    And thither the laurel-leaf.'   15

Winter

How large that thrush looks on the bare thorn-tree!
    A swarm of such, three little months ago,
    Had hidden in the leaves and let none know
Save by the outburst of their minstrelsy.
A white flake here and there – a snow-lily   5
    Of last night's frost – our naked flower-beds hold;
    And for a rose-flower on the darkling mould
The hungry redbreast gleams. No bloom, no bee.

The current shudders to its ice-bound sedge:
    Nipped in their bath, the stark reeds one by one   10
    Flash each its clinging diamond in the sun:
'Neath winds which for this Winter's sovereign pledge
Shall curb great king-masts to the ocean's edge
    And leave memorial forest-kings o'erthrown.

Spring

Soft-littered is the new-year's lambing-fold,
  And in the hollowed haystack at its side
  The shepherd lies o' nights now, wakeful-eyed
At the ewes' travailing call through the dark cold.
The young rooks cheep 'mid the thick caw o' the old: 5
  And near unpeopled stream-sides, on the ground,
  By her spring-cry the moorhen's nest is found,
Where the drained flood-lands flaunt their marigold.

Chill are the gusts to which the pastures cower,
  And chill the current where the young reeds stand   10
  As green and close as the young wheat on land:
Yet here the cuckoo and the cuckoo-flower
Plight to the heart Spring's perfect imminent hour
  Whose breath shall soothe you like your dear one's hand.

Untimely Lost

OLIVER MADOX BROWN. BORN 1855; DIED 1874

Upon the landscape of his coming life
  A youth high-gifted gazed, and found it fair:
  The heights of work, the floods of praise, were there.
What friendships, what desires, what love, what wife? —
All things to come. The fanned springtide was rife   5
  With imminent solstice; and the ardent air
  Had summer sweets and autumn fires to bear; —
Heart's ease full-pulsed with perfect strength for strife.

A mist has risen: we see the youth no more:
  Does he see on and strive on? And may we   10
  Late-tottering world-worn hence, find *his* to be
The young strong hand which helps us up that shore?
Or, echoing the No More with Nevermore,
Must Night be ours and his? We hope: and he?

Proserpina

(FOR A PICTURE)

Afar away the light that brings cold cheer
   Unto this wall, – one instant and no more
   Admitted at my distant palace-door.
Afar the flowers of Enna from this drear
Dire fruit, which, tasted once, must thrall me here.   5
   Afar those skies from this Tartarean grey
   That chills me; and afar, how far away,
The nights that shall be from the days that were.

Afar from mine own self I seem, and wing
   Strange ways in thought, and listen for a sign: 10
   And still some heart unto some soul doth pine,
(Whose sounds mine inner sense is fain to bring,
Continually together murmuring,) –
   'Woe's me for thee, unhappy Proserpine!'

Proserpina

(PER UN QUADRO)

Lungi è la luce che in sù questo muro
   Rifrange appena, un breve istante scorta
   Del rio palazzo alla soprana porta.
Lungi quei fiori d'Enna, O lido oscuro,
Dal frutto tuo fatal che omai m'è duro.   5
   Lungi quel cielo dal tartareo manto
   Che quì mi cuopre: e lungi ahi lungi ahi quanto
Le notti che saran dai dì che furo.

Lungi da me mi sento; e ognor sognando
   Cerco e ricerco, e resto ascoltatrice;   10
   E qualche cuore a qualche anima dice,
(Di cui mi giunge il suon da quando in quando.
Continuamente insieme sospirando,) –
   'Oimè per te, Proserpina infelice!'

La Bella Mano
(FOR A PICTURE)

O lovely hand, that thy sweet self dost lave
  In that thy pure and proper element,
  Whence erst the Lady of Love's high advènt
Was born, and endless fires sprang from the wave: –
Even as her Loves to her their offerings gave,   5
  For thee the jewelled gifts they bear; while each
  Looks to those lips, of music-measured speech
The fount, and of more bliss than man may crave.

In royal wise ring-girt and bracelet-spann'd,
  A flower of Venus' own virginity,   10
Go shine among thy sisterly sweet band;
  In maiden-minded converse delicately
  Evermore white and soft; until thou be,
O hand! heart-handsel'd in a lover's hand.

La Bella Mano
(PER UN QUADRO)

O bella Mano, che ti lavi e piaci
  In quel medesmo tuo puro elemento
  Donde la Dea dell' amoroso avvento
Nacque, (e dall' onda s'infuocar le faci
Di mille inispegnibili fornaci): –   5
  Come a Venere a te l'oro e l'argento
  Offron gli Amori; e ognun riguarda attento
La bocca che sorride e te che taci.

In dolce modo dove onor t' invii
  Vattene adorna, e porta insiem fra tante   10
  Di Venere e di vergine sembiante;
Umilemente in luoghi onesti e pii
Bianca e soave ognora; infin che sii,
  O Mano, mansueta in man d'amante.

Francesca da Rimini

DANTE

When I made answer, I began: 'Alas!
  How many sweet thoughts and how much desire
Led these two onward to the dolorous pass!'
  Then turned to them, as who would fain inquire,
And said: 'Francesca, these thine agonies   5
  Wring tears for pity and grief that they inspire:
But tell me, – in the season of sweet sighs,
  When and what way did Love instruct you so
That he in your vague longings made you wise?'
  Then she to me: 'There is no greater woe   10
Than the remembrance brings of happy days
  In misery; and this thy guide doth know.
But if the first beginnings to retrace
  Of our sad love can yield thee solace here,
So will I be as one that weeps and says.   15
  One day we read, for pastime and sweet cheer,
Of Lancelot, how he found Love tyrannous:
  We were alone and without any fear.
Our eyes were drawn together, reading thus,
  Full oft, and still our cheeks would pale and glow;   20
But one sole point it was that conquered us.
  For when we read of that great lover, how
He kissed the smile which he had longed to win, –
  Then he whom nought can sever from me now
For ever, kissed my mouth, all quivering.   25
  A Galahalt was the book, and he that writ:
Upon that day we read no more therein.'
  At the tale told, while one soul uttered it,
The other wept: a pang so pitiable
  That I was seized, like death, in swooning-fit,   30
And even as a dead body falls, I fell.

For
The Holy Family, by Michelangelo
in the National Gallery[1]

Turn not the prophet's page, O Son! He knew
  All that thou hast to suffer, and hath writ.
  Not yet thine hour of knowledge. Infinite
The sorrows that thy manhood's lot must rue
And dire acquaintance of thy grief. That clue   5
  The spirits of thy mournful ministerings
  Seek through yon scroll in silence. For these things
The angels have desired to look into.

Still before Eden waves the fiery sword, –
  Her Tree of Life unransomed: whose sad Tree   10
  Of Knowledge yet to growth of Calvary
  Must yield its Tempter, – Hell the earliest dead
Of Earth resign, – and yet, O Son and Lord,
  The Seed o' the woman bruise the serpent's head.

1 In this picture the Virgin Mother is seen withholding from the Child Saviour the prophetic writings in which his sufferings are foretold. Angelic figures beside them examine a scroll.

La Pia
(DANTE)

'And when on earth thy voice again is heard,
  And thou from the long road hast rested thee,'
After the second spirit said the third,
  'Remember me who am La Pia. Me
Siena, me Maremma, made, unmade.   5
  He knoweth this thing in his heart – even he
With whose fair jewel I was ringed and wed.'

The Bride's Prelude

'Sister,' said busy Amelotte
    To listless Aloÿse;
'Along your wedding-road the wheat
Bends as to hear your horse's feet,
And the noonday stands still for heat.'   5

Amelotte laughed into the air
    With eyes that sought the sun:
But where the walls in long brocade
Were screened, as one who is afraid
Sat Aloÿse within the shade.   10

And even in shade was gleam enough
    To shut out full repose
From the bride's 'tiring-chamber, which
Was like the inner altar-niche
Whose dimness worship has made rich.   15

Within the window's heaped recess
    The light was counterchanged
In blent reflexes manifold
From perfume-caskets of wrought gold
And gems the bride's hair could not hold   20

All thrust together: and with these
    A slim-curved lute, which now,
At Amelotte's sudden passing there,
Was swept in somewise unaware,
And shook to music the close air.   25

Against the haloed lattice-panes
    The bridesmaid sunned her breast;
Then to the glass turned tall and free,
And braced and shifted daintily
Her loin-belt through her cote-hardie.   30

The belt was silver, and the clasp
    Of lozenged arm-bearings;
A world of mirrored tints minute

The rippling sunshine wrought into 't,
That flushed her hand and warmed her foot.   35

At least an hour had Aloÿse, –
    Her jewels in her hair, –
Her white gown, as became a bride,
Quartered in silver at each side, –
Sat thus aloof, as if to hide.   40

Over her bosom, that lay still,
    The vest was rich in grain,
With close pearls wholly overset:
Around her throat the fastenings met
Of chevesayle and mantelet.   45

Her arms were laid along her lap
    With the hands open: life
Itself did seem at fault in her:
Beneath the drooping brows, the stir
Of thought made noonday heavier.   50

Long sat she silent; and then raised
    Her head, with such a gasp
As while she summoned breath to speak
Fanned high that furnace in the cheek
But sucked the heart-pulse cold and weak.   55

(Oh gather round her now, all ye
    Past seasons of her fear, –
Sick springs, and summers deadly cold!
To flight your hovering wings unfold,
For now your secret shall be told.   60

Ye many sunlights, barbed with darts
    Of dread detecting flame, –
Gaunt moonlights that like sentinels
Went past with iron clank of bells, –
Draw round and render up your spells!)   65

'Sister,' said Aloÿse, 'I had
    A thing to tell thee of
Long since, and could not. But do thou
Kneel first in prayer awhile, and bow
Thine heart, and I will tell thee now.'   70

Amelotte wondered with her eyes;

But her heart said in her:
'Dear Aloÿse would have me pray
Because the awe she feels to-day
Must need more prayers than she can say.'   75

So Amelotte put by the folds
    That covered up her feet,
And knelt, – beyond the arras'd gloom
And the hot window's dull perfume, –
Where day was stillest in the room.   80

'Queen Mary, hear,' she said, 'and say
    To Jesus the Lord Christ,
This bride's new joy, which He confers,
New joy to many ministers,
And many griefs are bound in hers.'   85

The bride turned in her chair, and hid
    Her face against the back,
And took her pearl-girt elbows in
Her hands, and could not yet begin,
But shuddering, uttered, 'Urscelyn!'   90

Most weak she was; for as she pressed
    Her hand against her throat,
Along the arras she let trail
Her face, as if all heart did fail,
And sat with shut eyes, dumb and pale.   95

Amelotte still was on her knees
    As she had kneeled to pray.
Deeming her sister swooned, she thought,
At first, some succour to have brought;
But Aloÿse rocked, as one distraught.   100

She would have pushed the lattice wide
    To gain what breeze might be;
But marking that no leaf once beat
The outside casement, it seemed meet
Not to bring in more scent and heat.   105

So she said only: 'Aloÿse,
    Sister, when happened it
At any time that the bride came
To ill, or spoke in fear of shame
When speaking first the bridegroom's name?'   110

A bird had out its song and ceased
    Ere the bride spoke. At length
She said: 'The name is as the thing: –
Sin hath no second christening,
And shame is all that shame can bring.   115

'In divers places many an while
    I would have told thee this;
But faintness took me, or a fit
Like fever. God would not permit
That I should change thine eyes with it.   120

'Yet once I spoke, hadst thou but heard: –
    That time we wandered out
All the sun's hours, but missed our way
When evening darkened, and so lay
The whole night covered up in hay.   125

'At last my face was hidden: so,
    Having God's hint, I paused
Not long; but drew myself more near
Where thou wast laid, and shook off fear,
And whispered quick into thine ear   130

'Something of the whole tale. At first
    I lay and bit my hair
For the sore silence thou didst keep:
Till, as thy breath came long and deep,
I knew that thou hadst been asleep.   135

'The moon was covered, but the stars
    Lasted till morning broke.
Awake, thou told'st me that thy dream
Had been of me, – that all did seem
At jar, – but that it was a dream.   140

'I knew God's hand and might not speak.
    After that night I kept
Silence and let the record swell:
Till now there is much more to tell
Which must be told out ill or well.'   145

She paused then, weary, with dry lips
    Apart. From the outside
By fits there boomed a dull report

From where i' the hanging tennis-court
The bridegroom's retinue made sport.   150

The room lay still in dusty glare,
    Having no sound through it
Except the chirp of a caged bird
That came and ceased: and if she stirred,
Amelotte's raiment could be heard.   155

Quoth Amelotte: 'The night this chanced
    Was a late summer night
Last year! What secret, for Christ's love,
Keep'st thou since then? Mary above!
What thing is this thou speakest of?   160

'Mary and Christ! Lest when 'tis told
    I should be prone to wrath, –
This prayer beforehand! How she errs
Soe'er, take count of grief like hers,
Whereof the days are turned to years!'   165

She bowed her neck, and having said,
    Kept on her knees to hear;
And then, because strained thought demands
Quiet before it understands,
Darkened her eyesight with her hands.   170

So when at last her sister spoke,
    She did not see the pain
O' the mouth nor the ashamèd eyes,
But marked the breath that came in sighs
And the half-pausing for replies.   175

This was the bride's sad prelude-strain: –
    'I' the convent where a girl
I dwelt till near my womanhood,
I had but preachings of the rood
And Aves told in solitude   180

'To spend my heart on: and my hand
    Had but the weary skill
To eke out upon silken cloth
Christ's visage, or the long bright growth
Of Mary's hair, or Satan wroth.   185

'So when at last I went, and thou,
    A child not known before,

Didst come to take the place I left, –
My limbs, after such lifelong theft
Of life, could be but little deft   190

'In all that ministers delight
      To noble women: I
Had learned no word of youth's discourse,
Nor gazed on games of warriors,
Nor trained a hound, nor ruled a horse.   195

'Besides, the daily life i' the sun
      Made me at first hold back.
To thee this came at once; to me
It crept with pauses timidly;
I am not blithe and strong like thee.   200

'Yet my feet liked the dances well,
      The songs went to my voice,
The music made me shake and weep;
And often, all night long, my sleep
Gave dreams I had been fain to keep.   205

'But though I loved not holy things,
      To hear them scorned brought pain, –
They were my childhood; and these dames
Were merely perjured in saints' names
And fixed upon saints' days for games.   210

'And sometimes when my father rode
      To hunt with his loud friends,
I dared not bring him to be quaff'd,
As my wont was, his stirrup-draught,
Because they jested so and laugh'd.   215

'At last one day my brothers said,
      "The girl must not grow thus, –
Bring her a jennet, – she shall ride."
They helped my mounting, and I tried
To laugh with them and keep their side.   220

'But brakes were rough and bents were steep
      Upon our path that day:
My palfrey threw me; and I went
Upon men's shoulders home, sore spent,
While the chase followed up the scent.   225

'Our shrift-father (and he alone
    Of all the household there
Had skill in leechcraft,) was away
When I reached home. I tossed, and lay
Sullen with anguish the whole day.   230

'For the day passed ere some one brought
    To mind that in the hunt
Rode a young lord she named, long bred
Among the priests, whose art (she said)
Might chance to stand me in much stead.   235

'I bade them seek and summon him:
    But long ere this, the chase
Had scattered, and he was not found.
I lay in the same weary stound,
Therefore, until the night came round.   240

'It was dead night and near on twelve
    When the horse-tramp at length
Beat up the echoes of the court:
By then, my feverish breath was short
With pain the sense could scarce support.   245

'My fond nurse sitting near my feet
    Rose softly, – her lamp's flame
Held in her hand, lest it should make
My heated lids, in passing, ache;
And she passed softly, for my sake.   250

'Returning soon, she brought the youth
    They spoke of. Meek he seemed,
But good knights held him of stout heart.
He was akin to us in part,
And bore our shield, but barred athwart.   255

'I now remembered to have seen
    His face, and heard him praised
For letter-lore and medicine,
Seeing his youth was nurtured in
Priests' knowledge, as mine own had been.'   260

The bride's voice did not weaken here,
    Yet by her sudden pause
She seemed to look for questioning;

Or else (small need though) 'twas to bring
Well to her mind the bygone thing.   265

Her thought, long stagnant, stirred by speech,
   Gave her a sick recoil;
As, dip thy fingers through the green
That masks a pool, – where they have been
The naked depth is black between.   270

Amelotte kept her knees; her face
   Was shut within her hands,
As it had been throughout the tale;
Her forehead's whiteness might avail
Nothing to say if she were pale.   275

Although the lattice had dropped loose,
   There was no wind; the heat
Being so at rest that Amelotte
Heard far beneath the plunge and float
Of a hound swimming in the moat.   280

Some minutes since, two rooks had toiled
   Home to the nests that crowned
Ancestral ash-trees. Through the glare
Beating again, they seemed to tear
With that thick caw the woof o' the air.   285

But else, 'twas at the dead of noon
   Absolute silence; all,
From the raised bridge and guarded sconce
To green-clad places of pleasaunce
Where the long lake was white with swans.   290

Amelotte spoke not any word
   Nor moved she once; but felt
Between her hands in narrow space
Her own hot breath upon her face,
And kept in silence the same place.   295

Aloÿse did not hear at all
   The sounds without. She heard
The inward voice (past help obey'd)
Which might not slacken nor be stay'd,
But urged her till the whole were said.   300

Therefore she spoke again: 'That night
   But little could be done:

My foot, held in my nurse's hands,
He swathed up heedfully in bands,
And for my rest gave close commands.   305

'I slept till noon, but an ill sleep
    Of dreams: through all that day
My side was stiff and caught the breath;
Next day, such pain as sickeneth
Took me, and I was nigh to death.   310

'Life strove, Death claimed me for his own,
    Through days and nights: but now
'Twas the good father tended me,
Having returned. Still, I did see
The youth I spoke of constantly.   315

'For he would with my brothers come
    To stay beside my couch,
And fix my eyes against his own,
Noting my pulse; or else alone,
To sit at gaze while I made moan.   320

'(Some nights I knew he kept the watch,
    Because my women laid
The rushes thick for his steel shoes.)
Through many days this pain did use
The life God would not let me lose.   325

'At length, with my good nurse to aid,
    I could walk forth again:
And still, as one who broods or grieves,
At noons I'd meet him and at eves,
With idle feet that drove the leaves.   330

'The day when I first walked alone
    Was thinned in grass and leaf,
And yet a goodly day o' the year:
The last bird's cry upon mine ear
Left my brain weak, it was so clear.   335

'The tears were sharp within mine eyes.
    I sat down, being glad,
And wept; but stayed the sudden flow
Anon, for footsteps that fell slow;
'Twas that youth passed me, bowing low.   340

'He passed me without speech; but when,
    At least an hour gone by,
Rethreading the same covert, he
Saw I was still beneath the tree,
He spoke and sat him down with me.   345

'Little we said; nor one heart heard
    Even what was said within;
And, faltering some farewell, I soon
Rose up; but then i' the autumn noon
My feeble brain whirled like a swoon.   350

'He made me sit. "Cousin, I grieve
    Your sickness stays by you."
"I would," said I, "that you did err
So grieving. I am wearier
Than death, of the sickening dying year."   355

'He answered: "If your weariness
    Accepts a remedy,
I hold one and can give it you."
I gazed: "What ministers thereto,
Be sure," I said, "that I will do."   360

'He went on quickly: – 'Twas a cure
    He had not ever named
Unto our kin lest they should stint
Their favour, for some foolish hint
Of wizardry or magic in't: 365

'But that if he were let to come
    Within my bower that night,
(My women still attending me,
He said, while he remain'd there,) he
Could teach me the cure privily.   370

'I bade him come that night. He came;
    But little in his speech
Was cure or sickness spoken of,
Only a passionate fierce love
That clamoured upon God above.   375

'My women wondered, leaning close
    Aloof. At mine own heart
I think great wonder was not stirr'd.

I dared not listen, yet I heard
His tangled speech, word within word. 380

'He craved my pardon first, – all else
  Wild tumult. In the end
He remained silent at my feet
Fumbling the rushes. Strange quick heat
Made all the blood of my life meet. 385

'And lo! I loved him. I but said,
  If he would leave me then,
His hope some future might forecast.
His hot lips stung my hand: at last
My damsels led him forth in haste.' 390

The bride took breath to pause; and turned
  Her gaze where Amelotte
Knelt, – the gold hair upon her back
Quite still in all its threads, – the track
Of her still shadow sharp and black. 395

That listening without sight had grown
  To stealthy dread; and now
That the one sound she had to mark
Left her alone too, she was stark
Afraid, as children in the dark. 400

Her fingers felt her temples beat;
  Then came that brain-sickness
Which thinks to scream, and murmureth;
And pent between her hands, the breath
Was damp against her face like death. 405

Her arms both fell at once; but when
  She gasped upon the light,
Her sense returned. She would have pray'd
To change whatever words still stay'd
Behind, but felt there was no aid. 410

So she rose up, and having gone
  Within the window's arch
Once more, she sat there, all intent
On torturing doubts, and once more bent
To hear, in mute bewilderment. 415

But Aloÿse still paused. Thereon
  Amelotte gathered voice

In somewise from the torpid fear
    Coiled round her spirit. Low but clear
She said: 'Speak, sister; for I hear.'   420

But Aloÿse threw up her neck
    And called the name of God: –
'Judge, God, 'twixt her and me to-day!
She knows how hard this is to say,
Yet will not have one word away.'   425

Her sister was quite silent. Then
    Afresh: – 'Not she, dear Lord!
Thou be my judge, on Thee I call!'
She ceased, – her forehead smote the wall
'Is there a God,' she said, 'at all?'   430

Amelotte shuddered at the soul,
    But did not speak. The pause
Was long this time. At length the bride
Pressed her hand hard against her side,
And trembling between shame and pride   435

Said by fierce effort: 'From that night
    Often at nights we met:
That night, his passion could but rave:
The next, what grace his lips did crave
I knew not, but I know I gave.'   440

Where Amelotte was sitting, all
    The light and warmth of day
Were so upon her without shade
That the thing seemed by sunshine made
Most foul and wanton to be said.   445

She would have questioned more, and known
    The whole truth at its worst,
But held her silent, in mere shame
Of day. 'Twas only these words came: –
'Sister, thou hast not said his name.'   450

'Sister,' quoth Aloÿse, 'thou know'st
    His name. I said that he
Was in a manner of our kin.
Waiting the title he might win,
They called him the Lord Urscelyn.'   455

The bridegroom's name, to Amelotte
    Daily familiar, – heard
Thus in this dreadful history, –
Was dreadful to her; as might be
Thine own voice speaking unto thee.   460

The day's mid-hour was almost full;
    Upon the dial-plate
The angel's sword stood near at One.
An hour's remaining yet; the sun
Will not decrease till all be done.   465

Through the bride's lattice there crept in
    At whiles (from where the train
Of minstrels, till the marriage-call,
Loitered at windows of the wall,)
Stray lute-notes, sweet and musical.   470

They clung in the green growths and moss
    Against the outside stone;
Low like dirge-wail or requiem
They murmured, lost 'twixt leaf and stem:
There was no wind to carry them.   475

Amelotte gathered herself back
    Into the wide recess
That the sun flooded: it o'erspread
Like flame the hair upon her head
And fringed her face with burning red.   480

All things seemed shaken and at change:
    A silent place o' the hills
She knew, into her spirit came:
Within herself she said its name
And wondered was it still the same.   485

The bride (whom silence goaded) now
    Said strongly, – her despair
By stubborn will kept underneath: –
'Sister, 'twere well thou didst not breathe
That curse of thine. Give me my wreath.'   490

'Sister,' said Amelotte, 'abide
    In peace. Be God thy judge,
As thou hast said – not I. For me,

I merely will thank God that he
Whom thou hast lovèd loveth thee.'   495

Then Aloÿse lay back, and laughed
   With wan lips bitterly,
Saying, 'Nay, thank thou God for this, –
That never any soul like his
Shall have its portion where love is.'   500

Weary of wonder, Amelotte
   Sat silent: she would ask
No more, though all was unexplained:
She was too weak; the ache still pained
Her eyes, – her forehead's pulse remained.   505

The silence lengthened. Aloÿse
   Was fain to turn her face
Apart, to where the arras told
Two Testaments, the New and Old,
In shapes and meanings manifold.   510

One solace that was gained, she hid.
   Her sister, from whose curse
Her heart recoiled, had blessed instead:
Yet would not her pride have it said
How much the blessing comforted.   515

Only, on looking round again
   After some while, the face
Which from the arras turned away
Was more at peace and less at bay
With shame than it had been that day.   520

She spoke right on, as if no pause
   Had come between her speech:
'That year from warmth grew bleak and pass'd,'
She said; 'the days from first to last
How slow, – woe's me! the nights how fast!   525

'From first to last it was not known:
   My nurse, and of my train
Some four or five, alone could tell
What terror kept inscrutable:
There was good need to guard it well.   530

'Not the guilt only made the shame,
   But he was without land

And born amiss. He had but come
To train his youth here at our home,
And, being man, depart therefrom.   535

'Of the whole time each single day
    Brought fear and great unrest:
It seemed that all would not avail
Some once, – that my close watch would fail,
And some sign, somehow, tell the tale.   540

'The noble maidens that I knew,
    My fellows, oftentimes
Midway in talk or sport, would look
A wonder which my fears mistook,
To see how I turned faint and shook.   545

'They had a game of cards, where each
    By painted arms might find
What knight she should be given to.
Ever with trembling hand I threw
Lest I should learn the thing I knew.   550

'And once it came. And Aure d'Honvaulx
    Held up the bended shield
And laughed: "Gramercy for our share! –
If to our bridal we but fare
To smutch the blazon that we bear!"   555

'But proud Denise de Villenbois
    Kissed me, and gave her wench
The card, and said: "If in these bowers
You women play at paramours,
You must not mix your game with ours.'   560

'And one upcast it from her hand:
    "Lo! see how high he'll soar!"
But then their laugh was bitterest;
For the wind veered at fate's behest
And blew it back into my breast.   565

'Oh! if I met him in the day
    Or heard his voice, – at meals
Or at the Mass or through the hall, –
A look turned towards me would appal
My heart by seeming to know all.   570

'Yet I grew curious of my shame,
    And sometimes in the church,
On hearing such a sin rebuked,
Have held my girdle-glass unhooked
To see how such a woman looked.   575

'But if at night he did not come,
    I lay all deadly cold
To think they might have smitten sore
And slain him, and as the night wore,
His corpse be lying at my door.   580

'And entering or going forth,
    Our proud shield o'er the gate
Seemed to arraign my shrinking eyes.
With tremors and unspoken lies
The year went past me in this wise.   585

'About the spring of the next year
    An ailing fell on me;
(I had been stronger till the spring;)
'Twas mine old sickness gathering,
I thought; but 'twas another thing.   590

'I had such yearnings as brought tears,
    And a wan dizziness:
Motion, like feeling, grew intense;
Sight was a haunting evidence
And sound a pang that snatched the sense.   595

'It now was hard on that great ill
    Which lost our wealth from us
And all our lands. Accursed be
The peevish fools of liberty
Who will not let themselves be free!   600

'The Prince was fled into the west:
    A price was on his blood,
But he was safe. To us his friends
He left that ruin which attends
The strife against God's secret ends.   605

'The league dropped all asunder, – lord,
    Gentle and serf. Our house
Was marked to fall. And a day came

When half the wealth that propped our name
Went from us in a wind of flame.   610

'Six hours I lay upon the wall
    And saw it burn. But when
It clogged the day in a black bed
Of louring vapour, I was led
Down to the postern, and we fled.   615

'But ere we fled, there was a voice
    Which I heard speak, and say
That many of our friends, to shun
Our fate, had left us and were gone,
And that Lord Urscelyn was one.   620

'That name, as was its wont, made sight
    And hearing whirl. I gave
No heed but only to the name:
I held my senses, dreading them,
And was at strife to look the same.   625

'We rode and rode. As the speed grew,
    The growth of some vague curse
Swarmed in my brain. It seemed to me
Numbed by the swiftness, but would be –
That still – clear knowledge certainly.   630

'Night lapsed. At dawn the sea was there
    And the sea-wind: afar
The ravening surge was hoarse and loud
And underneath the dim dawn-cloud
Each stalking wave shook like a shroud.   635

'From my drawn litter I looked out
    Unto the swarthy sea,
And knew. That voice, which late had cross'd
Mine ears, seemed with the foam uptoss'd:
I knew that Urscelyn was lost.   640

'Then I spake all: I turned on one
    And on the other, and spake:
My curse laughed in me to behold
Their eyes: I sat up, stricken cold,
Mad of my voice till all was told.   645

'Oh! of my brothers, Hugues was mute,
    And Gilles was wild and loud,

And Raoul strained abroad his face,
As if his gnashing wrath could trace
Even there the prey that it must chase.   650

'And round me murmured all our train,
      Hoarse as the hoarse-tongued sea;
Till Hugues from silence louring woke,
And cried: "What ails the foolish folk?
Know ye not frenzy's lightning stroke?"   655

'But my stern father came to them
      And quelled them with his look,
Silent and deadly pale. Anon
I knew that we were hastening on,
My litter closed and the light gone.   660

'And I remember all that day
      The barren bitter wind
Without, and the sea's moaning there
That I first moaned with unaware,
And when I knew, shook down my hair.   665

'Few followed us or faced our flight:
      Once only I could hear,
Far in the front, loud scornful words,
And cries I knew of hostile lords,
And crash of spears and grind of swords.   670

'It was soon ended. On that day
      Before the light had changed
We reached our refuge; miles of rock
Bulwarked for war; whose strength might mock
Sky, sea, or man, to storm or shock.   675

'Listless and feebly conscious, I
      Lay far within the night
Awake. The many pains incurred
That day, – the whole, said, seen or heard, –
Stayed by in me as things deferred.   680

'Not long. At dawn I slept. In dreams
      All was passed through afresh
From end to end. As the morn heaved
Towards noon, I, waking sore aggrieved,
That I might die, cursed God, and lived.   685

'Many days went, and I saw none
    Except my women. They
Calmed their wan faces, loving me;
And when they wept, lest I should see,
Would chaunt a desolate melody.   690

'Panic unthreatened shook my blood
    Each sunset, all the slow
Subsiding of the turbid light.
I would rise, sister, as I might,
And bathe my forehead through the night   695

'To elude madness. The stark wall
    Made chill the mirk: and when
We oped our curtains, to resume
Sun-sickness after long sick gloom,
The withering sea-wind walked the room.   700

'Through the gaunt windows the great gales
    Bore in the tattered clumps
Of waif-weed and the tamarisk-boughs;
And sea-mews, 'mid the storm's carouse,
Were flung, wild-clamouring, in the house.   705

'My hounds I had not; and my hawk,
    Which they had saved for me,
Wanting the sun and rain to beat
His wings, soon lay with gathered feet;
And my flowers faded, lacking heat.   710

'Such still were griefs: for grief was still
    A separate sense, untouched
Of that despair which had become
My life. Great anguish could benumb
My soul, – my heart was quarrelsome.   715

'Time crept. Upon a day at length
    My kinsfolk sat with me:
That which they asked was bare and plain:
I answered: the whole bitter strain
Was again said, and heard again.   720

'Fierce Raoul snatched his sword, and turned
    The point against my breast.
I bared it, smiling: "To the heart

Strike home," I said; "another dart
Wreaks hourly there a deadlier smart."   725

"'Twas then my sire struck down the sword,
     And said with shaken lips:
"She from whom all of you receive
Your life, so smiled; and I forgive."
Thus, for my mother's sake, I live.   730

'But I, a mother even as she,
     Turned shuddering to the wall:
For I said: "Great God! and what would I do,
When to the sword, with the thing I knew,
I offered not one life but two!"   735

'Then I fell back from them, and lay
     Outwearied. My tired sense
Soon filmed and settled, and like stone
I slept; till something made me moan,
And I woke up at night alone.   740

'I woke at midnight, cold and dazed;
     Because I found myself
Seated upright, with bosom bare,
Upon my bed, combing my hair,
Ready to go, I knew not where.   745

'It dawned light day, – the last of those
     Long months of longing days.
That noon, the change was wrought on me
In somewise, – nought to hear or see, –
Only a trance and agony.'   750

The bride's voice failed her, from no will
     To pause. The bridesmaid leaned,
And where the window-panes were white,
Looked for the day: she knew not quite
If there were either day or night.   755

It seemed to Aloÿse that the whole
     Day's weight lay back on her
Like lead. The hours that did remain
Beat their dry wings upon her brain
Once in mid-flight, and passed again.   760

There hung a cage of burnt perfumes
     In the recess: but these,

For some hours, weak against the sun,
Had simmered in white ash. From One
The second quarter was begun.   765

They had not heard the stroke. The air,
    Though altered with no wind,
Breathed now by pauses, so to say:
Each breath was time that went away, –
Each pause a minute of the day.   770

I' the almonry, the almoner,
    Hard by, had just dispensed
Church-dole and march-dole. High and wide
Now rose the shout of thanks, which cried
On God that He should bless the bride.   775

Its echo thrilled within their feet,
    And in the furthest rooms
Was heard, where maidens flushed and gay
Wove with stooped necks the wreaths alway
Fair for the virgin's marriage-day.   780

The mother leaned along, in thought
    After her child; till tears,
Bitter, not like a wedded girl's,
Fell down her breast along her curls,
And ran in the close work of pearls.   785

The speech ached at her heart. She said:
    'Sweet Mary, do thou plead
This hour with thy most blessed Son
To let these shameful words atone,
That I may die when I have done.'   790

The thought ached at her soul. Yet now: –
    'Itself – that life' (she said,)
'Out of my weary life – when sense
Unclosed, was gone. What evil men's
Most evil hands had borne it thence   795

'I knew, and cursed them. Still in sleep
    I have my child; and pray
To know if it indeed appear
As in my dream's perpetual sphere,
That I – death reached – may seek it there.   800

'Sleeping, I wept; though until dark
    A fever dried mine eyes
Kept open; save when a tear might
Be forced from the mere ache of sight.
And I nursed hatred day and night.   805

'Aye, and I sought revenge by spells;
    And vainly many a time
Have laid my face into the lap
Of a wise woman, and heard clap
Her thunder, the fiend's juggling trap.   810

'At length I feared to curse them, lest
    From evil lips the curse
Should be a blessing; and would sit
Rocking myself and stifling it
With babbled jargon of no wit.   815

'But this was not at first: the days
    And weeks made frenzied months
Before this came. My curses, pil'd
Then with each hour unreconcil'd,
Still wait for those who took my child.'   820

She stopped, grown fainter. 'Amelotte,
    Surely,' she said, 'this sun
Sheds judgment-fire from the fierce south:
It does not let me breathe: the drouth
Is like sand spread within my mouth.'   825

The bridesmaid rose. I' the outer glare
    Gleamed her pale cheeks, and eyes
Sore troubled; and aweary weigh'd
Her brows just lifted out of shade;
And the light jarred within her head.   830

'Mid flowers fair-heaped there stood a bowl
    With water. She therein
Through eddying bubbles slid a cup,
And offered it, being risen up,
Close to her sister's mouth, to sup.   835

The freshness dwelt upon her sense,
    Yet did not the bride drink;
But she dipped in her hand anon

And cooled her temples; and all wan
With lids that held their ache, went on.   840

'Through those dark watches of my woe,
        Time, an ill plant, had waxed
Apace. That year was finished. Dumb
And blind, life's wheel with earth's had come
Whirled round: and we might seek our home.   845

'Our wealth was rendered back, with wealth
        Snatched from our foes. The house
Had more than its old strength and fame:
But still 'neath the fair outward claim
I rankled, – a fierce core of shame.   850

'It chilled me from their eyes and lips
        Upon a night of those
First days of triumph, as I gazed
Listless and sick, or scarcely raised
My face to mark the sports they praised.   855

'The endless changes of the dance
        Bewildered me: the tones
Of lute and cithern struggled tow'rds
Some sense; and still in the last chords
The music seemed to sing wild words.   860

'My shame possessed me in the light
        And pageant, till I swooned.
But from that hour I put my shame
From me, and cast it over them
By God's command and in God's name   865

'For my child's bitter sake. O thou
        Once felt against my heart
With longing of the eyes, – a pain
Since to my heart for ever, – then
Beheld not, and not felt again!'   870

She scarcely paused, continuing: –
        'That year drooped weak in March;
And April, finding the streams dry,
Choked, with no rain, in dust: the sky
Shall not be fainter this July.   875

'Men sickened; beasts lay without strength;
        The year died in the land.

But I, already desolate,
Said merely, sitting down to wait, –
"The seasons change and Time wears late."   880

'For I had my hard secret told,
      In secret, to a priest;
With him I communed; and he said
The world's soul, for its sins, was sped,
And the sun's courses numberèd.   885

'The year slid like a corpse afloat:
      None trafficked, – who had bread
Did eat. That year our legions, come
Thinned from the place of war, at home
Found busier death, more burdensome.   890

'Tidings and rumours came with them,
      The first for months. The chiefs
Sat daily at our board, and in
Their speech were names of friend and kin:
One day they spoke of Urscelyn.   895

'The words were light, among the rest:
      Quick glance my brothers sent
To sift the speech; and I, struck through,
Sat sick and giddy in full view:
Yet did none gaze, so many knew.   900

'Because in the beginning, much
      Had caught abroad, through them
That heard my clamour on the coast:
But two were hanged; and then the most
Held silence wisdom, as thou know'st.   905

'That year the convent yielded thee
      Back to our home; and thou
Then knew'st not how I shuddered cold
To kiss thee, seeming to enfold
To my changed heart myself of old.   910

'Then there was showing thee the house,
      So many rooms and doors;
Thinking the while how thou wouldst start
If once I flung the doors apart
Of one dull chamber in my heart   915

'And yet I longed to open it;
   And often in that year
Of plague and want, when side by side
We've knelt to pray with them that died,
My prayer was, "Show her what I hide!"'   920

END OF PART I

Song and Music

O leave your hand where it lies cool
   Upon the eyes whose lids are hot:
Its rosy shade is bountiful
   Of silence, and assuages thought.
O lay your lips against your hand   5
   And let me feel your breath through it,
While through the sense your song shall fit
   The soul to understand.

The music lives upon my brain
   Between your hands within mine eyes;   10
It stirs your lifted throat like pain,
   An aching pulse of melodies.
Lean nearer, let the music pause:
   The soul may better understand
Your music, shadowed in your hand,   15
   Now while the song withdraws.

Place de la Bastille, Paris

How dear the sky has been above this place!
   Small treasures of this sky that we see here
   Seen weak through prison-bars from year to year;
Eyed with a painful prayer upon God's grace
To save, and tears that stayed along the face   5
   Lifted at sunset. Yea, how passing dear,
   Those nights when through the bars a wind left clear
The heaven, and moonlight soothed the limpid space!

So was it, till one night the secret kept
Safe in low vault and stealthy corridor   10
Was blown abroad on gospel-tongues of flame.
O ways of God, mysterious evermore!
How many on this spot have cursed and wept
That all might stand here now and own Thy Name.

Wellington's Funeral

18TH NOVEMBER 1852

'VICTORY!'
So once more the cry must be.
Duteous mourning we fulfil
In God's name; but by God's will,
Doubt not, the last word is still
            'Victory!'

Funeral,
In the music round this pall,
Solemn grief yields earth to earth;
But what tones of solemn mirth   10
In the pageant of new birth
            Rise and fall?

For indeed,
If our eyes were openèd,
Who shall say what escort floats   15
Here, which breath nor gleam denotes, –
Fiery horses, chariots
            Fire-footed?

Trumpeter,
Even thy call he may not hear;   20
Long-known voice for ever past,
Till with one more trumpet-blast
God's assuring word at last
            Reach his ear.

Multitude,   25
Hold your breath in reverent mood:
For while earth's whole kindred stand
Mute even thus on either hand,

This soul's labour shall be scann'd
  And found good.   30

  Cherubim,
Lift ye not even now your hymn?
Lo! once lent for human lack,
Michael's sword is rendered back.
Thrills not now the starry track,   35
  Seraphim?

  Gabriel,
Since the gift of thine 'All hail!'
Out of Heaven no time hath brought
Gift with fuller blessing fraught   40
Than the peace which this man wrought
  Passing well.

  Be no word
Raised of bloodshed Christ-abhorr'd.
Say: "Twas thus in His decrees   45
Who Himself, the Prince of Peace,
For His harvest's high increase
  Sent a sword.'

  Veterans,
He by whom the neck of France   50
Then was given unto your heel,
Timely sought, may lend as well
To your sons his terrible
  Countenance.

  Waterloo!   55
As the last grave must renew,
Ere fresh death, the banshee-strain, –
So methinks upon thy plain
Falls some presage in the rain,
  In the dew.   60

  And O thou,
Watching with an exile's brow
Unappeased, o'er death's dumb flood: –
Lo! the saving strength of God
In some new heart's English blood   65
  Slumbers now.

Emperor,
Is this all thy work was for? –
Thus to see thy self-sought aim,
Yea thy titles, yea thy name   70
In another's shame, to shame
        Bandied o'er?[1]

Wellington,
Thy great work is but begun.
With quick seed his end is rife   75
Whose long tale of conquering strife
Shows no triumph like his life
        Lost and won.

1 Date of the *Coup d'État*: 2nd December 1851.

The Church Porch I

Sister, first shake we off the dust we have
    Upon our feet, lest it defile the stones
    Inscriptured, covering their sacred bones
Who lie i' the aisles which keep the names they gave,
Their trust abiding round them in the grave;   5
    Whom painters paint for visible orisons,
    And to whom sculptors pray in stone and bronze;
Their voices echo still like a spent wave.

Without here, the church-bells are but a tune,
And on the carven church-door this hot noon   10
    Lays all its heavy sunshine here without:
But having entered in, we shall find there
Silence, and sudden dimness, and deep prayer,
    And faces of crowned angels all about.

The Church Porch II

Sister, arise: We have no more to sing
  Or say. The priest abideth as is meet
  To minister. Rise up out of thy seat
Though peradventure 'tis an irksome thing
To cross again the threshold of our King   5
  Where His doors stand against the evil street,
  And let each step increase upon our feet
The dust we shook from them at entering.

Must we of very sooth go home? The air,
  Whose heat outside makes mist that can be seen,   10
  Is very cool and clear where we have been.
  The priest abideth, ministering. Lo!
As he for service, why not we for prayer?
  It is so bidden, sister, let us go.

Words on the Window-Pane[1]

Did she in summer write it, or in spring,
  Or with this wail of autumn at her ears,
  Or in some winter left among old years
Scratched it through tettered cark? A certain thing
That round her heart the frost was hardening,   5
  Not to be thawed of tears, which on this pane
  Channelled the rime, perchance, in fevered rain,
For false man's sake and love's most bitter sting.

Howbeit, between this last word and the next
Unwritten, subtly seasoned was the smart,   10
  And here at least the grace to weep: if she,
Rather, midway in her disconsolate text,
Rebelled not, loathing from the trodden heart
  That thing which she had found man's love to be.

1 For a woman's fragmentary inscription.

Gioventù e Signorìa Youth and Lordship
(Italian Street-Song)

È giovine il signore,
  Ed ama molte cose, –
  I canti, le rose,
La forza e l'amore.

Quel che più vuole
  Ancor non osa:
Ahi più che il sole,
  Più ch' ogni rosa,
  La cara cosa,
Donna a gioire.

È giovine il signore,
  Ed ama quelle cose
  Che ardor dispose
In cuore all' amore.

Bella fanciulla,
  Guardalo in viso;
Non mancar nulla,
  Motto o sorriso;
  Ma viso a viso
Guarda a gradire.

È giovine il signore,
  Ed ama tutte cose,
  Vezzose, giojose,
Tenenti all' amore.

Prendilo in braccio
  Adesso o mai;
Per più mi taccio,
  Chè tu lo sai;
Bacialo e l'avrai,
  Ma non lo dire.

My young lord's the lover
  Of earth and sky above,
Of youth's sway and youth's play,
  Of songs and flowers and love.

Yet for love's desires   5
  Green youth lacks the daring;
Though one dream of fire,
  All his hours ensnaring,
  Burns the boy past bearing –
The dream that girls inspire.   10

My young lord's the lover
  Of every burning thought
That Love's will, that Love's skill
  Within his breast has wrought.

Lovely girl, look on him   15
  Soft as music's measure;
Yield him, when you've won him,
  Joys and toys at pleasure;
  But to win your treasure,
Softly look upon him.   20

My young lord's the lover
  Of every tender grace
That woman, to woo man,
  Can wear in form or face.

Take him to your bosom   25
  Now, girl, or never;
Let not your new blossom
  Of sweet kisses sever;
  Only guard for ever
Your boast within your bosom.   30

È giovine il signore,
   Ed ama ben le cose
   Che Amor nascose,
Che mostragli Amore.

Deh trionfando
   Non farne pruova;
Ahimè! che quando
   Gioja più giova,
   Allor si trova
Presso al finire.

È giovine il signore,
   Ed ama tante cose,
   Le rose, le spose,
Quante gli dona Amore.

My young lord's the lover
   Of every secret thing,
Love-hidden, love-bidden
   This day to banqueting.

Lovely girl, with vaunting   35
   Never tempt to-morrow:
From all shapes enchanting
   Any joy can borrow,
   Still the spectre Sorrow
Rises up for haunting.   40

And now my lord's the lover
   Of ah! so many a sweet, —
Of roses, of spouses,
   As many as love may greet.

Soothsay

Let no man ask thee of anything
Not yearborn between Spring and Spring.
More of all worlds than he can know,
Each day the single sun doth show.
A trustier gloss than thou canst give   5
From all wise scrolls demonstrative,
The sea doth sigh and the wind sing.

Let no man awe thee on any height
Of earthly kingship's mouldering might.
The dust his heel holds meet for thy brow   10
Hath all of it been what both are now;
And thou and he may plague together
A beggar's eyes in some dusty weather
When none that is now knows sound or sight.

Crave thou no dower of earthly things   15
Unworthy Hope's imaginings.
To have brought true birth of Song to be
And to have won hearts to Poesy,
Or anywhere in the sun or rain
To have loved and then beloved again,   20
Is loftiest reach of Hope's bright wings.

The wild waifs cast up by the sea
Are diverse ever seasonably.
Even so the soul-tides still may land
A different drift upon the sand.   25
But one the sea is evermore:
And one be still, 'twixt shore and shore,
As the sea's life, thy soul in thee.

Say, hast thou pride? How then may fit
Thy mood with flatterers' silk-spun wit?   30
Haply the sweet voice lifts thy crest,
A breeze of fame made manifest.
Nay, but then chaf'st at flattery? Pause:
Be sure thy wrath is not because
It makes thee feel thou lovest it.   35

Let thy soul strive that still the same
Be early friendship's sacred flame.
The affinities have strongest part
In youth, and draw men heart to heart:
As life wears on and finds no rest,   40
The individual in each breast
Is tyrannous to sunder them.

In the life-drama's stern cue-call,
A friend's a part well-prized by all:
And if thou meet an enemy,   45
What art thou that none such should be?
Even so: but if the two parts run
Into each other and grow one,
Then comes the curtain's cue to fall.

Whate'er by other's need is claimed   50
More than by thine, – to him unblamed
Resign it: and if he should hold
What more than he thou lack'st, bread, gold,
Or any good whereby we live, –
To thee such substance let him give   55
Freely: nor he nor thou be shamed.

Strive that thy works prove equal: lest
That work which thou hast done the best
Should come to be to thee at length
(Even as to envy seems the strength   60
Of others) hateful and abhorr'd, –
Thine own above thyself made lord, –
Of self-rebuke the bitterest.

Unto the man of yearning thought
And aspiration, to do nought   65
Is in itself almost an act, –
Being chasm-fire and cataract
Of the soul's utter depths unseal'd.
Yet woe to thee if once thou yield
Unto the act of doing nought!   70

How callous seems beyond revoke
The clock with its last listless stroke!
How much too late at length! – to trace
The hour on its forewarning face,
The thing thou hast not dared to do!   75
Behold, this *may* be thus! Ere true
It prove, arise and bear thy yoke.

Let lore of all Theology
Be to thy soul what it *can* be:
But know, – the Power that fashions man   80
Measured not out thy little span
For thee to take the meting-rod
In turn, and so approve on God
Thy science of Theometry.

To God at best, to Chance at worst,   85
Give thanks for good things, last as first.
But windstrown blossom is that good
Whose apple is not gratitude.
Even if no prayer uplift thy face,
Let the sweet right to render grace   90
As thy soul's cherished child be nurs'd.

Didst ever say, 'Lo, I forget'?
Such thought was to remember yet.
As in a gravegarth, count to see
The monuments of memory.   95
Be this thy soul's appointed scope: –
Gaze onward without claim to hope,
Nor, gazing backward, court regret.

Rose Mary

Of her two fights with the Beryl-stone:
Lost the first, but the second won.

PART I

'Mary mine that art Mary's Rose,
Come in to me from the garden-close.
The sun sinks fast with the rising dew,
And we marked not how the faint moon grew;
But the hidden stars are calling you.   5

'Tall Rose Mary, come to my side,
And read the stars if you'd be a bride.
In hours whose need was not your own,
While you were a young maid yet ungrown,
You've read the stars in the Beryl-stone.   10

'Daughter, once more I bid you read;
But now let it be for your own need:
Because to-morrow, at break of day,
To Holy Cross he rides on his way,
Your knight Sir James of Heronhaye.   15

'Ere he wed you, flower of mine,
For a heavy shrift he seeks the shrine.
Now hark to my words and do not fear;
Ill news next I have for your ear;
But be you strong, and our help is here.   20

'On his road, as the rumour's rife,
An ambush waits to take his life.
He needs will go, and will go alone;
Where the peril lurks may not be known;
But in this glass all things are shown.'   25

Pale Rose Mary sank to the floor: —
'The night will come if the day is o'er!'
'Nay, heaven takes counsel, star with star,
And help shall reach your heart from afar:
A bride you'll be, as a maid you are.'   30

The lady unbound her jewelled zone
And drew from her robe the Beryl-stone.
Shaped it was to a shadowy sphere, —
World of our world, the sun's compeer,
That bears and buries the toiling year.   35

With shuddering light 'twas stirred and strewn
Like the cloud-nest of the wading moon:
Freaked it was as the bubble's ball,
Rainbow-hued through a misty pall
Like the middle light of the waterfall.   40

Shadows dwelt in its teeming girth
Of the known and unknown things of earth;
The cloud above and the wave around, —
The central fire at the sphere's heart bound,
Like doomsday prisoned underground.   45

A thousand years it lay in the sea
With a treasure wrecked from Thessaly;
Deep it lay 'mid the coiled sea-wrack,
But the ocean-spirits found the track:
A soul was lost to win it back.   50

The lady upheld the wondrous thing:—
'Ill fare' (she said) 'with a fiend's-fairing:
But Moslem blood poured forth like wine
Can hallow Hell, 'neath the Sacred Sign;
And my lord brought this from Palestine.   55

'Spirits who fear the Blessed Rood
Drove forth the accursed multitude
That heathen worship housed herein,—
Never again such home to win,
Save only by a Christian's sin.   60

'All last night at an altar fair
I burnt strange fires and strove with prayer;
Till the flame paled to the red sunrise,
All rites I then did solemnize;
And the spell lacks nothing but your eyes.'   65

Low spake maiden Rose Mary:—
'O mother mine, if I should not see!'
'Nay, daughter, cover your face no more,
But bend love's heart to the hidden lore,
And you shall see now as heretofore.'   70

Paler yet were the pale cheeks grown
As the grey eyes sought the Beryl-stone:
Then over her mother's lap leaned she,
And stretched her thrilled throat passionately,
And sighed from her soul, and said, 'I see.'   75

Even as she spoke, they two were 'ware
Of music-notes that fell through the air;
A chiming shower of strange device,
Drop echoing drop, once twice and thrice,
As rain may fall in Paradise.   80

An instant come, in an instant gone,
No time there was to think thereon.
The mother held the sphere on her knee:—
'Lean this way and speak low to me,
And take no note but of what you see.'   85

'I see a man with a besom grey
That sweeps the flying dust away.'

'Ay, that comes first in the mystic sphere;
But now that the way is swept and clear,
Heed well what next you look on there.'   90

'Stretched aloft and adown I see
Two roads that part in waste-country:
The glen lies deep and the ridge stands tall;
What's great below is above seen small,
And the hill-side is the valley-wall.'   95

'Stream-bank, daughter, or moor and moss,
Both roads will take to Holy Cross.
The hills are a weary waste to wage;
But what of the valley-road's presage?
That way must tend his pilgrimage.'   100

'As 'twere the turning leaves of a book,
The road runs past me as I look;
Or it is even as though mine eye
Should watch calm waters filled with sky
While lights and clouds and wings went by.'   105

'In every covert seek a spear;
They'll scarce lie close till he draws near.'
'The stream has spread to a river now;
The stiff blue sedge is deep in the slough,
But the banks are bare of shrub or bough.'   110

'Is there any roof that near at hand
Might shelter yield to a hidden band?'
'On the further bank I see but one,
And a herdsman now in the sinking sun
Unyokes his team at the threshold-stone.'   115

'Keep heedful watch by the water's edge, –
Some boat might lurk 'neath the shadowed sedge.'
'One slid but now 'twixt the winding shores,
But a peasant woman bent to the oars
And only a young child steered its course.   120

'Mother, something flashed to my sight! –
Nay, it is but the lapwing's flight. –
What glints there like a lance that flees? –
Nay, the flags are stirred in the breeze,
And the water's bright through the dart-rushes.   125

'Ah! vainly I search from side to side: –
Woe's me! and where do the foemen hide?
Woe's me! and perchance I pass them by,
And under the new dawn's blood-red sky
Even where I gaze the dead shall lie.'   130

Said the mother: 'For dear love's sake,
Speak more low, lest the spell should break.'
Said the daughter: 'By love's control,
My eyes, my words, are strained to the goal;
But oh! the voice that cries in my soul!'   135

'Hush, sweet, hush! be calm and behold.'
'I see two floodgates broken and old:
The grasses wave o'er the ruined weir,
But the bridge still leads to the breakwater:
And – mother, mother, O mother dear!'   140

The damsel clung to her mother's knee,
And dared not let the shriek go free;
Low she crouched by the lady's chair,
And shrank blindfold in her fallen hair,
And whispering said, 'The spears are there!'   145

The lady stooped aghast from her place,
And cleared the locks from her daughter's face.
'More's to see, and she swoons, alas!
Look, look again, ere the moment pass!
One shadow comes but once to the glass.   150

'See you there what you saw but now?'
'I see eight men 'neath the willow bough.
All over the weir a wild growth's spread:
Ah me! it will hide a living head
As well as the water hides the dead.   155

'They lie by the broken water-gate
As men who have a while to wait.
The chief's high lance has a blazoned scroll,
He seems some lord of tithe and toll
With seven squires to his bannerole.   160

'The little pennon quakes in the air,
I cannot trace the blazon there: –
Ah! now I can see the field of blue,

The spurs and the merlins two and two; –
It is the Warden of Holycleugh!'   165

'God be thanked for the thing we know!
You have named your good knight's mortal foe.
Last Shrovetide in the tourney-game
He sought his life by treasonous shame;
And this way now doth he seek the same.   170

'So, fair lord, such a thing you are!
But we too watch till the morning star.
Well, June is kind and the moon is clear:
Saint Judas send you a merry cheer
For the night you lie at Warisweir!   175

'Now, sweet daughter, but one more sight,
And you may lie soft and sleep to-night.
We know in the vale what perils be:
Now look once more in the glass, and see
If over the hills the road lies free.'   180

Rose Mary pressed to her mother's cheek,
And almost smiled but did not speak;
Then turned again to the saving spell,
With eyes to search and with lips to tell
The heart of things invisible.   185

'Again the shape with the besom grey
Comes back to sweep the clouds away.
Again I stand where the roads divide;
But now all's near on the steep hillside,
And a thread far down is the rivertide.'   190

'Ay, child, your road is o'er moor and moss,
Past Holycleugh to Holy Cross.
Our hunters lurk in the valley's wake,
As they knew which way the chase would take:
Yet search the hills for your true love's sake.'   195

'Swift and swifter the waste runs by,
And nought I see but the heath and the sky;
No brake is there that could hide a spear,
And the gaps to a horseman's sight lie clear;
Still past it goes, and there's nought to fear.' 200

'Fear no trap that you cannot see, –
They'd not lurk yet too warily.

Below by the weir they lie in sight,
And take no heed how they pass the night
Till close they crouch with the morning light.'   205

'The road shifts ever and brings in view
Now first the heights of Holycleugh:
Dark they stand o'er the vale below,
And hide that heaven which yet shall show
The thing their master's heart doth know.   210

'Where the road looks to the castle steep,
There are seven hill-clefts wide and deep:
Six mine eyes can search as they list,
But the seventh hollow is brimmed with mist:
If aught were there, it might not be wist.'   215

'Small hope, my girl, for a helm to hide
In mists that cling to a wild moorside:
Soon they melt with the wind and sun,
And scarce would wait such deeds to be done:
God send their snares be the worst to shun.'   220

'Still the road winds ever anew
As it hastens on towards Holycleugh;
And ever the great walls loom more near,
Till the castle-shadow, steep and sheer,
Drifts like a cloud, and the sky is clear.'   225

'Enough, my daughter,' the mother said,
And took to her breast the bending head;
'Rest, poor head, with my heart below,
While love still lulls you as long ago:
For all is learnt that we need to know.   230

'Long the miles and many the hours
From the castle-height to the abbey-towers;
But here the journey has no more dread;
Too thick with life is the whole road spread
For murder's trembling foot to tread.'   235

She gazed on the Beryl-stone full fain
Ere she wrapped it close in her robe again:
The flickering shades were dusk and dun,
And the lights throbbed faint in unison,
Like a high heart when a race is run.   240

As the globe slid to its silken gloom,
Once more a music rained through the room;
Low it splashed like a sweet star-spray,
And sobbed like tears at the heart of May,
And died as laughter dies away.   245

The lady held her breath for a space,
And then she looked in her daughter's face:
But wan Rose Mary had never heard;
Deep asleep like a sheltered bird
She lay with the long spell minister'd.   250

'Ah! and yet I must leave you, dear,
For what you have seen your knight must hear.
Within four days, by the help of God
He comes back safe to his heart's abode:
Be sure he shall shun the valley-road.'   255

Rose Mary sank with a broken moan,
And lay in the chair and slept alone,
Weary, lifeless, heavy as lead:
Long it was ere she raised her head
And rose up all discomforted.   260

She searched her brain for a vanished thing,
And clasped her brows, remembering;
Then knelt and lifted her eyes in awe,
And sighed with a long sigh sweet to draw: –
'Thank God, thank God, thank God I saw!'   265

The lady had left her as she lay
To seek the Knight of Heronhaye.
But first she clomb by a secret stair,
And knelt at a carven altar fair,
And laid the precious Beryl there.   270

Its girth was graved with a mystic rune
In a tongue long dead 'neath sun and moon:
A priest of the Holy Sepulchre
Read that writing and did not err;
And her lord had told its sense to her.   275

She breathed the words in an undertone: –
'None sees here but the pure alone.'
'And oh!' she said, 'what rose may be

In Mary's bower more pure to see
Than my own sweet maiden Rose Mary?'   280

BERYL-SONG

We whose home is the Beryl,
Fire-spirits of dread desire,
Who entered in
By a secret sin,
'Gainst whom all powers that strive with ours are sterile, –   285
We cry, Woe to thee, mother!
What hast thou taught her, the girl thy daughter,
That she and none other
Should this dark morrow to her deadly sorrow imperil?
What were her eyes   290
But the fiend's own spies,
O mother,
And shall We not fee her, our proper prophet and seër?
Go to her, mother,
Even thou, yea thou and none other,   295
Thou, from the Beryl:
Her fee must thou take her,
Her fee that We send, and make her,
Even in this hour, her sin's unsheltered avower.
Whose steed did neigh,   300
Riderless, bridleless,
At her gate before it was day?
Lo! where doth hover
The soul of her lover?
She sealed his doom, she, she was the sworn approver, –   305
Whose eyes were so wondrous wise,
Yet blind, ah! blind to his peril!
For stole not We in
Through a love-linked sin,
'Gainst whom all powers at war with ours are sterile, –   310
Fire-spirits of dread desire,
We whose home is the Beryl?

PART II

'Pale Rose Mary, what shall be done
With a rose that Mary weeps upon?'
'Mother, let it fall from the tree,   315

And never walk where the strewn leaves be
Till winds have passed and the path is free.'

'Sad Rose Mary, what shall be done
With a cankered flower beneath the sun?'
'Mother, let it wait for the night;   320
Be sure its shame shall be out of sight
Ere the moon pale or the east grow light.'

'Lost Rose Mary, what shall be done
With a heart that is but a broken one?'
'Mother, let it lie where it must;   325
The blood was drained with the bitter thrust,
And dust is all that sinks in the dust.'

'Poor Rose Mary, what shall I do,' –
I, your mother, that lovèd you?'
'O my mother, and is love gone?   330
Then seek you another love anon:
Who cares what shame shall lean upon?'

Low drooped trembling Rose Mary,
Then up as though in a dream stood she.
'Come, my heart, it is time to go;   335
This is the hour that has whispered low
When thy pulse quailed in the nights we know.

'Yet O my heart, thy shame has a mate
Who will not leave thee desolate.
Shame for shame, yea and sin for sin: 340
Yet peace at length may our poor souls win
If love for love be found therein.

'O thou who seek'st our shrift to-day,'
She cried, 'O James of Heronhaye –
Thy sin and mine was for love alone;   345
And oh! in the sight of God 'tis known
How the heart has since made heavy moan.

'Three days yet!' she said to her heart;
'But then he comes, and we will not part.
God, God be thanked that I still could see!   350
Oh! he shall come back assuredly,
But where, alas! must he seek for me?

'O my heart, what road shall we roam
Till my wedding-music fetch me home?
For love's shut from us and bides afar,   355

And scorn leans over the bitter bar
And knows us now for the thing we are.'

Tall she stood with a cheek flushed high
And a gaze to burn the heart-strings by.
'Twas the lightning-flash o'er sky and plain   360
Ere labouring thunders heave the chain
From the floodgates of the drowning rain.

The mother looked on the daughter still
As on a hurt thing that's yet to kill.
Then wildly at length the pent tears came;   365
The love swelled high with the swollen shame,
And their hearts' tempest burst on them.

Closely locked, they clung without speech,
And the mirrored souls shook each to each,
As the cloud-moon and the water-moon   370
Shake face to face when the dim stars swoon
In stormy bowers of the night's mid-noon.

They swayed together, shuddering sore,
Till the mother's heart could bear no more.
'Twas death to feel her own breast shake   375
Even to the very throb and ache
Of the burdened heart she still must break.

All her sobs ceased suddenly,
And she sat straight up but scarce could see.
'O daughter, where should my speech begin?   380
Your heart held fast its secret sin:
How think you, child, that I read therein?'

'Ah me! but I thought not how it came
When your words showed that you knew my shame:
And now that you call me still your own,   385
I half forget you have ever known,
Did you read my heart in the Beryl-stone?'

The lady answered her mournfully: –
'The Beryl-stone has no voice for me:
But when you charged its power to show   390
The truth which none but the pure may know,
Did naught speak once of a coming woe?'

Her hand was close to her daughter's heart,
And it felt the life-blood's sudden start:

A quick deep breath did the damsel draw,   395
Like the struck fawn in the oakenshaw:
'O mother,' she cried, 'but still I saw!'

'O child, my child, why held you apart
From my great love your hidden heart?
Said I not that all sin must chase   400
From the spell's sphere the spirits of grace,
And yield their rule to the evil race?

'Ah! would to God I had clearly told
How strong those powers, accurst of old:
Their heart is the ruined house of lies;   405
O girl, they can seal the sinful eyes,
Or show the truth by contraries!'

The daughter sat as cold as a stone,
And spoke no word but gazed alone,
Nor moved, though her mother strove a space   410
To clasp her round in a close embrace,
Because she dared not see her face.

'Oh!' at last did the mother cry,
'Be sure, as he loved you, so will I!
Ah! still and dumb is the bride, I trow;   415
But cold and stark as the winter snow
Is the bridegroom's heart, laid dead below!

'Daughter, daughter, remember you
That cloud in the hills by Holycleugh?
'Twas a Hell-screen, hiding truth away: 420
There, not i' the vale, the ambush lay,
And thence was the dead borne home to-day.'

Deep the flood and heavy the shock
When sea meets sea in the riven rock:
But calm is the pulse that shakes the sea   425
To the prisoned tide of doom set free
In the breaking heart of Rose Mary.

Once she sprang as the heifer springs
With the wolf's teeth at its red heart-strings.
First 'twas fire in her breast and brain,   430
And then scarce hers but the whole world's pain,
As she gave one shriek and sank again.

In the hair dark-waved the face lay white
As the moon lies in the lap of night;
And as night through which no moon may dart   435
Lies on a pool in the woods apart,
So lay the swoon on the weary heart.

The lady felt for the bosom's stir,
And wildly kissed and called on her;
Then turned away with a quick footfall,   440
And slid the secret door in the wall
And clomb the strait stair's interval.

There above in the altar-cell
A little fountain rose and fell:
She set a flask to the water's flow,   445
And, backward hurrying, sprinkled now
The still cold breast and the pallid brow.

Scarce cheek that warmed or breath on the air,
Yet something told that life was there.
'Ah! not with the heart the body dies!'   450
The lady moaned in a bitter wise;
Then wrung her hands and hid her eyes.

'Alas! and how may I meet again
In the same poor eyes the selfsame pain?
What help can I seek, such grief to guide?   455
Ah! one alone might avail,' she cried, –
'The priest who prays at the dead man's side.'

The lady arose, and sped down all
The winding stairs to the castle-hall.
Long-known valley and wood and stream,   460
As the loopholes passed, naught else did seem
Than the torn threads of a broken dream.

The hall was full of the castle-folk;
The women wept, but the men scarce spoke.
As the lady crossed the rush-strewn floor,   465
The throng fell backward, murmuring sore,
And pressed outside round the open door.

A stranger shadow hung on the hall
Than the dark pomp of a funeral.
'Mid common sights that were there alway,   470
As 'twere a chance of the passing day,

On the ingle-bench the dead man lay.

A priest who passed by Holycleugh
The tidings brought when the day was new.
He guided them who had fetched the dead;   475
And since that hour, unwearièd,
He knelt in prayer at the low bier's head.

Word had gone to his own domain
That in evil wise the knight was slain:
Soon the spears must gather apace   480
And the hunt be hard on the hunters' trace;
But all things yet lay still for a space.

As the lady's hurried step drew near,
The kneeling priest looked up to her.
'Father, death is a grievous thing;   485
But oh! the woe has a sharper sting
That craves by me your ministering.

'Alas for the child that should have wed
This noble knight here lying dead!
Dead in hope, with all blessed boon   490
Of love thus rent from her heart ere noon,
I left her laid in a heavy swoon.

'O haste to the open bower-chamber
That's topmost as you mount the stair:
Seek her, father, ere yet she wake;   495
Your words, not mine, be the first to slake
This poor heart's fire, for Christ's sweet sake!

'God speed!' she said as the priest passed through,
'And I ere long will be with you.'
Then low on the hearth her knees sank prone;   500
She signed all folk from the threshold-stone,
And gazed in the dead man's face alone.

The fight for life found record yet
In the clenched lips and the teeth hard-set;
The wrath from the bent brow was not gone,   505
And stark in the eyes the hate still shone
Of that they last had looked upon.

The blazoned coat was rent on his breast
Where the golden field was goodliest;

But the shivered sword, close-gripped, could tell   510
That the blood shed round him where he fell
Was not all his in the distant dell.

The lady recked of the corpse no whit,
But saw the soul and spoke to it:
A light there was in her steadfast eyes, –   515
The fire of mortal tears and sighs
That pity and love immortalize.

'By thy death have I learnt to-day
Thy deed, O James of Heronhaye!
Great wrong thou hast done to me and mine;   520
And haply God hath wrought for a sign
By our blind deed this doom of thine.

'Thy shrift, alas! thou wast not to win;
But may death shrive thy soul herein!
Full well do I know thy love should be   525
Even yet – had life but stayed with thee –
Our honour's strong security.'

She stooped, and said with a sob's low stir, –
'Peace be thine, – but what peace for her?'
But ere to the brow her lips were press'd,   530
She marked, half-hid in the riven vest,
A packet close to the dead man's breast.

'Neath surcoat pierced and broken mail
It lay on the blood-stained bosom pale.
The clot clung round it, dull and dense,   535
And a faintness seized her mortal sense
As she reached her hand and drew it thence.

'Twas steeped in the heart's flood welling high
From the heart it there had rested by:
'Twas glued to a broidered fragment gay, –   540
A shred by spear-thrust rent away
From the heron-wings of Heronhaye.

She gazed on the thing with piteous eyne: –
'Alas, poor child, some pledge of thine!
Ah me! in this troth the hearts were twain,   545
And one hath ebbed to this crimson stain,
And when shall the other throb again?'

She opened the packet heedfully;
The blood was stiff, and it scarce might be.
She found but a folded paper there,   550
And round it, twined with tenderest care,
A long bright tress of golden hair.

Even as she looked, she saw again
That dark-haired face in its swoon of pain:
It seemed a snake with a golden sheath   555
Crept near, as a slow flame flickereth,
And stung her daughter's heart to death.

She loosed the tress, but her hand did shake
As though indeed she had touched a snake;
And next she undid the paper's fold,   560
But that too trembled in her hold,
And the sense scarce grasped the tale it told.

'My heart's sweet lord,' ('twas thus she read,)
'At length our love is garlanded.
At Holy Cross, within eight days' space,   565
I seek my shrift; and the time and place
Shall fit thee too for thy soul's good grace.

'From Holycleugh on the seventh day
My brother rides, and bides away:
And long or e'er he is back, mine own,   570
Afar where the face of fear's unknown
We shall be safe with our love alone.

'Ere yet at the shrine my knees I bow,
I shear one tress for our holy vow.
As round these words these threads I wind,   575
So, eight days hence, shall our loves be twined
Says my lord's poor lady, JOCELIND.'

She read it twice, with a brain in thrall,
And then its echo told her all.
O'er brows low-fall'n her hands she drew: –   580
'O God!' she said, as her hands fell too, –
'The Warden's sister of Holycleugh!'

She rose upright with a long low moan
And stared in the dead man's face new-known.
Had it lived indeed? She scarce could tell: 585

'Twas a cloud where fiends had come to dwell, –
A mask that hung on the gate of Hell.

She lifted the lock of gleaming hair
And smote the lips and left it there.
'Here's gold that Hell shall take for thy toll!   590
Full well hath thy treason found its goal,
O thou dead body and damnèd soul!'

She turned, sore dazed, for a voice was near,
And she knew that some one called to her.
On many a column fair and tall   595
A high court ran round the castle-hall;
And thence it was that the priest did call.

'I sought your child where you bade me go,
And in rooms around and rooms below;
But where, alas! may the maiden be?   600
Fear nought, – we shall find her speedily, –
But come, come hither, and seek with me.'

She reached the stair like a lifelorn thing,
But hastened upward murmuring: –
'Yea, Death's is a face that's fell to see;   605
But bitterer pang Life hoards for thee,
Thou broken heart of Rose Mary!'

BERYL-SONG

We whose throne is the Beryl,
Dire-gifted spirits of fire,
    Who for a twin   610
    Leash Sorrow to Sin,
Who on no flower refrain to lour with peril, –
We cry, – O desolate daughter!
Thou and thy mother share newer shame with each other
    Than last night's slaughter.   615
  Awake and tremble, for our curses assemble!
  What more, that thou know'st not yet, –
  That life nor death shall forget?
No help from Heaven, – thy woes heart-riven are sterile!
    O once a maiden,   620
With yet worse sorrow can any morrow be laden?
    It waits for thee,
    It looms, it must be,

O lost among women, –
It comes and thou canst not flee.   625
Amen to the omen,
Says the voice of the Beryl.
Thou sleep'st? Awake, –
What dar'st thou yet for his sake,
Who each for other did God's own Future imperil?   630
Dost dare to live
'Mid the pangs each hour must give?
Nay, rather die, –
With him thy lover 'neath Hell's cloud-cover to fly, –
Hopeless, yet not apart,   635
Cling heart to heart,
And beat through the nether storm-eddying winds together?
Shall this be so?
There thou shalt meet him, but mayst thou greet him?
ah no!   640
He loves, but thee he hoped nevermore to see, –
He sighed as he died,
But with never a thought for thee.
Alone!
Alone, for ever alone, –   645
Whose eyes were such wondrous spies for the fate foreshown!
Lo! have not We leashed the twin
Of endless Sorrow to Sin, –
Who on no flower refrain to lour with peril, –
Dire-gifted spirits of fire,   650
We whose throne is the Beryl?

PART III

A swoon that breaks is the whelming wave
When help comes late but still can save.
With all blind throes is the instant rife, –
Hurtling clangour and clouds at strife, –   655
The breath of death, but the kiss of life.

The night lay deep on Rose Mary's heart,
For her swoon was death's kind counterpart:
The dawn broke dim on Rose Mary's soul, –
No hill-crown's heavenly aureole,   660
But a wild gleam on a shaken shoal.

Her senses gasped in the sudden air,
And she looked around, but none was there.

She felt the slackening frost distil
Through her blood the last ooze dull and chill: 665
Her lids were dry and her lips were still.

Her tears had flooded her heart again;
As after a long day's bitter rain,
At dusk when the wet flower-cups shrink,
The drops run in from the beaded brink,   670
And all the close-shut petals drink.

Again her sighs on her heart were rolled;
As the wind that long has swept the wold, –
Whose moan was made with the moaning sea, –
Beats out its breath in the last torn tree,   675
And sinks at length in lethargy.

She knew she had waded bosom-deep
Along death's bank in the sedge of sleep:
All else was lost to her clouded mind;
Nor, looking back, could she see defin'd   680
O'er the dim dumb waste what lay behind.

Slowly fades the sun from the wall
Till day lies dead on the sun-dial:
And now in Rose Mary's lifted eye
'Twas shadow alone that made reply   685
To the set face of the soul's dark sky.

Yet still through her soul there wandered past
Dread phantoms borne on a wailing blast, –
Death and sorrow and sin and shame;
And, murmured still, to her lips there came   690
Her mother's and her lover's name.

How to ask, and what thing to know?
She might not stay and she dared not go.
From fires unseen these smoke-clouds curled;
But where did the hidden curse lie furled?   695
And how to seek through the weary world?

With toiling breath she rose from the floor
And dragged her steps to an open door:
'Twas the secret panel standing wide,
As the lady's hand had led it bide   700
In hastening back to her daughter's side.

She passed, but reeled with a dizzy brain
And smote the door which closed again.

She stood within by the darkling stair,
But her feet might mount more freely there, –   705
'Twas the open light most blinded her.

Within her mind no wonder grew
At the secret path she never knew:
All ways alike were strange to her now, –
One field bare-ridged from the spirit's plough,   710
One thicket black with the cypress-bough.

Once she thought that she heard her name;
And she paused, but knew not whence it came.
Down the shadowed stair a faint ray fell
That guided the weary footsteps well   715
Till it led her up to the altar-cell.

No change there was on Rose Mary's face
As she leaned in the portal's narrow space:
Still she stood by the pillar's stem,
Hand and bosom and garment's hem,   720
As the soul stands by at the requiem.

The altar-cell was a dome low-lit,
And a veil hung in the midst of it:
At the pole-points of its circling girth
Four symbols stood of the world's first birth, –   725
Air and water and fire and earth.

To the north, a fountain glittered free;
To the south, there glowed a red fruit-tree;
To the east, a lamp flamed high and fair;
To the west, a crystal casket rare   730
Held fast a cloud of the fields of air.

The painted walls were a mystic show
Of time's ebb-tide and overflow;
His hoards long-locked and conquering key,
His service-fires that in heaven be,   735
And earth-wheels whirled perpetually.

Rose Mary gazed from the open door
As on idle things she cared not for, –
The fleeting shapes of an empty tale;
Then stepped with a heedless visage pale,   740
And lifted aside the altar-veil.

The altar stood from its curved recess
In a coiling serpent's life-likeness:
Even such a serpent evermore
Lies deep asleep at the world's dark core   745
Till the last Voice shake the sea and shore.

From the altar-cloth a book rose spread
And tapers burned at the altar-head;
And there in the altar-midst alone,
'Twixt wings of a sculptured beast unknown,   750
Rose Mary saw the Beryl-stone.

Firm it sat 'twixt the hollowed wings,
As an orb sits in the hand of kings:
And lo! for that Foe whose curse far-flown
Had bound her life with a burning zone,   755
Rose Mary knew the Beryl-stone.

Dread is the meteor's blazing sphere
When the poles throb to its blind career;
But not with a light more grim and ghast
Thereby is the future doom forecast,   760
Than now this sight brought back the past.

The hours and minutes seemed to whirr
In a clanging swarm that deafened her;
They stung her heart to a writhing flame,
And marshalled past in its glare they came, –   765
Death and sorrow and sin and shame.

Round the Beryl's sphere she saw them pass
And mock her eyes from the fated glass:
One by one in a fiery train
The dead hours seemed to wax and wane,   770
And burned till all was known again.

From the drained heart's fount there rose no cry,
There sprang no tears, for the source was dry.
Held in the hand of some heavy law,
Her eyes she might not once withdraw,   775
Nor shrink away from the thing she saw.

Even as she gazed, through all her blood
The flame was quenched in a coming flood:
Out of the depth of the hollow gloom
On her soul's bare sands she felt it boom, –   780
The measured tide of a sea of doom.

Three steps she took through the altar-gate,
And her neck reared and her arms grew straight:
The sinews clenched like a serpent's throe,
And the face was white in the dark hair's flow,   785
As her hate beheld what lay below.

Dumb she stood in her malisons, –
A silver statue tressed with bronze:
As the fabled head by Perseus mown,
It seemed in sooth that her gaze alone   790
Had turned the carven shapes to stone.

O'er the altar-sides on either hand
There hung a dinted helm and brand:
By strength thereof, 'neath the Sacred Sign,
That bitter gift o'er the salt sea-brine   795
Her father brought from Palestine.

Rose Mary moved with a stern accord
And reached her hand to her father's sword;
Nor did she stir her gaze one whit
From the thing whereon her brows were knit;   800
But gazing still, she spoke to it.

'O ye, three times accurst,' she said,
'By whom this stone is tenanted!
Lo! there ye came by a strong sin's might;
Yet a sinner's hand that's weak to smite   805
Shall send you hence ere the day be night.

'This hour a clear voice bade me know
My hand shall work your overthrow:
Another thing in mine ear it spake, –
With the broken spell my life shall break.   810
I thank Thee, God, for the dear death's sake!

'And he Thy heavenly minister
Who swayed erewhile this spell-bound sphere, –
My parting soul let him haste to greet,
And none but he be guide for my feet   815
To where Thy rest is made complete.'

Then deep she breathed, with a tender moan: –
'My love, my lord, my only one!

Even as I held the cursed clue,
When thou, through me, these foul ones slew, –   820
By mine own deed shall they slay me too!

'Even while they speed to Hell, my love,
Two hearts shall meet in Heaven above.
Our shrift thou sought'st, but might'st not bring:
And oh! for me 'tis a blessed thing   825
To work hereby our ransoming.

'One were our hearts in joy and pain,
And our souls e'en now grow one again.
And O my love, if our souls are three,
O thine and mine shall the third soul be, –   830
One threefold love eternally.'

Her eyes were soft as she spoke apart,
And the lips smiled to the broken heart:
But the glance was dark and the forehead scored
With the bitter frown of hate restored,   835
As her two hands swung the heavy sword.

Three steps back from her Foe she trod: –
'Love, for thy sake! In Thy Name, O God!'
In the fair white hands small strength was shown;
Yet the blade flashed high and the edge fell prone,   840
And she cleft the heart of the Beryl-stone.

What living flesh in the thunder-cloud
Hath sat and felt heaven cry aloud?
Or known how the levin's pulse may beat?
Or wrapped the hour when the whirlwinds meet   845
About its breast for a winding-sheet?

Who hath crouched at the world's deep heart
While the earthquake rends its loins apart?
Or walked far under the seething main
While overhead the heavens ordain   850
The tempest-towers of the hurricane?

Who hath seen or what ear hath heard
The secret things unregister'd
Of the place where all is past and done,
And tears and laughter sound as one   855
In Hell's unhallowed unison?

Nay, is it writ how the fiends despair
In earth and water and fire and air?
Even so no mortal tongue may tell
How to the clang of the sword that fell   860
The echoes shook the altar-cell.

When all was still on the air again
The Beryl-stone lay cleft in twain;
The veil was rent from the riven dome;
And every wind that's winged to roam   865
Might have the ruined place for home.

The fountain no more glittered free;
The fruit hung dead on the leafless tree;
The flame of the lamp had ceased to flare;
And the crystal casket shattered there   870
Was emptied now of its cloud of air.

And lo! on the ground Rose Mary lay,
With a cold brow like the snows ere May,
With a cold breast like the earth till Spring,
With such a smile as the June days bring   875
When the year grows warm for harvesting.

The death she had won might leave no trace
On the soft sweet form and gentle face:
In a gracious sleep she seemed to lie;
And over her head her hand on high   880
Held fast the sword she triumphed by.

'Twas then a clear voice said in the room: –
'Behold the end of the heavy doom.
O come, – for thy bitter love's sake blest;
By a sweet path now thou journeyest,   885
And I will lead thee to thy rest.

'Me thy sin by Heaven's sore ban
Did chase erewhile from the talisman:
But to my heart, as a conquered home,
In glory of strength thy footsteps come   890
Who hast thus cast forth my foes therefrom.

'Already thy heart remembereth
No more his name thou sought'st in death:
For under all deeps, all heights above, –

So wide the gulf in the midst thereof, –   895
Are Hell of Treason and Heaven of Love.

'Thee, true soul, shall thy truth prefer
To blessed Mary's rose-bower:
Warmed and lit is thy place afar
With guerdon-fires of the sweet Love-star   900
Where hearts of steadfast lovers are: –

'Though naught for the poor corpse lying here
Remain to-day but the cold white bier,
But burial-chaunt and bended knee,
But sighs and tears that heaviest be,   905
But rent rose-flower and rosemary.'

BERYL-SONG

We, cast forth from the Beryl,
Gyre-circling spirits of fire,
   Whose pangs begin
   With God's grace to sin,   910
For whose spent powers the immortal hours are sterile, –
   Woe! must We behold this mother
Find grace in her dead child's face, and doubt of none other
But that perfect pardon, alas! hath assured her guerdon?
   Woe! must We behold this daughter,   915
Made clean from the soil of sin wherewith We had fraught her,
   Shake off a man's blood like water?
     Write up her story
   On the Gate of Heaven's glory,
Whom there We behold so fair in shining apparel,   920
   And beneath her the ruin
   Of our own undoing!
   Alas, the Beryl!
   We had for a foeman
   But one weak woman;   925
   In one day's strife,
  Her hope fell dead from her life;
   And yet no iron,
   Her soul to environ,
Could this manslayer, this false soothsayer imperil!   930
   Lo, where she bows
   In the Holy House!
Who now shall dissever her soul from its joy for ever,
   While every ditty

Of love and plentiful pity   935
  Fills the White City,
And the floor of Heaven to her feet for ever is given?
  Hark, a voice cries 'Flee!'
Woe! woe! what shelter have We,
  Whose pangs begin   940
  With God's grace to sin,
For whose spent powers the immortal hours are sterile,
  Gyre-circling spirits of fire,
  We, cast forth from the Beryl?

Chimes

I

Honey-flowers to the honey-comb
And the honey-bee's from home.

A honey-comb and a honey-flower,
And the bee shall have his hour.

A honeyed heart for the honey-comb,   5
And the humming bee flies home.

A heavy heart in the honey-flower,
And the bee has had his hour.

II

A honey-cell's in the honeysuckle,
And the honey-bee knows it well.   10

The honey-comb has a heart of honey,
And the humming bee's so bonny.

A honey-flower's the honeysuckle,
And the bee's in the honey-bell.

The honeysuckle is sucked of honey,   15
And the bee is heavy and bonny.

III

Brown shell first for the butterfly
And a bright wing by and by.

Butterfly, good-bye to your shell,
And, bright wings, speed you well.   20

Bright lamplight for the butterfly
And a burnt wing by and by.

Butterfly, alas for your shell,
And, bright wings, fare you well.

IV

Lost love-labour and lullaby, 25
And lowly let love lie.

Lost love-morrow and love-fellow
And love's life lying low.

Lovelorn labour and life laid by
And lowly let love lie. 30

Late love-longing and life-sorrow
And love's life lying low.

V

Beauty's body and benison
With a bosom-flower new-blown.

Bitter beauty and blessing bann'd 35
With a breast to burn and brand.

Beauty's bower in the dust o'erblown
With a bare white breast of bone.

Barren beauty and bower of sand
With a blast on either hand. 40

VI

Buried bars in the breakwater
And bubble of the brimming weir.

Body's blood in the breakwater
And a buried body's bier.

Buried bones in the breakwater 45
And bubble of the brawling weir.

Bitter tears in the breakwater
And a breaking heart to bear.

VII

Hollow heaven and the hurricane
And hurry of the heavy rain. 50

Hurried clouds in the hollow heaven
And a heavy rain hard-driven.

The heavy rain it hurries amain
And heaven and the hurricane.

Hurrying wind o'er the heaven's hollow   55
And the heavy rain to follow.

A Sea-Spell

(FOR A PICTURE)

Her lute hangs shadowed in the apple-tree,
  While flashing fingers weave the sweet-strung spell
  Between its chords; and as the wild notes swell,
The sea-bird for those branches leaves the sea.
But to what sound her listening ear stoops she?   5
  What netherworld gulf-whispers doth she hear,
  In answering echoes from what planisphere,
Along the wind, along the estuary?

She sinks into her spell: and when full soon
  Her lips move and she soars into her song,   10
  What creatures of the midmost main shall throng
In furrowed surf-clouds to the summoning rune:
Till he, the fated mariner, hears her cry,
And up her rock, bare-breasted, comes to die?

Parted Presence

Love, I speak to your heart,
  Your heart that is always here.
  Oh draw me deep to its sphere,
Though you and I are apart;
And yield, by the spirit's art,   5
  Each distant gift that is dear.
  O love, my love, you are here!

Your eyes are afar to-day,
  Yet, love, look now in mine eyes.
  Two hearts sent forth may despise   10

All dead things by the way.
All between is decay,
  Dead hours and this hour that dies,
  O love, look deep in mine eyes!

Your hands to-day are not here,   15
  Yet lay them, love, in my hands.
  The hourglass sheds its sands
All day for the dead hours' bier;
But now, as two hearts draw near,
  This hour like a flower expands.   20
  O love, your hands in my hands!

Your voice is not on the air,
  Yet, love, I can hear your voice:
  It bids my heart to rejoice
As knowing your heart is there, –   25
A music sweet to declare
  The truth of your steadfast choice.
  O love, how sweet is your voice!

To-day your lips are afar,
  Yet draw my lips to them, love.   30
  Around, beneath, and above,
Is frost to bind and to bar;
But where I am and you are,
  Desire and the fire thereof.
  O kiss me, kiss me, my love!   35

Your heart is never away,
  But ever with mine, for ever,
  For ever without endeavour,
To-morrow, love, as to-day;
Two blent hearts never astray,   40
  Two souls no power may sever,
  Together, O my love, for ever!

A Death-Parting

Leaves and rain and the days of the year,
  (Water-willow and wellaway,)
All these fall, and my soul gives ear,
And she is hence who once was here.
  (With a wind blown night and day.)   5

Ah! but now, for a secret sign,
  (The willow's wan and the water white,)
In the held breath of the day's decline
Her very face seemed pressed to mine.
  (With a wind blown day and night.)   10

O love, of my death my life is fain;
  (The willows wave on the water-way,)
Your cheek and mine are cold in the rain,
But warm they'll be when we meet again.
  (With a wind blown night and day.)   15

Mists are heaved and cover the sky;
  (The willows wail in the waning light,)
O loose your lips, leave space for a sigh, –
They seal my soul, I cannot die.
  (With a wind blown day and night.)   20

Leaves and rain and the days of the year,
  (Water-willow and wellaway,)
All still fall, and I still give ear,
And she is hence, and I am here.
  (With a wind blown night and day.)   25

Three Shadows

I looked and saw your eyes
  In the shadow of your hair,
As a traveller sees the stream
  In the shadow of the wood;
And I said, 'My faint heart sighs,   5
  Ah me! to linger there,
To drink deep and to dream
  In that sweet solitude.'

I looked and saw your heart
   In the shadow of your eyes,   10
As a seeker sees the gold
   In the shadow of the stream;
And I said, 'Ah me! what art
   Should win the immortal prize,
Whose want must make life cold   15
   And Heaven a hollow dream?'

I looked and saw your love
   In the shadow of your heart,
As a diver sees the pearl
   In the shadow of the sea;   20
And I murmured, not above
   My breath, but all apart, –
'Ah! you can love, true girl,
   And is your love for me?'

Adieu

Waving whispering trees,
What do you say to the breeze
   And what says the breeze to you?
'Mid passing souls ill at ease,
Moving murmuring trees,   5
   Would ye ever wave an Adieu?

Tossing turbulent seas,
Winds that wrestle with these,
   Echo heard in the shell, –
'Mid fleeting life ill at ease,   10
Restless ravening seas, –
   Would the echo sigh Farewell?

Surging sumptuous skies,
For ever a new surprise,
   Clouds eternally new, –   15
Is every flake that flies,
Widening wandering skies,
   For a sign – Farewell, Adieu?

Sinking suffering heart
That know'st how weary thou art, –   20
    Soul so fain for a flight, –
Aye, spread your wings to depart,
Sad soul and sorrowing heart, –
    Adieu, Farewell, Good-night.

Astarte Syriaca

(FOR A PICTURE)

Mystery! lo! betwixt the sun and moon
    Astarte of the Syrians: Venus Queen
    Ere Aphrodite was. In silver sheen
Her twofold girdle clasps the infinite boon
Of bliss whereof the heaven and earth commune: 5
    And from her neck's inclining flower-stem lean
    Love-freighted lips and absolute eyes that wean
The pulse of hearts to the spheres' dominant tune.

Torch-bearing, her sweet ministers compel
    All thrones of light beyond the sky and sea   10
    The witnesses of Beauty's face to be:
That face, of Love's all-penetrative spell
Amulet, talisman, and oracle, –
    Betwixt the sun and moon a mystery.

Fiammetta

(FOR A PICTURE)

Behold Fiammetta, shown in Vision here.
    Gloom-girt 'mid Spring-flushed apple-growth she stands;
    And as she sways the branches with her hands,
Along her arm the sundered bloom falls sheer,
In separate petals shed, each like a tear;   5
    While from the quivering bough the bird expands
    His wings. And lo! thy spirit understands
Like shaken and shower'd and flown, and Death drawn near.

All stirs with change. Her garments beat the air:
    The angel circling round her aureole   10

Shimmers in flight against the tree's grey bole:
While she, with reassuring eyes most fair,
A presage and a promise stands; as 'twere
On Death's dark storm the rainbow of the Soul.

The White Ship

HENRY I OF ENGLAND – 25TH NOVEMBER 1120

By none but me can the tale be told,
The butcher of Rouen, poor Berold.
    (Lands are swayed by a King on a throne.)
'Twas a royal train put forth to sea,
Yet the tale can be told by none but me.   5
    (The sea hath no King but God alone.)

King Henry held it as life's whole gain
That after his death his son should reign.

'Twas so in my youth I heard men say,
And my old age calls it back to-day.   10

King Henry of England's realm was he,
And Henry Duke of Normandy.

The times had changed when on either coast
'Clerkly Harry' was all his boast.

Of ruthless strokes full many an one   15
He had struck to crown himself and his son;
And his elder brother's eyes were gone.

And when to the chase his court would crowd,
The poor flung ploughshares on his road,
And shrieked: 'Our cry is from King to God!'   20

But all the chiefs of the English land
Had knelt and kissed the Prince's hand.

And next with his son he sailed to France
To claim the Norman allegiance:

And every baron in Normandy   25
Had taken the oath of fealty.

'Twas sworn and sealed, and the day had come
When the King and the Prince might journey home:

For Christmas cheer is to home hearts dear,
And Christmas now was drawing near.   30

Stout Fitz-Stephen came to the King, –
A pilot famous in seafaring;

And he held to the King, in all men's sight,
A mark of gold for his tribute's right.

'Liege Lord! my father guided the ship   35
From whose boat your father's foot did slip
When he caught the English soil in his grip,

'And cried: "By this clasp I claim command
O'er every rood of English land!"

'He was borne to the realm you rule o'er now   40
In that ship with the archer carved at her prow:

'And thither I'll bear, an it be my due,
Your father's son and his grandson too.

'The famed White Ship is mine in the bay;
From Harfleur's harbour she sails to-day,   45

'With masts fair-pennoned as Norman spears
And with fifty well-tried mariners.'

Quoth the King: 'My ships are chosen each one,
But I'll not say nay to Stephen's son.

'My son and daughter and fellowship   50
Shall cross the water in the White Ship.'

The King set sail with the eve's south wind,
And soon he left that coast behind.

The Prince and all his, a princely show,
Remained in the good White Ship to go.   55

With noble knights and with ladies fair,
With courtiers and sailors gathered there,
Three hundred living souls we were:

And I Berold was the meanest hind
In all that train to the Prince assign'd.   60

The Prince was a lawless shameless youth;
From his father's loins he sprang without ruth:

Eighteen years till then he had seen,
And the devil's dues in him were eighteen.

And now he cried: 'Bring wine from below;   65
Let the sailors revel ere yet they row:

'Our speed shall o'ertake my father's flight
Though we sail from the harbour at midnight.'

The rowers made good cheer without check;
The lords and ladies obeyed his beck;   70
The night was light, and they danced on the deck.

But at midnight's stroke they cleared the bay,
And the White Ship furrowed the water-way.

The sails were set, and the oars kept tune
To the double flight of the ship and the moon: 75

Swifter and swifter the White Ship sped
Till she flew as the spirit flies from the dead:

As white as a lily glimmered she
Like a ship's fair ghost upon the sea.

And the Prince cried, 'Friends, 'tis the hour to sing!   80
Is a songbird's course so swift on the wing?'

And under the winter stars' still throng,
From brown throats, white throats, merry and strong,
The knights and the ladies raised a song.

A song, – nay, a shriek that rent the sky,   85
That leaped o'er the deep! – the grievous cry
Of three hundred living that now must die.

An instant shriek that sprang to the shock
As the ship's keel felt the sunken rock.

'Tis said that afar – a shrill strange sigh –   90
The King's ships heard it and knew not why.

Pale Fitz-Stephen stood by the helm
'Mid all those folk that the waves must whelm.

A great King's heir for the waves to whelm,
And the helpless pilot pale at the helm!   95

The ship was eager and sucked athirst,
By the stealthy stab of the sharp reef pierc'd:

And like the moil round a sinking cup
The waters against her crowded up.

A moment the pilot's senses spin, –   100
The next he snatched the Prince 'mid the din,
Cut the boat loose, and the youth leaped in.

A few friends leaped with him, standing near.
'Row! the sea's smooth and the night is clear!'

'What! none to be saved but these and I?'   105
'Row, row as you'd live! All here must die!'

Out of the churn of the choking ship,
Which the gulf grapples and the waves strip,
They struck with the strained oars' flash and dip.

'Twas then o'er the splitting bulwarks' brim   110
The Prince's sister screamed to him.

He gazed aloft, still rowing apace,
And through the whirled surf he knew her face.

To the toppling decks clave one and all
As a fly cleaves to a chamber-wall.   115

I Berold was clinging anear;
I prayed for myself and quaked with fear,
But I saw his eyes as he looked at her.

He knew her face and he heard her cry,
And he said, 'Put back! she must not die!'   120

And back with the current's force they reel
Like a leaf that's drawn to a water-wheel.

'Neath the ship's travail they scarce might float,
But he rose and stood in the rocking boat.

Low the poor ship leaned on the tide: 125
O'er the naked keel as she best might slide,
The sister toiled to the brother's side.

He reached an oar to her from below,
And stiffened his arms to clutch her so.

But now from the ship some spied the boat,   130
And 'Saved!' was the cry from many a throat.

And down to the boat they leaped and fell:
It turned as a bucket turns in a well,
And nothing was there but the surge and swell.

The Prince that was and the King to come,   135
There in an instant gone to his doom,

Despite of all England's bended knee
And maugre the Norman fealty!

He was a Prince of lust and pride;
He showed no grace till the hour he died.   140

When he should be King, he oft would vow,
He'd yoke the peasant to his own plough.
O'er him the ships score their furrows now.

God only knows where his soul did wake,
But I saw him die for his sister's sake.   145

By none but me can the tale be told,
The butcher of Rouen, poor Berold.
    (Lands are swayed by a King on a throne.)
'Twas a royal train put forth to sea,
Yet the tale can be told by none but me.   150
    (The sea hath no King but God alone.)

And now the end came o'er the waters' womb
Like the last great Day that's yet to come.

With prayers in vain and curses in vain,
The White Ship sundered on the mid-main: 155

And what were men and what was a ship
Were toys and splinters in the sea's grip.

I Berold was down in the sea;
And passing strange though the thing may be,
Of dreams then known I remember me.   160

Blithe is the shout on Harfleur's strand
When morning lights the sails to land:

And blithe is Honfleur's echoing gloam
When mothers call the children home:

And high do the bells of Rouen beat   165
When the Body of Christ goes down the street.

These things and the like were heard and shown
In a moment's trance 'neath the sea alone;

And when I rose, 'twas the sea did seem,
And not these things, to be all a dream.   170

The ship was gone and the crowd was gone,
And the deep shuddered and the moon shone:

And in a strait grasp my arms did span
The mainyard rent from the mast where it ran;
And on it with me was another man.   175

Where lands were none 'neath the dim sea-sky
We told our names, that man and I.

'O I am Godefroy de l'Aigle hight,
And son I am to a belted knight.'

'And I am Berold the butcher's son   180
Who slays the beasts in Rouen town.'

Then cried we upon God's name, as we
Did drift on the bitter winter sea.

But lo! a third man rose o'er the wave,
And we said, 'Thank God! us three may He save!'   185

He clutched to the yard with panting stare,
And we looked and knew Fitz-Stephen there.

He clung, and 'What of the Prince?' quoth he.
'Lost, lost!' we cried. He cried, 'Woe on me!'
And loosed his hold and sank through the sea.   190

And soul with soul again in that space
We two were together face to face:

And each knew each, as the moments sped,
Less for one living than for one dead:

And every still star overhead   195
Seemed an eye that knew we were but dead.

And the hours passed; till the noble's son
Sighed, 'God be thy help! my strength's foredone!

'O farewell, friend, for I can no more!'
'Christ take thee!' I moaned; and his life was o'er.   200

Three hundred souls were all lost but one,
And I drifted over the sea alone.

At last the morning rose on the sea
Like an angel's wing that beat tow'rds me.

Sore numbed I was in my sheepskin coat;   205
Half dead I hung, and might nothing note,
Till I woke sun-warmed in a fisher-boat.

The sun was high o'er the eastern brim
As I praised God and gave thanks to Him.

That day I told my tale to a priest,   210
Who charged me, till the shrift were releas'd,
That I should keep it in mine own breast.

And with the priest I thence did fare
To King Henry's court at Winchester.

We spoke with the King's high chamberlain,   215
And he wept and mourned again and again,
As if his own son had been slain:

And round us ever there crowded fast
Great men with faces all aghast:

And who so bold that might tell the thing   220
Which now they knew to their lord the King?
Much woe I learnt in their communing.

The King had watched with a heart sore stirred
For two whole days, and this was the third:

And still to all his court would he say,   225
'What keeps my son so long away?'

And they said: 'The ports lie far and wide
That skirt the swell of the English tide;

'And England's cliffs are not more white
Than her women are, and scarce so light   230
Her skies as their eyes are blue and bright;

'And in some port that he reached from France
The Prince has lingered for his pleasaùnce.'

But once the King asked: 'What distant cry
Was that we heard 'twixt the sea and sky?'   235

And one said: 'With suchlike shouts, pardie!
Do the fishers fling their nets at sea.'

And one: 'Who knows not the shrieking quest
When the sea-mew misses its young from the nest?'

'Twas thus till now they had soothed his dread,   240
Albeit they knew not what they said:

But who should speak to-day of the thing
That all knew there except the King?

Then pondering much they found a way,
And met round the King's high seat that day: 245

And the King sat with a heart sore stirred,
And seldom he spoke and seldom heard.

'Twas then through the hall the King was 'ware
Of a little boy with golden hair,

As bright as the golden poppy is   250
That the beach breeds for the surf to kiss:

Yet pale his cheek as the thorn in Spring,
And his garb black like the raven's wing.

Nothing heard but his foot through the hall,
For now the lords were silent all.   255

And the King wondered, and said, 'Alack!
Who sends me a fair boy dressed in black?

'Why, sweet heart, do you pace through the hall
As though my court were a funeral?'

Then lowly knelt the child at the dais,   260
And looked up weeping in the King's face.

'O wherefore black, O King, ye may say,
For white is the hue of death to-day.

'Your son and all his fellowship
Lie low in the sea with the White Ship.'   265

King Henry fell as a man struck dead;
And speechless still he stared from his bed
When to him next day my rede I read.

There's many an hour must needs beguile
A King's high heart that he should smile, –   270

Full many a lordly hour, full fain
Of his realm's rule and pride of his reign: –

But this King never smiled again.

By none but me can the tale be told,
The butcher of Rouen, poor Berold.   275
   (Lands are swayed by a King on a throne.)
'Twas a royal train put forth to sea,
Yet the tale can be told by none but me.
   (The sea hath no King but God alone.)

Five English Poets

I THOMAS CHATTERTON

With Shakspeare's manhood at a boy's wild heart, –
   Through Hamlet's doubt to Shakspeare near allied,
   And kin to Milton through his Satan's pride, –
At Death's sole door he stooped, and craved a dart;
And to the dear new bower of England's art, –   5
   Even to that shrine Time else had deified,
   The unuttered heart that soared against his side, –
Drove the fell point, and smote life's seals apart.

Thy nested home-loves, noble Chatterton;
   The angel-trodden stair thy soul could trace   10
   Up Redcliffe's spire; and in the world's armed space
Thy gallant sword-play: – these to many an one
Are sweet for ever; as thy grave unknown
   And love-dream of thine unrecorded face.

II WILLIAM BLAKE

(TO FREDERICK SHIELDS, ON HIS SKETCH OF BLAKE'S WORKROOM AND
DEATH-ROOM, 3, FOUNTAIN COURT, STRAND)

This is the place. Even here the dauntless soul,
   The unflinching hand, wrought on; till in that nook,
   As on that very bed, his life partook
New birth, and passed. Yon river's dusky shoal,
Whereto the close-built coiling lanes unroll,   5
   Faced his work-window, whence his eyes would stare,
   Thought-wandering, unto nought that met them there,
But to the unfettered irreversible goal.

This cupboard, Holy of Holies, held the cloud
   Of his soul writ and limned; this other one,   10
His true wife's charge, full oft to their abode
   Yielded for daily bread the martyr's stone,
   Ere yet their food might be that Bread alone,
The words now home-speech of the mouth of God.

III SAMUEL TAYLOR COLERIDGE

His Soul fared forth (as from the deep home-grove
   The father-songster plies the hour-long quest,)
   To feed his soul-brood hungering in the nest;
But his warm Heart, the mother-bird, above
   Their callow fledgling progeny still hove   5
   With tented roof of wings and fostering breast
Till the Soul fed the soul-brood. Richly blest
From Heaven their growth, whose food was Human Love.

Yet ah! Like desert pools that show the stars
   Once in long leagues, – even such the scarce-snatched hours   10
   Which deepening pain left to his lordliest powers: –
Heaven lost through spider-trammelled prison-bars.
   Six years, from sixty saved! Yet kindling skies
   Own them, a beacon to our centuries.

IV JOHN KEATS

The weltering London ways where children weep
   And girls whom none call maidens laugh, – strange road
   Miring his outward steps, who inly trode
The bright Castalian brink and Latmos' steep: –
Even such his life's cross-paths; till deathly deep   5
   He toiled through sands of Lethe; and long pain,
   Weary with labour spurned and love found vain,
In dead Rome's sheltering shadow wrapped his sleep.

O pang-dowered Poet, whose reverberant lips
And heart-strung lyre awoke the Moon's eclipse, –   10
   Thou whom the daisies glory in growing o'er, –
Their fragrance clings around thy name, not writ
But rumour'd in water, while the fame of it
   Along Time's flood goes echoing evermore.

V PERCY BYSSHE SHELLEY

(INSCRIPTION FOR THE COUCH, STILL PRESERVED, ON WHICH HE PASSED
THE LAST NIGHT OF HIS LIFE)

'Twixt those twin worlds, – the world of Sleep, which gave
  No dream to warn, – the tidal world of Death,
  Which the earth's sea, as the earth, replenisheth, –
Shelley, Song's orient sun, to breast the wave,
Rose from this couch that morn. Ah! did he brave   5
  Only the sea? – or did man's deed of hell
  Engulph his bark 'mid mists impenetrable? . . . .
No eye discerned, nor any power might save.

When that mist cleared, O Shelley! what dread veil
  Was rent for thee, to whom far-darkling Truth   10
  Reigned sovereign guide through thy brief ageless youth?
Was the Truth *thy* Truth, Shelley? – Hush! All-Hail,
Past doubt, thou gav'st it; and in Truth's bright sphere
Art first of praisers, being most praisèd here.

The Day-Dream

(FOR A PICTURE)

The thronged boughs of the shadowy sycamore
  Still bear young leaflets half the summer through;
  From when the robin 'gainst the unhidden blue
Perched dark, till now, deep in the leafy core,
The embowered throstle's urgent wood-notes soar   5
  Through summer silence. Still the leaves come new;
  Yet never rosy-sheathed as those which drew
Their spiral tongues from spring-buds heretofore.

Within the branching shade of Reverie
Dreams even may spring till autumn; yet none be   10
  Like woman's budding day-dream spirit-fann'd.
Lo! tow'rd deep skies, not deeper than her look,
She dreams; till now on her forgotten book
  Drops the forgotten blossom from her hand.

For
Spring, by Sandro Botticelli
in the Accademia of Florence

What masque of what old wind-withered New-Year
   Honours this Lady?[1] Flora, wanton-eyed
   For birth, and with all flowrets prankt and pied:
Aurora, Zephyrus, with mutual cheer
Of clasp and kiss: the Graces circling near,   5
   'Neath bower-linked arch of white arms glorified:
   And with those feathered feet which hovering glide
O'er Spring's brief bloom, Hermes the harbinger.

Birth-bare, not death-bare yet, the young stems stand,
   This Lady's temple-columns: o'er her head   10
   Love wings his shaft. What mystery here is read
Of homage or of hope? But how command
   Dead Springs to answer? And how question here
   These mummers of that wind-withered New-Year?

1 The same lady, here surrounded by the masque of Spring, is evidently the subject
of a portrait by Botticelli formerly in the Pourtalès collection in Paris. This portrait
is inscribed 'Smeralda Bandinelli.'

The Last Three from Trafalgar
AT THE ANNIVERSARY BANQUET, 21ST OCTOBER 187*

In grappled ships around The Victory,
   Three boys did England's Duty with stout cheer,
   While one dread truth was kept from every ear,
More dire than deafening fire that churned the sea:
For in the flag-ship's weltering cockpit, he   5
   Who was the Battle's Heart without a peer,
   He who had seen all fearful sights save Fear,
Was passing from all life save Victory.

And round the old memorial board to-day,
   Three greybeards – each a warworn British Tar –   10
   View through the mist of years that hour afar:
Who soon shall greet, 'mid memories of fierce fray,

The impassioned soul which on its radiant way
Soared through the fiery cloud of Trafalgar.

Insomnia

Thin are the night-skirts left behind
  By daybreak hours that onward creep,
  And thin, alas! the shred of sleep
That wavers with the spirit's wind:
But in half-dreams that shift and roll   5
  And still remember and forget,
My soul this hour has drawn your soul
    A little nearer yet.

Our lives, most dear, are never near,
  Our thoughts are never far apart,   10
  Though all that draws us heart to heart
Seems fainter now and now more clear.
To-night Love claims his full control,
  And with desire and with regret
My soul this hour has drawn your soul   15
    A little nearer yet.

Is there a home where heavy earth
  Melts to bright air that breathes no pain,
  Where water leaves no thirst again
And springing fire is Love's new birth?   20
If faith long bound to one true goal
  May there at length its hope beget,
My soul that hour shall draw your soul
    For ever nearer yet.

Tiber, Nile, and Thames

The head and hands of murdered Cicero,
  Above his seat high in the Forum hung,
  Drew jeers and burning tears. When on the rung
Of a swift-mounted ladder, all aglow,
Fulvia, Mark Antony's shameless wife, with show
  Of foot firm-poised and gleaming arm upflung,

Bade her sharp needle pierce that god-like tongue
Whose speech fed Rome even as the Tiber's flow.

And thou, Cleopatra's Needle, that hadst thrid
Great skirts of Time ere she and Antony hid   10
   Dead hope! – hast thou too reached, surviving death,
A city of sweet speech scorned, – on whose chill stone
Keats withered, Coleridge pined, and Chatterton,
   Breadless, with poison froze the God-fired breath?

Alas, So Long!

Ah! dear one, we were young so long,
   It seemed that youth would never go,
For skies and trees were ever in song
   And water in singing flow
In the days we never again shall know.   5
      Alas, so long!
   Ah! then was it all Spring weather?
   Nay, but we were young and together.

Ah! dear one, I've been old so long,
   It seems that age is loth to part,   10
Though days and years have never a song,
   And oh! have they still the art
That warmed the pulses of heart to heart?
      Alas, so long!
   Ah! then was it all Spring weather?   15
   Nay, but we were young and together.

Ah! dear one, you've been dead so long, –
   How long until we meet again,
Where hours may never lose their song
   Nor flowers forget the rain   20
In glad noonlight that never shall wane?
      Alas, so long!
   Ah! shall it be then Spring weather,
   And ah! shall we be young together?

'Found'
(FOR A PICTURE)

'There is a budding morrow in midnight:' –
  So sang our Keats, our English nightingale.
    And here, as lamps across the bridge turn pale
In London's smokeless resurrection-light,
Dark breaks to dawn. But o'er the deadly blight   5
  Of Love deflowered and sorrow of none avail,
  Which makes this man gasp and this woman quail,
Can day from darkness ever again take flight?

Ah! gave not these two hearts their mutual pledge,
Under one mantle sheltered 'neath the hedge   10
  In gloaming courtship? And, O God! to-day
He only knows he holds her; – but what part
Can life now take? She cries in her locked heart, –
  'Leave me – I do not know you – go away!'

Czar Alexander the Second
(13TH MARCH 1881)

From him did forty million serfs, endow'd
  Each with six feet of death-due soil, receive
  Rich freeborn lifelong land, whereon to sheave
Their country's harvest. These to-day aloud
Demand of Heaven a Father's blood, – sore bow'd   5
  With tears and thrilled with wrath; who, while they grieve,
  On every guilty head would fain achieve
All torment by his edicts disallow'd.

He stayed the knout's red-ravening fangs; and first
  Of Russian traitors, his own murderers go   10
  White to the tomb. While he, – laid foully low
With limbs red-rent, with festering brain which erst
Willed kingly freedom, – 'gainst the deed accurst
  To God bears witness of his people's woe.

The King's Tragedy

JAMES I OF SCOTS. — 20TH FEBRUARY 1437

NOTE

Tradition says that Catherine Douglas, in honour of her heroic act when she barred the door with her arm against the murderers of James the First of Scots, received popularly the name of 'Barlass.' This name remains to her descendants, the Barlas family, in Scotland, who bear for their crest a broken arm. She married Alexander Lovell of Bolunnie.

A few stanzas from King James's lovely poem, known as *The King's Quair*, are quoted in the course of this ballad. The writer must express regret for the necessity which has compelled him to shorten the ten-syllabled lines to eight syllables, in order that they might harmonize with the ballad metre.

I Catherine am a Douglas born,
  A name to all Scots dear;
And Kate Barlass they've called me now
  Through many a waning year.

This old arm's withered now. 'Twas once   5
  Most deft 'mong maidens all
To rein the steed, to wing the shaft,
  To smite the palm-play ball.

In hall adown the close-linked dance
  It has shone most white and fair;   10
It has been the rest for a true lord's head,
And many a sweet babe's nursing-bed,
  And the bar to a King's chambère.

Aye, lasses, draw round Kate Barlass,
  And hark with bated breath   15
How good King James, King Robert's son,
  Was foully done to death.

Through all the days of his gallant youth
  The princely James was pent,
By his friends at first and then by his foes,   20
  In long imprisonment.

For the elder Prince, the kingdom's heir,
  By treason's murderous brood
Was slain; and the father quaked for the child
  With the royal mortal blood.   25

I' the Bass Rock fort, by his father's care,
   Was his childhood's life assured;
And Henry the subtle Bolingbroke,
Proud England's King, 'neath the southron yoke
   His youth for long years immured.   30

Yet in all things meet for the kingly man
   Himself did he approve;
And the nightingale through his prison-wall
   Taught him both lore and love.

For once, when the bird's song drew him close   35
   To the opened window-pane,
In her bower beneath a lady stood,
A light of life to his sorrowful mood,
   Like a lily amid the rain.

And for her sake, to the sweet bird's note,   40
   He framed a sweeter Song,
More sweet than ever a poet's heart
   Gave yet to the English tongue.

She was a lady of royal blood;
   And when, past sorrow and teen,   45
He stood where still through his crownless years
   His Scotish realm had been,
At Scone were the happy lovers crowned,
   A heart-wed King and Queen.

But the bird may fall from the bough of youth,   50
   And song be turned to moan,
And Love's storm-cloud to the shadow of Hate,
When the tempest-waves of a troubled State
   Are beating against a throne.

Yet well they loved; and the god of Love,   55
   Whom well the King had sung,
Might find on the earth no truer hearts
   His lowliest swains among.

From the days when first she rode abroad
   With Scotish maids in her train,   60
I Catherine Douglas won the trust
   Of my mistress sweet Queen Jane.

And oft she sighed, 'To be born a King!'
  And oft along the way
When she saw the homely lovers pass 65
  She has said, 'Alack the day!'

Years waned, – the loving and toiling years:
  Till England's wrong renewed
Drove James, by outrage cast on his crown,
  To the open field of feud. 70

'Twas when the King and his host were met
  At the leaguer of Roxbro' hold,
The Queen o' the sudden sought his camp
  With a tale of dread to be told.

And she showed him a secret letter writ 75
  That spoke of treasonous strife,
And how a band of his noblest lords
  Were sworn to take his life.

'And it may be here or it may be there,
  In the camp or the court,' she said:
'But for my sake come to your people's arms 80
  And guard your royal head.'

Quoth he, ''Tis the fifteenth day of the siege,
  And the castle's nigh to yield.'
'O face your foes on your throne,' she cried, 85
  'And show the power you wield;
And under your Scotish people's love
  You shall sit as under your shield.'

At the fair Queen's side I stood that day
  When he bade them raise the siege, 90
And back to his Court he sped to know
  How the lords would meet their Liege.

But when he summoned his Parliament,
  The louring brows hung round,
Like clouds that circle the mountain-head 95
  Ere the first low thunders sound.

For he had tamed the nobles' lust
  And curbed their power and pride,
And reached out an arm to right the poor
  Through Scotland far and wide; 100
And many a lordly wrong-doer
  By the headsman's axe had died.

'Twas then upspoke Sir Robert Græme,
  The bold o'ermastering man: –
'O King, in the name of your Three Estates   105
  I set you under their ban!

'For, as your lords made oath to you
  Of service and fealty,
Even in like wise you pledged your oath
  Their faithful sire to be: –   110

'Yet all we here that are nobly sprung
  Have mourned dear kith and kin
Since first for the Scotish Barons' curse
  Did your bloody rule begin.'

With that he laid his hands on his King: –   115
  'Is this not so, my lords?'
But of all who had sworn to league with him
  Not one spake back to his words.

Quoth the King: – 'Thou speak'st but for one Estate,
  Nor doth it avow thy gage.   120
Let my liege lords hale this traitor hence!'
  The Græme fired dark with rage: –
'Who works for lesser men than himself,
  He earns but a witless wage!'

But soon from the dungeon where he lay   125
  He won by privy plots,
And forth he fled with a price on his head
  To the country of the Wild Scots.

And word there came from Sir Robert Græme
  To the King at Edinbro': –   130
'No Liege of mine thou art; but I see
From this day forth alone in thee
  God's creature, my mortal foe.

'Through thee are my wife and children lost,
  My heritage and lands;   135
And when my God shall show me a way,
Thyself my mortal foe will I slay
  With these my proper hands.'

Against the coming of Christmastide
  That year the King bade call   140
I' the Black Friars' Charterhouse of Perth
  A solemn festival.

And we of his household rode with him
  In a close-ranked company;
But not till the sun had sunk from his throne   145
  Did we reach the Scotish Sea.

That eve was clenched for a boding storm,
  'Neath a toilsome moon half seen;
The cloud stooped low and the surf rose high;
And where there was a line of the sky,   150
  Wild wings loomed dark between.

And on a rock of the black beach-side,
  By the veiled moon dimly lit,
There was something seemed to heave with life
  As the King drew nigh to it.   155

And was it only the tossing furze
  Or brake of the waste sea-wold?
Or was it an eagle bent to the blast?
When near we came, we knew it at last
  For a woman tattered and old.   160

But it seemed as though by a fire within
  Her writhen limbs were wrung;
And as soon as the King was close to her,
  She stood up gaunt and strong.

'Twas then the moon sailed clear of the rack   165
  On high in her hollow dome;
And still as aloft with hoary crest
  Each clamorous wave rang home,
Like fire in snow the moonlight blazed
  Amid the champing foam.   170

And the woman held his eyes with her eyes: —
  'O King, thou art come at last;
But thy wraith has haunted the Scotish Sea
  To my sight for four years past.

'Four years it is since first I met,   175
  'Twixt the Duchray and the Dhu,

A shape whose feet clung close in a shroud,
   And that shape for thine I knew.

'A year again, and on Inchkeith Isle
   I saw thee pass in the breeze,   180
With the cerecloth risen above thy feet
   And wound about thy knees.

'And yet a year, in the Links of Forth,
   As a wanderer without rest,
Thou cam'st with both thine arms i' the shroud   185
   That clung high up thy breast.

'And in this hour I find thee here,
   And well mine eyes may note
That the winding-sheet hath passed thy breast
   And risen around thy throat.   190

'And when I meet thee again, O King,
   That of death hast such sore drouth, –
Except thou turn again on this shore, –
The winding-sheet shall have moved once more
   And covered thine eyes and mouth.   195

'O King, whom poor men bless for their King,
   Of thy fate be not so fain;
But these my words for God's message take,
And turn thy steed, O King, for her sake
   Who rides beside thy rein!'   200

While the woman spoke, the King's horse reared
   As if it would breast the sea,
And the Queen turned pale as she heard on the gale
   The voice die dolorously.

When the woman ceased, the steed was still,   205
   But the King gazed on her yet,
And in silence save for the wail of the sea
   His eyes and her eyes met.

At last he said: – 'God's ways are His own;
   Man is but shadow and dust.   210
Last night I prayed by His altar-stone;
To-night I wend to the Feast of His Son;
   And in Him I set my trust.

'I have held my people in sacred charge,
   And have not feared the sting   215

Of proud men's hate, – to His will resign'd
Who has but one same death for a hind
   And one same death for a King.

'And if God in His wisdom have brought close
   The day when I must die,   220
That day by water or fire or air
My feet shall fall in the destined snare
   Wherever my road may lie.

'What man can say but the Fiend hath set
   Thy sorcery on my path,   225
My heart with the fear of death to fill,
And turn me against God's very will
   To sink in His burning wrath?'

The woman stood as the train rode past,
   And moved nor limb nor eye;   230
And when we were shipped, we saw her there
   Still standing against the sky.

As the ship made way, the moon once more
   Sank slow in her rising pall;
And I thought of the shrouded wraith of the King,   235
   And I said, 'The Heavens know all.'

And now, ye lasses, must ye hear
   How my name is Kate Barlass: –
But a little thing, when all the tale
   Is told of the weary mass   240
Of crime and woe which in Scotland's realm
   God's will let come to pass.

'Twas in the Charterhouse of Perth
   That the King and all his Court
Were met, the Christmas Feast being done,   245
   For solace and disport.

'Twas a wind-wild eve in February,
   And against the casement-pane
The branches smote like summoning hands,
   And muttered the driving rain.   250

And when the wind swooped over the lift
   And made the whole heaven frown,
It seemed a grip was laid on the walls
   To tug the housetop down.

And the Queen was there, more stately fair   255
  Than a lily in garden set;
And the King was loth to stir from her side;
For as on the day when she was his bride,
  Even so he loved her yet.

And the Earl of Athole, the King's false friend,   260
  Sat with him at the board;
And Robert Stuart the chamberlain
  Who had sold his sovereign Lord.

Yet the traitor Christopher Chaumber there
  Would fain have told him all,   265
And vainly four times that night he strove
  To reach the King through the hall.

But the wine is bright at the goblet's brim
  Though the poison lurk beneath;
And the apples still are red on the tree   270
Within whose shade may the adder be
  That shall turn thy life to death.

There was a knight of the King's fast friends
  Whom he called the King of Love;
And to such bright cheer and courtesy   275
  That name might best behove.

And the King and Queen both loved him well
  For his gentle knightliness;
And with him the King, as that eve wore on,
  Was playing at the chess.   280

And the King said, (for he thought to jest
  And soothe the Queen thereby;) –
'In a book 'tis writ that this same year
  A King shall in Scotland die.

'And I have pondered the matter o'er,   285
  And this have I found, Sir Hugh, –
There are but two Kings on Scotish ground,
  And those Kings are I and you.

'And I have a wife and a newborn heir,
  And you are yourself alone;   290
So stand you stark at my side with me
  To guard our double throne.

'For here sit I and my wife and child,
    As well your heart shall approve,
In full surrender and soothfasteness,   295
    Beneath your Kingdom of Love.'

And the Knight laughed, and the Queen too smiled;
    But I knew her heavy thought,
And I strove to find in the good King's jest
    What cheer might thence be wrought.   300

And I said, 'My Liege, for the Queen's dear love
    Now sing the song that of old
You made, when a captive Prince you lay,
And the nightingale sang sweet on the spray,
    In Windsor's castle-hold.'   305

Then he smiled the smile I knew so well
    When he thought to please the Queen;
The smile which under all bitter frowns
    Of fate that rose between
For ever dwelt at the poet's heart   310
    Like the bird of love unseen.

And he kissed her hand and took his harp,
    And the music sweetly rang;
And when the song burst forth, it seemed
    'Twas the nightingale that sang.   315

'Worship, ye lovers, on this May:
    Of bliss your kalends are begun:
Sing with us, Away, Winter, away!
    Come, Summer, the sweet season and sun!
    Awake for shame, – your heaven is won, –   320
And amorously your heads lift all:
Thank Love, that you to his grace doth call!'

But when he bent to the Queen, and sang
    The speech whose praise was hers,
It seemed his voice was the voice of the Spring   325
    And the voice of the bygone years.

'The fairest and the freshest flower
That ever I saw before that hour,
To which o' the sudden made to start
The blood of my body to my heart.   330

* * * * *

Ah sweet, are ye a worldly creature
Or heavenly thing in form of nature?'

And the song was long, and richly stored
   With wonder and beauteous things;   335
And the harp was tuned to every change
   Of minstrel ministerings;
But when he spoke of the Queen at the last
   Its strings were his own heart-strings.

'Unworthy but only of her grace,   340
   Upon Love's rock that's easy and sure,
In guerdon of all my love's space
   She took me her humble creäture.
   Thus fell my blissful aventure
In youth of love that from day to day   345
Flowereth aye new, and further I say.

'To reckon all the circumstance
   As it happed when lessen gan my sore,
Of my rancour and woful chance,
   It were too long, – I have done therefor.   350
   And of this flower I say no more,
But unto my help her heart hath tended
And even from death her man defended.'

'Aye, even from death,' to myself I said;
   For I thought of the day when she,   355
Had borne him the news, at Roxbro' siege,
   Of the fell confederacy.

But Death even then took aim as he sang
   With an arrow deadly bright;
And the grinning skull lurked grimly aloof,   360
And the wings were spread far over the roof
   More dark than the winter night.

Yet truly along the amorous song
   Of Love's high pomp and state,
There were words of Fortune's trackless doom   365
   And the dreadful face of Fate.

And oft have I heard again in dreams
    The voice of dire appeal
In which the King then sang of the pit
    That is under Fortune's wheel.   370

'And under the wheel beheld I there
    An ugly Pit as deep as hell,
That to behold I quaked for fear:
    And this I heard, that who therein fell
    Came no more up, tidings to tell: 375
Whereat, astound of the fearful sight,
I wist not what to do for fright.'

And oft has my thought called up again
    These words of the changeful song: –
'Wist thou thy pain and thy travàil   380
To come, well might'st thou weep and wail!'
    And our wail, O God! is long.

But the song's end was all of his love;
    And well his heart was grac'd
With her smiling lips and her tear-bright eyes   385
    As his arm went round her waist.

And on the swell of her long fair throat
    Close clung the necklet-chain
As he bent her pearl-tir'd head aside,
And in the warmth of his love and pride   390
    He kissed her lips full fain.

And her true face was a rosy red,
    The very red of the rose
That, couched on the happy garden-bed,
    In the summer sunlight glows.   395

And all the wondrous things of love
    That sang so sweet through the song
Were in the look that met in their eyes,
    And the look was deep and long.

'Twas then a knock came at the outer gate,   400
    And the usher sought the King.
'The woman you met by the Scotish Sea,
    My Liege, would tell you a thing;
And she says that her present need for speech
    Will bear no gainsaying.'   405

And the King said: 'The hour is late
   To-morrow will serve, I ween.'
Then he charged the usher strictly, and said:
   'No word of this to the Queen.'

But the usher came again to the King.   410
   'Shall I call her back?' quoth he:
'For as she went on her way, she cried,
   "Woe! Woe! then the thing must be!"'

And the King paused, but he did not speak.
   Then he called for the Voidee-cup: 415
And as we heard the twelfth hour strike,
There by true lips and false lips alike
   Was the draught of trust drained up.

So with reverence meet to King and Queen,
   To bed went all from the board;   420
And the last to leave of the courtly train
Was Robert Stuart the chamberlain
   Who had sold his sovereign lord.

And all the locks of the chamber-door
   Had the traitor riven and brast;   425
And that Fate might win sure way from afar,
He had drawn out every bolt and bar
   That made the entrance fast.

And now at midnight he stole his way
   To the moat of the outer wall,   430
And laid strong hurdles closely across
   Where the traitors' tread should fall.

But we that were the Queen's bower-maids
   Alone were left behind;
And with heed we drew the curtains close   435
   Against the winter wind.

And now that all was still through the hall,
   More clearly we heard the rain
That clamoured ever against the glass
   And the boughs that beat on the pane.   440

But the fire was bright in the ingle-nook,
   And through empty space around
The shadows cast on the arras'd wall

'Mid the pictured kings stood sudden and tall
  Like spectres sprung from the ground.   445

And the bed was dight in a deep alcove;
  And as he stood by the fire
The King was still in talk with the Queen
  While he doffed his goodly attire.

And the song had brought the image back   450
  Of many a bygone year;
And many a loving word they said
With hand in hand and head laid to head;
  And none of us went anear.

But Love was weeping outside the house,   455
  A child in the piteous rain;
And as he watched the arrow of Death,
He wailed for his own shafts close in the sheath
  That never should fly again.

And now beneath the window arose   460
  A wild voice suddenly:
And the King reared straight, but the Queen fell back
  As for bitter dule to dree;
And all of us knew the woman's voice
  Who spoke by the Scotish Sea.   465

'O King,' she cried, 'in an evil hour
  They drove me from thy gate;
And yet my voice must rise to thine ears;
  But alas! it comes too late!

'Last night at mid-watch, by Aberdour,   470
  When the moon was dead in the skies,
O King, in a death-light of thine own
  I saw thy shape arise.

'And in full season, as erst I said,
  The doom had gained its growth;   475
And the shroud had risen above thy neck
  And covered thine eyes and mouth.

'And no moon woke, but the pale dawn broke,
  And still thy soul stood there;
And I thought its silence cried to my soul   480
  As the first rays crowned its hair.

'Since then have I journeyed fast and fain
  In very despite of Fate,
Lest Hope might still be found in God's will:
  But they drove me from thy gate.   485

'For every man on God's ground, O King,
  His death grows up from his birth
In a shadow-plant perpetually;
And thine towers high, a black yew-tree,
  O'er the Charterhouse of Perth!'   490

That room was built far out from the house;
  And none but we in the room
Might hear the voice that rose beneath,
  Nor the tread of the coming doom.

For now there came a torchlight-glare,   495
  And a clang of arms there came;
And not a soul in that space but thought
  Of the foe Sir Robert Græme.

Yea, from the country of the Wild Scots,
  O'er mountain, valley, and glen,   500
He had brought with him in murderous league
  Three hundred armèd men.

The King knew all in an instant's flash;
  And like a King did he stand;
But there was no armour in all the room,   505
  Nor weapon lay to his hand.

And all we women flew to the door
  And thought to have made it fast;
But the bolts were gone and the bars were gone
  And the locks were riven and brast.   510

And he caught the pale pale Queen in his arms
  As the iron footsteps fell, –
Then loosed her, standing alone, and said,
  'Our bliss was our farewell!'

And 'twixt his lips he murmured a prayer,   515
  And he crossed his brow and breast;
And proudly in royal hardihood
Even so with folded arms he stood, –
  The prize of the bloody quest.

Then on me leaped the Queen like a deer: –   520
   'O Catherine, help!' she cried.
And low at his feet we clasped his knees
   Together side by side.
'Oh! even a King, for his people's sake,
   From treasonous death must hide!'   525

'For *her* sake most!' I cried, and I marked
   The pang that my words could wring.
And the iron tongs from the chimney-nook
   I snatched and held to the king: –
'Wrench up the plank! and the vault beneath   530
   Shall yield safe harbouring.'

With brows low-bent, from my eager hand
   The heavy heft did he take;
And the plank at his feet he wrenched and tore;
And as he frowned through the open floor,   535
   Again I said, 'For her sake!'

Then he cried to the Queen, 'God's will be done!'
   For her hands were clasped in prayer.
And down he sprang to the inner crypt;
And straight we closed the plank he had ripp'd   540
   And toiled to smooth it fair.

(Alas! in that vault a gap once was
   Wherethro' the King might have fled:
But three days since close-walled had it been
By his will; for the ball would roll therein   545
   When without at the palm he play'd.)

Then the Queen cried, 'Catherine, keep the door,
   And I to this will suffice!'
At her word I rose all dazed to my feet,
   And my heart was fire and ice.   550

And louder ever the voices grew,
   And the tramp of men in mail;
Until to my brain it seemed to be
As though I tossed on a ship at sea
   In the teeth of a crashing gale.   555

Then back I flew to the rest; and hard
   We strove with sinews knit

To force the table against the door;
  But we might not compass it.

Then my wild gaze sped far down the hall   560
  To the place of the hearthstone-sill;
And the Queen bent ever above the floor,
  For the plank was rising still.

And now the rush was heard on the stair,
  And 'God, what help?' was our cry.   565
And was I frenzied or was I bold?
I looked at each empty stanchion-hold,
  And no bar but my arm had I!

Like iron felt my arm, as through
  The staple I made it pass: –   570
Alack! it was flesh and bone – no more!
'Twas Catherine Douglas sprang to the door,
  But I fell back Kate Barlass.

With that they all thronged into the hall,
  Half dim to my failing ken;   575
And the space that was but a void before
  Was a crowd of wrathful men.

Behind the door I had fall'n and lay,
  Yet my sense was wildly aware,
And for all the pain of my shattered arm   580
  I never fainted there.

Even as I fell, my eyes were cast
  Where the King leaped down to the pit;
And lo! the plank was smooth in its place,
  And the Queen stood far from it.   585

And under the litters and through the bed
  And within the presses all
The traitors sought for the King, and pierced
  The arras around the wall.

And through the chamber they ramped and stormed   590
  Like lions loose in the lair,
And scarce could trust to their very eyes, –
  For behold! no King was there.

Then one of them seized the Queen, and cried, –
  'Now tell us, where is thy lord?'   595

And he held the sharp point over her heart:
She drooped not her eyes nor did she start,
  But she answered never a word.

Then the sword half pierced the true true breast:
  But it was the Græme's own son   600
Cried, 'This is a woman, – we seek a man!'
  And away from her girdle zone
He struck the point of the murderous steel;
  And that foul deed was not done.

And forth flowed all the throng like a sea   605
  And 'twas empty space once more;
And my eyes sought out the wounded Queen
  As I lay behind the door.

And I said: 'Dear Lady, leave me here,
  For I cannot help you now;   610
But fly while you may, and none shall reck
  Of my place here lying low.'

And she said, 'My Catherine, God help thee!'
  Then she looked to the distant floor,
And clasping her hands, 'O God help *him*,'   615
  She sobbed, 'for we can no more!'

But God He knows what help may mean,
  If it mean to live or to die;
And what sore sorrow and mighty moan
  On earth it may cost ere yet a throne   620
  Be filled in His house on high.

And now the ladies fled with the Queen;
  And through the open door
The night-wind wailed round the empty room
  And the rushes shook on the floor.   625

And the bed drooped low in the dark recess
  Whence the arras was rent away;
And the firelight still shone over the space
  Where our hidden secret lay.

And the rain had ceased, and the moonbeams lit   630
  The window high in the wall, –
Bright beams that on the plank that I knew
  Through the painted pane did fall,

And gleamed with the splendour of Scotland's crown
  And shield armorial.   635

But then a great wind swept up the skies
  And the climbing moon fell back;
And the royal blazon fled from the floor,
  And nought remained on its track;
And high in the darkened window-pane   640
  The shield and the crown were black.

And what I say next I partly saw
  And partly I heard in sooth,
And partly since from the murderers' lips
  The torture wrung the truth.   645

For now again came the armèd tread,
  And fast through the hall it fell;
But the throng was less; and ere I saw,
  By the voice without I could tell
That Robert Stuart had come with them   650
  Who knew that chamber well.

And over the space the Græme strode dark
  With his mantle round him flung;
And in his eye was a flaming light
  But not a word on his tongue.   655

And Stuart held a torch to the floor,
  And he found the thing he sought;
And they slashed the plank away with their swords;
  And O God! I fainted not!

And the traitor held his torch in the gap,   660
  All smoking and smouldering;
And through the vapour and fire, beneath
  In the dark crypt's narrow ring,
With a shout that pealed to the room's high roof
  They saw their naked King.   665

Half naked he stood, but stood as one
  Who yet could do and dare:
With the crown, the King was stript away, –
The Knight was 'reft of his battle-array, –
  But still the Man was there.   670

From the rout then stepped a villain forth, –
  Sir John Hall was his name;

With a knife unsheathed he leapt to the vault
  Beneath the torchlight-flame.

Of his person and stature was the King   675
  A man right manly strong,
And mightily by the shoulder-blades
  His foe to his feet he flung.

Then the traitor's brother, Sir Thomas Hall,
  Sprang down to work his worst;   680
And the King caught the second man by the neck
  And flung him above the first.

And he smote and trampled them under him;
  And a long month thence they bare
All black their throats with the grip of his hands   685
  When the hangman's hand came there.

And sore he strove to have had their knives,
  But the sharp blades gashed his hands.
Oh James! so armed, thou hadst battled there
  Till help had come of thy bands;   690
And oh! once more thou hadst held our throne
  And ruled thy Scotish lands!

But while the King o'er his foes still raged
  With a heart that nought could tame,
Another man sprang down to the crypt;   695
And with his sword in his hand hard-gripp'd,
  There stood Sir Robert Græme.

(Now shame on the recreant traitor's heart
  Who durst not face his King
Till the body unarmed was wearied out   700
  With two-fold combating!

Ah! well might the people sing and say,
  As oft ye have heard aright: –
'O Robert Græme, O Robert Græme,
Who slew our King, God give thee shame!'   705
  For he slew him not as a knight.)

And the naked King turned round at bay,
  But his strength had passed the goal,
And he could but gasp: – 'Mine hour is come;
But oh! to succour thine own soul's doom,   710
  Let a priest now shrive my soul!'

And the traitor looked on the King's spent strength,
    And said: – 'Have I kept my word? –
Yea, King, the mortal pledge that I gave?
No black frair's shrift thy soul shall have,   715
    But the shrift of this red sword!'

With that he smote his King through the breast;
    And all they three in that pen
Fell on him and stabbed and stabbed him there
    Like merciless murderous men.   720

Yet seemed it now that Sir Robert Græme,
    Ere the King's last breath was o'er,
Turned sick at heart with the deadly sight
    And would have done no more.

But a cry came from the troop above: –   725
    'If him thou do not slay,
The price of his life that thou dost spare
    Thy forfeit life shall pay!'

O God! what more did I hear or see,
    Or how should I tell the rest?   730
But there at length our King lay slain
    With sixteen wounds in his breast.

O God! and now did a bell boom forth,
    And the murderers turned and fled; –
Too late, too late, O God, did it sound! –   735
And I heard the true men mustering round,
    And the cries and the coming tread.

But ere they came, to the black death-gap
    Somewise did I creep and steal;
And lo! or ever I swooned away,   740
Through the dusk I saw where the white face lay
    In the Pit of Fortune's Wheel.

And now, ye Scotish maids who have heard
    Dread things of the days grown old, –
Even at the last, of true Queen Jane   745
    May somewhat yet be told,
And how she dealt for her dear lord's sake
    Dire vengeance manifold.

'Twas in the Charterhouse of Perth,
  In the fair-lit Death-chapelle,
That the slain King's corpse on bier was laid   750
  With chaunt and requiem-knell.

And all with royal wealth of balm
  Was the body purified;
And none could trace on the brow and lips   755
  The death that he had died.

In his robes of state he lay asleep
  With orb and sceptre in hand;
And by the crown he wore on his throne
  Was his kingly forehead spann'd.   760

And, girls 'twas a sweet sad thing to see
  How the curling golden hair,
As in the day of the poet's youth,
  From the King's crown clustered there.

And if all had come to pass in the brain   765
  That throbbed beneath those curls,
Then Scots had said in the days to come
That this their soul was a different home
  And a different Scotland, girls!

And the Queen sat by him night and day,   770
  And oft she knelt in prayer,
All wan and pale in the widow's veil
  That shrouded her shining hair.

And I had got good help of my hurt:
  And only to me some sign   775
She made; and save the priests that were there,
  No face would she see but mine.

And the month of March wore on apace;
  And now fresh couriers fared
Still from the country of the Wild Scots   780
  With news of the traitors snared.

And still as I told her day by day,
  Her pallor changed to sight,
And the frost grew to a furnace-flame
  That burnt her visage white.   785

And evermore as I brought her word,
  She bent to her dead King James,
And in the cold ear with fire-drawn breath
  She spoke the traitors' names.

But when the name of Sir Robert Græme   790
  Was the one she had to give,
I ran to hold her up from the floor;
For the froth was on her lips, and sore
  I feared that she could not live.

And the month of March wore nigh to its end, 795
  And still was the death-pall spread;
For she would not bury her slaughtered lord
  Till his slayers all were dead.

And now of their dooms dread tidings came,
  And of torments fierce and dire;   800
And nought she spake, – she had ceased to speak, –
  But her eyes were a soul on fire.

But when I told her the bitter end
  Of the stern and just award,
She leaned o'er the bier, and thrice three times 805
  She kissed the lips of her lord.

And then she said, – 'My King, they are dead!'
  And she knelt on the chapel-floor,
And whispered low with a strange proud smile, –
  'James, James, they suffered more!'   810

Last she stood up to her queenly height,
  But she shook like an autumn leaf,
As though the fire wherein she burned
Then left her body, and all were turned
  To winter of life-long grief.   815

And 'O James!' she said, – 'My James!' she said, –
  'Alas for the woful thing,
That a poet true and a friend of man,
In desperate days of bale and ban,
  Should needs be born a King!'   820

Possession

There is a cloud above the sunset hill,
   That wends and makes no stay,
For its goal lies beyond the fiery west;
A lingering breath no calm can chase away,
The onward labour of the wind's last will;   5
A flying foam that overleaps the crest
Of the top wave: and in possession still
A further reach of longing; though at rest
   From all the yearning years,
Together in the bosom of that day   10
Ye cling, and with your kisses drink your tears.

Spheral Change

In this new shade of Death, the show
   Passes me still of form and face;
Some bent, some gazing as they go,
   Some swiftly, some at a dull pace,
   Not one that speaks in any case.   5

If only one might speak! – the one
   Who never waits till I come near;
But always seated all alone
   As listening to the sunken air,
   Is gone before I come to her.   10

O dearest! while we lived and died
   A living death in every day,
Some hours we still were side by side,
   When where I was you too might stay
   And rest and need not go away.   15

O nearest, furthest! Can there be
   At length some hard-earned heart-won home,
Where, – exile changed for sanctuary, –
   Our lot may fill indeed its sum,
   And you may wait and I may come?   20

Poems
published posthumously

On Certain Elizabethan Revivals

O ruff-embastioned vast Elizabeth,
  Bush to these bushel-bellied casks of wine,
  Home-growth, 'tis true, but rank as turpentine –
What would we with such skittle-plays at death?
Say, must we watch these brawlers' brandished lathe,   5
  Or to their reeking wit our ears incline,
  Because all Castaly flowed crystalline
In gentle Shakspeare's modulated breath?

What! must our drama with the rat-pie vie,
  Nor the scene close while one is left to kill?   10
    Shall this be poetry? And thou – thou man
    Of blood, thou cannibalic Caliban,
What shall be said of thee? A poet? – Fie!
'An honourable murderer, if you will.'

Raleigh's Cell in the Tower

Here writ was the World's History by his hand
  Whose steps knew all the earth; albeit his world
  In these few piteous paces then was furl'd.
Here daily, hourly, have his proud feet spann'd
This smaller speck than the receding land   5
  Had ever shown his ships; what time he hurl'd
  Abroad o'er new-found regions spiced and pearl'd
His country's high dominion and command.

Here dwelt two spheres. The vast terrestrial zone
  His spirit traversed; and that spirit was   10
    Itself the zone celestial, round whose birth
    The planets played within the zodiac's girth;
  Till hence, through unjust death unfeared, did pass
His spirit to the only land unknown.

Mnemosyne
(FOR A PICTURE)

Thou fill'st from the winged chalice of the soul
Thy lamp, O Memory! fire-winged to its goal.

To Philip Bourke Marston,
inciting me to Poetic Work

Sweet Poet, thou of whom these years that roll
  Must one day yet the burdened birthright learn,
  And by the darkness of thine eyes discern
How piercing was the sight within thy soul; –
Gifted apart, thou goest to the great goal,   5
  A cloud-bound radiant spirit, strong to earn,
  Light-reft, that prize for which fond myriads yearn
Vainly light-blest, – the Seër's aureole.

And doth thine ear, divinely dowered to catch
  All spheral sounds in thy song blent so well,   10
  Still hearken for my voice's slumbering spell
With wistful love? Ah! let the Muse now snatch
My wreath for thy young brows, and bend to watch
  Thy veiled transfiguring sense's miracle.

For
An Annunciation
Early German

The lilies stand before her like a screen
  Through which, upon this warm and solemn day,
  God surely hears. For there she kneels to pray
Who wafts our prayers to God – Mary the Queen.
She was Faith's Present, parting what had been   5
  From what began with her, and is for aye.
  On either hand, God's twofold system lay:
With meek bowed face a Virgin prayed between.

So prays she, and the Dove flies in to her,
   And she has turned. At the low porch is one   10
   Who looks as though deep awe made him to smile.
Heavy with heat, the plants yield shadow there;
   The loud flies cross each other in the sun;
   And the aisled pillars meet the poplar-aisle.

At the Sun-Rise in 1848

God said, Let there be light; and there was light.
   Then heard we sounds as though the Earth did sing
   And the Earth's angels cried upon the wing:
We saw priests fall together and turn white:
And covered in the dust from the sun's sight,   5
   A king was spied, and yet another king.
   We said: 'The round world keeps its balancing;
On this globe, they and we are opposite, –
If it is day with us, with them 'tis night.'
   Still, Man, in thy just pride, remember this: –   10
      Thou hadst not made that thy sons' sons shall ask
      What the word *king* may mean in their day's task,
   But for the light that led: and if light is,
It is because God said, Let there be light.

Autumn Song

   Know'st thou not at the fall of the leaf
   How the heart feels a languid grief
      Laid on it for a covering,
      And how sleep seems a goodly thing
   In Autumn at the fall of the leaf?   5

   And how the swift beat of the brain
   Falters because it is in vain,
      In Autumn at the fall of the leaf
      Knowest thou not? and how the chief
   Of joys seems – not to suffer pain?   10

Know'st thou not at the fall of the leaf
How the soul feels like a dried sheaf
    Bound up at length for harvesting,
    And how death seems a comely thing
In Autumn at the fall of the leaf?   15

The Lady's Lament

Never happy any more!
Aye, turn the saying o'er and o'er,
It says but what it said before,
And heart and life are just as sore.
The wet leaves blow aslant the floor   5
In the rain through the open door.
    No, no more.

Never happy any more!
The eyes are weary and give o'er,
But still the soul weeps as before.   10
And always must each one deplore
Each once, nor bear what others bore?
This is now as it was of yore.
    No, no more.

Never happy any more!   15
Is it not a sorry lore
That says, 'Take strength, the worst is o'er'?
Shall the stars seem as heretofore?
The day wears on more and more –
While I was weeping the day wore.   20
    No, no more.

Never happy any more!
In the cold behind the door
That was the dial striking four:
One for joy the past hours bore,   25
Two for hope and will cast o'er,
One for the naked dark before.
    No, no more.

Never happy any more!
Put the light out, shut the door,   30
Sweep the wet leaves from the floor.

Even thus Fate's hand has swept her floor,
Even thus Love's hand has shut the door
Through which his warm feet passed of yore.
Shall it be opened any more? 35
No, no, no more.

Vox Ecclesiae, Vox Christi

*I saw under the altar the souls of them that were slain for the word of
God, and for the testimony which they held; and they cried with a loud
voice, saying How long, O Lord, holy and true, dost Thou not judge and
avenge blood on them that dwell on the earth? – REV. vi. 9, 10.*

Not 'neath the altar only, – yet, in sooth,
    There more than elsewhere, – yet is the cry 'How long?'
    The right sown there hath still borne fruit in wrong –
The wrong waxed fourfold. Thence (in hate of truth)
O'er weapons blessed for carnage, to fierce youth 5
    From evil age, the word hath hissed along: –
    'Ye are the Lord's: go forth, destroy, be strong:
Christ's Church absolves ye from Christ's law of ruth.'

Therefore the wine-cup at the altar is
    As Christ's own blood indeed, and as the blood 10
    Of Christ's elect, at divers seasons spilt
On the altar-stone, that to man's church, for this,
    Shall prove a stone of stumbling, – whence it stood
    To be rent up ere the true Church be built.

The Staircase of Notre Dame, Paris

As one who, groping in a narrow stair,
    Hath a strong sound of bells upon his ears,
    Which, being at a distance off, appears
Quite close to him because of the pent air:
So with this France. She stumbles file and square 5
    Darkling and without space for breath: each one
    Who hears the thunder says: 'It shall anon
Be in among her ranks to scatter her.'

This may be; and it may be that the storm
  Is spent in rain upon the unscathed seas,   10
  Or wasteth other countries ere it die:
Till she, – having climbed always through the swarm
  Of darkness and of hurtling sound, – from these
  Shall step forth on the light in a still sky.

Near Brussels – A Half-way Pause

The turn of noontide has begun.
  In the weak breeze the sunshine yields.
  There is a bell upon the fields.
On the long hedgerow's tangled run
  A low white cottage intervenes: 5
  Against the wall a blind man leans,
And sways his face to have the sun.

Our horses' hoofs stir in the road,
  Quiet and sharp. Light hath a song
  Whose silence, being heard, seems long.   10
The point of noon maketh abode,
  And will not be at once gone through.
  The sky's deep colour saddens you,
And the heat weighs a dreamy load.

The Mirror

She knew it not: – most perfect pain
  To learn: this too she knew not. Strife
    For me, calm hers, as from the first.
    'Twas but another bubble burst
  Upon the curdling draught of life, –   5
My silent patience mine again.

As who, of forms that crowd unknown
  Within a distant mirror's shade,
    Deems such an one himself, and makes
    Some sign; but when the image shakes   10

No whit, he finds his thought betray'd,
And must seek elsewhere for his own.

During Music

O cool unto the sense of pain
   That last night's sleep could not destroy;
   O warm unto the sense of joy,
That dreams its life within the brain.

What though I lean o'er thee to scan   5
   The written music cramped and stiff; –
   'Tis dark to me, as hieroglyph
On those weird bulks Egyptian.

But as from those, dumb now and strange,
   A glory wanders on the earth,   10
   Even so thy tones can call a birth
From these, to shake my soul with change.

O swift, as in melodious haste
   Float o'er the keys thy fingers small;
   O soft, as is the rise and fall   15
Which stirs that shade within thy breast.

English May

Would God your health were as this month of May
   Should be, were this not England, – and your face
   Abroad, to give the gracious sunshine grace
And laugh beneath the budding hawthorn-spray.
But here the hedgerows pine from green to grey   5
   While yet May's lyre is tuning, and her song
   Is weak in shade that should in sun be strong;
And your pulse springs not to so faint a lay.

If in my life be breath of Italy,
   Would God that I might yield it all to you!   10
   So, when such grafted warmth had burgeoned through
The languor of your Maytime's hawthorn-tree,

My spirit at rest should walk unseen and see
The garland of your beauty bloom anew.

Dawn on the Night-Journey

Till dawn the wind drove round me. It is past
  And still, and leaves the air to lisp of bird,
  And to the quiet that is almost heard
Of the new-risen day, as yet bound fast
In the first warmth of sunrise. When the last   5
  Of the sun's hours to-day shall be fulfilled,
  There shall another breath of time be stilled
For me, which now is to my senses cast
As much beyond me as eternity,
  Unknown, kept secret. On the newborn air   10
The moth quivers in silence. It is vast,
Yea, even beyond the hills upon the sea,
  The day whose end shall give this hour as sheer
As chaos to the irrevocable Past.

To Thomas Woolner
First Snow 9 February 1853

Woolner, to-night it snows for the first time.
  Our feet knew well the path, where in this snow
  Mine leave one track: how all the ways we know
Are hoary in the long-unwonted rime!
Grey as the ghosts which now in your new clime   5
  Must haunt you while those singing spirits reap
  All night the field of hospitable sleep –
Whose song, past the whole sea, finds counter-chime.

Can the year change, and I not think of thee,
  With whom so many changes of the year   10
So many years were watched, – our love's degree
Alone the same? Ah, still for thee and me,
  Winter or summer, Woolner, here or there,
One grief, one joy, one loss, one victory.

The Seed of David

Christ sprang from David Shepherd, and even so
From David King, being born of high and low.
The Shepherd lays his crook, the King his crown,
Here at Christ's feet, and high and low bend down.

Dennis Shand

The shadows fall along the wall,
   It's night at Haye-la-Serre;
The maidens weave since day grew eve,
   The lady's in her chair.

O passing slow the long hours go   5
   With time to think and sigh,
When weary maidens weave beneath
   A listless lady's eye.

It's two days that Earl Simon's gone
   And it's the second night;   10
At Haye-la-Serre the lady's fair,
   In June the moon is light.

O it's 'Maids, ye'll wake till I come back,'
   And the hound's i' the lady's chair:
No shuttles fly, the work stands by,   15
   It's play at Haye-la-Serre.

The night is worn, the lamp's forlorn,
   The shadows waste and fail;
There's morning air at Haye-la-Serre,
   The watching maids look pale.   20

O all unmarked the birds at dawn
   Where drowsy maidens be;
But heard too soon the lark's first tune
   Beneath the trysting tree.

'Hold me thy hand, sweet Dennis Shand,'   25
   Says the Lady Joan de Haye,
'That thou to-morrow do forget
   To-day and yesterday.

'For many a weary month to come
   My lord keeps house with me,   30
And sighing summer must lie cold
   In winter's company.

'And many an hour I'll pass thee by
   And see thee and be seen;
Yet not a glance must tell by chance   35
   How sweet these hours have been.

'We've all to fear; there's Maud the spy,
   There's Ann whose face I scor'd,
There's Blanch tells Huot everything,
   And Huot loves my lord.   40

'But O and it's my Dennis'll know,
   When my eyes look weary dim,
Who finds the gold for his girdle-fee
   And who keeps love for him.'

The morrow's come and the morrow-night,   45
   It's feast at Haye-la-Serre,
And Dennis Shand the cup must hand
   Beside Earl Simon's chair.

And still when the high pouring's done
   And cup and flagon clink,   50
Till his lady's lips have touched the brim
   Earl Simon will not drink.

But it's, 'Joan my wife,' Earl Simon says,
   'Your maids are white and wan.'
And it's, 'O,' she says, 'they've watched the night   55
   With Maud's sick sister Ann.'

But it's, 'Lady Joan and Joan my bird,
   Yourself look white and wan.'
And it's, 'O, I've walked the night myself
   To pull the herbs for Ann: 60

'And some of your knaves were at the hutch
   And some in the cellarage,
But the only one that watched with us
   Was Dennis Shand your page.

'Look on the boy, sweet honey lord,   65
    How drooped his eyelids be:
The rosy colour's not yet back
    That paled in serving me.'

O it's, 'Wife, your maids are foolish jades,
    And you're a silly chuck,   70
And the lazy knaves shall get their staves
    About their ears for luck:

'But Dennis Shand may take the cup
    And pour the wine to his hand;
Wife, thou shalt touch it with thy lips,   75
    And drink thou, Dennis Shand!'

After the French Liberation of Italy

As when the last of the paid joys of love
    Has come and gone, and with a single kiss
    At length, and with one laugh of satiate bliss
The wearied man one minute rests above
The wearied woman, no more urged to move   5
    In those long throes of longing, till they glide
    Now lightlier clasped, each to the other's side,
    In joys past acting, not past dreaming of.

So Europe now beneath this paramour
    Lies for a little out of use – full oft   10
Submissive to his lust, a loveless whore.
    He wakes, she sleeps, the breath falls slow and soft.
Wait: the bought body holds a birth within,
An harlot's child, to scourge her for her sin!

After the German Subjugation of France, 1871

Lo the twelfth year – the wedding-feast come round
    With years for months – and lo the babe new-born;
    Out of the womb's rank furnace cast forlorn,
And with contagious effluence seamed and crown'd.
To hail this birth, what fiery tongues surround   5

Hell's Pentecost – what clamour of all cries
That swell, from Absalom's scoff to Shimei's,
One scornful gamut of tumultuous sound!

For now the harlot's heart on a new sleeve
   Is prankt; and her heart's lord of yesterday   10
   (Spurned from her bed, whose worm-spun silks o'erlay
Such fretwork as that other worm can weave)
Takes in his ears the vanished world's last yell,
And in his flesh the closing teeth of Hell.

The Question
(FOR A DESIGN)

I

This sea, deep furrowed as the face of Time,
   Mirrors the ghost of the removed moon;
   The peaks stand bristling round the waste lagoon;
While up the difficult summit steeply climb
Youth, Manhood, Age, one triple labouring mime;   5
   And to the measure of some mystic rune
   Hark how the restless waters importune
These echoing steps with chime and counter-chime.

What seek they? Lo, upreared against the rock
   The Sphinx, Time's visible silence, frontleted   10
   With Psyche wings, with eagle plumes arched o'er.
Ah, when those everlasting lips unlock
   And the old riddle of the world is read,
   What shall man find? or seeks he evermore?

II

Lo, the three seekers! Youth has sprung the first
   To question the Unknown: but see! he sinks
   Prone to the earth – becomes himself a sphinx, –
A riddle of early death no love may burst.
Sorely anhungered, heavily athirst   5
   For knowledge, Manhood next to reach the Truth
   Peers in those eyes; till haggard and uncouth
Weak Eld renews that question long rehearsed.

Oh! and what answer? From the sad sea brim
  The eyes o' the Sphinx stare through the midnight spell,   10
  Unwavering, – Man's eternal quest to quell:
While round the rock-steps of her throne doth swim
Through the wind-serried wave the moon's faint rim,
  Some answer from the heaven invisible.

Notebook fragments
and verses

The Orchard-Pit

Piled deep below the screening apple-branch
   They lie with bitter apples in their hands:
And some are only ancient bones that blanch,
And some had ships that last year's wind did launch,
   And some were yesterday the lords of lands.   5

In the soft dell, among the apple-trees,
   High up above the hidden pit she stands,
And there for ever sings, who gave to these,
That lie below, her magic hour of ease,
   And those her apples holden in their hands.   10

This in my dreams is shown me; and her hair
   Crosses my lips and draws my burning breath;
Her song spreads golden wings upon the air,
Life's eyes are gleaming from her forehead fair,
   And from her breasts the ravishing eyes of Death.   15

Men say to me that sleep hath many dreams,
   Yet I knew never but this dream alone:
There, from a dried-up channel, once the stream's,
The glen slopes up; even such in sleep it seems
   As to my waking sight the place well known.   20

         *   *   *   *   *

My love I call her, and she loves me well:
   But I love her as in the maelstrom's cup
The whirled stone loves the leaf inseparable
That clings to it round all the circling swell,
   And that the same last eddy swallows up.   25

To Art

I loved thee ere I loved a woman, Love.

On Burns

In whomsoe'er, since Poesy began,
A Poet most of all men we may scan,
Burns of all poets is the most a Man.

Fin di Maggio

Oh! May sits crowned with hawthorn-flower,
    And is Love's month, they say;
And Love's the fruit that is ripened best
    By ladies' eyes in May.

And the Sibyl, you know. I saw her with my own eyes at Cumæ, hanging in a
jar; and when the boys asked her, 'What would you, Sibyl?' she answered, 'I
would die.' – PETRONIUS

'I saw the Sibyl at Cumæ'
    (One said) 'with mine own eye.
She hung in a cage, and read her rune
    To all the passers-by.
Said the boys, "What wouldst thou, Sibyl?"
    She answered, "I would die." '

As balmly as the breath of her you love
When deep between her breasts it comes to you.

With golden mantle, rings, and necklace fair,
    It likes her best to wear
Only a rose within her golden hair.

A golden robe, yet will she wear
Only a rose in her golden hair.

An ant-sting's prickly at first,
But the pain soon dies away;
A gnat-sting's worse the next day;
But a wasp 'tis that stings the worst.

O thou whose name, being alone, aloud
I utter oft, and though thou art not there,
Toward thine imaged presence kiss the air.

As much as in a hundred years, she's dead:
Yet is to-day the day on which she died.

Who shall say what is said in me,
With all that I might have been dead in me?

'Was it a friend or foe that spread these lies?'
'Nay, who but infants question in such wise?
'Twas one of my most intimate enemies.'

   At her step the water-hen
Springs from her nook, and skimming the clear stream,
Ripples its waters in a sinuous curve,
And dives again in safety.

Would God I knew there were a God to thank
When thanks rise in me!

I shut myself in with my soul,
And the shapes come eddying forth.

———————

She bound her green sleeve on my helm,
    Sweet pledge of love's sweet meed:
Warm was her bared arm round my neck
    As well she bade me speed;
And her kiss clings still between my lips,
    Heart's beat and strength at need.

Memory

Is Memory most of miseries miserable,
Or the one flower of ease in bitterest hell?

NOTES

Dates of composition are as given by W. M. Rossetti except where evidence indicates otherwise. Archaic and unfamiliar words not annotated are in the Concise Oxford and other reliable dictionaries. Key to abbreviations used is on page ix.

Poems first published 1848–62

MY SISTER'S SLEEP
text A 1850; text B 1870
wr. 1847–8; pub. *La Belle Assemblée*, September 1848; *Germ* January 1850, as 'Songs of One Household No. 1 My Sister's Sleep'; rev. and re-pub. *Poems* 1870, 1881

WMR 1911, 660 describes this as 'a very early performance ... still earlier, I apprehend, than "The Blessed Damozel" '. But in September 1848 DGR described *My Sister's Sleep* as 'one of the last things I have written' (DW 37). In 1869, DGR was intending to omit it from *Poems* 1870 until ACS wrote: 'Don't cut My Sister's Sleep or I will put up a public wail for the author's best piece.' (See DW 928 no. 4.) In revision, the poem lost much of its original Anglo-Catholic flavour and symbolism.

MARY'S GIRLHOOD: FOR A PICTURE
text part I 1870; part II 1849
wr. 1849; pub. 1849, on picture frame and in catalogue of Free Exhibition, to accompany painting entitled *The Girlhood of Mary Virgin*; part I rev. and re-pub. *Poems* 1870 as 'Mary's Girlhood (For a Picture)'; part II re-pub. in William Sharp, *Dante Gabriel Rossetti* (1882). For a discussion of other symbols and the painting this double sonnet was written to

accompany, see TG 1984, no. 15.
Part I original (1849) lines read:
3 Was young in Nazareth of Galilee.
4 Her kin she cherished with devout respect:
5 her gifts were simpleness of intellect
8 Strong in grave peace; in duty circumspect.
16 Tripoint: symbolic of the Trinity.

THE BLESSED DAMOZEL
text A 1850; text B 1870
wr. 1847–8; pub. *Germ* February 1850; *Oxford & Cambridge Magazine* November 1856 and *Crayon* (New York) February 1857; rev. and re-pub. 1870, 1881

In 1873, DGR asked his mother if she still had the earliest handwritten version of this famous piece, and if so, whether it was dated (DW 1340). No such MS is known to survive, but the pencilled date '1847' is appended to a later MS copy. In 1880, DGR described it as a poem he wrote '(and have altered little since)' when he was 18, which would mean it was composed before May 1847. WMR 1911, 647 endorsed this date, adding that 'the very first form of the poem appears to have been lost; it was seriously revised in printed shape more than once'. When in March 1848 DGR sent some of his compositions to Leigh Hunt, it can be inferred from the reply that *The Blessed Damozel* was among them; two or three unidentified stanzas were added in

1849, immediately prior to publication in the *Germ*. David Riede (*Victorian Poetry* 20, 188) argues that the 'legend' of DGR's precocity as a poet has led to contradictions, since it makes better work precede weaker pieces and obscures his literary development.

DGR also claimed to have written it in conscious emulation of Edgar Allan Poe, whose *Poems written in Youth* appeared in 1845. In 1876–9 and 1879 DGR produced two similar oil paintings (VS 244) based on the poem, which itself inspired Claude Debussy's *La demoiselle élue* (1887).

THE CARILLON: ANTWERP AND BRUGES

text 1850
wr. 1849; pub. *Germ* March 1850 (where dated 'October, 1849')

DGR travelled with WHH from Paris to Belgium in October 1849, chiefly to see early Flemish art. Hans Memlinc (d.1494) and Jan van Eyck (d.1441) were the painters whose work they most wished to see. Here DGR uses anglicized versions of their names. In WMR 1886, the piece is reprinted in slightly different form from DGR's MS.

FROM THE CLIFFS: NOON / THE SEA LIMITS

text A 1850; text B 1870
wr. 1849–50; pub. *Germ* March 1850; rev. and re-pub. *Poems* 1870 (as 'Song XI: The Sea-Limits'); 1881 (as 'The Sea-Limits')

Probably conceived at Boulogne in September 1849, during DGR's journey from London to Paris with WHH.

PAX VOBIS / WORLD'S WORTH

text A 1850; text B 1881
wr. 1849–50; pub. *Germ* April 1850 (as 'Pax Vobis'); rev. and re-pub. *Poems* 1881 (as 'World's Worth')

Inspired by DGR's visit to Ghent in 1849 with WHH (see 'The Carillon' above). Considered for inclusion in *Poems* 1870 but not used (see DW 929).

AN ALLEGORICAL DANCE OF WOMEN / BY ANDREA MANTEGNA (IN THE LOUVRE)

text 1870
wr. 1849; pub. *Germ* April 1850 (as 'Sonnets for Pictures. 3. / A Dance of Nymphs, by Andrea Mantegna; in the Louvre'); rev. and re-pub. *Poems* 1870, 1881

In 1850 the following note was attached to the poem:
'*It is necessary to mention, that this picture would appear to have been in the artist's mind an allegory, which the modern spectator may seek vainly to interpret.'

Revising for publication in 1870, DGR amended title and text. Variant lines in 1850 version:
3 Sharp through his brain, a distinct rapid pang,
5 But I believe he just leaned passively
6 And felt their hair carried
7 As each nymph passed him;
10 To see the dancers.
12 A portion of most secret life: to wit: –
13 Each human pulse shall keep

DGR first visited the Louvre in Paris in autumn 1849, with WHH, where he saw this work, correctly entitled *Parnassus*, by Italian artist Andrea Mantegna (*c.* 1431–1506), court painter at Mantua from 1460. A depiction of the home of the Muses, it includes Mars and Venus, together with Apollo and Pegasus as well as nine female Muses dancing in their grove on Mt Helicon. WMR 1911, 665, notes that DGR, apparently unaware of the picture's title, starting with the notion of 'a quasi-allegory not readily interpretable' used it to say 'that the emotion of the artist, which produced the picture, is manifest, but not the particular thought which governed it'.

A VIRGIN AND CHILD, BY HANS MEMMELING / IN THE ACADEMY OF BRUGES

text 1850
wr. 1849; pub. *Germ* April 1850 as

'Sonnets for Pictures I'

Sonnet for a painting seen by DGR in Bruges in October 1849. In WMR 1886, it was reprinted with amendments taken from DGR's MS.

Hans Memlinc was active in Bruges 1465–94. Depictions of the Virgin and Child were frequently commissioned from his workshop; examples in the National Gallery, London include nos. 686, 709 and 6275. A familiar motif shows the Christ Child holding or taking a fruit offered by an angel.

A MARRIAGE OF ST KATHARINE BY THE SAME / IN THE HOSPITAL OF ST JOHN AT BRUGES
text 1850
wr. 1849 pub. *Germ* April 1850 as 'Sonnets for Pictures. 2.'

WMR 1886 reprints this with minor amendments, altering the saint's name to 'Catherine'. WMR 1911, 666 quotes DGR's admiration for the triptych of which this is the central panel, seen in Bruges in October 1849. Many of Memlinc's works were commissioned by the Hospital of St John, including this depiction of the Mystic Marriage of St Catherine (a scene sometimes known as a Sacred Conversation) in which the Christ Child is shown placing a ring on the saint's finger, symbolic of her devotion as 'Bride of Christ'. Traditionally, the Virgin is shown reading, while the attendant saints named here are St John the disciple and gospel author ('whom He loved'), and St John Baptist ('His harbinger'.)

A VENETIAN PASTORAL / BY GIORGIONE / IN THE LOUVRE
text A 1850; text B 1870
wr. 1849; pub. *Germ* April 1850 (as 'Sonnets for Pictures. 4. / A Venetian Pastoral, by Giorgione; in the Louvre'); rev. and re-pub. *Poems* 1870, 1881

Venetian painter Giorgione (c. 1477–1510) is held to be one of the earliest artists for whom aesthetic beauty took precedence over subject, and as forerunner of Titian (c.

1485–1576) to whom this picture, *Concert Champêtre*, is now attributed. In the early 1850s, DGR sketched a proposed composition (VS 695) showing Giorgione at the easel, painting a young woman. The celebrated *Déjeuner sur l'herbe* by Edouard Manet (1832–83) was partly inspired by the Louvre picture.

RUGGIERO AND ANGELICA / BY INGRES
text 1870
wr. 1849; pub. *Germ* April 1850, (as 'Sonnets for Pictures. 5. / "Angelica rescued from the Sea-monster", by Ingres; in the Luxembourg / [and] 6. The same.'); rev. and re-pub. *Poems* 1870, 1881

Seen in the Luxembourg Palace on DGR's visit to Paris in 1849 and now one of the most celebrated nineteenth-century works in the Louvre, this painting by Jean-Auguste Dominique Ingres (1780–1867) shows Ruggiero, hero in *Orlando Furioso* (1516) by Ludovico Ariosto (1474–1533), rescuing the naked Angelica, roped to a rock, from a dragon-like sea-monster. WMR 1911, 666 notes of ll.25–6 that DGR 'had forgotten his Ariosto. The sea-monster does not become a "dead thing" through the prowess of Ruggiero [but] survives to be afterwards exterminated by Roland.' WMR also quotes DGR as complaining in 1869 that these sonnets 'are merely picturesque, and which stupid people are sure to like better than better things'.

4 **geomaunt and teraphim**: loosely used to denote geomancy and divination. Variant lines in 1850 version read:
4 Hell-spurge of geomaunt
22–3 ellipses between octave and sestet

THE CARD-DEALER
text 1870
wr. 1848; pub. *Athenaeum* 23 October 1852 (as 'The Card Dealer: or, Vingt-Et-Un. From A Picture'); rev. and re-pub. *Poems* 1870, 1881

Mentioned in DW 37 to WHH in September 1848, where called *Vingt-et-*

un and elucidated thus: ' "Vingt-et-un"
is, as you of course know, the title of
a game of cards, at which I have
supposed the lady of the picture
(personifying, according to me,
intellectual enjoyment) to be playing,
since twenty-one is the age at which
the mind is most liable to be beguiled
for a time from its proper purpose.'
DGR reached twenty-one, the
contemporary age of majority, in May
1849.

In the *Athenaeum*, the poem was
prefaced by an epigraph, attributed to
the 'Calendrier de la Vie, 1630':
'Ambition, Cupidité, / Et délicieuse
Volupté, / Sont les sœurs de la
Destinée, / Après la vingt-première
année.' ('Ambition, Cupidity and
delicious Voluptuousness are the sisters
of Destiny, after the 21st year) which
WMR believed was DGR's 'own
invention' (WMR 1911, 672).

It was also attended by a note
reading: '*The picture is one painted
by the late Theodore von Holst and
represents a beautiful woman, richly
dressed, who is sitting at a lamp-lit
table, dealing out cards, with a
peculiar fixedness of expression.' This
refers to *The Wish* (1840) by Theodor
von Holst (1810–44) which in the late
1840s was in the Thirlestane House
collection of Lord Northwick.

WMR 1911, 664 notes that like
Sister Helen, on first publication this
poem bore the signature 'H.H.H.'
'because (as Rossetti said) people
alleged that his style was hard', and
HHH designates the hardest form of
graphite pencil for drawing.

Revising the text for re-publication
in 1869 DGR added the final stanza
and altered the following lines, saying
the piece was now 'divested of
trivialities' (DW 866):
2 yet, through their splendour
3 Into the lamplight
5 eyes are wide and clear, as if
6 They saw the stars
10 magic silence
deleted 1852 stanza after line 12:
    Some music surely fans the sense,
    A breath like closing plumes:

You know it by the spark called up
    From her eyes' purple glooms;
You almost feel the instant thrill
    Pulse the lighted rooms.
13 And surely, where
14 now pants
18 a heart
19 let them through
23 Crimson and orange, green
27 me: I search her secret will
28 All deem her bosom grand.
32 Whose substance is as breath
33 one lying down
38 that does but
39 more, being fed
44 With *him*, 'tis
45 With *him* ... with *him*
46 is not yet
48 The game of Twenty-One.

SISTER HELEN
text 1881
wr. 1851–2, 1880; pub. *Düsseldorf
Artists' Album* 1854; rev. and re-pub.
Poems 1870; enlarged and re-pub.
Poems 1881

WMR 1911, 650 gives the
publication history of this piece,
noting that its signature in 1854 was
H.H.H., 'the designation of a very
hard lead pencil' (cf. *The Card-
Dealer*). New stanzas were added in
1880, introducing the woman not
present in earlier versions, who has
become the wife of Helen's faithless
lover (see DW 2142) whose presence,
according to DGR 'helps, I think, to
humanize Helen, besides lifting the
tragedy to a yet sterner height'.

Style and subject derive from ballads
in traditional form such as those
published in Thomas Percy's *Reliques
of Early English Poetry* (3 vols. 1765)
and Walter Scott's *Minstrelsy of the
Scottish Border* (3 vols, 1802–3)

THE BURDEN OF NINEVEH
text 1870
wr. 1850–1; pub. *Oxford & Cambridge
Magazine*, September 1856; *Crayon*
(New York) January 1857; rev. and re-
pub. *Poems* 1870, 1881

Inspired by witnessing in 1847 the
arrival at the British Museum in

London of the huge human-headed winged bull from ancient Assyria excavated by Sir Henry Layard, now on view with its companion, a human-headed winged lion. At the time this was regarded as dating from the ninth century BC and an impressive complement to the Greek sculptures from the Parthenon acquired by Lord Elgin (see lines 2–5). Layard's account of his first excavations was *Nineveh and its remains* (1849). For the Biblical account of Nineveh, see the Book of Jonah.

60 **Sardanapalus**: name given to last king of Nineveh, legendary for luxurious effeminacy and subject of large painting by Eugène Delacroix (1798–1863) in the Louvre.
62 **Sennacherib**: Assyrian king who invaded Judah in the time of Hezekiah.
63 **Semiramis**: ancient Egyptian queen
88 **unblest abode**: British Museum
110 **Thebes**: in ancient Egypt
144 **lustres**: five-year periods
164 **ranks in gypsum**: rows of figures carved in plaster, like relief sculptures.

WMR 1911, 649 notes 'attentive revision' to the text in 1869–70, which can be seen to have removed many topical notes contrasting with the immense antiquity of the main subject. Variant lines in 1856 version (see also Sharp, 1882, 328–30) read:
1–6 I have no taste for polyglot:
At the Museum 'twas my lot,
Just once, to jot and blot and rot
In Babel for I know not what.
  I went at two, I left at three.
Round those still floors I tramped, to win
7 the last door
21 Some colour'd Arab straw matting
22 Half-ripp'd, was still upon
51 On London stones its shape lay scored
52 That day when, nigh the gates, the Lord
61–5
Here cold-pinch'd clerks on yellow days

Shall stop and peer; and in sun-haze
Small clergy crimp their eyes to gaze;
And misses titter in their stays
Just fresh from "Layard's Nineveh."
71–5
Here, while the Antique-students lunch
Shall Art be slang'd o'er cheese-and-hunch,
Whether the great R.A.'s a bunch
Of gods, or dogs and whether Punch
Is right about the P.R.B.
89 An elder scarce more
92 this pigmy pile
94 Since thy vast temple
104 A pilgrim. Nay, but even to some
105 Of these thou wert
141 harlot! – eldest grown
142 Of earthly queens! thou on thy throne
151–60
Then waking up, I turn'd because
That day my spirit might not pause
O'er any dead thing's doleful laws;
That day all hope with glad applause
  Through miles of London beckoned me:
And all the wealth of Life's free choice
Love's ardour, friendship's equipoise
And Ellen's gaze and Philip's voice
And all that evening's curtain'd joys
  Struck pale my dream of Nineveh.
161 Yet while I walk'd, my sense

THE STAFF AND SCRIP
text 1870
wr. 1851–2; pub. *Oxford & Cambridge Magazine*, December 1856; *Crayon* (New York) March 1857; rev. and re-pub. *Poems* 1870, 1881
  In 1856 epigraph (from *Hamlet*; cf. *An Old Song Ended*):
'How should I your true love know
From another one?
By his cockle-hat and staff
And his sandal-shoon.'
  C.F. Murray wrote: 'Rossetti himself gave me the date 1851–2 for the Staff & Scrip when he sent me the manuscript' (Delaware, 1980, 143). But first mentioned to WMR in September 1849 (DW 43) as a suitable subject for versifying from the *Gesta Romanorum*,

a collection of fables in Latin compiled around 1300.

WMR 1911, 649 states that it is based on the story 'Of Ingratitude' whose theme DGR 'wholly transmuted' altering both sentiment and significance of the medieval text, in which, having been restored to prosperity, the lady disposes of the pilgrim's staff and scrip on marriage, forgetting her vow. The harsher narrative elements apparently introduced in 1856 would seem to derive from DGR's reading that year of Jean Froissart's History of the Hundred Years' War.

27 **combed**: carded
54 **grame**: grief or harm
88 **blent**: blended, mixed
Variant lines in 1856 version read:
13 Thou'll fly
14 thy blood
16 thy head
47 waste. To meet
48 all fear. This
63 Remains. God
74 'To-night thou'lt bid
after 90 additional stanza:
> So, arming, through his soul there
> pass'd
> Thoughts of all depth and height:
> But more than other things at last
> Seem'ed to the armed knight
> The joy to fight.
91 The skies, by sunset all unseal'd
92 Long lands
106–10 stanza not in 1856 version
128 held her brows
153 East, and West, and North, and
South
154 Fair flew these folds
179 Pink shells, a torpid
187 chaunts in chapel

SUDDEN LIGHT
text 1870
wr. 1854; pub. *Poems: An offering to Lancashire*, 1862; *Poems* 1870 (as 'Song IV'), 1881
Contributed to an anthology edited by Isa Craig Knox as part of the fund-raising appeal to relieve unemployment in the cotton manufacturing districts caused by the interrupted supply of raw materials during the US Civil War. Printed by the Victoria Press, the anthology contained contributions from DGR's sister Christina and other poets of his acquaintance. Artist friends sent works to a sale exhibition for the same cause. See also below, *Lost Days*, sonnet 86 in *HofL*, first published in *A Welcome to the Princess of Wales*, anthology edited by Emily Faithfull for the Victoria Press (1863).

Fiction, published 1850

HAND AND SOUL
text 1850
wr. December 1849; first pub. *Germ* January 1850; re-pub. with slight revisions *Fortnightly Review*, December 1870
DGR's only completed piece of prose fiction, largely written in one night against the deadline for the first issue of the PRB magazine *The Germ*. Revived and slightly revised in accordance with WMR's objections (e.g. that St Rocco or Roch was a historical figure of a later period than that in which Chiaro's tale is set) with a view to inclusion in *Poems* 1870 but ultimately omitted, only to be published separately in the *Fortnightly* (proof-sheets from this being later used as the basis for a spurious 'privately printed' booklet edition produced by T. J. Wise.)

The epigraph, from a canzonetta by Urbiciani, was translated by DGR in *Early Italian Poets* (1861): 'I turn to where I heard / That whisper in the night; / And there a breath of light / Shines like a silver star. / The same is mine own soul.' It may indicate that the poem provided the initial impulse for the tale.

Reissuing the *Germ* in facsimile in 1901, WMR offered the following explication of *Hand and Soul*: 'Though the form of this fable is that of romantic metaphor, its substance is a very serious manifesto of art-dogma. It amounts to saying, The only satisfactory works of art are those which exhibit the very soul of the artist. To work for fame or self-display is a failure, and to work for direct moral proselytizing is a failure; but to paint that which your own perceptions and emotions urge you to paint promises to be a success for yourself, and hence a benefit to the mass of beholders. This was the core of the "Praeraphaelite" [sic] creed...'

The pseudo-scholarly mixture of historical fact with fictional detail is characteristic of this tale, and most of the names are invented. In the final section, 'Manus Animam pinxit' means 'the hand painted the soul'; 'schizzo d'autore incerto' means sketch by unknown artist; 'yards of Guido' refers to the Baroque painter Guido Reni; and the Italian students joke about the crazy English liking for mysterious, mystical things due to their foggy homeland, while the French student observes that if something is not comprehensible, it cannot contain anything of significance.

From *Early Italian Poets*, published 1861

Early Italian Poets from Ciullo D'Alcamo to Dante Alighieri ... translated by D. G. Rossetti, began as a series of translations in 1845–50, revised and arranged in 1858–9 and published at the end of 1861. It was re-ordered and re-issued as *Dante and his Circle* in 1874, with one additional canzone by Dante.

The 1861 Preface here printed offers a statement of DGR's aims in verse translation.

p. 61, l. 1 **first epoch**: late twelfth- and thirteenth-century poets, translations of whose work formed the first section of *EIPs*.

p. 62, l. 12 **matter which may not meet with universal approval**: language or themes deemed vulgar, coarse or indecent.

p. 62, l. 43 **my father's devoted studies**: DGR's father Prof. G. Rossetti published scholarly commentaries on Dante.

p. 63, l. 6 **other pursuits**: DGR's main career as a painter.

FROM PART I: POETS CHIEFLY BEFORE DANTE

Those few poems selected here represent a small fraction (11 out of 100 by 44 authors) of those in Part I. The notes here largely derive from DGR's own notes in *EIPs*.

Guido Guinicelli: DGR gives 1220 as the approximate date of this Bolognese poet's birth, noting that Dante bestowed the highest praise on his work in the *Commedia*, the *Convito* and in *De Vulgari Eloquio*; this ode is his most famous.

Jacopo da Lentino: DGR gives 1250 as approximate date of this Sicilian poet (also known as the Notary of Lentino) adding that the low estimate of his work given by Dante in the *Purgatorio* (canto 24) must relate to his lack of linguistic purity and nobility but asserting that 'there is a peculiar charm in the sonnet which stands first [here'].

Niccolò degli Albizzi: DGR notes that this 'vivid and admirable' sonnet is the only one by this Florentine author (fl. 1300) known to him.

Giacomino Pugliesi: identifying him as a 'Knight of Prato' around 1250, DGR adds 'of this poet there seems nothing to be learnt, but he deserves special notice as possessing rather more individuality than usual, and also as furnishing the only instance, among Dante's predecessors, of a poem (and a very beautiful one) written on a lady's death.'

45 **Almayn**: Germany
46 **Saint Sophia**: chief church in Constantinople/Byzantium.

Fra Guittone d'Arezzo: fl. 1250, not a monk but member of the fraternity Cavalieri Gaudenti. The final line of this sonnet was borrowed by Petrarch in *Trionfi d'Amore*.

Fazio degli Uberti (1326–60): as DGR explains, the grandfather of this author (whose full name is Bonifazio) is among the personages encountered in Dante's *Inferno* (canto 10) and was himself among those exiled from Florence in 1287. Fazio was also author of the unfinished *Il Dittamondo (Song of the World*, a sort of earthly complement to the *Divine Comedy*). His poem here translated was of such excellence that it was often attributed to Dante. 'This contested *canzone* is well worth fighting for,' comments DGR; 'and the victor would deserve by right to receive his prize at the hands of a peerless Queen of Beauty, for never was beauty better described.' DGR himself used the poem as reference point for his picture *Fazio's Mistress* (VS 164)

Franco Sacchetti, born 1335, died c. 1400: DGR gave his reason for including this Florentine author's poems in his anthology, 'partly because their attraction was irresistible, but also because he is the earliest Italian poet with whom playfulness is the chief characteristic'. Those printed were written for music. Present-day readers may discern resemblances between Sacchetti's pastoral songs and certain poems by DGR's sister Christina Rossetti.

FROM PART II: DANTE AND HIS CIRCLE
Here DGR includes Dante's *Vita Nuova (New Life)*, the account of his love for the lady Beatrice, as well as over 100 poems by Dante and his contemporaries.

INTRODUCTION TO PART II: [INTRODUCTION TO THE *VITA NUOVA*]
Although DGR alludes here to the puzzling nature of many passages in the *Vita Nuova*, he ignores the argument contentiously advanced by his father, that the figure of Beatrice is allegorical rather than romantic.

DGR's footnotes, however (e.g. p. 88, n.2; p. 123, n. 1), indicate his awareness of such debates and his own conviction that doubled or ambiguous meanings are usually intended (e.g. that Beatrice is for Dante both a real person and a personification of ideal beauty and goodness). Beyond that, Dante's text being much concerned with strange visions and dreams as well as purportedly everyday events, DGR relishes the mysterious and ambiguous for its own sake.

THE NEW LIFE
The italicised expositions introducing the poems within the *Vita Nuova* were translated by WMR, who in 1886 added this note: 'The translation of the *Vita Nuova* had been done at a very early date, probably 1847–8, when [DGR] was more inclined to consult his own preferences in the way of translating than to be at the rigid beck of his original. When he had to prepare the work, 1860, for publication, he felt that he had taken too great a liberty and asked me to supply what was wanted to these expositions, etc.'

It is not feasible to add explanatory notes to the translation. Those studying Dante are advised to use a modern scholarly edition of the *Vita Nuova* rather than to rely on DGR's version.

p. 83 l. 7 **sirvent:** Provençal poetic form usually used for satirical subjects.

p. 88 l. 15 **vulgar tongue:** vernacular Italian, contrasted with the polite, educated Latin of Love's previous remark.

p. 104 l. 16 ff. **the vision of Beatrice's death:** the subject of DGR's three pictures in oil and watercolour of Dante's Dream at the time of the death of Beatrice (VS 81) includes one with predella panels depicting Dante sleeping and waking.

p. 108 l. 13 **John who went before the True Light:** St John Baptist.

p. 113 l. 33 **Queen Mary:** mother of Christ

p. 115 l. 17 **words of Jeremias:** quotation

from the Biblical Lamentations of
Jeremiah.
p. 126 l. 25 **House of St James**: Santiago
de Compostela, in Galicia, Spain.
p. 126 l. 27 **Palmers**: pilgrims to
Jerusalem.

POEMS BY DANTE ALIGHIERI,
GUIDO CAVALCANTI AND CINO DA
PISTOIA: FROM *INTRODUCTION
TO PART II*
As well as the *Vita Nuova*, *EIPs*
contains 104 poems by Dante and
fourteen other authors, of which a
selection of those by Guido Cavalcanti
and Cino da Pistoia is reprinted here,
together with the appropriate section
of DGR's introduction. The
biographical accounts, while not
immediately relevant to the poems, are
included as examples of DGR's prose
writing.

Poems first published 1870

(excluding *The House of Life*)
in approximate order of original
composition

The volume *Poems* 1870 carried the
following Author's Note: 'Many
poems in this volume were written
between 1847 and 1853. Others are of
recent date, and a few belong to the
intervening period. It has been thought
unnecessary to specify the earlier
work, as nothing is included which the
author believes to be immature.'

THE PORTRAIT
text 1870
begun 1847–8; rev. 1860, 1869; pub.
Poems 1870, 1881
   WMR 1911, 663, states that the first
draft (1847) was entitled 'On Mary's
Portrait, which I painted six years
ago', adding that in 1841 DGR was
aged 13 'and there was no Mary'. This
draft was presumably that about which
DGR enquired in 1873, asking his
mother if, along with the first MS
'long and long ago' of *The Blessed*

Damozel, she still possessed the MS of
'a poem about a portrait. Have you
these ancient documents, and ... What
is the date thereof?' (DW 1340).
However, by 1873 the present poem
was already published. The PRB
Journal for 16 February 1850 contains
a reference to a poem by DGR called
'Jane's Portrait', complete and similar
to Thomas Woolner's *My Lady in
Death*. It would seem that either
both 'Mary's Portrait' and 'Jane's
Portrait' were revised in preparation
for the aborted 'Dante at Verona and
Other Poems' of 1862, in relation to
which volume DGR told WA on 22
November 1860: 'The one of any
length I most thought of omitting is
the *Portrait*, which is rather spoon-
meat, but ... perhaps I may leave it.'
(DW 350) Nine years later, on 30
October 1869, DGR told ACS he had
'condensed' the piece 'and made a
good short poem out of it.' (DW 893)
The context indicates that this was one
of the poems recovered from the
exhumed notebook.
   In 1911, 663, WMR printed a stanza
about the Archangel Raphael from the
MS 'On Mary's Portrait'.

AVE
text 1870
wr. 1847–8; rev. 1860, 1869; pub.
Poems 1870, 1881
   WMR 1911, 661–2 states that this
was composed 'when DGR was more
than vague in point of religious faith'.
The original text, entitled 'Mater
Pulchrae Delectionis' was printed in
full in 1911. However, as a hymn to
the Virgin Mary it is as reliant as the
sonnets on *Mary's Girlhood* on the
contemporary Anglo-Catholic revival
of Marian symbolism, and would seem
to have been one of those included in
the sub-title 'Songs of an Art-Catholic'
which DGR gave his verses in 1849.
In this respect *Ave* may be compared
with James Collinson's *The Child
Jesus*, published in *Germ*, February
1850.
   Consulting WA in 1860 on the
contents of his projected volume

'Dante at Verona and Other Poems', DGR wrote: '[I] have myself no prejudice in favour of *Ave*, but should be smothered by certain friends it has if it did not go in. Are your objections to it on poetic or dogmatic grounds?' (DW 350). The poem's 'friends' may have been DGR's mother and sisters.

20 **the sea**: when WMR pointed out that Nazareth was far from the sea, DGR dismissed this as pedantry, on the grounds that early Renaissance painters would never have worried about such literal details.

40–70: DGR designed several pictures to scenes from the Life of the Virgin alluded to here, including the Passover in the Holy Family (VS 78); an *Annunciation* showing Mary washing clothes in a stream (VS 69); and *Mary in the House of St John* after the Crucifixion (VS 110).

112 **Mary Virgin, full of grace**: opening line of the Ave Maria prayer.

A LAST CONFESSION
text 1870
wr. 1848–9, 1858–60, 1869; pub. *Poems* 1870, 1881

According to DGR 'the first nucleus of the *Confession* was the *very* earliest thing in the whole [1870] book, and was the simple and genuine result of my having passed my whole boyhood among people just like the speaker in the poem. / Browning by travel and cultivation, imported the same sort of thing into English poetry on a much larger scale; but this subject, if any, was my absolute birth-right, and the poem was conceived and in a manner begun long before 1848 (the date afterwards put to it, as characteristic of patriotic struggles) and at a time when Byron and Shelley were about the limits of my modern English poetic studies.' (DW 1420) Among the pieces prepared for publication in 1860–1 and buried with DGR's wife, it was revised in 1869, when DGR told ACS he had added 130 lines to the recovered text, 'and also a translation of the Italian song in it.' At this point he regarded it with 'great

affection' as 'the best of all my doings ... It is the outcome of the Italian part of me, and I am glad it is not lost.' (DW 893)

WMR 1911, 649 notes that the form 'is partly derived from Byron's "Giaour" ' and the style and method 'show a trace of Browning'. In fact, the work is a dramatic monologue much indebted to Browning; and may be compared with *The Italian in England*. A comparison between a surviving MS draft and the 1870 text shows how DGR expunged religious themes and imagery from the earlier version.

1 WMR notes in respect of the location that 'Every one except Dante Rossetti knows that Lombardy has no coast: however, the "Regno Lombardo-Veneto" ... has a coast in its Venetian section. My brother was reckless, and also ignorant, in matters of this kind. The place-name "Iglio", further on, is an invention.' For the first half of the nineteenth century, the province of Lombardo-Veneto was ruled by the Austro-Hungarian Empire, whose army was the enemy to Italian patriots such as the young narrator of the poem.

4 **German**: Austrian
145 **flying Love**: a Cupid
183 **Metternich**: the most powerful figure in Austro-Hungary, in charge of foreign policy, who fell from power in 1848.
353 **Monza**: town near Milan
354 **Duomo**: cathedral
378 **Iron Crown**: symbol of independence, a gift from Pope Gregory I to the rulers of Lombardy, dating from the fifth century AD.

DANTE AT VERONA
text 1870
wr. 1848–52; rev. 1860; pub. *Poems* 1870, 1881

Recorded as 'in progress' on 15 May 1849 (PRB Journal); prepared as lead poem in 'Dante at Verona, and other Poems', the volume planned for publication in 1862; buried that year; following exhumation, revised for publication. WMR 1911, 647 states 'The commencement of this poem dates very early, perhaps even before 1848. It may have been substantially completed towards 1852; but was modified in various regards prior to 1870.' He added that the piece was so reliant on knowledge of Dante's life and writings, that 'a thorough relish for "Dante at Verona" can only be attained by readers who come to it well imbued with the subject-matter.'

25 **Sacred Song:** the *Divine Comedy*
30 in 1301/2 Dante was among those exiled from Florence owing to internecine strife between Black and White Guelph factions. He died on an embassy to Venice in 1321.
34 **laurel-crown:** poetic/literary honour, as in 'laureate'.
66 **Can Grande della Scala:** Cangrande I, head of Scaliger dynasty, powerful rulers of Verona 1260–1387, who died in 1329.
72 **'Even I . . .':** Beatrice's words to Dante in *Purgatorio*.
89 **ghostly guild:** religious order (ghostly = spiritual)
123 **Giotto:** the Florentine painter.
142 **lilies:** Florence's city emblem is the lily.
164 **palm-playing:** *jeu de paume*, a sort of handball.
173 **the song:** *Vita Nuova*.
260 **port:** Verona is inland, on the Adige river.
324 **Gian . . . Giacomo:** as, for example, John and Jim.
438 **first words:** thus because Dante was the first major poet to write in the vernacular Italian language.

ON REFUSAL OF AID BETWEEN NATIONS
text 1870
wr. 1849; pub. *Poems* 1870, 1881
WMR 1911, 664: 'This sonnet refers to the apathy with which other countries witnessed the national struggles of Italy and Hungary against Austria. In MS, the title is 'On the

Refusal of aid to Hungary by the European powers / 1849'. By this date, despotic forces prevailed over democratic hopes in Germany, Austro-Hungary, Italy, France and Britain. When preparing the poem for publication in 1869, DGR considered re-titling it 'On the Refusal of Aid to Hungary 1849, to Poland 1861, to Crete 1867' to encompass later failures of international solidarity.

A YOUNG FIR-WOOD
text 1870
wr. 1850; pub. *Poems* 1870 (as Song X'); 1881
WMR 1911, 666 notes that one MS is inscribed 'Between Ightham and Sevenoaks, November 1850.' In this month DGR was staying with WHH in Sevenoaks, Kent, painting a wooded landscape background in Knole Park.

FOR 'OUR LADY OF THE ROCKS' BY LEONARDO DA VINCI
text 1870
wr. 1851?; pub. *Poems* 1870, 1881
Dating this to 1848, WMR 1911, 663 quotes DGR as saying this was written 'in front of the picture in the British Institution many years' before 1869, and thereby disproving the claim that it was written for the picture in the Louvre. Now in the National Gallery, London, the Leonardo *Madonna of the Rocks* cartoon was then owned by Lord Suffolk. Gail Weinberg, 'Looking Backward: opportunities for the Pre-Raphaelites to see "pre-Raphaelite" art', in M. F. Watson ed., *Collecting the Pre-Raphaelites: the Anglo-American Enchantment*, 1997, 55–6, states that this work was exhibited at the British Institution in 1851 and 1858. If it was not on show in London earlier, the Louvre version is the first DGR would have seen, in 1849. But the poem was not printed in *Germ*, alongside others inspired by Louvre pictures. As there is no reason to doubt DGR's memory, it would seem reasonable to ascribe

the poem to 1851. However, in *Poems* 1870, it was placed first in the section entitled 'Sonnets for Pictures and Other Sonnets', ahead of those relating to Louvre paintings. If revised for *Poems* 1870, the present text may have been influenced by Walter Pater's celebrated essay 'Notes on Leonardo da Vinci' in *Fortnightly Review*, 1 November 1869, which DGR is known to have read.

ON THE 'VITA NUOVA' OF DANTE
text 1870
wr. 1852; pub. *Poems* 1870, 1881
5 **threefold charm**: the three parts of the *Divine Comedy: Inferno, Purgatorio, Paradiso*. See also extract from DGR's preface to his *Vita Nuova* translation above, on his perception of the relation between Dante's works.

PENUMBRA
text 1870
wr. 1853; pub. *Poems* 1870 (as 'Song VII'), 1881

THE HONEYSUCKLE
text 1870
wr. 1853; pub. *Poems* 1870 (as 'Song IX'), 1881
In 1853 DGR spent some days walking in Warwickshire, visiting Kenilworth, Warwick, Stratford-on-Avon, Charlecote, etc.

A MATCH WITH THE MOON
text 1870
wr. 1854; pub. *Poems* 1870, 1881
Apparently inspired by DGR's Warwickshire walking tour of 1853.

STRATTON WATER
text 1870
wr. 1854, 1860; rev. 1869; pub. *Poems* 1870, 1881
Inspired by floods seen in Warwickshire in summer 1853, and by Scott's *Minstrelsy of the Scottish Border*, for which DGR and Elizabeth Siddal were designing illustrations. The

first version was composed October 1854 (see DW 187 where DGR admits incorporating 'an unimportant phrase here and there' from old ballad texts.) Some stanzas following 'The nags were in the hall' were added c. 1860, to give the gradual impression of Lord Sands slowly recognizing the woman he thought dead. The whole was in the buried MS and re-worked for publication in 1870, when DGR wrote: 'I have revised the additional verses to *Stratton Water* which were rather in the rough, and have added one further on about the priest in a funk.' (DW 869)

LOVE'S NOCTURN
text 1870
wr. 1854, 1869; pub. *Poems* 1870, 1881
Re-writing this poem in 1869, DGR wrote: 'The first conception of this poem was of a man not yet in love who dreams vaguely of a woman who he thinks must exist for him. This is not very plainly expressed and not I think very valuable, and it might be better to refer the love to a known woman whom he wishes to approach.' (DW 869) For more details of revisions at this date see DW 866 and Peattie 163–5. Atmospherically, it recalls Milton's *Arcades* and *Comus*.

1 **Master**: Love, the unnamed power to whom the ode is addressed.

THE WOODSPURGE
text 1870
wr. 1856; pub. *Poems* 1870 (as 'Song VIII'), 1881
WMR 1911, 667 stated that the poem 'expresses, I have no doubt, some actual moment in my brother's life, of distressful experience and harrowing thought' and conjectured this had to do with Elizabeth Siddal's ill-health. Mary Robinson, in *Harper's New Monthly Magazine*, 1882, 696, drew on information from the Rossetti family to ascribe the poem to 1856, describing how 'after an aimless city walk', DGR came back to his studio

late one evening, picked up a book of botanical illustrations and, chancing upon the woodspurge, drafted the poem. It would however seem also to relate to Ruskin's remarks on the Pathetic Fallacy in *Modern Painters III*, published January 1856, about 'the man who perceives rightly in spite of his feelings, and to whom the primrose is forever nothing else than itself – a little flower apprehended in the very plain and leafy fact of it, whatever and how many so ever the associations and passions that may crowd around it.' (John Ruskin, *Collected Works*, vol. 5, 209)

BEAUTY AND THE BIRD
text 1870
wr. 1858?; pub. *Poems* 1870, 1881
WMR 1911 dates this to 1855, but it appears to have been inspired by seeing actress Ruth Herbert feed her pet bull-finch in this manner; an inscribed drawing dated 25 June 1858 commemorates this event (see Virginia Surtees, *The Actress and the Brewer's Wife*, 1997, 42–4). Shortly before this, DGR saw for the first time the wardrobe which in spring 1858 EBJ decorated with scenes from Chaucer's *Prioress's Tale* relating the legend in which the Virgin Mary lays a grain on the tongue of a boy martyr, enabling him to continue singing her praises – the source of the allusion in ll. 9–11.

JENNY
text 1870
wr. 1848, 1858–9; rev. 1869; pub. *Poems* 1870, 1881
WMR 1911, 649 states that 'this much-discussed poem was begun at an extremely youthful age – may even have been before the end of 1847', adding that at this date it consisted of 'general reflection'. It was re-drafted as a dramatic monologue 'towards 1858' and again revised late in 1869. DGR himself stated (12 March 1880) that 'in a first form' it was 'written almost as early as the "Blessed Damozel" ' but

later 'completely' re-written. In 1871 he said it was 'written some thirteen years ago' (*Athenaeum* 16 December 1871), which fixes the text now known as the work of 1858. Among the poems contained in the exhumed notebook, it was revised 1869–70 (see DW 893).

An early draft, inscribed '1847–48' (composed in stanzas of 6–8 couplets followed by a triad) carries the epigraph: ' "What, still here! / In this enlightened age, too, since you have been / Proved not to exist!" / Shelley, from Goethe.' The final epigraph, from *The Merry Wives of Windsor*, was inserted in 1869, when DGR told ACS: 'I want to put Mrs. Q (instead of *Merry Wives* etc) at the end of the sentence to remind the virtuous reader strongly whose words they are that his own mind is echoing at the moment.' (DW 904) More discussion on the revisions is to be found in other correspondence with ACS around this date.

1 **Jenny**: a name that used to rhyme more closely with 'guinea'.
18 **full of grace**: in Christian prayers the chief attribute of the Virgin.
100 **lilies of the field**: see Sermon on the Mount, Matt. 6.28; see also Shakespeare sonnet 94.
142 **Haymarket**: street in central London theatre district notorious in the nineteenth century for prostitutes and their clients.
166 **Lethe**: river of oblivion in Hades.
207–8 allusion here to Adam and Eve as ancestors of all mankind, and the Fall/Expulsion from Eden, followed by reference to the Last Judgment.
258 **psyche-wings**: butterfly, symbol of the soul.
316 **wise virgin**: see Matt. 25.
362 **Paphian**: Paphos, city sacred to Venus, hence symbolic of sexual indulgence and especially prostitution.
366 **Priapus**: god of procreation, personification of male libido.

376 **Danaë**: mythical woman raped by Zeus in a shower of gold.

EVEN SO
text 1870
wr. 1858–9; pub. *Poems* 1870, 1881
  WMR 1911, 668, states that poet Coventry Patmore observed that stanza 3 'seems scratched with an adamantine pen upon a slab of agate.' DGR used the same image of fishing boats like flies in a letter from Hastings in summer 1854.

A NEW YEAR'S BURDEN
text 1870
wr. 1859; pub. *Poems* 1870, 1881
  'Burden' is here used to mean refrain, or chief motif in a traditional song.

A LITTLE WHILE
text 1870
wr. 1859; pub. *Poems* 1870 (as 'Song V'), 1881

AN OLD SONG ENDED
text 1870
wr. 1858–9?; pub. *Poems* 1870, 1881
  WMR 1911, dates composition to 1869, but the poem seems stylistically to relate to the 1850s. Its opening stanza is the first in Ophelia's song in *Hamlet* Act 4, scene 5, which modulates into cruder verses about seduction and betrayal. Thus in Shakespeare the 'old song' ends thus:

  By Gis and by Saint Charity,
  Alack and fie for shame!
  Young men will do't, if they come to't
  By Cock, they are to blame.

  Quoth she, 'Before you tumbled me
  You promis'd me to wed.'
  'So would I 'a done, by yonder sun,
  An thou hadst not come to my bed.'

In 1857–8 DGR designed an elaborate drawing of Ophelia returning Hamlet's betrothal gifts (VS 108) and in 1864 a watercolour of the scene in which she sings. (VS 169)

THE SONG OF THE BOWER
text 1870
wr. 1860; pub. *Poems* 1870 (as 'Song VI'), 1881
  CFM claimed to have seen 'early dated copies' from around 1855 (Delaware, 1980, 143) but both style and sentiment accord better with the sensuous mode of DGR's work in both poetry and painting that began in 1859, and WMR 1911 dates the piece to 1860. Diction and metre are similar to those of ACS's work in early 1860s. Compare also the sentiment with the ending of *Jenny*.

JOHN OF TOURS (OLD FRENCH)
text 1870
wr. 1860?; pub. *Poems* 1870, 1881
  CFM claimed to have transcribed this and *My Father's Close* when both poems were recalled verbatim by EBJ, presumably in the late 1860s. DGR heard of and borrowed CFM's copies, having none of his own, and thus they were included in *Poems* 1870 (Delaware no. 161). The most likely date for their composition is around 1858–61, when GBJ and her sisters frequently played and sang from a collection of old French songs. According to CFM, DGR's original title for this piece was 'John of Harth', and it would appear to be an original composition.

MY FATHER'S CLOSE (OLD FRENCH)
text 1870
wr. 1860?; pub. *Poems* 1870, 1881
  See *John of Tours* above; both poems may be compared with comparably 'archaic' pieces in William Morris's first volume *The Defence of Guenevere* (1858).

DANTIS TENEBRAE (IN MEMORY OF MY FATHER)
text 1870
wr. 1861; pub. *Poems* 1870, 1881
  DGR's father died in 1854. See preface to *Early Italian Poets*, in which DGR wrote of his 'first associations' relating to his father's devoted studies of Dante. Later re-

ordered, DGR's baptismal names were
Gabriel (for his father) Charles (for his
godfather) and Dante (for the poet). In
Latin the title means 'the darkness of
Dante' but the idea here may be the
most solemn *tenebrae* (dark masses) of
the Catholic liturgy sung to mark the
Crucifixion of Christ.

ASPECTA MEDUSA
text 1870
wr. 1865–7; pub. *Poems* 1870, 1881
   In 1867 DGR secured a commission
to paint Perseus and Andromeda with
the severed head of the Gorgon
Medusa, whose direct gaze turned
viewers to stone, according to the
ancient Greek legend. The poem
describes the design (VS 183) which
was laid aside when the purchaser
changed his mind.

PLIGHTED PROMISE
text 1870
wr. 1865; pub. *Poems* 1870 (as 'Song
III'), 1881
   In 1865 DGR gave the title 'Aurora'
to a half-length picture of a young
woman at her toilet in watercolour
(VS 202 and see DW 615 for correct
date). Aurora is the classical name for
Dawn; Venus here is both a star and
the goddess of love; Dian is both the
moon and the goddess of chastity.

VENUS VERTICORDIA
text 1870
wr. 1865; pub. *Poems* 1870 as 'Venus
(For a Picture)'; 1881
   Composed to accompany the
painting of the same name, begun in
1864, which depicts a half-length nude
figure holding an apple and an arrow
(VS 173). Slightly different texts exist,
one dated '16 Jan. 1865' (in *Rossetti
Papers*, ed. WMR, 1903, 296) and one
inscribed on the chalk study for the
painting (VS 173A; see also TG 1984,
130). The title derives from DGR's
error in thinking the classical
appellation 'verticordia' means 'turner
of hearts' towards love when in fact it
denotes a particular attribute of Venus

impelling devotees towards virtue.
1 apple: that awarded to Paris,
   provoking the Trojan War. Paris is
   also the Phrygian boy in l. 11.

THE PASSOVER IN THE HOLY
FAMILY (FOR A DRAWING)
text 1870
wr. 1867?; pub. *Poems* 1870, 1881
   WMR 1911, 668 states that the
watercolour (VS 78) for which this
sonnet was written was begun in 1855,
for Ruskin, and was intended to form
part of a triptych, flanked by 'Mary
planting a Lily and a Rose', and 'Mary
in the House of St John.' As such it
relates to the sequence of events
alluded to in *Ave*, and the elaborate
typologies favoured in Anglo-Catholic
circles. There is no obvious reason
why the sonnet should have been
composed in 1867, as stated by WMR,
especially since there was at that date
no notion of the volume that became
Poems 1870. The quotation within the
text is from Exodus 12, in which the
Passover rituals are prescribed, and the
subject is conceived as the Holy
Family performing the ceremony as
devout Jews. 'John' is the future
Baptist, and Zachary is his father. For
more on the drawing, see TG 1984,
no. 209.

MARY MAGDALENE AT THE DOOR
OF SIMON THE PHARISEE (FOR A
DRAWING)
text 1870
wr. 1869; pub. *Poems* 1870, 1881
   Written for DGR's elaborate ink
drawing of the same name inscribed
1858 (VS 109) which was re-produced
in oil at a later date. Mary Magdalen,
traditionally said to have anointed
Jesus's feet with oil and dried them
with her hair, is conceived as the type
of the repentant sinner, who turns to
Christ, forswearing her previous
licentiousness. In the mid-nineteenth
century re-training schemes for former
prostitutes were often called 'Magdalen
Homes'.
9 Bridegroom: Christ.

CASSANDRA (FOR A DRAWING)
text 1870
wr. 1869; pub. *Poems* 1870, 1881
Written for DGR's elaborate ink drawing inscribed 1861 (VS 127). In the *Iliad*, it is the fate of Cassandra – Hector's sister – that her always accurate warnings are never heeded.

PANDORA (FOR A PICTURE)
text 1870
wr. 1869; pub. *Poems* 1870, 1881
DGR began drawing from Jane Morris at the end of 1868 for a projected picture of Pandora, who in classical mythology was sent to Prometheus by Jupiter with a box containing all evils or mischiefs, which escaped when the box was opened, with the exception of Hope (see VS 224; TG 1984, no. 245).

FOR 'THE WINE OF CIRCE' BY EDWARD BURNE JONES
text 1870
wr. 1869–70; pub. *Poems* 1870, 1881
In the Odyssey, Circe is an enchantress who turns Ulysses' crew into swine – taken in the nineteenth-century as an allegory of the bestial character of the emotions and behaviour induced by material and sensual lusts. EBJ's stunning picture was exhibited at the Old Water-Colour Society in spring 1869. Sending a draft of the poem to ACS on 15 March 1870, DGR wrote: 'I wanted to have some record of his work in my book. I have tried in the first lines to give some notion of the colour, and in the last some impression of the scope of the work – taking the transformed beasts as images of ruined passion – the torn seaweed of the sea of pleasure. You will remember that in the picture the window shows a view of the sea and the galleys which bear the new lovers and victims of the enchantress.' (DW 946)
5 Helios, Hecate: alternative names for Sun and Moon.

THREE TRANSLATIONS FROM FRANÇOIS VILLON, 1450

I. THE BALLAD OF DEAD LADIES
text 1870
wr. 1869–70; pub. *Poems* 1870, 1881

II. TO DEATH, OF HIS LADY
text 1870
wr. 1869–70; pub. *Poems* 1870, 1881

III. HIS MOTHER'S SERVICE TO OUR LADY
text 1870
wr. 1869–70; pub. *Poems* 1870, 1881

ONE GIRL (A COMBINATION FROM SAPPHO)
text 1870
wr. 1869?; pub. *Poems* 1870, 1881 (as 'Beauty')
DGR, with a limited knowledge of classical Greek, was probably introduced to the fragmentarily-known works of Sappho by ACS.

LOVE-LILY
text 1870
wr. 1869; pub. *Poems* 1870 (as 'Song I'), 1881

FIRST LOVE REMEMBERED
text 1870
wr. 1869; pub. *Poems* 1870 (as 'Song II'), 1881

TROY TOWN
text 1870
wr. 1869; pub. *Poems* 1870, 1881
Composed autumn 1869, while DGR was staying at Penkill in Ayrshire (see DW 876) and based on a legend that Helen, while wife to Menelaus of Sparta, dedicated a goblet to Venus moulded to the shape of her breast – one of the antecedent acts of the Trojan War. In 1864 Browning told a friend that in his 'last good days at Rome' (1859–60) he had the idea of a poem on this theme, and 'on mentioning this to my friend Rossetti, "I'll paint it," said he – and there it is, archaically treated indeed.' Browning did not write such a poem and despite his words, DGR did not paint it

either, though he did make a rough compositional sketch (VS 219). When beginning the poem in 1869, he wrote to Browning, who replied in May 1870, saying he believed the source to lie in Pausanias. DGR's main classical reference book was Lemprière's Dictionary of Classical Mythology.

50 **three**: allusion to the Judgement of Paris, when Venus/Aphrodite was deemed more beautiful than her rival goddesses Hera and Athena. Venus then awarded Paris his choice of the most beautiful woman on earth, and his taking Helen led to war between Greeks and Trojans and hence to the destruction of Troy evoked in the poem's refrain.

EDEN BOWER
text 1870
wr. 1869; pub. *Poems* 1870, 1881
  Composed autumn 1869, during DGR's journey from Ayrshire to London (see DW 874–5) and inspired by the apocryphal legend of Lilith, first wife to Adam, often represented as a sorceress or witch (cf. *Body's Beauty, HofL* 78). Here Lilith is re-conceived as a rejected partner seducing the Serpent-devil in order to take his shape and tempt Eve, thus precipitating the Expulsion from Eden and Fall of mankind. In 1866–8 DGR painted 'a modern Lilith', a voluptuous figure of vanity, combing luxuriant hair and gazing into a mirror (VS 205) to which *Eden Bower* is only loosely linked. Keats's *Lamia* is a more plausible comparison. A rough sketch of a long-haired woman embracing a snake is reproduced as no. 30 in *JPRAS*, ii:2, 1989 (1991) and as no. 20 in *VP*, 1982.

THE STREAM'S SECRET
text 1870
wr. 1869–70; pub. *Poems* 1870, 1881
  Ode inspired by the Penwhapple burn, by Penkill castle, Ayrshire, where DGR stayed in summer 1869, but largely composed spring 1870 while at Scalands Gate, Sussex. WMR 1911, 659, states that some of the verses were written down in a cave in the Penwhapple glen.

NB: The following poems were published in *Poems*, 1870 but not there included in the *HofL* sequence:

Saint Luke the Painter (For a Drawing) (HofL 74) wr. 1849;
Autumn Idleness (HofL 69) wr. 1850;
Lost Days (HofL 86) wr. 1862;
Lilith (For a Picture) (HofL 78 'Body's Beauty') wr. 1867;
Sibylla Palmifera (For a Picture) (HofL 77 'Soul's Beauty') wr. 1867;
Farewell to the Glen (HofL 84) wr. 1869;
The Monochord (Written during Music) (HofL 79) wr. 1870.

The House of Life, 1881

A posthumously published note from DGR's memorandum book reads: 'To the Reader of The House of Life. The "life" involved is neither my life nor your life, but life representative, tripled with love and death.' (WMR 1911, 638) In *DGR as Designer & Writer*, WMR offered a prose-paraphrase of *HofL*, 'aware that some persons pronounced it to be partly obscure, sometimes doubtfully intelligible.' (See WMR 1911, 650.) Other studies of the sequence include Paull Baum's *House of Life* (1928), W. E. Fredeman's 'An Elegiac Reading of the House of Life', (*Bulletin of the John Rylands Library*, 1965) and the forthcoming edition by R. C. Lewis. The present editor suggests that the best way of approaching the alleged difficulties in DGR's sonnet sequence is to recall his view of the sonnet form as 'condensed and concentrated' and to see them in the tradition of Shakespeare's. The inspiration and arrangement of the sequence are indebted to Dante's *Vita Nuova*, where however poems are

interspersed with a prose narrative
lacking in *HofL*. According to WMR
1911, 651, DGR never volunteered an
explanation for his title, which has
been interpreted as analogous to
astrological notions of the sun being
'in the house of Aries' etc., but would
appear obliquely to allude to John
Donne's *Canonization*:

> We can die by it, if not live by
> love,
>   And if unfit for tombs and hearse
> Our legend be, it will be fit for
> verse;
>   And if no piece of chronicle we
> prove,
>   We'll build in sonnets pretty
> rooms;

When DGR conceived the sequence's
title in 1869, Donne was not included
among his favourite English poets,
although in *Poems* 1870 he introduced
the first versions of his own sonnets
under the heading 'Sonnets and Songs
Towards a Work to be called "The
House of Life"', which may implicitly
acknowledge the 'Songs and Sonets' of
Donne's earliest editions. Additionally,
it should be noted that in Italian
'stanza' means 'room', so that a poem
with many parts could well be likened
to a house. Sharp, 409, notes that 'the
series is as much a poem of interlinked
stanzas as if the latter followed each
other without break of page.'

INTRODUCTORY SONNET
wr. 1880, pub. *B&S* 1881
  On 6 February 1880 DGR told
TWD he had 'be-sonneted The Sonnet
itself at last' (DW 2187). The text was
then incorporated in a design for his
mother's 80th birthday on 27 April
(VS 258). WMR 1911, 652, quotes
DGR on the design: 'The Soul is
instituting the "memorial to one dead
deathless hour"; a ceremony easily
effected by placing a winged hour-
glass in a rose-bush, at the same time
that she touches the fourteen-stringed
harp of the sonnet, hanging round her
neck. On the rose-branches trailing
over in the opposite corner is seen

hanging the Coin, which is the second
symbol used for the sonnet. Its "face"
bears the soul, expressed in the
butterfly; its "converse" the Serpent of
Eternity enclosing the Alpha and
Omega.'

I LOVE ENTHRONED
wr. 1871, pub. *B&S* 1881

II BRIDAL BIRTH
wr. 1869, pub. *Poems* 1870, *B&S* 1881
9 (1870) Now, shielded . . .

III LOVE'S TESTAMENT
wr. 1869, pub. *Poems* 1870 (as 'Love's
Redemption'); rev. and re-pub. *B&S*
1881.
Original title 'Flammifera' (DW 951);
amendments made after 1870 owing to
Fleshly attack (see Sharp, 413) so that
central metaphor of 'love's sacrament'
as Christian eucharist was altered to
an indeterminate, pagan, ceremony.
Original 1870 octave:
> O thou who are Love's hour
> ecstatically
>   Unto my lips dost evermore
> present
>   The body and blood of Love in
> sacrament;
> Whom I have neared and felt thy
>   breath to be
> The inmost incense of his
> sanctuary;
>   Who without speech hast owned
> him, and intent
>   Upon his will, thy life with mine
> hast blent,
> And murmured o'er the cup,
>   Remember me!

IV LOVESIGHT
wr. 1869, pub. *Poems* 1870, *B&S* 1881

V HEART'S HOPE
wr. 1871; pub. *B&S* 1881

VI THE KISS
wr. 1869, pub. *Poems* 1870, 1881

7 **laurelled Orpheus**: legendary author
  of lyrical verse, whose song was
  almost able to draw his dead wife
  back from the underworld.

VIA NUPTIAL SLEEP
wr. 1858–9?, rev. 1869, pub. *Poems* 1870

Original title 'Placatâ Venere' (Venus Appeased). WMR 1911 dates composition to 1870, but there is evidence to infer earlier date, as the sonnet was not new to WMR in 1869 when it was proposed for *Poems* 1870 under original title, and when both title and text were discussed by him and DGR (see Peattie 161, 162, 166, where for example, WMR objected to 'chirped' as first word in l.8, 'as Leigh Huntish – or perhaps more rightly Browningish.') There is no way of knowing when it was first drafted (or exactly what its text then was) but insofar as it is a graphic account of coition, it may plausibly be ascribed to 1859, alongside *Eden Bower* and *On the French Liberation*, whose date is secure. It is possible that as *Placatâ Venere* it was written during DGR's marriage; but the title, which WMR thought even more indelicate than the sonnet itself, does not exactly suggest conjugal joys. Neither tenor nor imagery accord with the poems written in 1869–70. After the critical attack by Buchanan, the poem was omitted from re-publication in 1881; see WMR 1911, 652, where a long account of the sonnet's role in the Fleshly School controversy includes a reference to Palgrave's claim that its 'passion and imaginative power' impressed Tennyson deeply.

VII SUPREME SURRENDER
wr. 1870, pub. *Poems* 1870, *B&S* 1881
1870 version:
2 love-sown fallowfield...

VIII LOVE'S LOVERS
wr. 1869, pub. *B&S* 1881

IX PASSION AND WORSHIP
wr. 1870, pub. *Poems* 1870, *B&S* 1881
1 flame-winged: Passion; white-winged: Worship
6 hautboy: oboe
14 voluntary: musical solo in church service

X THE PORTRAIT
wr. 1868, pub. *Poems* 1870, *B&S* 1881

Apparently inspired by Jane Morris' sittings for portrait and subject paintings in 1868–9 when DGR was at work inter alia with the oil portrait now known as 'Mrs Morris in a Blue Silk Dress' (VS 372) which bears the inscription 'Conjuge clara poeta et praeclarissima vultu, denique pictura clara sit illa mea' (Famous for her poet-husband, and more famous for her face, may she also be famous for my picture). When finished, the portrait hung in the Morrises' home.
1870 version:
9 the long lithe throat

XI THE LOVE-LETTER
wr. 1870, pub. *Poems* 1870, *B&S* 1881

XII THE LOVERS' WALK
wr. 1871, pub. *B&S* 1881
Sent from Kelmscott on 13 August 1871 (see DW 1150).

XIII YOUTH'S ANTIPHONY
wr. 1871, pub. *B&S* 1881

XIV YOUTH'S SPRING-TRIBUTE
wr. 1870, pub. *B&S* 1881

XV THE BIRTH-BOND
wr. 1854, pub. *Poems* 1870, *B&S* 1881

XVI A DAY OF LOVE
wr. 1870, pub. *Poems* 1870, *B&S* 1881

XVII BEAUTY'S PAGEANT
wr. 1871, pub. *B&S* 1881
4 encomiast: one who praises or flatters
11 galiot: small boat, apparently here envisaged as a Venetian-style gondola

XVIII GENIUS IN BEAUTY
wr. 1871, pub. *B&S* 1881
When re-printing in 1886, WMR silently emended last word in line 6 to 'bequeaths' having previously failed to persuade DGR this was correct spelling. DGR's insistence on 'bequeathes' indicates his desire for the

word to rhyme exactly with 'breathes'. Similarly, WMR urged DGR to print 'in likewise' (line 12) and altered the punctuation in 1886 (see VP 1982, 19).
3 **Michael**: Michelangelo

XIX SILENT NOON
wr. 1871, pub. *B&S* 1881

XX GRACIOUS MOONLIGHT
wr. 1871, pub. *B&S* 1881
12 **Queen Dian**: the moon

XXI LOVE-SWEETNESS
wr. 1870, pub. *Poems* 1870, *B&S* 1881
2 **thy face**: the poet appears to be speaking of/to himself

XXII HEART'S HAVEN
wr. 1871, pub. *B&S* 1881
Sent from Kelmscott on 13 August 1871.
14 **roundelay**: simple repetitive song

XXIII LOVE'S BAUBLES
wr. 1870, pub. *Poems* 1870, *B&S* 1881

XXIV PRIDE OF YOUTH
wr. 1871, pub. *B&S* 1881

XXV WINGED HOURS
wr. 1869, pub. *Poems* 1870, *B&S* 1881
One of first sonnets written after the resumption of verse, and ready for publication in the *Fortnightly Review* by 24 January 1869 (see RP, 380).
1870 version:
8 Through our contending kisses oft unheard

XXVI MID-RAPTURE
wr. 1871, pub. *B&S* 1881

XXVII HEART'S COMPASS
wr. 1871, pub. *B&S* 1881
13 **gage**: pledge

XXVIII SOUL-LIGHT
wr. 1871, pub. *B&S* 1881
5 **glamour**: apparently used to mean light or glimmer.

XXIX THE MOONSTAR
wr. 1869, pub. *B&S* 1881

Though dated to 1871 by WMR, this was originally included in the texts set in type in 1869.

XXX LAST FIRE
wr. 1871, pub. *B&S* 1881

XXXI HER GIFTS
wr. 1871, pub. *B&S* 1881
1 **dower**: endowment, gift

XXXII EQUAL TROTH
wr. 1871, pub. *B&S* 1881
1 **mete**: measure.

XXXIII VENUS VICTRIX
wr. 1871, pub. *B&S* 1881
The title means 'Love Victorious' and alludes to the Judgement of Paris in which the beautiful mortal man awarded the prize to Venus, goddess of Love.

XXXIV THE DARK GLASS
wr. 1871, pub. *B&S* 1881
Sent from Kelmscott on 13 August 1871.

XXXV THE LAMP'S SHRINE
wr. 1871, pub. *B&S* 1881
8 **chrysoprase**: golden- or apple-green gemstone.

XXXVI LIFE-IN-LOVE
wr. 1870, pub. *Poems* 1870, *B&S* 1881

XXXVII THE LOVE-MOON
wr. 1869, pub. *Poems* 1870, *B&S* 1881
7 **Love's philtred euphrasy**: an elaborate conceit built on the medical term euphrasy (from the Greek word for gladness) to denote the eyebright plant used to treat weak or sore eyes, coupled with the idea of a philtre or love-potion.

XXXVIII THE MORROW'S MESSAGE
wr. 1869, pub. *Poems* 1870, *B&S* 1881
9 **malisons**: curses

XXXIX SLEEPLESS DREAMS
wr. 1868–9, pub. 1869, *Poems* 1870, *B&S* 1881
Probably written in December 1868

and ready for publication in the *Fortnightly Review* (March 1869) by 24 January 1869 (RP 380).

7 **Ruth:** Pity

XL SEVERED SELVES
wr. 1871, pub. *B&S* 1881

XLI THROUGH DEATH TO LOVE
wr. 1871, pub. *B&S* 1881
Sent from Kelmscott on 13 August 1871.

XLII HOPE OVERTAKEN
wr. 1871, pub. *B&S* 1881
1 **grey:** traditionally, green is the symbolic colour for hope.

XLIII LOVE AND HOPE
wr. 1871, pub. *B&S* 1881

XLIV CLOUD AND WIND
wr. 1871, pub. *B&S* 1881

XLV SECRET PARTING
wr. 1869, pub. *Poems* 1870, *B&S* 1881

XLVI PARTED LOVE
wr. 1869, pub. *Poems* 1870, *B&S* 1881

XLVII BROKEN MUSIC
wr. 1852, pub. 1869, *Poems* 1870, *B&S* 1881
Among those first printed in *Fortnightly Review* (March 1869).

XLVIII DEATH-IN-LOVE
wr. 1869, pub. *Poems* 1870, *B&S* 1881
2 **gonfalon:** banner
3 **web:** woven fabric
MS version has annotation 'Dies atra [black day] 1st May 1869' apparently in reference to the stillbirth of DGR's daughter in 1861.

XLIV–LII WILLOWWOOD
wr. 1868, pub. 1869, *Poems* 1870, *B&S* 1881
Dated 1869 by WMR 1911, but recorded by him as complete on 18 December 1868 (*RP* 339) 'about the finest thing he has done' and among the earliest of the sonnets written after DGR resumed verse at the end of

1868. Printed in *Fortnightly Review* (March 1869). CGR's *An Echo from Willowwood* quotes the first line of sonnet iii as epigraph.
'Willow-wood' appears to homophonically indicate 'widow-hood'.
sonnet iii, 10 tear-spurge . . . blood-wort: the spurges are plants with bitter or irritant properties, the blood-worts have red leaves or roots.

LIII WITHOUT HER
wr. 1871, pub. *B&S* 1881
THC records DGR saying that this sonnet was wrung from him 'at a terrible moment' after his wife's death in 1862. WMR 1911 dates its composition to 1871, which, as it was not included in *Poems* 1870, seems more likely. However, Sharp, 1882, 425, also deriving from a comment by DGR, states it 'was the outcome of the poet's own most bitter personal sorrow, and it has hence an added significance and pathos'.

LIV LOVE'S FATALITY
wr. 1871, pub. *B&S* 1881
2 **gyves:** fetters

LV STILLBORN LOVE
wr. 1869, pub. *B&S* 1881
Though WMR 1911 gives 1870 as date of composition and 1871 for first publication, the sonnet was included in the texts set in type in 1869 and then omitted from *Poems* 1870.

LVI TRUE WOMAN (HERSELF)
wr. 1880, pub. *B&S* 1881
WMR 1911, 654, states that these three sonnets were written 'towards September 1881' and were thus 'the latest-composed of all Dante Rossetti's published work'. But all three were sent by DGR to Jane Morris in November–December 1880, as 'forming a trio with which I intend to wind up the first part of the House of Life'. He added that the feeling expressed in sonnet 56 (*Herself*) 'is as fresh and unchanged in me towards you as ever' (Bryson 122, 124).

6 **Philomel:** classical maiden turned into nightingale

LVII TRUE WOMAN (HER LOVE)
wr. 1880, pub. *B&S* 1881

LVIII TRUE WOMAN (HER HEAVEN)
wr. 1880, pub. *B&S* 1881
2 **Seer:** according to DGR 'The *seer* in the sonnet is Swedenborg, and the saying a very fine one' (see Bryson 124).

LIX LOVE'S LAST GIFT
wr. 1871, pub. *B&S* 1881

LX TRANSFIGURED LIFE
wr. 1871, pub. *B&S* 1881
    WMR 1911, 654, says that this sonnet sets forth what DGR believed the truth concerning good poetry, that a poem is the essential self of the author developed into words under the control of art. 'Abundant rain' is glossed as an allusion to I Kings 18, where the cloud like a man's hand heralds abundance of rain. W. E. Fredeman dates the sonnet to 1873 (see *Bulletin of the John Rylands Library*, Manchester, vol. 47, 1965, 303).

LXI THE SONG-THROE
wr. 1880, pub. *B&S* 1881
    WMR 1911, 655 says this was written in April 1880, and was therefore a late but important affirmation of DGR's view concerning good poetry.
9 **Song-god/Sun-god:** Apollo

LXII THE SOUL'S SPHERE
wr. 1873, pub. *B&S* 1881

LXIII INCLUSIVENESS
wr. 1869, pub. 1869, *Poems* 1870, *B&S* 1881
    First published in *Fortnightly Review* (March 1869). WMR 1911, 655 glosses the title as 'many-sidedness' or 'divergent identity'.

LXIV ARDOUR AND MEMORY
wr. 1879, pub. *B&S* 1881
    Dated by WMR to 1873, and

therefore regarded as the first sonnet written on DGR's recovery from his breakdown of 1872, but sent as 'Pleasure and Memory' to William Davies at the end of 1879 described as 'a sonnet written just now' (DW 2164). Sharp 1882, 426, while stating that it was written in December 1880, on facing page reproduces poem in MS, inscribed 'Dante G. Rossetti / Xmas 1879.' As Sharp comments, the last line is syntactically 'without sense' but in MS line 13 ends with a comma rather than the semi-colon of the printed text, allowing the rose-tree's autumn leaves to hold or inspire 'ditties and dirges'.

LXV KNOWN IN VAIN
wr. 1853, pub. 1869, *Poems* 1870, *B&S* 1881
    WMR 1911, 655 says this sonnet was written January 1853, the same month as a purchaser was secured for DGR's painting *Ecce Ancilla*, exhibited in 1850. First printed in *Fortnightly Review* (March 1869).

LXVI THE HEART OF THE NIGHT
wr. 1873, pub. *B&S* 1881

LXVII THE LANDMARK
wr. 1855, pub. 1869, *Poems* 1870, *B&S* 1881
    First printed in *Fortnightly Review* (March 1869).

LXVIII A DARK DAY
wr. 1855, pub. *Poems* 1870, *B&S* 1881
    First versions in letters to WA and WHH, January 1855 (DW 196 and 197) show relatively minor variations. 'Does this smack of [Martin] Tupper at all?' DGR asked WA. 'The last simile I heard as a fact common in some parts of the country.'

LXIX AUTUMN IDLENESS
wr. 1850, pub. *Poems* 1870, *B&S* 1881
    In *Poems* 1870, this was not printed in the *HofL* sequence but as a free-standing piece. MS version bears note: 'A Sunny Day at the close of Autumn dated Sevenoaks, Nov. 1850.'

LXX THE HILL SUMMIT
wr. 1853, pub. *Poems* 1870, *B&S* 1881

LXXI–LXXIII THE CHOICE I, II, III
wr. 1848, pub. *Poems* 1870, *B&S* 1881
WMR 1911, 655 states that before
printing in *Poems* 1870, 'some
juvenilities of expression' were
removed from the texts.

LXXIV–LXXVI OLD AND NEW ART
WMR 1911, 656: 'This trio of sonnets
forms a manifesto – perhaps the best
manifesto it ever received in writing –
of the Praeraphaelite movement, begun
in the autumn of 1848.'

i ST LUKE THE PAINTER
wr. 1849, pub. *Poems* 1870, *B&S* 1881
In *Poems* 1870, this was not within
the *HofL* sequence, but a free-standing
sonnet called 'St Luke the Painter (for
a Drawing)'. Traditionally, Luke is the
patron saint of painters.

ii NOT AS THESE
wr. 1848, pub. *B&S* 1881
MS is dated 1848.

iii THE HUSBANDMEN
wr. 1848–9, pub. *B&S* 1881
Originally entitled 'To the Young
Painters of England, in memory of
those before Raphael.' In spring 1880
DGR wrote: 'I have run ... "St Luke
the Painter" into a sequence with 2
more not yet printed, and given the 3
a general title of Old & New Art as
well as special titles to each. I shall
annex them to the *House of Life*' (see
VP 1982, 206).

LXXVII SOUL'S BEAUTY
wr. 1867, pub. 1868, *Poems* 1870 as
'Sibylla Palmifera (For a Picture)'; re-
pub. *B&S* 1881 in *HofL*.

LXXVIII BODY'S BEAUTY
wr. 1867, pub. 1868, *Poems* 1870 as
'Lilith (For a Picture)'; re-pub. *B&S*
1881 in *HofL*.
WMR 1911, 656 cities DGR's
painting *Lady Lilith* (VS 205) dated
1868, and Goethe's lines from *Faust*

(as translated by Shelley) where
Mephistopheles warns Faust against
Lilith: 'Beware of her fair hair, for she
excels All women in the magic of her
locks ...' cf. *Eden Bower* above. In
1870 DGR told a correspondent that
the idea 'of the perilous principle in
the world being female from the first'
was 'about the most essential notion of
the sonnet' (DW 992).

LXXIX THE MONOCHORD
wr. 1870, pub. *Poems* 1870, *B&S* 1881
In *Poems* 1870, this was not
included in the *HofL* sequence.
WMR 1911, 656: 'Of all the sonnets
in "The House of Life" this is the one
which seems to me the most obscure.'
1870 version:
1 Is it the moved air or the moving
   sound

LXXX FROM DAWN TO NOON
wr. 1873, pub. *B&S* 1881

LXXXI MEMORIAL THRESHOLDS
wr. 1873, pub. *B&S* 1881

LXXXII HOARDED JOY
wr. 1870, pub. *Poems* 1870, *B&S* 1881

LXXXIII BARREN SPRING
wr. 1870, pub. *Poems* 1870, *B&S* 1881
2 **sails balanced:** owing to voluminous
   crinoline

LXXXIV FAREWELL TO THE GLEN
wr. 1869, pub. *Poems* 1870, *B&S* 1881
In *Poems* 1870 this was not included
in *HofL*. Written 27 September 1869,
at Penkill Castle in Ayrshire, home of
Alice Boyd and W. B. Scott (Sharp,
429); cf. *The Stream's Secret*.

LXXXV VAIN VIRTUES
wr. 1869, pub. *Poems* 1870, *B&S* 1881

LXXXVI LOST DAYS
wr. 1862, pub. 1863, *Poems* 1870, *B&S*
1881
First published in *A Welcome to the
Princess of Wales*, anthology edited by
Emily Faithfull for the Victoria Press.
In May 1880, DGR said he altered

line 8 from 'The throats of men in Hell, who thirst alway' to avoid repeating 'in' in successive lines.

LXXXVII DEATH'S SONGSTERS
wr. 1870, pub. *Poems* 1870, *B&S* 1881
   WMR 1911, 657 notes that 'except for its last two lines, the sonnet consists entirely of a reference to two acts of self-discipline recorded of Ulysses,' when he resists the wiles of Helen and the song of the Sirens.

LXXXVIII HERO'S LAMP
wr. 1875, pub. *B&S* 1881
   In classical legend, Leander, lover of Hero, was drowned swimming the Hellespont to meet her, as she held aloft a lamp to guide him. Anteros, son of Venus and brother of Cupid, had an altar dedicated to him in Athens. The Avernian lake is the legendary entrance to the classical Underworld. In 1875-6 DGR projected a picture showing Hero, derived from his composition for *Astarte Syriaca* (VS 249).

LXXXIX THE TREES OF THE GARDEN
wr. 1875, pub. *B&S* 1881
   When DGR was resident at Bognor Regis, winter 1875-6, a great storm felled several ancient trees in the garden of his rented house.

XC 'RETRO ME, SATHANA!'
wr. 1847, pub. *Poems* 1870, *B&S* 1881
   The title means 'Get thee behind me, Satan!' - a traditional saying when confronted with sinful temptation. According to WMR 1911, 657, this was the earliest of all the sonnets later making up *HofL*; it was composed in 1847-8 when DGR was painting an oil picture of the same title, which was soon abandoned; its design survives as VS 37, dated July 1848, which may be the original date of the sonnet, though the poem bears no other relation to the picture. The present text does not have the flavour of an early work.

XCI LOST ON BOTH SIDES
wr. 1854, pub. 1869, *Poems* 1870, *B&S*
1881
   First printed in *Fortnightly Review* (March 1869). WMR 1911, 657 suggests this refers to DGR's aspirations as poet and painter. The original text is contained in a letter of August 1854 (DW 177) where the sestet reads:

> So separate hopes, that in a soul
>   had wooed
>   The same one Peace, strove with
>   each other long
>   And Peace before their faces,
>   perish'd since;
> So from that soul, in mindful
>   brotherhood,
>   (When silence may not be)
>   sometimes they throng
>   Through high streets and at many
>   dusty inns.

XCII THE SUN'S SHAME I
wr. 1869, pub. *Poems* 1870, *B&S* 1881

XCIII THE SUN'S SHAME II
wr. 1873, pub. *B&S* 1881

XCIV MICHELANGELO'S KISS
wr. 1881, pub. *B&S* 1881
   WMR 1911, 657-8 refers to an incident recorded by Michelangelo's biographer Condivi. Towards the end of 1872, DGR projected translating Michelangelo's sonnets, which he was currently reading.
6 **Colonna**: Vittoria Colonna, Michelangelo's model and supposed beloved, and held by DGR to resemble Jane Morris.
9 **Buonarruoti**: WMR 1911, 658 explains that DGR erroneously took the artist's family name (now usually spelt Buonarroti) to derive from 'buon-a-ruote' or 'good-at-wheels'; hence the allusion in lines 9-10 (see DW 2390, n. 1).

XCV THE VASE OF LIFE
wr. 1869, pub. 1869, *Poems* 1870, *B&S*
1881
   First printed in *Fortnightly Review* (March 1869). WMR, 1911, 658 suggests that this sonnet was inspired by the career of John Everett Millais,

DGR's companion in the PRB and 'early colleague in the race of life and of art'. The original title was 'Run and Won' (see DW 951).

XCVI LIFE THE BELOVED
wr. 1873, pub. *B&S* 1881

XCVII A SUPERSCRIPTION
wr. 1869, pub. 1869, *Poems* 1870, *B&S* 1881
Dated 1868 by WMR, but described as 'newly written' on 24 January 1869 (*RP*, p. 380) and printed in *Fortnightly Review* (March 1869).

XCVIII HE AND I
wr. 1870, pub. *Poems* 1870, *B&S* 1881
WMR 1911, 658-9 offers a full paraphrase for readers who find this 'an insoluble riddle'.

XCIX-C NEWBORN DEATH
wr. 1868, pub. 1869, *Poems* 1870, *B&S* 1881
First printed in *Fortnightly Review* (March 1869). WMR 1911, 659 notes: 'My brother never grew old; he wrote the verses in December 1868, when his age was forty.' Presumed to be the linked sonnets DGR sent to WA for comments on 23 December 1868, saying 'It seems to me doubtful whether the second adds anything of much value to the first, and whether it (the second) is not in itself rather far-fetched and obscure. I wish you would tell me what you think.' (DW 801)

CI THE ONE HOPE
wr. 1870, pub. *Poems* 1870, *B&S* 1881
WMR 1911, 659 glosses 'the one Hope's one name' as 'the name of the woman supremely beloved on earth.'

Prose, published 1871

THE STEALTHY SCHOOL OF CRITICISM
text 1872
wr. 1871; pub. *Athenaeum*, 16 December 1872

Written in response to 'The Fleshly School of Poetry', a pseudonymous attack (by Robert Buchanan over the name Thomas Maitland) on *Poems* 1870 published in the *Contemporary Review*, October 1871, this represents DGR's most sustained defence of his poetic intentions, albeit coloured by anxiety to rebut allegations of sensuality, especially in poems like *Eden Bower, Jenny* and *Nuptial Sleep* from *HofL*. Following Buchanan's re-publication of *The Fleshly School of Poetry* in an expanded form in May 1872, DGR's mental equilibrium collapsed, and he gave up painting (for some 3-4 months) and writing (for 6-7 years.) When preparing *HofL* for re-publication as a full sequence in 1880, he omitted *Nuptial Sleep*.

p. 329, l. 2 other writers: ACS and William Morris were included by name in the 'Fleshly School' article.
p. 329, l. 6 Sidney Colvin: art and literary critic friendly to DGR who promised (but failed) to counter-attack on his behalf.
p. 330, l. 9-10 Nos. 2, 8, 11, 17, 28: as the *HofL* numbering was changed in 1881, it is necessary to state that in *Poems* 1870 these were as follows: *Love's Redemption* (see above: *Love's Testament*); *Passion and Worship*; *The Birth-Bond*; *The Love-Moon*; *Stillborn Love*.
p. 330, l. 35 Sonnets 29, 30, 31, 39, 40, 41, 43: *Inclusiveness*; *Known in Vain*; *The Landmark*; *Vain Virtues*; *Lost Days*; *Death's Songsters*; *Lost on Both Sides*.
p. 332, l. 32 a treatment from without: i.e. to describe (and judge) the narrator of *Jenny* rather than present a first-person voice.
p. 333, l. 6 plagiarism: Buchanan's own verses included monologues in the voices of 'common' Londoners such as flower-girls and clerks, and his article suggested that *Jenny* was in this respect partly derivative.
p. 334, l. 6 what more inspiring: here DGR defends his work against the charge of 'art for art's sake' without moral message by claiming moral

intention for his poems.

p. 335, l. 6   **Robert-Thomas:** i.e. Buchanan/Maitland.

Poems published 1871–82

in order of publication

ON THE SITE OF A MULBERRY-TREE; PLANTED BY WM. SHAKSPEARE; FELLED BY THE REV. F. GASTRELL

text 1882

wr. 1853; pub. *Academy* 15 February 1871 where datelined 'Stratford-on-Avon'; re-pub. Sharp, 404.

Included in 1869 proofs but not *Poems* 1870. The text in BL Ashley MS 1397 is inscribed 'Stratford on Avon – July 1853'. DGR visited Stratford-on-Avon in 1853 and 1867.

7   **Sheppard, Turpin:** Jack Sheppard and Dick Turpin were notorious eighteenth-century criminals, both hanged. In MS, and the versions published by WMR, the last line begins 'Some Starveling's . . .' in allusion to the character in *A Midsummer Night's Dream*. WMR 1911, 677 recalled being told that DGR's 'real reason for not publishing the sonnet in either of his volumes [1870 and 1881] was to avoid hurting the feelings of some sensitive member or members of the tailoring craft.'

DOWN STREAM

text 1881

wr. 1871; pub. *Poems* 1881

This Hardyesque narrative, originally entitled 'The River's Record', was written at Kelmscott and first published October 1871 in *The Dark Blue*, vol. ii, 211, with design by F. M. Brown. *The Dark Blue* has been described as an 'arch and pretentious' university magazine emanating from Oxford (Ronald Pearsall, *Collapse of Stout Party*, 1975, 114).

WMR 1911, 669 quotes a letter from DGR to his mother: 'I doubt not you will note the intention to make

the first half of each verse, expressing the landscape, tally with the second expressing the emotion, even to the repetition of phrases.' To Madox Brown, he wrote: 'I *meant* my unheroic hero for an Oxford swell.' (DW 1175)

THE CLOUD CONFINES

text 1881

wr. 1871; pub. *Fortnightly Review*, January 1872; re-pub. *B&S* 1881

Written at Kelmscott in August 1871, the poem was sent to WMR on 10 September 1871, as 'one short thing I have done, not meant to be a trifle. I want your advice about the close . . . But at first I had meant to answer the question in a way, on the theory hardly of annihilation but of absorption.' (DW 1165) WMR 1911, 669, quotes DGR's remark on the question of personal immortality: 'I cannot suppose that any particle of life is "extinguished" though its permanent individuality may be more than questionable. Absorption is not annihilation; and it is even a real retributive future for the special atom of life to be re-embodied (if so it were) in a world which its own former identity had helped to fashion for pain or pleasure.'

In late 1872 or early 1873 DGR composed two additional stanzas for the poem, which he intended to place as sts. 3 and 4, but were not included in the published version (see DW 1310).

The refrain echoes Byron's famous lines in *Childe Harold's Pilgrimage* quoting Socrates: 'Well didst thou speak, Athena's wisest son! "All that we know is, nothing can be known." '

SUNSET WINGS

text 1881

wr. 1871; pub. *Athenaeum* 24 May 1873; *B&S* 1881

Written at Kelmscott in August 1871. 'It is one I wrote when first I came here, and embodies a habit of the starlings which quite amounts to a local phenomenon, and is most beautiful and interesting daily towards sunset for months together in summer and autumn,' DGR told his mother on 20 May 1873 (DW 1340). To the *Athenaeum* editor Thomas Purnell he explained: 'It was new to Morris also – a great rural observer – and might perhaps seem strange to some readers, but is very exactly described. The noise is, as said, just like the wheels of a water-mill or (more prosaically) like a factory in full spin.' (9 May 1873, UT) It seems odd that as a Londoner DGR had not observed the same phenomenon of starlings swarming at dusk in the city; moreover, it is notably used by Dante in the *Inferno* (canto 5) as a figure for whirling souls in hell.

TWO LYRICS, FROM NICCOLÒ TOMMASEO
I THE YOUNG GIRL; II A FAREWELL
text 1874
wr. 1848?; pub. 1874
    Published in *Athenaeum*, 13 June 1874, when DGR sent a note to the editor: 'In your late obituary notice (*Ath.* May 16) of Niccolò Tommaseo, a passing allusion is made to his earlier lyrical poetry. Any countryman of his, looking, years ago, when it appeared, into the slender collection of these verses, must have been struck by their not being chiefly concerned with public events and interests; inevitably a rare exception in those dark yearning-days of the Italian Muse. Perhaps the two translated specimens which I offer of their delicate and romantic tone may not be unacceptable to some of your readers.' (See also DW 1499.)
    Niccolò Tommaseo (1802–74) was an Italian poet, patriot and lexicographer. It is not clear which slim volume of lyric poetry DGR referred to, but Tommaseo's collected *Poesie* were published in 1872.

THE LEAF – LEOPARDI
text 1881
wr. 1869; pub. *Poems* 1881
    Translated from the Italian of Giacomo Leopardi (1798–1837)

according to DGR. However, WMR 1886, ii, 518 notes: 'thus entitled in my brother's own volume. But the lyric, as given by Leopardi, is only a translation from the French of Arnauld.'

WINTER
text 1881
wr. 1874; pub. 1874, *B&S* 1881
    'I'll enclose a Winter Sonnet written lately', wrote DGR from Kelmscott on 23 February 1874 (DW 1458). First published in *Athenaeum*, 30 May 1874.

SPRING
text 1881
wr. 1873; pub. 1874, *B&S* 1881
    First published in *Athenaeum* 30 May 1874, and suggested by lambing-time at Kelmscott the previous year, when DGR observed a sheepfold 'thatched and walled with straw, and adjoining a scooped-out haystack in which the shepherd sleeps.' (DW 1298)

UNTIMELY LOST – OLIVER MADOX BROWN
text 1881
wr. 1874; pub. 1874, *B&S* 1881
    First published in *Athenaeum*, 21 November 1874. Oliver, only surviving son of Ford and Emma Madox Brown, DGR's oldest friends, died aged 20 in October 1874, having already given promise of talent in both painting and fiction. While appreciating DGR's condolences in this poem, as a convinced atheist, Brown was annoyed by the evocation of posthumous reunion in the sestet.

PROSERPINA (FOR A PICTURE)
text 1881
wr. 1872; pub. 1875, *B&S* 1881
    First published in *Athenaeum* 28 August 1875; English version of the Italian text below.
    The legendary Proserpina or Persephone is the nymph captured at Enna and imprisoned by the god of the Underworld, whose temporary return to earth each year is symbolic of Spring.

[printed here for convenience]
PROSERPINA (PER UN QUADRO)
text 1881
wr. 1872; pub. *B&S* 1881
  Sent to WMR autumn 1872, and
inscribed on the picture entitled
Proserpina (VS 233) then being
painted.

LA BELLA MANO (FOR A PICTURE)
text 1881
wr. 1875; pub. 1875, *B&S* 1881
  First published in *Athenaeum* 28
August 1875; English version of Italian
text below. 'La bella mano' means 'the
fair hand', and the picture represents a
woman attended by two angelic figures
washing her hands before admitting
her lover. In line 14 'handsel'd' is a
way of saying 'given'.

[printed here for convenience]
LA BELLA MANO (PER UN QUADRO)
text 1881
wr. 1875; pub. *B&S* 1881
  To accompany the painting of the
same title (VS 240).

FRANCESCA DA RIMINI (DANTE)
text 1881
wr. 1878; pub. 1879, *Poems* 1881
  First published in *Athenaeum* 11
January 1879. Translated from Dante's
Inferno (canto 5) where Francesca da
Rimini and her brother-in-law Paolo
Malatesta are doomed to spend
eternity for their adulterous love,
occasioned by reading the romance of
Lancelot and Guinevere. The narrator
is Dante, and his guide (line 12) is
Virgil. In line 26 'Galahalt' is a
translation of the Italian word
(*galeotto*) for a go-between or pander,
using the archaic French version of the
same.
  DGR used the motif several times in
visual art (see VS 75), the earliest
depiction of the lovers dating from
around 1846. In November 1849 he
was recorded as working seriously on
the design: 'He intends that the picture
should be in three compartments. In
the middle Paolo and Francesca
kissing; on the left, Dante and Virgil

in the second circle; on the right the
spirits blowing to and fro.'
  Watercolour versions from 1855 and
1862 bear quotations from Dante (in
Italian) while that of 1867 carries the
following translation on the frame:
                                    One day
  For our delight we read of
      Lancelot,
  How him love thralled. Alone we
      were, and no
  Suspicion near us. Oft times by
      that reading
  Our eyes were drawn together, and
      the hue
  Fled from our altered cheek. But at
      one point
  Alone we fell. When of that smile
      we read,
  The wicked smile so rapturously
      kiss'd
  By one so deep in love, then he,
      who ne'er
  From me shall separate, at once my
      lips
  All trembling kiss'd.

FOR 'THE HOLY FAMILY' (BY
MICHELANGELO)
text 1881
wr. 1880; pub. 1881, *B&S* 1881
  First published *Athenaeum* 1
January 1881. DGR wrote on 23
December 1880: 'In this picture the
Virgin is withdrawing from the Child
the book which contains the prophecy
of his sufferings – I suppose that of
Isaiah. The idea is a most beautiful
one; and behind this group are angels
perusing a scroll. [F. J.] Shields was
helpful to me in the interpretation of
this. I possess another photograph,
having the same intention in the
actions of the Virgin and Child, by
Sandro Botticelli; but whether the
motif was a usual one I do not further
know.' (DW 2368)

LA PIA (DANTE)
text 1886
wr. 1880–1; pub. 1881 and 1886
  Part published in *Athenaeum* 26

February 1881; in full in WMR 1886, ii, 406.

Translation from canto 5 of Dante's *Purgatorio* which describes the meeting with Pia de' Tolomei, from Siena, who died confined to a fortress in the Maremma by her husband. The lines were quoted in an article (approved in proof by DGR) in the *Athenaeum*, 26 February 1881, around the time DGR completed his painting of the same subject begun in 1868 and finished at the end of 1880 (VS 207; see also DW 2395). In the article, the lines, said to be 'placed on the frame of the picture' had line 3 in brackets, a semi-colon in place of the period in line 4; and line 6 read 'This in his inmost heart well knoweth he.' For a discussion of the painting, see TG 1984, no. 153.

THE BRIDE'S PRELUDE / PART I
text 1881
wr. 1848–9 and 1859–60; pub. *Poems* 1881

Earlier titles in MS: 'Bride-chamber Talk' and 'The Bride's Chamber'. In one early MS fragment (on paper watermarked *1847*) the sisters are named Amelotte and Hélénon. First mentioned in September 1849 (DW 43) this may have been inspired by the 'old romaunts' DGR read in the British Museum: cf. *The Staff and Scrip*. Re-worked in the late 1850s (when it is suggested Elizabeth Siddal's drawing *The Woeful Victory* was designed to illustrate the proposed conclusion) it was taken up again in 1869 with a view to inclusion in *Poems* 1870, but not proceeded with, and so finally published in unfinished form as 'Part I' in 1881. According to WMR 1911, 647, DGR stated that his 1860 drawing *How They Met Themselves* (VS 118) was suggested by a stanza in 'Bride-chamber Talk'; though no exact passage can be identified, both works share some common motifs. According to DGR in the projected sequel: 'the mere passionate frailty of Aloyse's first love would be followed by a true and noble love, rendered calamitous by Urscelyn, who then (having become a powerful soldier of fortune) solicits the hand of Aloyse. Thus the horror which she expresses against him to her sister on the bridal morning wd. be fully justified. Of course Aloyse wd. confess her fault to her second lover, whose love wd. nevertheless endure. The poem wd. gain so greatly by this sequel that I suppose I must set to and finish it one day ...' WMR 1911, 647–8 remarks that the never-finished text proceeds too slowly: 'if only an hour was remaining yet, the heart-sore bride would surely have made more haste' in her confession. But this is to demand realism from a romance narrative.

45 **chevesayle**: embroidered collar
226 **shrift-father**: priest
239 **stound**: stupefaction
255 **barred athwart**: i.e. with bar sinister, indicating descent from illegitimate branch of family
552 **bended shield**: as in line 255
591 **yearnings**: indicating pregnancy
740 **alone**: Aloyse's child has been taken away at birth.
773 **church-dole and march-dole**: charitable distribution by church and army

SONG AND MUSIC
text 1881
wr. 1849; pub. *B&S* 1881

PLACE DE LA BASTILLE, PARIS
text 1881
wr. 1849; pub. *B&S* 1881

Written during visit to Paris with WHH, at the same time as sonnets to pictures in the Louvre (see above) published in the *Germ*, and among the verse included in letters to WMR. The Place de la Bastille is the site of the notorious prison whose destruction became a symbol of the French Revolution and is commemorated in the national celebration of Bastille Day on 14 July.

WELLINGTON'S FUNERAL
text 1881
wr. 1852, rev. and pub. *Poems* 1881

As DGR told WA on 22 November 1860 that he 'never meant, I believe, to print ... the *Duke of Wellington*' (DW 350) it would appear that this early piece was rejected for the aborted 1862 collection, and only resurrected for the new edition of *Poems* in 1881.

British commander at the victorious battle of Waterloo in 1815 and later Prime Minister, Wellington was the greatest national hero, and his death on 18 November 1852 was marked by a state funeral. Original copies of the poem give merely the date as title, confident that this would be immediately understood. In 1849, like most British tourists to Belgium, DGR and WHH visited the Waterloo battlefield outside Brussels where, a generation before, his uncle John Polidori had purchased various military souvenirs.

34 and 37 Michael, Gabriel: archangels
67 Emperor: Napoleon I, defeated at Waterloo.
72 footnote refers to seizure of power in France by Louis Napoleon, who assumed title of Emperor as Napoleon III.

THE CHURCH PORCH I
text 1881
wr. 1853; pub. *B&S* 1881 as 'The Church Porch'.

Addressed to Maria Francesca Rossetti, DGR's elder sister. Reprinted by WMR, it bore the title 'The Church-Porches, Sonnet 1'.

THE CHURCH PORCH II
text 1882 [printed here for convenience]
wr. 1853; pub. 1882

Addressed to Christina Georgina Rossetti, DGR's younger sister, and published soon after DGR's death in the *Century Magazine*. Reprinted by WMR it bore the title 'The Church-Porches, sonnet 2'.

WORDS ON THE WINDOW-PANE
wr. 1853; pub. *B&S* 1881

GIOVENTÙ E SIGNORIA / YOUTH AND LORDSHIP
text 1881
wr. 1871; pub. *Poems* 1881

According to WMR 1886, 523, the 'street-song' supposedly given and translated here was in both languages DGR's original composition.

SOOTHSAY
text 1881
wr. 1871/79; pub. *B&S* 1881

Sts 1–3 written at Kelmscott as 'Commandments', and copied out on 2 September 1871 (DW 1150). Taken up eight years later, it was 'nearly doubled in size' by 23 December 1879 (DW 2153).

WMR 1911, 669 quotes Walter Pater's remark that this poem 'testifies – more clearly even than the "Nineveh" – to the reflective force, the dry reason, always at work behind [DGR's] imaginative creations, which at no time dispensed with a genuine intellectual structure.'

ROSE MARY
text 1881
wr. 1871/79; pub. *B&S* 1881

Using a title previously employed 'long ago for some rubbish destroyed', by 10 September 1871 DGR had written fifty-one stanzas of this poem, 'a story of my own, good, I think, turning of course on the innocence required in the seer ... with, I hope, good emotions and surprises in it' (DW 1165, 1167). A fortnight later 160 stanzas were complete (DW 1172). The 'beryl-stone' central to the supernatural narrative was suggested by a magic crystal, reputedly once owned by Elizabethan necromancer Dr John Dee, belonging to a neighbour in Chelsea and known as the magic beryl. DGR confessed he 'had no idea what the stone was really like, but perceived that for my purpose the elements must be somehow mystically condensed in it as a sort of mimic world' (DW 1169).

Other contributing sources include the *Arabian Nights*, the tale of Fair Geraldine and the Earl of Surrey, and Walter Scott's Waverley novels, which DGR re-read while working on *Rose Mary*.

Laid aside in 1872, the poem was resumed eight years later, when to the three parts DGR added the interlude passages. 'I've done a Beryl-Song and am going on to the two others,' he wrote on 25 January 1880. 'They will be a great gain to the scheme of the poem. Of course they are quite short – about thirty lines each.' (DW 2176) Three days later all three Beryl-Songs were complete: 'they are of course less songs than lyrical chaunts proceeding from the spirits of the Beryl. I thought them needed especially to eludicate the great transition of feeling between Parts I and II, and to explain the altered position of mother and daughter. The third song is also useful as giving some hint of the mother's finding the dead daughter ... I have this minute finished reading Keats's *Endymion*, which I had never really read through in my life. It is a brilliant labyrinth – a sort of magic toy. The interview with Diana, however, in Book II is as human as it needs must be, but artfully interspersed with supernatural invocation, so as to give the unearthly element.' (DW 2178, DW 2179)

WMR 1911, 660, observes: 'The "Beryl-songs" are a later addition, say 1879. The general opinion has been that they were better away; I cannot but agree with it, and indeed the author did so eventually. I have heard my brother say that he wrote them to show he was not incapable of the daring rhyming and rhythmical exploits of some other poets. As to this point readers must judge. It is at any rate true that in making the word "Beryl" the pivot of his experiment, a word to which there are the fewest possible rhymes, my brother weighted himself heavily.'

509 fabled head: Medusa
563 levin: lightning flash

CHIMES
text 1881
wr. 1871/8; pub. *B&S* 1881

Originally written at Kelmscott, these verses were intended as 'a running and very varied burden' within *Rose Mary*, 'with one line after the couplet and one after the triplet of each stanza' but omitted when the poem grew 'too long and intricate' (DW 1166). Another sequence from the burdens was later incorporated in *A Death-Parting*. Dating *Chimes* to 1878, WMR seems to have been unaware of their first incarnation, describing it in 1911, 670, as 'clearly an exercise in alliterative verse [representing] rather than aught else a number of thoughts and images passing through the writer's mind in dreary dimness, when he was already too prone to gloomy impressions.'

A SEA-SPELL
text 1881
wr. 1869?; pub. *B&S* 1881

Dated to 1869 by WMR, this would rather seem to have been composed to accompany DGR's picture of the same name executed in 1875–7 and originally intended to represent Coleridge's 'damsel with a dulcimer' from *Kubla Khan* (VS 248). In the poem, the figure with spell-binding song is evidently one of the Sirens who lured Ulysses and his crew towards shipwreck.

PARTED PRESENCE
text 1881
wr. 1875; pub. *B&S* 1881

This and the three following pieces have been linked to the end of DGR's intimacy with Jane Morris in 1876.

A DEATH-PARTING
text 1881
wr. 1876; pub. *B&S* 1881

The refrains ('Water-willow and wellaway' etc.) were originally couplets in the drafts of *Rose Mary* written at Kelmscott in 1871, alongside those later incorporated in *Chimes*.

THREE SHADOWS

text 1881
wr. 1876; pub. *B&S* 1881

ADIEU

text 1881
wr. 1876; pub. *B&S* 1881

ASTARTE SYRIACA (FOR A PICTURE)

text 1881
wr. 1877; pub. *B&S* 1881

Written for the painting with the same title reproduced 1876–7 (VS 249) depicting Astarte, which is one of the names given to the classical goddess Aphrodite/Venus. Syriaca denotes her origins in the even more ancient Middle Eastern cultures.

FIAMMETTA (FOR A PICTURE)

text 1881
wr. 1878; pub. *B&S* 1881

DGR finished the painting *A Vision of Fiammetta* in summer 1878 (VS 252).

THE WHITE SHIP (HENRY I OF ENGLAND)

text 1881
wr. 1880; pub. *B&S* 1881

Dated 1878–80 by WMR, his own diary for 12 April 1880 records DGR having looked up 'some scraps written long ago of an intended ballad' on the loss of the ship carrying the son and daughter of Henry I. The next day DGR asked WMR: 'when y next come, wd. y bring any book that gives a good account of the *White Ship* matter? After you went away I wrote some more verses of it; but am rather at a loss for some of the particulars . . .' (DW 2233). It was completed on 26 April 1880, and according to DGR 'every incident, including that of the boy at the end' was taken from a historical source (DW 2252). It is assumed that the italicised refrains were intended to be repeated with each pair of couplets (sometimes triplets).

FIVE ENGLISH POETS

I THOMAS CHATTERTON

text 1881
wr. 1880; pub. *B&S* 1881

WMR 1911, 670, states that 'it was only in his closing year that my brother paid minute attention to [Chatterton's] writings, and then he admired them enormously, and felt a remarkable degree of sympathy with Chatterton, his performances, and his personality.' Interest was sparked by TWD's commission (see DW 2250) to write an article on Chatterton (1752–70) who came from Redcliffe in Bristol and committed suicide.

II WILLIAM BLAKE

text 1881
wr. 1880; pub. *B&S* 1881

Text sent to F. J. Shields, dated 20 May 1880 (DW 2264). An early admirer of Blake (1757–1827), DGR had helped compile Alexander Gilchrist's biography and selections published in 1863, and in 1880 collaborated again on the re-issue.

Artist Frederic James Shields (1833–1911) was friend and companion to DGR in the last years.

III SAMUEL TAYLOR COLERIDGE

text 1881
wr. 1880; pub. *B&S* 1881

The line 'six years, from sixty saved' appears to assert that the only works of significant value by Coleridge (1772–1834) came from the period around the publication (with Wordsworth) of *Lyrical Ballads* in 1798 and Coleridge's departure for Malta in 1804.

IV JOHN KEATS

text 1881
wr. 1880; pub. *B&S* 1881

WMR 1911, 670 notes that the poetry of Keats (1795–1821) first became known to DGR 'in 1844, or perhaps 1845. He delighted in it then, and ever afterwards.'

Writing to THC in February 1880, DGR sent his own early adaptation of

NOTES

509

Keats' 'self-chosen epitaph' ('Here lies one whose name was writ in water.') A month later he forwarded the present sonnet, saying it was 'again concerned with the epitaph, and perhaps my reviving the latter in writing you was the cause of the sonnet.'
4 **Castalian:** of the Muses
8 **Rome:** where Keats died.

V PERCY BYSSHE SHELLEY
text 1881
wr. 1881; pub. *B&S* 1881
Shelley (1792–1822) drowned while sailing in Mediterranean; his couch or sofa was subsequently acquired by WMR, his editor and biographer.

THE DAY-DREAM
text 1881
wr. 1880; pub. *B&S* 1881
Written to accompany the picture of the same name painted 1879–80 (VS 259) showing a woman with Jane Morris's features sitting with a book in the branches of a sycamore tree.

FOR 'SPRING' (BY SANDRO BOTTICELLI)
text 1881
wr. 1880; pub. *B&S* 1881
Written for the famous painting usually known as *Primavera*.

THE LAST THREE FROM TRAFALGAR
text 1881
wr. 1880; pub. *B&S* 1881
The naval battle at Trafalgar off the coast of Spain, in which Admiral Lord Nelson was killed, took place on 21 October 1805 and as a patriotic victory remained second only to Waterloo through the nineteenth century. The reference in DGR's sub-title line to 'the Anniversary Banquet, 21st October 187–' invites the inference that the poem was prompted by an earlier anniversary in the 1870s. But although WMR 1911, xxix dates this text to 1878, his own diary entry for 7 November 1880 notes that DGR 'read a sonnet he has just composed on the survivors of Trafalgar ... who

dined together on the recent anniversary of the victory' (*VP*, 1982, 231). In 1880 WMR's diary entry indicates there were then five survivors of Trafalgar; possibly by the time the poem was sent to the printer the following year their number had dwindled to three.
The Victory was the British fleet flagship. 'England's Duty' refers to Nelson's pre-battle message saying 'England expects that every man will do his duty.'

INSOMNIA
text 1881
wr. 1881; pub. *B&S* 1881
'With me, Sonnets mean Insomnia,' wrote DGR in January 1881 (DW 2390).

TIBER, NILE, AND THAMES
text 1881
wr. 1881; pub. *B&S* 1881
'I send another just written last night', DGR wrote on 19 January 1881 (DW 2390). Originally entitled 'Cleopatra's Needle in London', this was inspired by the installation on the Thames Embankment in central London of the Egyptian hierogylph column popularly dubbed 'Cleopatra's Needle', and used as an occasion for a contrived and somewhat tortuous lament for the scorn and neglect suffered by eloquence in ancient Rome and modern Britain.

ALAS, SO LONG!
text 1881
wr. 1881; pub. *B&S* 1881

'FOUND' (FOR A PICTURE)
text 1881
wr. 1881; pub. *B&S* 1881
Written to accompany the picture of the same title (VS 64) begun in 1854 and still in progress at DGR's death.

CZAR ALEXANDER II
text 1881
wr. 1881; pub. *B&S* 1881
The liberation of the Russian serfs

took place under Alexander II, who was assassinated on 13 March 1881.

THE KING'S TRAGEDY (JAMES I OF SCOTS)
text 1881
wr. 1881; pub. B&S 1881

'[P]robably the best thing I ever did,' DGR wrote on 6 March 1881 (Bryson 133). The poetic narrative of the murder of James I (1394–1437) is closely based on historical sources, including a medieval prose chronicle translated by James Shirley and available in a Maitland Club reprint, 1837; Walter Scott's *Tales of a Grandfather*, 1828; and Charles Rogers, ed. *Poetical Remains of James I of Scotland*, 1873 (see Dwight & Helen Culler, 'The Sources of "The King's Tragedy"', *Studies in Philology*, 41, 1944, 427ff.). James was poet as well as king, author of *The Kingis Quair* (first printed 1783) from which DGR borrowed the italicised stanzas of his own poem, adapting the rime royal lines to fit the ballad metre.

POSSESSION
text 1881
wr. 1881; pub. B&S 1881

SPHERAL CHANGE
text 1881
wr. 1881; pub. B&S 1881

Poems published posthumously

in order of publication

ON CERTAIN ELIZABETHAN REVIVALS
text 1911
wr. 1860?; pub. 1882

Considered for *Poems* 1870 but rejected with several 'of semi-comic sort' (DW 929). WMR 1886, I, 521 says it was considered in 1881 for publication in *Sonnets of Three Centuries* edited by THC, but dropped as not in keeping with DGR's other

contributions, and therefore first printed in Hall Caine's *Recollections of DGR* (1882). In MS line 11 reads 'Write thus, and be a poet! Hark, thou man'.

RALEIGH'S CELL IN THE TOWER
text 1911
wr. 1881; pub. 1882

Published in *Sonnets of Three Centuries*, ed. Thomas Hall Caine (1882). The subject is Sir Walter Raleigh, Elizabethan explorer, naval commander and poet, author of *The History of the World* (1614), who was imprisoned in the Tower of London for thirteen years and finally executed in 1618 after a disastrous expedition to Guiana.

MNEMOSYNE
text 1882
wr. 1881; pub. 1882

Lines to accompany the painting of the same name (VS 261) similar in composition to *Astarte Syriaca*; inscribed on the frame, they were first printed Sharp 1882, 261. Mnemosyne, shown holding a lamp, is Memory, mother of the Muses.

TO PHILIP BOURKE MARSTON
text 1881
wr. 1878; pub. 1882

Published in Sharp, 405. Philip Bourke Marston (1850–87) was a poet known to DGR from 1870, son of dramatist J. Westland Martson, and blind from boyhood. DGR wrote on 11 October 1878: 'I heard the other day from Philip Marston with a Sonnet addressed to me urging further poetry! This is truly Tuscan and must be replied to in kind' (DW 1975). By 'Tuscan' he alluded to the exchange of sonnets between Dante and his associates, as demonstrated in *Early Italian Poets*. In MS in line 4 the word 'sight' is given as 'light'. The reference in line 11 to DGR's 'slumbering' voice relates to the cessation of poetic composition 1872–9. Philip Marston's *Collected Poems* appeared in 1892.

FOR AN ANNUNCIATION, EARLY
GERMAN
wr. 1847; pub. WMR 1886
   Considered but rejected for
inclusion in *Poems 1881*. WMR 1886,
I, 522, cites this as 'perhaps the
earliest of all the Sonnets on Pictures.'
The otherwise unidentified
Annunciation picture is thought to
have been seen in a London auction
room, or exhibition gallery.

AT THE SUN-RISE IN 1848
text 1886
wr. 1848; pub. WMR 1886
   WMR 1911, 663 notes that this
shows how DGR 'shared the
aspirations and exultations of the year
of vast European upheavals'. To
qualify this statement, read the
doggerel satire *The English Revolution
of 1848* (WMR 1911, 261), in which
DGR mocked the Chartist
demonstrators:

   O thou great Spirit of the World!
      shall not the lofty things
   He saith be borne until all time for
      noble lessonings?
   Shall not our sons tell to their sons
      what we could do and dare
   In this great year Forty-Eight and
      in Trafalgar Square?
   . . .

   Upon what point of London, say,
      shall our next vengeance burst?
   Shall the Exchange, or Parliament,
      be immolated first?
   Which of the Squares shall we burn
      down? which of the Palaces?
               (*The speaker is nailed by*
   a policeman)
   Oh please sir, don't! It isn't me.
      It's him. Oh don't sir, please?

AUTUMN SONG
text 1911
wr. 1848 (as 'The Fall of the Leaf');
pub. WMR 1886
   WMR 1886, I, 518 notes that this
lyric was set to music by DGR's
acquaintance Edward Dannreuther.

THE LADY'S LAMENT
text 1911
wr. 1848; pub. *CW* 1886

VOX ECCLESIAE, VOX CHRISTI
text 1911
wr. 1849; pub. WMR 1886, i, 265
   Proposed for the *Germ* on 26
August 1849, but not there published.
WMR 1886, I, 520 says it was written
as pendant to his own sonnet, *The
Evil under the Sun* on the collapse of
revolutionary hopes in Europe in 1848
(see *Germ* iv). It would also seem to
be companion to DGR's *On the
Refusal of Aid between Nations* (see p.
218) published in *Poems 1870*. The
title means 'Voice of the Church,
Voice of Christ', used to underline the
wrongful invocation of religion by
armed forces engaged in suppressing
political reform.

THE STAIRCASE OF NOTRE DAME,
PARIS
text 1911
wr. 1849; pub. WMR 1886, i, 261
   While travelling with WHH in
France and Belgium, DGR sent letters
home largely written in blank verse
(see WMR 1911, 176–88) interspersed
with sonnets, including this and *Place
de la Bastille* (see p. 375). Here the
image of emerging into light has
political resonance, following the
events of 1848.

NEAR BRUSSELS – A HALF-WAY
PAUSE
text 1911
wr. 1849; pub. WMR 1886, i, 262
   Another complete piece from
DGR's travels in 1849.

THE MIRROR
text 1911
wr. 1850; pub. WMR 1886, i, 272
   WMR 1886, I, 520 notes that
though this poem was never published
by DGR, he 'had a certain liking for
it'. DGR's remark to WA on 22
November 1860: '*The Mirror* I will
sacrifice to you' (DW 350) indicates it
was considered for publication in the
aborted 1862 collection.

DURING MUSIC
text 1911
wr. 1851; pub. WMR 1886, i, 273

ENGLISH MAY
text 1911
wr. 1854?; pub. WMR 1886, i, 286
  WMR, 1886, I, 521 dates the
composition to 1854, linking it with
Elizabeth Siddal, but the text would
seem to relate equally well to DGR's
concern with Jane Morris's health in
spring 1870.

DAWN ON THE NIGHT JOURNEY
text 1911
wr. 1855?; pub. WMR 1886, i, 303

TO THOMAS WOOLNER / FIRST
SNOW 9 FEBRUARY 1853
text 1911
wr. 1853; pub. 1895
  Included (with slightly different
punctuation) in a letter sent on 16
April 1853 to Thomas Woolner
(1825–92), fellow member of the PRB,
in Australia 1852–4. 'This is the only
verse I think (or almost) that I have
written since you left – except
something de rigueur on the Duke of
Wellington,' DGR wrote (DW 104).
Published by WMR in 1895, the text
was included in A. Woolner, Thomas
Woolner: His Life & Letters, 1917.

THE SEED OF DAVID
text 1911
wr. 1864; pub. 1895
  WMR 1911, 668 notes that this, the
first verses following Elizabeth Siddal's
death in 1862, was composed for the
altarpiece in Llandaff Cathedral (VS
105). Considered for inclusion in
Poems 1870, but omitted at the last
minute (see BL Ashley 1400 and DW
965).

DENNIS SHAND
text 1911
wr. 1850?; pub. 1904
  Considered for inclusion in 'Dante
at Verona and Other Poems' (see DW

350) and prepared for publication in
Poems 1870, but omitted on the
grounds that 'it deals trivially with a
base amour' (see WMR 1911, 666)

AFTER THE FRENCH LIBERATION OF
ITALY
text 1911
wr. 1859; pub. 1904
  WMR 1911, 667 states that the
'strong form of imagery and words'
precluded this from earlier publication,
and explains the political subject: 'This
sonnet was written in 1859, after
Napoleon III, seconded by the
Piedmontese army, had expelled the
Austrians from Lombardy, and had
concluded the Peace of Villafranca,
whereby Venetia was left
unenfranchised from the Austrian
yoke, and all the rest of Italy had to
shift for itself as best it might, while
France secured Savoy and Nice, and
garrisoned the Pope in Rome.' He
adds that DGR 'had of course no
objection – quite the contrary – to
Napoleon's action in liberating
Lombardy: but he objected to the
other features of his Italian policy and
wrote this sonnet to commemorate his
forecast of bad times for Europe
generally.' According to a note by
ACS, however, DGR also stated that
the octave was written 'simply through
his wish to do into verse his
experience of the animal sensation' and
that the political metaphor and sestet
were 'an afterthought' (MS note, 27
November 1886, Princeton University
Library).

AFTER THE GERMAN SUBJUGATION
OF FRANCE, 1871
text 1911
wr. 1871; pub. 1904
  Written soon after the end of the
siege of Paris during the Franco-
Prussian War 1870–1, this mainly
consists of an attack on Napoleon III.
Absalom and Shimei (who cursed
David with the words 'Come out,
come out, thou bloody man') are
found in 2 Samuel ch. 15–16.

THE QUESTION
text 1967
wr. 1882; pub. 1967

Written four days before DGR's
death in April 1882, in explication of
his 1875 design of the same title (VS
241 and DW 2615). Of the subject,
thought to have been inspired by the
death of Oliver Madox Brown (see p.
346), DGR wrote: 'the idea is that of
Man questioning the Unknown, and I
shall call it either *The Question* or *The
Sphinx and her Questioners* ... The
subject is in fact the same as my little
poem *The Cloud Confines*: / "And
eyes fixed ever in vain / on the pitiless
eyes of Fate." ' (Bryson 37–9)

Notebook fragments and

verses

Copied from DGR's memorandum
books and published in WMR 1886
and 1911. All date from the last years
of DGR's life.

SELECT BIBLIOGRAPHY

WORKS BY D. G. ROSSETTI

The Early Italian Poets from Ciullo d'Alcamo to Dante Alighieri 1100–1200–1300, together with Dante's Vita Nuova, translated by D. G. Rossetti, London 1861. Reissued as *Dante and his Circle*, London, 1874.

Poems, London, 1870. Re-issued in different format, London, 1881.

Ballads and Sonnets, London, 1881.

The Works of Dante Gabriel Rossetti, ed. with introduction and notes by William Michael Rossetti, London, 1911.

The Complete Writings and Pictures of Dante Gabriel Rossetti: a Hypermedia Research Archive, ed. Jerome J. McGann, University of Michigan Press, online 1999 at ‹http://jefferson.village.edu/rossetti/rossetti.ht›

see also Alexander Gilchrist, *Life of William Blake*, London, 1863, reissued 1880, to which Rossetti contributed a supplementary chapter and commentaries on poems and designs, including *Job* and *Jerusalem*

OTHER WORKS

Ainsworth, Maryan W., ed., *Dante Gabriel Rossetti and the Double Work of Art*, New Haven, 1976.

Allen, Vivien, ed., *The Correspondence of Dante Gabriel Rossetti and Thomas Hall Caine*, Sheffield University Press, 2000.

Bentley, D. M. R., 'Rossetti's "Ave" and Related Pictures', *Victorian Poetry* 15 (1977) 21ff.

Boos, Florence, *The Poetry of Dante Gabriel Rossetti: A Critical and Source Study*, The Hague, 1976.

Bowra, C. M. *The Romantic Imagination*, London, 1947.

Bryson, John, ed., *Dante Gabriel Rossetti and Jane Morris: Their Correspondence*, Oxford: Clarendon Press, 1976.

Buchanan, R. W., *The Fleshly School of Poetry and Other Phenomena of the Day*, London, 1872. A preliminary version of this essay appeared in the *Contemporary Review*, October 1871.

Buckley, Jerome H., *The Pre-Raphaelites*, New York, 1968.

—— 'Pre-Raphaelite Past and Present: the Poetry of the Rossettis', *Victorian Poetry*, ed. M. Bradbury and D. Palmer, London, 1972.

Butterworth, Walter, *Dante Gabriel Rossetti in relation to Dante Alighieri*, London, 1912.

Doughty, Oswald, *A Victorian Romantic: Dante Gabriel Rossetti*, London, 1949 and 1960.

Eliot, T. S., *The Use of Poetry and the Use of Criticism: Studies in the Relation of Criticism to Poetry in England*, London, 1933.

Fennell, Francis F., *Dante Gabriel Rossetti: An Annotated Bibliography*, New York, 1982.

Fredeman, W. E., *Pre-Raphaelitism: A Bibliocritical Study*, Oxford, 1965.

—— 'Rossetti's "In Memoriam": an Elegiac Reading of *The House of Life*', *Bulletin of the John Rylands Library*, Manchester, 47 (1965) 298ff.

—— 'The Pre-Raphaelites', *The Victorian Poets: A Guide to Research*, ed. F. Faverty, Harvard University Press, 1968, 251ff.

—— 'What is wrong with Rossetti? A Centenary Assessment', *Victorian Poetry* 20 (1982).

Fredeman, W. E., ed., *The Collected Letters of Dante Gabriel Rossetti*, forthcoming.

Ghose, S. N., *Dante Gabriel Rossetti and Contemporary Criticism 1849–1882*, Dijon, 1929.

Gitter, Elizabeth J., 'Rossetti's translations of Early Italian Lyrics', *Victorian Poetry* 12 (1974) 351ff.

Harris, Daniel, 'D.G. Rossetti's "Jenny": Sex, Money and the Interior Monologue', *Victorian Poetry* 22 (1984) 197ff.

Harrison, Antony, *The Victorian Poets and Romantic Poems: Intertextuality and Ideology*, Virginia University Press, 1990.

Hough, Graham, *The Last Romantics*, London, 1949.

Howard, Ronnalie, *The Dark Glass: Vision and Technique in the Poetry of Dante Gabriel Rossetti*, Ohio University Press, 1972.

Hunt, John Dixon, *The Pre-Raphaelite Imagination 1848–1900*, London, 1968.

Johnston, R. D., *Dante Gabriel Rossetti*, New York, 1969.

Lucas, F. L., *Eight Victorian Poets*, Cambridge, 1930.

McGann, Jerome J., 'Rossetti's Significant Details', *Victorian Poetry* 7 (1969) 41ff.

—— 'Dante Gabriel Rossetti and the Betrayal of Truth', *Victorian Poetry* 26 (1988) 339ff.

—— *Rossetti and the Game that Must be Lost*, forthcoming.

McSweeney, Kerry, *Supreme Attachments: Studies in Victorian Love Poetry*, London: Ashgate Publishing, 1998.

Megroz, R. M., *Dante Gabriel Rossetti: Painter Poet of Heaven in Earth*, London, 1928.

Myers, F. W. H., *Essays: Modern*, London, 1885.

Pater, Walter, *Appreciations*, London, 1889.

Paolucci, Anne, 'Ezra Pound and Dante Gabriel Rossetti as translators of Guido Cavalcanti', *Romantic Review* 51 (1960) 256ff.

Peattie, Robert, ed., *The Selected Letters of William Michael Rossetti*, Pennsylvania State University Press, 1991

Pound, Ezra, *Literary Essays*, London, 1954.

Rees, Joan, *The Poetry of Dante Gabriel Rossetti: Modes of Self-Expression*, Cambridge, 1981.

Richardson, James, *Vanishing Lives: Style and Self in Tennyson, D.G. Rossetti, Swinburne and Yeats*, Virginia University Press, 1981.

Riede, David G., *Dante Gabriel Rossetti and the Limits of Victorian Vision*, Cornell University Press, 1983.

———— *Dante Gabriel Rossetti Revisited*, New York, 1992.

Rossetti, William Michael, *Dante Gabriel Rossetti as Designer and Writer*, 2 vols, London 1889.

Sambrook, James, ed., *Pre-Raphaelites: A Collection of Critical Essays*, Chicago University Press, 1974.

Sharp, William, *Dante Gabriel Rossetti: A Record and a Study*, London, 1882.

Sheets, Robin, 'Pornography and Art: the Case of "Jenny" ', *Critical Inquiry* 14 (1988) 315ff.

Stein, Richard L., *The Ritual of Interpretation: Literature and Art in Ruskin, Rossetti and Pater*, Harvard University Press, 1975.

Swinburne, Algernon C., 'The Poetry of Dante Gabriel Rossetti', *Fortnightly Review*, 1870, 551ff., reprinted in *the Complete Works of Algernon Charles Swinburne*, 20 vols., London 1925-7.

Victorian Poetry: An Issue devoted to the works of Dante Gabriel Rossetti, vol. 20 (1982).

Wetherby, H. L., 'Problems of Form and Content in the Poetry of Dante Gabriel Rossetti', *Victorian Poetry* 2 (1964) 11ff.

INDEX OF TITLES AND FIRST LINES